THE CHAMBERLAIN HITLER COLLUSION

The Chamberlain-Hitler Collusion

by

Clement Leibovitz

and

Alvin Finkel

MERLIN PRESS

JAMES LORIMER & Company

First published in UK by

Merlin Press Ltd
2 Rendlesham Mews,
Rendlesham, Woodbridge,
Suffolk IP12 2EA
085036 468 X

First published in Canada by

James Lorimer & Company
5502 Atlantic Street
Halifax, N.S.
Canada B3H 1G4
1 55028 578 5

Printed by WSOY in Finland

To Elvira Leibovitz and Carol Taylor and our sons, Boris, David and Yair Leibovitz and Antony and Kieran Finkel

*****

The authors have enjoyed advice and encouragement from a variety of friends and colleagues, and only a few of our debts can be acknowledged here. Dr. Larry Pratt and Dr. Gordon Fearn played a particularly important role in encouraging Dr. Leibovitz's research from the early stages of this project. Mr. Noubar Martayan provided important materials on France's behaviour in the early months of the war without which Chapter 9 could not have been written. Dr. Michael Carley provided glimpses of yet-to-be-published work that strengthened our understanding of French attitudes towards the Soviets in the inter-war period. Steve Boddington, Ph.D. candidate at the University of Alberta, did a thorough check of references and quotations; Athabasca University provided funds to permit Steve's work as a research assistant to this project and release time to allow Dr. Finkel to write this manuscript.

Dr. Alvin Finkel

Born in Winnipeg, Canada, in 1949, Alvin Finkel is Professor of History at Athabasca University in Alberta, Canada, an open-learning institute modelled on Britain's Open University. He joined the university in 1978.

Dr. Finkel earned his B.A. and M.A. at the University of Manitoba and his Ph.D. at the University of Toronto and has taught at Brandon University, the University of Manitoba, Queen's University, and the University of Alberta. He is the author of *Business and Social Reform in the Thirties* (1979) and *The Social Credit Phenomenon in Alberta* (1989) and co-author of the two-volume *History of the Canadian Peoples* (1993, 2nd edition 1997). His articles on Canadian history, comparative social policy-making in industrial countries, and distance education have appeared in a variety of Canadian and international journals.

Active in the New Democratic Party and in left-wing movements, Dr. Finkel first met Dr. Leibovitz as a fellow member of Jews for Peace in the Middle East. In 1994, he was persuaded by Dr. Leibovitz to collaborate on converting Dr. Leibovitz's extensive research, first compiled as The *Chamberlain-Hitler Deal* (1993) to produce the current manuscript.

Alvin Finkel is married to Carol Taylor and has two sons, Antony and Kieran.

*****

Dr. Clement Leibovitz

Clement Leibovitz was born in Egypt in 1923 into a Jewish family and educated in French-language schools. Forced to leave school at age 12, he worked in a variety of trades, principally as a radio technician. In 1959, he moved to Israel, where, after twenty years of interruption, he resumed his studies. He earned a

B.Sc., M.Sc., and D.Sc. from the Haifa Technion Institute of Technology. His thesis was in general relativity and cosmology. He moved to Canada in 1969 with his wife, Elvira, and three sons and worked in Computing Services at the University of Alberta until his retirement.

In 1976 Dr. Leibovitz was diagnosed with prostate cancer and, despite treatment, the tumour became active again four years later and metastased to several other organs. He was told that he had only one year to live. He spent the next six months producing a philosophical and dramatic work, *Memoirs of God*. He also joined other progressive Jews in Edmonton to form the organization, Jews for Peace in the Middle East, after the Israeli invasion of Lebanon, and pursued his peace activities.

Still feeling hale and hearty, Dr. Leibovitz spent eight years doing research on the events leading to World War 2. The results of his research first appeared in The *Chamberlain-Hitler Deal*, the prototype of the current manuscript. In 1995 his doctors declared him free of cancer. He is currently working to produce books on socialist philosophy.

CONTENTS

INTRODUCTION

by Christopher Hitchens

To call Neville Chamberlain an appeaser in 1938 was to flatter him by presuming that his objective was the avoidance of war. His mistake, in other words, was only an excess of compassion and naiveté and an imprudent unwillingness to consider the use of force. Churchill's famous comment on the betrayal of Czechoslovakia – that Britain had resorted to disgrace to avoid war but would have the disgrace and the war also – captured the essence of the view that dithering, cowardice and irresolution held Chamberlain and his colleagues back. During the Cold War, this image proved serviceable to those who argued for "peace through strength."

Yet consider for a moment: the Tories were never renowned for their pacifism nor yet for their isolationism. Their attitude to the use of violence when their own interest was involved could be described without exaggeration as unsentimental. And yet they were assumed to have pursued a policy, heedless of that very self-interest, which later led to a war being fought on less favourable terms.

Was it simply dithering and cowardice that caused the Baldwin-Chamberlain establishment to give Mussolini a free hand in Abyssinia, Franco a free hand in Spain, Hitler a free hand in Austria and the Sudeten territories of Czechoslovakia? They traded armaments to Hitler, conducted anti-Communist diplomacy with him at various European watering places, and very frequently announced to the world that his grievances, while often expressed in a tone regrettably lacking in reserve, were nonetheless genuine. What if the motivation were not capitulation? What if the disaster of the Second World War resulted not from an underestimate of the evils of Nazism but from a consistent attempt to cooperate with it?

It is the argument of this important book that the documentary record demands affirmative answers to both of these questions.

That is, until the last moments of the crisis over Poland, and well through the Munich agreement, the chief objectives of Hitler and Chamberlain were more or less explicitly the same: an agreed division of Europe, an immunity of the British Empire from Nazi claims, and the isolation and eventual destruction of the Soviet Union and the communist threat generally.

The present text uses the official record to reveal the collusion of the leaders of Britain and, to a degree, France, with Hitler's Nazi regime. It helps to explain the findings of other researchers that, on their own, might seem inexplicable. For example, it has now been demonstrated that the celebrated Kim Philby, a Soviet mole in the highest reaches of the British Secret Service, secured the confidence of those he needed to impress in the British establishment by the simple trick of acting like a Nazi sympathizer. He attended swastika-bedecked evenings sponsored by the Anglo-German League, an upper crust front organization in sympathy with "The New Germany," and having gone to Spain to report from the side of the fascist mutineers, he accepted a decoration from Franco.

Philby's success in penetrating the Secret Service by posing as a fascist sympathizer will seem unsurprising after reading Leibovitz and Finkel's account of ruling-class thinking in Britain in the 1930s. Sir Nevile Henderson, British ambassador to Germany during the decisive years between 1937 and 1939, could write in October 1939: "There are in fact many things in the Nazi organization and social institutions, as distinct from its rabid nationalism and ideology, which we might study and adapt to our own nation and old democracy." *The Chamberlain-Hitler Collusion* reveals how common such views were among those who counted in foreign-policy-making in Britain in the 1930s and how it affected the policies they arrived at. Leibovitz and Finkel present a veritable anthology of upper-class enthusiasms for fascism and Nazism, demonstrating carefully how these sympathies for extremist authoritarian means of protecting existing privilege shaped the making of foreign policy.

In January 1997 the *New York Review of Books* published a lengthy and detailed essay by Thomas Powers. The subject was a new tranche of books on the resistance to Hitler among the German establishment. Two of these books in particular had made exhaustive use of newly-opened German and British archives. *Plotting Hitler's Death*, by the conservative Frankfurt editor Joachim Fest, and *The Unnecessary War: Whitehall and the German Resistance to Hitler* by Patricia Meehan, had reached essentially identical conclusions by empirically different routes. There had been a high-level resistance to Hitler's fantasy of world domination; this resistance had made appeals to principle as well as self-interest; it had been ready to take grave risks and it had been sabotaged by the Chamberlain-Halifax regime. Not always to be confused with the much later and more celebrated "July Plot" of the Stauffenberg conspirators, this resistance was capably summarized by Powers in the following words:

> Of the many circles of those who opposed Hitler during the 1930s three may be identified as central...a group of religious and philosophical opponents centring on Helmuth von Moltke, a great grandnephew of the famous nineteenth-century general, whose ancestral estate in Silesia (now part of Poland) gave the group its name, "the Kreisau circle;" the nexus of German Foreign Office and military intelligence officials around Admiral Wilhelm Canaris, commander of the Abwehr, the Geman military intelligence service, and his close ally in the Foreign Office, Ernst von Weizsacker; and a loosely knit, constantly fluctuating group of civilian politicians and high-ranking military officers centring on the former mayor of Leipzig, Carl Goerdeler, and General Ludwig Beck, who resigned as Army chief of staff in 1938 in protest against Hitler's planned invasion of Czechoslovakia.

This not unimpressive movement directed most of its energies and initiatives towards London. It was prepared to go to considerable lengths. In the period immediately preceding the betrayal of Czechoslovakia, for instance, high-level envoys were talking to Lord Halifax, assuring him that they had serious plans for a coup against Hitler (which indeed they did) and beseeching him to stand firm and thereby convince the German public that the removal of Hitler would be a deliverance from war.

Powers' review, added to the Fest and Meehan books, represent non-perishable additions to the school of "read it and weep." Yet here is how Powers chooses to evoke the unfolding of the drama:

> Despite knowing of this and other contacts, Chamberlain, in Scotland for the annual grouse-shooting, could not steel himself for the blunt public challenge the German conspirators wanted. He wrote to his advisers that if Hitler marched "a very serious situation would arise and it might be necessary to call ministers together to consider it. But I have a notion that it won't come to that." These are not the words of a man who needed to be taken seriously.

On the contrary, they are the words of a man who needed to be taken very seriously indeed; a man who had a settled conviction that an agreement had already been reached, and a man who was not going to deviate for the sake of something as immaterial (to him) as the idea of a German opposition. In full possession of the facts, he flew straight to Munich. In the words of one of the surviving German resistance members, a few days after that famous handshake the anti-Hitlerites "sat around Witzleben's fireplace and tossed our lovely plan and projects into the fire. We spent the rest of the evening meditating, not on Hitler's triumph, but on the calamity that had befallen Europe."

Even though it was probably too late, some heroic Germans were prepared to try again with the same tactic when Prague had been occupied and it came the turn of Poland. Weizsacker actually asked Sir Nevile Henderson to find a British general who would assure Hitler beyond doubt that a move on Warsaw would mean war. Again Powers:

> But while the clock ticked away during the final days of peace no words of resolution came from Chamberlain, who was fishing in Scotland...or from the foreign secretary Lord Halifax, who had asked

> before accepting the job whether he could still shoot
> on Saturdays; or from the permanent head of the
> British Foreign Office, Alexander Cadogan, who was
> playing golf at Le Touquet. *The dithering continued
> until the end* (my italics).

There is something in the image of 'dither,' of Chamberlain's umbrella and droopy moustache and chronic moral nullity, that seems to meet a widespread psychological want. Together with its corollary of languid upper-class blood sports, it ministers to a certain impression of drawling British complacency and impressive teak-headedness that is beloved by Hollywood and some writers of fiction. Powers, even with all the evidence in front of him, seems unable to dispense with this trope. He concludes by denouncing something that is a mere theoretical construct: the Chamberlain government's miserable failure to resist Hitler stoutly when that might have been enough to prevent the war.

Miserable though it undoubtedly was, this Tory statecraft can only with the most unhistorical lenience be described as a failure. Those who read Clement Leibovitz and Alvin Finkel's account will run into Chamberlain and Halifax and Cadogan not once but many times. They will also learn about that same British ambassador to Berlin, who so coldly repelled the overtures of German patriots and democrats. They will understand, in effect, that the Chamberlain-Hitler regime took a position some measurable distance to the Right of many members of the German general staff. Within a few years of Munich, British strategy was – in the fullest battledress of moral authority – making war on German civilians and calmly levelling entire cities. The bombers would do to the German people what the political establishment had declined, even in the most limited fashion, to do to the Nazi party. We still live with the consequences of the titanic historical betrayal of the leaders of the democracies in the 1930s.

PREFACE

During World War Two a great deal of public anger in Great Britain was directed against the political leaders of the 1930s whom public opinion held guilty of having been duped by the European dictators and of having failed to rearm the country sufficiently to make it possible easily to defeat the Axis powers. President Roosevelt and some of his key foreign policy advisors shared the view of the Soviet authorities that the ruling elites of Britain and France had cooperated with Hitler in the belief that he would make war upon the Soviet Union. The governments of Britain and France had offered Hitler a "free hand" in central and eastern Europe in return for guarantees that Hitler would leave the West and the British Empire alone. German control over all of eastern Europe could ultimately pose a threat to the British Empire but elite fear and loathing of communism was such that Hitler, who made a great show of his anti-Bolshevism, was seen as worthy of their trust. Only when it became abundantly clear that Hitler would not live up to his side of the deal to leave the West alone did the British turn against him. Within Britain itself Churchill had, for several years before the war, denounced what looked to him like government attempts to grant Germany a free hand in the East. So did Robert Vansittart, the Permanent Under-Secretary for Foreign Affairs before Chamberlain came into office and kicked him upstairs to a largely ceremonial position.

After the war the conservative forces in Britain tried to defend themselves against the "guilty men" thesis. Taking advantage of the Cold War, they denounced suggestions that they had, formally or tacitly, given the Nazis a free hand in the East as an invention of Soviet propaganda. While this conveniently ignored the equal conviction of the American leadership that the free hand had been offered, it provided the opportunity to rehabilitate the political leadership of the 1930s as honourable men interested in peace and unable to fathom the true nature of the Hitler regime. The historical literature on the 1930s soon began to be coloured by this conception of the political leaders in the years that preceded the war. By the time Donald Cameron Watt wrote his supposedly definitive *How War Came* in 1989, the "guilty men" thesis had been largely discarded.

Yet the historical works were filled with paradoxes. A.J.P. Taylor, while claiming to find no evidence of a pact with Hitler

1

to attack the Soviet Union, conceded that Britain and France did not care what happened to eastern Europe and suggested that they had been swept up by events to go to war over Poland about which they cared little and did not do much to defend. Simon Newman documented the cynicism with which Britain approached its guarantee to Poland in 1939 and Watt, for his part, admitted that Germany believed the Anglo-German Naval Agreement of 1935 constituted a free hand. Wesley Wark revealed that the military chiefs from 1933 onwards were quite happy to grant Germany a free hand in the East. Yet all of these historians are prepared to defend the actions of the British government towards Germany from 1933 to 1939 to a large degree and to offer excuses for British and French "appeasement" of the Nazi regime.

Opponents of the "guilty men" approach warn that it is important not to read history backwards, not to assume that Baldwin, Chamberlain, Daladier and others could have known about Hitler and the Nazis what we know now. They had to judge the authoritarian regime in Germany, extreme as it might appear to be, by what it said, and its promises that it meant only to seek justice for German-speaking peoples in other lands rang true to the British and French leaders. While such a position seems moderate and reasonable at first blush, it has often lead to an uncritical approach to the question: what did the British and French leaders know? What did they expect of Hitler? Why did they remain friendly to him as he remilitarized his country furiously? As he marched into the Rhineland? Into Austria? Into Czechoslovakia?

This book does not read history backwards. Its concern is not what the leaders of Britain and France should have known but what they did know and what they did with that knowledge. We believe that the historical record demonstrates beyond the shadow of a doubt that Roosevelt and his associates, Churchill and Vansittart, not to mention Stalin and his associates, were right. Though diplomatic niceties caused the British leaders to denounce the phrase "free hand," they believed in its substance. They understood the Anglo-German Naval Agreement in the same way that Hitler did and during the three meetings that Neville Chamberlain held with Hitler in September 1938, they attempted to cement the understanding between Nazi Germany and Imperial Britain that would make these two nations

2

everlasting allies and joint enemies of the Soviet Union and international communism.

A reader might well ask how could we come to such radically different conclusions from those of our predecessors who have examined this era. We would encourage the reader to reread the earlier historians in the light of our evidence here. We suggest that she or he will find no evidence to contradict the well-documented argument of this book. Instead what will be found are assertions about the character of Chamberlain and other leaders and a large number of public and private documents that demonstrate concern about Germany's behaviour but an unwillingness to react too hastily to German aggression.

The Chamberlain-Hitler Collusion examines critically the entire documentary record of the behaviour of the political elites of this period with especial emphasis on the British political establishment. Our concern is not simply to uncover documents that demonstrate flagrantly the desire of the British leadership to strike a devil's pact with Hitler in order to rid the European continent of the Communist movement which the leaders dreaded. Instead our goal is to examine dispassionately all the official and unofficial correspondence, conference notes, Cabinet minutes, and diaries available from this period to determine the ideas that motivated policy-makers. We contend that in many cases, the discourse of the politicians, civil servants, military men, and ambassadors has assumptions built in which all individuals "in the know" could readily understand. Diplomatic and political niceties dictated that use of plain language was rare and that the simplest of statements requires a microscopic analysis to determine the nuances of its message.

We suggest that an acquaintance with the context of these statements makes it easier to determine what individuals were really saying. Ultimately we find no contradiction between documents, usually of a private nature, where the willingness to grant Hitler a free hand in central and eastern Europe and the desire to have Hitler make war on the Soviets are plainly stated, and the larger documentary record. Indeed we pay close attention to the way that various documents are linked. What went on at Munich, an event which historian Ronald Blythe is hardly alone in calling a "baffling" meeting, makes perfect sense in light of the minutes of the two earlier meetings between

Chamberlain and Hitler as well as more generally the events from Hitler's accession to power onwards.

The authenticity of the documents in this book is not in question. Indeed, though the book is based largely on primary sources, much of the evidence used here can be found scattered about through the many books and articles that have been produced on this period. What is new here is the gathering together in one place of all the evidence about what the political leaders of Britain and, to a lesser degree, France, thought they could accomplish by cooperating with Hitler from 1933 to 1939. The synthesis provided here may seem radical. But, as we have already observed, many leading politicians in several countries shared its main tenets in the 1930s. So did the well-respected historians Gaetano Salvemini and Frederick L. Schuman who came to their conclusions at a period before the full documentary record had become available. In any case, the accuracy of our conclusions cannot be judged by how many writers and politicians in the past have shared our perspective. Rather it must be judged on the basis of the evidence presented, evidence which we invite the reader once again to compare with the evidence contained in the works of such authors as Taylor, Newman, and Watt.

The present work is based largely on an earlier and lengthier publication by Clement Leibovitz entitled *The Chamberlain-Hitler Deal* and published by Les Editions Duval in Edmonton in 1993. Though the earlier work is voluminous and unedited and could discourage a general reader, its argumentation in several areas is more fully developed than in the present work.

Clement Leibovitz
Alvin Finkel

4

CHAPTER ONE
THE MYTH OF APPEASEMENT

Britain had declared war on Germany just over two months earlier when Lord Lloyd of Dolobran published a sixty-page pamphlet entitled "The British Case" in November 1939.[1] Lord Halifax, the Secretary of State for Foreign Affairs, provided the enthusiastic introduction that left no doubt that this pamphlet expressed the views of the Chamberlain government.

It was a peculiar introduction to a peculiar pamphlet. Halifax did not denounce or even mention Germany, Nazism or fascism. Instead he instructed readers that Dolobran would reveal that the war was a defence of "the Christian conception of freedom" against enemies of this conception.[2] And Lord Lloyd did just that. While the declaration of war against Germany in September 1939 had cited the German invasion of Poland as the cause, Dolobran focused on an event that occurred in August: the German-Soviet pact. This was "Herr Hitler's final apostasy. It was the betrayal of Europe."[3]

Indeed, in "The British Case," it would seem that the war for "the Christian conception of freedom" was really being fought against the Soviet Union rather than Germany, though Britain had declared war on the latter and not on the former. Germany's crime was to have thrown in its lot, in however expedient a fashion, with the Bolshevik state. Lord Lloyd was unsparing in his criticism not only of Bolshevik philosophy but of Soviet external policies upon which he heaped "the main responsibility for European unrest" in the decade following the peace treaties that concluded World War One. Soviet manipulations and the insidious Communist doctrines had created chaos in Finland, Estonia, Bulgaria, Hungary, Poland, Italy, Germany, and Spain. "Russian agents and Russian money were busy all over Europe."[4]

Fascism, wrote Dolobran, with the unreserved endorsement of the British government's second most important member, served the purpose of combating this Bolshevik threat. The government

---

[1]   Lord Lloyd of Dolobran, *The British Case* (Toronto: W.M. Collins Sons and Company, Canada, 1940).
[2]   *Ibid.,* p. 10.
[3]   *Ibid.,* p. 53.
[4]   *Ibid.,* p. 36.

had no quarrel with fascist or Nazi ideology as such since it was an internal matter how a country beat back the Communist threat and equally an internal matter how it dealt with racial questions. But the Nazis, thought this British lord, had *betrayed* their principles by collaborating with Stalin. Britain therefore had to react and react strongly if "European civilization" were to be maintained.

This was hardly the only defence of fascism produced in the early wartime period by individuals with strong links to the British government. Writing in October 1939, Nevile Henderson, British Ambassador to Germany from 1937 till the outbreak of war in 1939, was sycophantic in his praise of fascist dictators such as Italy's Mussolini and Portugal's Salazar. He also lauded National Socialism and suggested that Hitler was a tragic figure who had saved his country from the socialist threat but had overstepped certain bounds: "Nor would the world have failed to acclaim Hitler as a great German if he had known when and where to stop: even, for instance, after Munich and the Nuremberg decrees for the Jews."[5]

Halifax and Henderson held their high positions under Prime Minister Neville Chamberlain, whose fondness for Herr Hitler and whose disappointment with the Soviet-German pact matched their own. In turn, Chamberlain, leader of the British Conservatives, had become leader of his party and the government with the support of a broad section of the ruling classes in Britain who, while sometimes having reservations about fascist regimes, admired their ability to crush Communism.

Chamberlain and his associates, argues the present book, went well beyond an admiration for fascists, an admiration which was rarely as public as in the Henderson and Dolobran books because public disgust with the ruthless dictators of the continent made it inadvisable for politicians, however conservative, to associate themselves publicly with the likes of Hitler, Mussolini, Franco and Salazar. Indeed they had an understanding with Hitler. They would allow Germany to rearm and, in return, Hitler would use his reinvigorated armed forces to destroy the mutual enemy of Nazism and the British Empire: Soviet Communism. To this end Britain was prepared to allow

[5] Nevile Henderson, *Failure of a Mission* (New York: G.P. Putnam's Sons, 1939), p. 12.

6

Germany a "free hand" in its dealings with eastern European countries. But Hitler, events would prove, was unwilling to limit his territorial aspirations to eastern Europe or at least was unwilling to trust that the West would not replace his friends with leaders who would attack Germany from the west while she was engaged in war on the eastern front. Having allowed Hitler to rearm, the British leaders felt a strong sense of betrayal when they realized that Hitler might not be a defender of "the Christian conception of freedom" after all. Otherwise, how could he plan an attack on the West, as their intelligence in early 1939 informed them he was doing? How could he eventually make a pact with the Soviet devil and plan attacks on the capitalist democracies of the continent?

Ultimately then the argument here is that "appeasement" – the notion that a war-weary Britain humoured Hitler with small countries that he wished to gobble up in order to avoid another European-wide slaughter – is a myth. Chamberlain and his friends were not trying to avoid a war; indeed their whole intention was to have Hitler carry out a bloody confrontation with the Soviet Union to end Bolshevism in its heartland. He was to have a "free hand" in eastern Europe so that this common end could be achieved. Appeasement was a public front meant to "appease" public disgust with the Nazis and their treatment of minorities such as the Jews and small nations such as Czechoslovakia and Austria. It was not appeasement, which never existed, that failed, but the devils' pact between the British and Nazi German leaders. Hitler suspected that if he limited his military sights on central and eastern Europe, the Western armies would take advantage of German forces while they were engaged on eastern fronts. In the end, Hitler was not willing to gamble the future of his Third Reich on the ability of Chamberlain to deliver.

Yet, even as the war began to rage, the Halifaxes and Hendersons, with Chamberlain's endorsement, desperately attempted to revive the old anti-Communist understanding between themselves and Hitler. They made clear that they did not wish to fight fascism as such and that indeed they admired many aspects of fascism. The German occupation of Norway and the fall of France discredited the Chamberlainites and brought Winston Churchill to power. Churchill had been the leading spokesman for the minority within the British ruling class who had sensed from the beginning that Britain could not do business with Hitler and his cronies, that they were indeed a great threat to the British Empire.[6] While not without admiration for Mussolini or fear and loathing of communists, Churchill recognized that Hitler was unlikely to restrict his ambitions to eastern Europe. Like President Roosevelt in the United States and a section of the ruling political class in France, Churchill and his supporters recognized that a "common front" with Hitler against Communism was an insane proposition. But Chamberlainites were included in the Churchill Cabinet and, without Churchill's knowledge, secret negotiations with the Nazi regime continued for a period after he took office. They did not come to a complete halt until the Americans entered the war and scuttled such efforts.[7]

Over the years it would become accepted that the battle between Chamberlain and his supporters, on the one hand, and Churchill, Anthony Eden, and their supporters on the other, had been about appeasement. As this book shows, that allows the Chamberlainites, who represented majority opinion among Britain's bankers, industrialists, and landed aristocrats off the hook as bumbling fools. Like Lord Darlington in the novel *Remains of the Day*, they are presented as amateurs who are fooled by German protestations of peaceful intent, kind dolts who think that avoiding war at any cost will save humankind from another slaughter. The argument here is rather that the ruling group before May 10, 1940 were bloody-minded protectors of privilege whose fixation with destroying communists and communism led them to make common cause with fascists. They were not honest idiotic patriots; they were liars and traitors who would sacrifice human lives in their defence of property and privilege.

Ironically, on any rational account, the real threat posed by Soviet Communism to aristocratic and bourgeois privilege in Britain and other western countries in the interwar period was

[6] A recent Churchill biographer charges however that even Churchill was wildly inconsistent on the key issues of the period. Though he was a strong supporter of rearmament, he supported both the Anglo-German Naval Agreement of 1935 and Britain's encouragement of France to look the other way as Hitler marched into the Rhineland in 1936. If only because he was anxious to be reappointed to Cabinet, Churchill was unwilling to oppose policies that implied support for a "free hand" for Germany in the East. Clive Ponting, *Churchill* (London: Sinclair-Stevenson, 1994), p. 378.

[7] John Loftus and Mark Aarons, *The Secret War Against the Jews: How Western Espionage Betrayed the Jewish People* (New York: St. Martin's Press, 1994), pp. 89-91.

probably slight. But that did not stop aristocrats and industrial magnates from regarding the Soviet Union as a plague that could spread its poisonous message abroad to the discomfort of wealthy elites. The Allied attempt to overthrow Communist Russia between 1918 and 1921 had failed but the obsession with this goal did not go away. It was, by no means, restricted to the British ruling class. The next chapter discusses the origins and the extent of the hysteria about Bolsheviks and the degree to which it led to sympathy and support for fascism among political and economic leaders of the democracies. Without an understanding of the depths of outrage the propertied classes felt at the Soviet experiment which had eliminated their counterparts in the Russian Empire, much of British official policy in the interwar period makes little sense. We begin however with an outline of where the logic of an anti-Communist front of the remaining democracies with fascism led the British leaders.

***

As early as 1923, in *Mein Kampf*, his manifesto for the future, Adolf Hitler had made clear his intention that Germany rearm in defiance of the Versailles Treaty of 1919 in which the victors of World War One specifically forbade German rearmament. He also made clear his desire for a German Empire. An early target for conquest would be Ukraine, the breadbasket of the Soviet Union.

By the end of 1933, having imprisoned or murdered his opponents and established a dictatorship, Hitler, as German chancellor, had moved determinedly to fulfil the ambitions set out in his madman's manifesto. The British government was aware by November 1933, as Anthony Eden would later write, that Nazi Germany would soon be an "armed menace." The annual report of the British Chiefs of Staff concluded that the purpose of German rearmament was solely "to make it possible for her to secure a revision of frontiers in the East."[8] (Eden claims that early on, he feared that Hitler also had ambitions in western Europe though, in practice, he was in the ranks of the appeasers until shortly before he left the government in February 1938). While such a "revision" would violate the independence of existing nations and the rearmament necessary to achieve it would violate the Versailles Treaty, Britain pointedly refused to act.

[8]   Anthony Eden, *Facing The Dictators* (London: Cassell, 1962), pp. 47-48.

On October 24, 1933, Hitler tested the waters by informing Sir Eric Phipps, the British Ambassador to Germany, "that he sought 'a certain expansion in eastern Europe.' "[9] Silence speaks loudly in diplomacy between nations, the lack of a denunciation of the stated aims of one nation by another being interpreted as a tacit acceptance. It was indeed with silence that Britain responded to this candid statement of intentions by Hitler. France was in a position militarily to prevent further rearmament (it had already allowed a modicum of rearmament in the pre-Hitler period in violation of Versailles but Germany remained militarily quite weak). A section of the French political leadership was anxious to have Britain join it in using threats and if necessary force to thwart Hitler's aggressive policies which France believed would ultimately be directed against their nation. Instead Britain restrained France.

Silence soon gave way to cautious public endorsements of German rearmament by the British government. In the House of Commons in July 1934 Conservative leader Stanley Baldwin defended Germany's right to recreate an air force. "She has every argument in her favour, from her defenceless position in the air, to try to make herself secure."[10] Baldwin's party completely dominated the National government over which Ramsay MacDonald presided as a figurehead; one year later Baldwin assumed the prime ministership.

Britain intended initially to maintain its military superiority over Germany. But it also intended to violate the Versailles agreement. After Hitler declared that Germany would not be bound by the disarmament provisions of the treaty, Britain had met with France and Italy at Stresa to discuss a joint reaction of the European victors of World War One. Britain acted unilaterally however in moving to accommodate Hitler. While Germany rearmed, Chamberlain and other members of the Baldwin government declared that Germany's intentions were pacific and ought not to be opposed. On June 18, 1935, Britain concluded a naval accord with Germany that allowed Germany to build up her naval force to 35 percent of Britain's. The accord was denounced by the Baltic states who recognized immediately that such a large German naval force would give that nation

[9] *Ibid.*, p. 149.
[10] Gaetano Salvemini, *Prelude to World War Two* (London: Victor Gollancz Ltd., 1953), p. 165.

control of the Baltic and the ability to determine the fate of the nations bordering that sea. Perhaps more importantly, the British-German accord, which left Versailles in tatters, placed no limits on the expansion of Germany's land forces. A free hand was to be given to Germany's expansion into central and eastern Europe.

In March 1936 Hitler had tested the West's resolve to prevent him from creating a menacing military force. He remilitarized the Rhineland in blatant violation of the Treaty of Locarno. France, still anxious to limit German rearmament and unconvinced that it would limit its appetite to small countries to the East, prepared to demand demilitarization of the Rhineland and force it upon Hitler if necessary with British armed help. But Baldwin, by then prime minister, was not only opposed to helping out such an operation; he actively worked against it. As he told his Cabinet, if the French succeeded in their aims, the Hitler government would fall. In his opinion, the chaos that would then ensue would give the advantage to the German Communists.[11] With the only alternatives (in his mind anyway) being the Nazis and the Communists, Baldwin had no difficulty choosing. The Nazis were supporters of private property.

Indeed, preparations were being made for a Baldwin-Hitler meeting before the former resigned his prime ministership in favour of Neville Chamberlain. The intention was that this meeting would produce an open British-German political and military front against the Soviets. At the last minute however it was decided that British public opinion was not ready for a formal alliance with the German dictator. But that did not stop secret encouragement of Hitler to proceed with his policy of arming to attack the Soviets and detach Ukraine from Communist control. There were no warnings to Hitler to reverse his course.

Yet, in February 1937, the Committee of Imperial Defence (C.I.D.), which combined the wisdom of the military and Cabinet, confirmed that the rulers of Britain were aware that Hitler was bent on wars of territorial expansion. In a report which the Cabinet approved, the Committee concluded that Germany had "expansion eastward in her mind." It was unlikely to sign a "treaty of mutual guarantees" with the four other "Western Powers" unless the treaty was "constructed in such a

[11] Great Britain, Cabinet Minutes, CAB 23/81, p. 292, March 11, 1936.

form as to leave her free to pursue a policy of expansion in Eastern and Central Europe, which, in conjunction with her antagonism to Communism, clearly tends to lead Germany into conflict with the U.S.S.R." The C.I.D. was not bothered by German military intentions in the east *per se* but it was concerned that French pacts with the Soviet Union and other central and eastern European countries might produce a war between France and Germany when an eastern country was attacked. Though the C.I.D. was certain that Germany was not yet a military match for Britain and France, it was aware that this could change in a year or two. But it saw no reasons for antagonism with Germany, concluding instead that more work should be done to get a five-power anti-Soviet agreement for western Europe – an agreement that it conceded was not possible without giving Hitler a free hand in eastern and central Europe.[12]

Nine months after the C.I.D. report, Halifax met with Hitler (November 1937). Halifax gave the Führer fulsome praise for having made Germany "a bulwark of the West against Bolshevism."[13] He focused on the need for a formal treaty between Britain and Germany though Hitler indicated his reticence regarding a British government's ability to fulfil its pledges when party political considerations played such a large role in the life of a democracy.

But Chamberlain and his associates were still not prepared to pay heed to Churchill and Eden, among others, who believed that Germany must be brought to heel before it achieved military parity with Britain. The Chamberlain government attempted to justify Germany's invasion of Austria in February 1938 by claiming that the two countries had decided peacefully to unite. Secretly, the government also decided to do nothing should Hitler, who was claiming a right of interference because of the large Sudeten German population, invade Czechoslovakia. While Churchill, Eden, the Labour Party and even some Cabinet members called for massive rearmament and clear warnings to Hitler about the consequences of aggression, Chamberlain pressed for a four-party agreement on the future of Europe. The

---

[12] *Documents on British Foreign Policy,* 2nd Series, Vol 18, pp. 965-987.
[13] *Documents and Materials Relating to the Eve of the Second World War,* Volume One (Salisbury, North Carolina: Documentary Publications, 1978), p. 20.

four parties were Britain, Germany, France and Italy. The exclusion of the Soviet Union was quite deliberate.

***

In September 1938, Neville Chamberlain had three separate meetings, lasting several days each, with Adolf Hitler. Ostensibly the purpose of the meetings was to determine the fate of Czechoslovakia, particularly the Sudeten region where the German-speaking ethnic minority of Czechoslovakia formed a regional majority. But the British Cabinet had resolved six months earlier not to use force under any circumstances to defend Czechoslovakia from German aggression. The Czech issue alone would not have been a reason for marathon meetings with the Nazi leader. Rather, Chamberlain's purpose, as he explained privately in letters to the king and his sister, was to secure a broader "understanding" with Hitler.

On 13 September 1938, two days before meeting Hitler at Berchtesgaden, Chamberlain wrote King George VI that his aim was "the establishment of an Anglo-German understanding preceded by a settlement of the Czecho-Slovakian question." Such an understanding must be deemed possible to achieve because Germany and England were "the two pillars of European peace and buttresses against communism."[14] In the same letter, Chamberlain informed the king that reliable sources confirmed that "Herr Hitler has made up his mind to attack Czecho-Slovakia and then to proceed further East." Only by negotiations could Britain determine with Hitler how the latter could achieve his objectives without having to use violence against the Czechs. He must be able "to proceed further East" without having to resort to war.[15]

This anti-Communist "peace," he admitted candidly, required giving Hitler satisfaction on the Czechoslovak issue. "Your Majesty's representative in Berlin," that is, Nevile Henderson, had informed Chamberlain that Hitler insisted on a solution to

[14] It is interesting that France is not included as one of the pillars of peace. France, after all, was supposed to be Britain's closest ally in Europe. Presumably the election of the Popular Front government in 1936, which caused consternation among British Conservatives, caused Chamberlain to believe that France could no longer be counted upon to preserve the established social order in Europe.

[15] J. W. Wheeler-Bennett, *King George VI* (Toronto: Macmillan, 1958), p. 346.

the Czech crisis "satisfactory to himself." If that solution could be obtained peacefully, well and good. But if necessary, "he is ready to march if he should so decide." At Berchtesgaden Chamberlain accepted Hitler's point of view, agreeing to pressure Czechoslovakia to accept Germany's territorial demands. Also at this meeting, as Chamberlain would recall at a Cabinet meeting on 3 May 1939: "The Prime Minister said that the first time the idea of a free hand in Eastern Europe had been mentioned was, he thought, at his interview with Herr Hitler at Berchtesgaden."[16]

This was somewhat misleading. As we shall see, the "idea of a free hand in eastern Europe" for Germany emerged in Anglo-German relations early in the Nazi period. It underlay the Naval Treaty between the two countries in 1935 and much of the Cabinet's strategic thinking from 1933 to 1939. But Chamberlain and Hitler had not met until Berchtesgaden and so it was technically correct that the first time Chamberlain had heard about the "free hand" *from Hitler personally* was at Berchtesgaden.

At Berchtesgaden Chamberlain praised Hitler for having "carried through the renaissance of the German nation with extraordinary success" and stated that he had "the greatest respect for this man."[17] He let the dictator know that his goal was to "work further for an Anglo-German rapprochement." Hitler suggested that the point of the Anglo-German Naval Agreement of 1935, from Nazi Germany's perspective, was for the two nations to renounce the use of force one against the other forever.

Germany had only agreed to have inferior naval forces to Britain on the understanding that the two countries had no reason ever to clash. It was not necessary for Hitler to point out to Chamberlain the obvious point that Germany had informed the British government well before the Naval Agreement of its

---

[16] Minutes of the British Cabinet (CAB) 23/99 0.122.
[17] *Documents on British Foreign Policy (DBFP)*, 3rd Series, Vol. 2, Doc. 895. *DBFP* includes two accounts of the Berchtesgaden meeting. The one consists of notes made by Chamberlain after the meeting. The other was made at the meeting by the noted German translator Dr. Paul Schmidt. The reliability of translations by Schmidt, who was a member of an anti-Nazi group, is unanimously accepted by historians. In the discussions that follow of the meeting, all references are to the Schmidt translation except where otherwise indicated.

desire to have a free hand in Eastern Europe. What he told him instead was that Germany would cancel the agreement if there was no longer an understanding between the two nations that assured the impossibility of a clash. Both men understood that this meant that Hitler believed that the Naval Agreement signified Britain's agreement to a free hand and any new agreement between the two countries had to reinforce that free hand. There were in short in Hitler's mind two keys to the free hand: the Naval Agreement and an understanding between the two nations that they would never, under any circumstances make war on one another.

Chamberlain admitted that Hitler's interpretation of the Naval Agreement was correct. Without mentioning a free hand, he conceded that Germany would have no reason to respect the Anglo-German Naval Agreement if it believed Britain would stand in the way of its foreign policy goals. But he demurred at that point to say unconditionally that Britain would never use force against Germany. He knew that there still were bones of contention between the two countries one of them being Germany's expressed desire to recover her pre-war colonies.

But he tried to reassure Hitler that his government had never seriously considered armed intervention against Germany. Indirectly admitting the hypocrisy of his government which soothed anti-fascist public opinion by an occasional belligerent statement regarding Germany, he suggested that "no proper distinction was made on the German side between a threat and a warning." His government had issued warnings but no threats and should be seen as desirous of peace with Germany. Hitler did not think Chamberlain was going far enough and repeated his view that the Naval Agreement, which assured the British that German naval strength would be inferior to their own, required both sides to renounce war against the other in all circumstances. Otherwise the two sides should abrogate the agreement.

Though Chamberlain did not give the requested undertaking, he gave Hitler satisfaction on the Czech question. As Chamberlain wrote in his own notes, Hitler "would not feel safe unless the Sudeten Germans were incorporated in the Reich." He also demanded the abrogation of the mutual assistance pact between Czechoslovakia and the Soviet Union. Chamberlain's response:

> I said: 'Supposing it were modified, so that Czechoslovakia were no longer bound to go to the assistance of Russia if Russia was attacked, and on the other hand Czechoslovakia was debarred from giving asylum to Russian forces in her aerodromes or elsewhere; would that remove your difficulty?

Chamberlain clearly did not wish Hitler to face any "difficulty" when Germany attacked Russia. He used "if" and did not say who might be attacking Russia. But it is clear from his letter to the king that he knew – as he had indeed known for several years – that Hitler desired control over all of central and eastern Europe. "The two pillars of European peace and buttresses against communism," hoped Chamberlain, could come to an agreement that would encourage Germany to make war on Russia while allowing Czechoslovakia, shorn of the Sudeten, a limited national existence under the German thumb.

The two leaders came closer to an "understanding" during two days of meetings at Godesberg on 22 and 23 September. As their second day of meetings concluded at 2 a.m., "Hitler thanked Chamberlain for his efforts for peace," as Dr. Paul Schmidt wrote in a memoir of the meeting. Schmidt was a translator whose translations have been accepted by post-war historians, particularly because of his anti-Nazi connections. Acting as translator, Schmidt was the only third party in the room. He wrote further:

> Hitler also spoke about a German-Anglo rapprochement and cooperation. It was clearly noticeable that it was important for him to have a good relation with the Englishman. He went back to his old tune: 'Between us there should be no conflict,' he said to Chamberlain, *we will not stand in the way of your pursuit of your non-European interests and you may without harm let us have a free hand on the European continent in central and South-East Europe.*[18] Sometime we will have to solve the colonial question; but this has time, and war is not to be considered in this case.'[19]

---

[18] Here is the original German text of the italicized sentence. "wir werden Ihnen bei der Verfolgung Ihrer auereuropaishen Interessen nicht im Wege stehen, und Sie konnen uns ohne Schaden auf dem europaischen Festlande in Mittel-und Sudosteuropa freie Hand lassen."
[19] Author translation from Dr. Paul Schmidt, *Statist auf Diplomatischer Buhne 1923-45* (Bonn: Athenaum-Verlag, 1949), pp. 406-407.

After this conversation, noted Schmidt, the mood of the meeting, which had been quite positive all along, became especially buoyant. Chamberlain did not disabuse Hitler of the notion that he had a "free hand" in central and eastern Europe. Rather he allowed the comment to stand without a direct response.

Back in Britain after Godesberg, Chamberlain, still jubilant, told his Cabinet that he had established real influence with Hitler. The Cabinet minutes note: "Herr Hitler had said that if we got this [Czech] question out of the way without conflict, it would be a turning point in Anglo-German relations. That to the Prime Minister, was the big thing of the present issue."[20] Chamberlain said nothing to the Cabinet of the "turning point" envisioned by Hitler. He did not repeat to his colleagues Hitler's insistence on a deal which gave Germany a free hand in central and eastern Europe.

At Munich Chamberlain colluded with Hitler to provide the deal offered by Hitler at Berchtesgaden and fleshed out at Godesberg. The declaration issued by Hitler and Chamberlain on September 30, 1938 at the end of a private meeting following the signing of the Munich agreement is very revealing. The two leaders said: "We regard the agreement signed last night and the Anglo-German Naval Agreement as symbolic of the desire of our two peoples never to go to war with one another again."[21]

This declaration had been prepared by Chamberlain. It was made just two weeks after Hitler had insisted at Berchtesgaden that the spirit of the Anglo-German Naval Agreement was that both sides had to renounce the use of force against the other no matter the circumstances. As Chamberlain later admitted to his Cabinet, it was at Berchtesgaden that Hitler requested a free hand in eastern Europe. Yet nowhere in the minutes of that meeting was there any direct reference to the free hand. Rather, both leaders understood that the Anglo-German Naval Agreement combined with a declaration of both sides never to go to war with each other amounted to the granting to Germany of a free hand in the East. One week later Hitler had made as plain as possible his view that a proper tit for tat between the two countries was a German avowal never to resort to aggression against any part of the British Empire in return for a British granting of a free hand

[20] Ian Colvin, *The Chamberlain Cabinet* (London: Victor Gollancz, 1971), p. 162.
[21] *DBFP*, Series 3, Vol. 2, annex to Doc. 1228, p. 640.

in central and eastern Europe to Germany. Yet Chamberlain's declaration with Hitler repeated Hitler's language from Berchtesgaden which Chamberlain recognized amounted to the granting of a free hand. Munich, which included Italy and France along with Germany and Britain, provided the crowning touch to the "Anglo-German understanding" that emerged from the earlier two meetings. It formalized, at the level of the German and British leaders, the understanding that Britain had informally (though as the Naval Agreement suggested, not always passively) given Germany that it had a free hand in eastern Europe and was welcome to do what it could to destroy the Soviet Union. Chamberlain's promise to the king to cement an alliance between the two "buttresses against communism" appeared to have been fulfilled.

But by early 1939 British military intelligence was confirming the Churchill-Eden view that Hitler was planning aggression in western Europe as well as eastern Europe. Chamberlain was concerned but held doggedly to his alliance with Germany. On 15 March 1939, when it became clear that Hitler had broken the Munich Agreement and seized the parts of Czechoslovakia that he had not been handed on a plate six months earlier, Chamberlain made a mealy-mouthed and completely non-bellicose statement to the House of Commons. Czechoslovakia, he noted, had ceased to exist and therefore the British agreement to defend the Czech state was null and void. Peaceful settlement of disputes, not war, must remain the foreign policy goal of Britain.

Two days later however he reversed himself and Halifax sent to Ambassador Henderson in Berlin a stern note for the German government which claimed Germany's military actions in Czechoslovakia were "devoid of any basis of legality." What had happened in between? Chamberlain had heard the shocking word not of yet another German conquest but of a German surrender of sorts. Germany had agreed to cede the former Czech province of Ruthenia (Carpatho-Ukraine) to Hungary. Ruthenia had long been seen as the focal point of a German conquest of the Ukraine. Its cession to Hungary suggested, presumably even to the Hitler-beguiled Chamberlain, that the military assessment that Hitler planned to move westwards rather than eastwards was correct.

Shortly afterwards, Britain gave its famous unilateral guarantee to Poland against a German assault, though ironically Germany's claim to Danzig, unlike its claims to Austria and Czechoslovakia, had some merit. The merit of claims was not the British concern: Britain wanted to insure that if it was attacked by Germany, Germany would face a battle on two fronts. Poland, as anticipated, later agreed to a reciprocal guarantee with Britain that meant that if Germany attacked Britain, it would face a two-front war with Britain and Poland.

But the British government of the day had not given up its attempts to restore their earlier agreement with Germany. In early June Adam Von Trott, a former Rhodes scholar, was sent by Germany to England on a fact-finding mission. He met with government leaders and recorded in a memorandum to the German government the conciliatory position of the British. Halifax indicated that after Munich "he had seen the way open for a new consolidation of Powers, in which Germany would have the preponderance in Central and South East Europe, a 'not too unfriendly Spain and Italy' would leave unthreatened British positions in the Mediterranean and the Middle East, and with pacification in the Far East also becoming possible."[22]

Lord Lothian, one of Chamberlain's closest advisors, defended Germany's invasion of Czechoslovakia as a means of achieving her "vital rights."[23] He accepted that Germany needed to expand but suggested that some means had to be found to preserve the national identity of the Czechs so as to appease public opinion in Britain. Like Halifax, he supported the notion of spheres of influence as a solution to the growing impasse between Britain and Nazi Germany. Central and eastern Europe would be conceded to Germany.

Chamberlain had done all he could to shore up his shattered agreement with Hitler to allow German conquest in the East in return for a guarantee of peaceful relations between Germany and Britain. Circumventing the Foreign Office where, Halifax notwithstanding, Munich had been received as an appalling surrender, Chamberlain used a personal envoy to maintain a post-Munich dialogue with German Foreign Minister Joachim von Ribbentrop. Through George F. Steward, his press advisor,

---

[22] *Documents on German Foreign Policy*, Series D, Vol. 6, Doc. 497, pp. 674-685.
[23] *Ibid.*

Chamberlain kept a line open to von Ribbentrop via Dr. Fritz Hesse, a representative of the German Foreign Minister in London. The British prime minister promised to work to prevent the forces for rearmament within the government and the country from having their way but indicated this was only possible if Germany resisted the urge to boast about the results of Munich as a victory and emphasized its intention never again to threaten Britain with war.

Like Lothian and Halifax, Chamberlain was disappointed that Germany in 1939 seemed to be preparing for war in the West rather than just the East. His government made efforts throughout 1939, even after the war had begun, to revive its plan for an alliance of the non-Communist nations against the Soviets in which the Germans would do all or most of the fighting and gain the spoils of war. Only the events that replaced Chamberlain with Churchill and removed most of the Chamberlainites from high office ended the sordid collusion from the top with the Nazis that had allowed Hitler to rearm Germany with impunity. Before his fall, however, Chamberlain, along with French Prime Minister Edouard Daladier, had attempted to divert concern from Nazi Germany's depredations to the Soviet danger. Using Soviet presssure on Finland as a pretext, France and Britain planned an assault on Soviet territory while doing nothing to combat Germany upon whom they had declared war.

Blame for the tragedy of World War Two, including the Holocaust, must rest partly with Stanley Baldwin, Neville Chamberlain, Lord Halifax, and their close associates who, far from being naive appeasers anxious to avoid wars in Europe, were visceral anti-Communists who single-mindedly pursued an alliance with Hitler. Their desire to overthrow the Soviet Union, not because of its totalitarian character but because it symbolized forces that appeared to threaten the privileges of capitalists and imperialists, led them away from nipping in the bud the plans of an evil German government which openly embodied an unspeakable anti-humanist philosophy.

***

The attempt to decipher the motivations of foreign policy-makers requires some understanding of the language these individuals tend to use. While British officials used the

English language to make known their views, they gave terms special meanings that were clear only to those in the know. Coded messages were prevalent in public addresses meant to shape public opinion and usually prevailed in diplomatic documents as well. The word "peace" constitutes one example. In plain English, it means the absence of war. In the mouths and pens of British officialdom it meant something rather different. It meant the absence of war in western Europe with no concern whether Germany was making war in eastern Europe. "Self-determination" for German speakers outside Germany might, in plain English, imply the right of these people to determine their own fate. In officialdom's code it meant the right of the German government to rule all speakers of German.

It is useful then to examine a document that combined coded meanings with plain English to see how this diplomatic code worked. Writing to the Foreign Office on 10 May 1937, Nevile Henderson, the new British ambassador to Germany, provided his views on the political situation.[24] Though he made some use of diplomatic code throughout his document, Henderson was aware that he was writing for a restricted audience and could be somewhat candid. By the end of the letter, his plain English betrays the real meanings of certain coded words.

Henderson begins by observing that there are two fundamental principles of British foreign policy. The first is the defence of Great Britain and the British Empire. The second is the maintenance of peace in Europe and throughout the world. "Our conceptions of moral principles," writes the ambassador, must guide foreign policy. Britain's attitudes to German aspirations must be predicated upon "peace and peaceful evolution." To this point Henderson sounds like a noble-minded pacifist. But, as the rest of his letter reveals, that is because he is writing in code. The italicized words in the section we now quote show a transition from misleading official language to plain English.

> On the other hand, though Germany must be regarded
> as the most formidable menace of all at the present
> moment, there is no reason, provided she does not
> *ruthlessly* disregard the vital principles of the League
> of Nations or revert to a policy of naval and overseas
> rivalry or of a renewed *push to the West*, or
> deliberately threatens us by air, why – *restless and*

[24] *Documents on British Foreign Policy*, 2nd Series, Vol.19, Doc 53 (enclosure), p. 98.

21

> *troublesome though she is bound to be* – she should
> perpetually constitute a danger of war *for us.*

It begins to become clear that Henderson recognizes that
Germany does not have peaceful intentions towards all nations.
But he is optimistic that Germany intends no harm "for us,"
meaning Britain and her Empire as well as the West. Yet he goes
on to speak of Germany's "inevitable urge towards unity and
expansion." This plain English statement of Germany's
"inevitable" behaviour raises questions about the statement that
Britain is committed to "peace and peaceful evolution" in its
dealings with Germany. How can one negotiate peace with
people who have an inevitable urge to attack the right of other
nations to exist? The answer is found in Henderson's plain
English viewpoint that Germany does not "constitute a danger of
war for us." In plain English Britain is committed only to peace
for itself, its Empire and Western Europe.

Henderson then goes on to discuss the problems posed for good
Anglo-German relations by France's mutual assistance pact with
the Soviet Union in which each guaranteed the other aid in case
of a military attack by a third party. He suggests that a solution
would be "a direct Anglo-German understanding based on
French security and integrity but including some guarantee of
neutrality in the event of a Russo-German conflict." Here is an
almost-plain-English indication of Henderson's advocacy of a
free hand for Germany to attack the Soviets. "Peace and
peaceful evolution," the official words for Britain's relations
with Germany, give way to discussion of an arrangement that
insures Germany can attack the Soviet Union free from any fears
that France would intervene on the Soviets' behalf.

On goes this advocate of "peace." Recalling the valedictory
speech of his predecessor, Sir Eric Phipps, Henderson outlines
Germany's foreign policy aims as: the annexation of
German-speaking nations such as Austria and territories such as
Czechoslovakia's Sudetenland; "expansion in the east;" and
"recovery of colonies." "In themselves none of these aims need
injure purely British national interest," writes Henderson. It now
becomes clear that there is a "British national interest" that is
separate from the international peace aims mentioned earlier as
constituting an aim of British foreign policy. Germany can grab
countries in eastern Europe and recover some old colonies
without violating "British national interest."

Henderson finishes off by being very blunt in stating that Britain should allow Germany to make war against eastern European countries provided that it makes no threat against the British Empire. In a letter that started off in a high-minded tone, he finishes off by revealing a narrow notion of national interest, a racist attitude to Slavs, and a willingness to let Germany get her way through warfare.

> To put it quite bluntly, Eastern Europe emphatically is neither definitely settled for all time nor is it a vital British interest and the German is certainly more civilized than the Slav, and in the end, if properly handled, also less potentially dangerous to British interests – One might even go so far as to assert that it is not even just to endeavour to prevent Germany from completing her unity or from being prepared for war against the Slav provided her preparations are such as to reassure the British Empire that they are not simultaneously designed against it.

Apart from what it reveals about the differences between official language and plain English, this memo is important because, in plain English, it parallels the views, usually expressed with more coded language, of the leaders of the British government and military at the time. Throughout this book, we are often forced to try to translate official language into plain English because, while Henderson's views were typical of those of the elite, customary politeness and/or the need to mollify public opinion necessitated the use of opaque language.

CHAPTER TWO

AN OBSESSION WITH COMMUNISM

The ruling classes throughout western Europe had watched with horror as Marxian and other socialist doctrines spread among members of the burgeoning working class from the late nineteenth century onwards. The takeover of the Russian Empire by committed Marxists as the Czar's rule collapsed during World War One confirmed the propertied classes' worst nightmare: a disciplined organization of the "inferior" members of society could destroy the power and privileges of traditional elites.

The Bolsheviks were viewed in the circles of the powerful as a "virus" that infected the working class in every country. Worker unrest, growing electoral support for Communist and socialist parties, and the spread of socialist ideas throughout European nations' non-European colonies were all blamed on the new rulers of Russia. Little attention need be paid to the complaints of exploitation by workers and peasants at home or in the colonies when unrest could be explained in terms of "Soviet propaganda." Indeed vilification of the Soviets went hand in hand with strident defences of the existing economic order and a growing resentment that workers were using the liberties won for average citizens during the previous century to demand a redistribution of wealth and power. Fascism in this context was welcomed because it put the people in their place and defended, however thuggishly, the view that property rights and the right to colonial possessions, not democracy and equality, were the central values of Western civilization.

But how could the uninformed and impressionable masses be convinced that existing property relations were superior to those they might imagine to exist in Soviet Russia and their conservative rulers a better bet than the leaders of labour-based parties? Western rulers early developed the habit of simply telling lies in order to mask their visceral hatred of the Marxist doctrine. The idea was to discredit the Russian Marxist rulers in the eyes of the peoples of western Europe by focusing attention on their supposed betrayals of the norms of international political behaviour. There were some real betrayals of these norms: the publication of secret treaties and the carrying out of

25

open diplomacy, for example. But public indignation could hardly be aroused by emphasizing such 'betrayals.'

The strategy of telling lies was employed almost immediately after the Bolsheviks seized power in October 1917. The czar had been overthrown in an earlier coup in February 1917 that established a government lead by Alexander Kerensky, a bourgeois politician. A change of government was greeted with equanimity and even relief by the Allies who recognized that the country was prostrate before Germany and on the verge of total chaos. Kerensky pledged his government's willingness to pursue the military obligations to the Allies undertaken by the czar. This pledge was welcomed by Russia's wartime allies but it was also taken to be *pro forma*. It was well understood that the Russian military was in disarray and could make no useful contribution to the Allied cause. The Bolsheviks, who had opposed the war all along as an imperialist battle, recognized the war weariness of the troops and the country as a whole and gained the support of important sections of the military rank-and-file by promising to pull Russia out of the war unilaterally if the two sides would not agree to an immediate peace.

The reaction of the British, American and French governments was sharp: the Bolshevik government was accused of betrayal of the Allies and this supposed betrayal became the pretext for providing support for various armies that formed within Russia to overthrow the new regime and replace it with a reactionary administration. Even when the war was over, the Allied governments used the memory of this Bolshevik decision to take Russia formally out of the war as an excuse not to establish normal relations with the Bolshevik government. They also claimed dubiously that recognition of the new government was impossible because it did not represent the Russian people, a requirement for recognition that they did not impose on other states.

But no one in the British government seriously believed that Russia by 1917 was capable of making a military contribution to the war effort. Nevertheless the British government withdrew its ambassador to Russia and appointed R.H. Bruce Lockhart, a former Consul-General in Moscow, as its Special Commissioner to determine the aims of the new government. Lockhart later recalled:

> I deprecated as sheer folly our militarist propaganda because it took no account of the war-weariness which had raised the Bolsheviks to the supreme power...

> I think that in their hearts the Cabinet realized that Russia was out of the war for good, but with an obstinate lack of logic they refused to accept the implications of their secret beliefs. *Hate of the revolution and fear of its consequences in England were the dominant reactions of the Conservatives.*[1]

Lockhart would have little impact on the government which had appointed him since it would seem they had determined early on to do all in their power to overthrow the Soviets. But Lockhart's views were confirmed in a report presented to Parliament in 1921 by the parliamentary Committee to Collect Information on Russia. Prepared by Lord Emmott, the report emphasized that the Russian military was a shambles by autumn 1916 and rife with talk of revolution as a result of the disorganization both at the front and in the rear and the enormous casualties sustained.[2] Discipline collapsed and the officers lost the respect of the rank-and-file. The Bolsheviks, in short, did nothing more than end the pretence that Russia was a military factor in the war. This was the conclusion of a committee dominated by MPs supporting the Lloyd George Coalition Government.

But that unmasking of military pretence had been enough to allow those who feared the spread of socialism to brand the Bolsheviks traitors to the Western military cause. It was convenient to try to convince the public, in which the working class loomed large, that the Russian leaders (and, after the creation of the Union of Soviet Socialist Republics in 1921, the Soviet leadership) were beyond the pale because they had allowed British, French and American boys to die while Russian boys no longer fought. That made it less necessary to admit that the real reason the ruling classes of western Europe hated the Soviet government was that it had brought into question the sanctity of private ownership of the means of production and large landed estates.

[1] Bruce Lockhart, *Memoirs of a British Agent* (London: Putman, 1932), p. 197.
[2] W. P. Coates and Zelda K. Coates, *Armed Intervention in Russia* (London: Victor Gollancz Ltd., 1935), pp.20-1.

Related to the charge that the Bolsheviks had abandoned their international military obligations and therefore earned invasion from the Allies was the fabricated claim that the Bolsheviks were cooperating with the Germans against the Allies. Lockhart also tried to dispel this mythology. In May 1918 he informed his American equivalent, Colonel Raymond Robins, of the many ways in which Leon Trotsky, chief military commander of the Soviet government, was cooperating with the Allied armies.[3] Lockhart, it should be noted, at the time of his appointment as Special Commissioner, was an advocate of Allied intervention to overthrow the Bolsheviks; so his dismissal of notions of Soviet-German cooperation was not influenced by a desire to make the Bolsheviks look good. Robins, head of the American Red Cross Mission in Russia,[4] and Commander H. G. Grenfell, British Naval Attaché to Russia, 1912-17,[5] among others, joined Lockhart in dismissing Allied claims of Soviet-German collaboration.

In March 1918, an opportunity occurred to bring Russia back into the Allied military fold. The revolutionary government had begun meetings with the Germans at Brest-Litovsk in December 1917 to negotiate peace. Despite the hostility of the Allies towards them, the Bolsheviks asked the Germans to allow the Allies to join in working out a peace agreement. They insisted on a clause in the armistice that no German division freed from battle in the east should be freed to fight in the west. The Germans were not in a mood to be generous to the new Russian regime and the Bolsheviks were shocked by the severity of the peace terms demanded by the Kaiser. The German peace proposals at Brest-Litovsk required that Russia cede Ukraine and the Baltic provinces to Germany. V.I. Lenin inquired of the American and British governments what military assistance Russia might expect should it reject the German treaty terms and re-enter the war on the Allied side.[6] Lockhart implored his

---

[3] Lockhart's letter to Robins appears in Coates, *Armed Intervention*, pp. 84-5.
[4] *Ibid.*, p. 29, quoting the *Times*, 9 March 1919.
[5] *Ibid.*, p. 29, quoting *Manchester Guardian*, 11 November 1919.
[6] General W.S. Graves quotes passages from a note from the Soviet Government, dated 5 March 1918, and included in the Congressional Record, 29 June 1919, in which the Soviet government asks pointedly:

> In case (a)the All-Russian congress of the Soviets will refuse to ratify the peace treaty with Germany, or (b) if the German Government, breaking the peace treaty, will renew the offensive in order to continue its robber's raid...

government to take the opportunity provided to prevent German paramountcy in Russia. The price, he suggested, would be to call off a proposed Japanese invasion of Siberia and to have the Chinese lift an embargo to Russia of foodstuffs.[7] D.R. Francis, the American Ambassador to Russia, cabled his government, echoing Lockhart's view that aid to Russia should be provided and that an invasion by Japan would be a fatal error.[8] But Britain, despite its official claims that it wanted no more from Russia than for it to fulfil its military obligations, ignored Lockhart. An All-Russian Congress of Soviets was called to decide whether to ratify or reject the Treaty of Brest-Litovsk. The mood of the Congress was for rejection. As Robins would later recall, Lenin was prepared to support rejection as well until it became clear that neither Lockhart nor Robins nor Francis had received a reply from their governments to the Russian request. Lenin then told the Congress that Russia's military position gave it no option but to sign the humiliating peace with Germany. The treaty was ratified by a majority of the delegates though many voted against ratification or abstained.

On the very same day that the Soviets voted on Brest-Litovsk, Lord Balfour, the British Foreign Secretary, addressed the Russian question in the House of Commons. He observed that while he believed the Bolsheviks sincerely wished to rebuild their army and fight Germany, he did not think they would succeed (an interesting observation since he had been so outraged that they withdrew Russia's tattered forces from the fray just a few months earlier).[9] His government joined the Japanese in an invasion of Siberia, part of the campaign to overthrow the Soviets. The Americans later joined this invasion.

> 1. Can the Soviet Government rely on the support of the United States of North America, Great Britain, and France in its struggle against Germany?
>
> 2. What kind of support could be furnished in the nearest future, and what conditions – military equipment, transportation supplies, living necessities?
>
> 3. What kind of support would be furnished particularly and especially by the United States?

William S. Graves, *America's Siberian Adventure* (New York: Jonathan Cape and Harrison Smith, 1931), pp. 22-3.
[7] W.P. Coates and Zelda K. Coates, *Armed Intervention in Russia*, pp. 64-5.
[8] Coates and Coates, *Armed Intervention in Russia*, p.67.
[9] Coates and Coates, pp. 70-71.

Interestingly, in February 1918, the French, breaking from the anti-Bolshevik mindset temporarily, had intimated to the Soviets that they would assist their government if Russia re-entered the war and had asked the Americans if they would consider doing the same. William Phipps, Assistant Secretary of State, scribbled on the French request: "It is out of the question. Submitted to President who says the same thing."[10] Lenin's government unsurprisingly was rebuffed when it asked the Americans to use their influence with Britain to call off the Siberian invasion. With their territory under Allied attack, the Bolsheviks concluded they had no choice but to sign the humiliating treaty with Germany.

The Allies did not restrict their lies to the question of the Bolsheviks' willingness to fulfil military obligations. They claimed that the major reason they did not wish to recognize the Bolshevik government in Russia was that it ruled undemocratically. Yet, lack of democracy on the part of the Czarist regime had proved no impediment to its inclusion among the Allied forces confronting the combined might of Germany and the Austro-Hungarian empire in 1914. Nor did Britain or France regard democracy as essential or even desirable for their colonial possessions.

But, for public consumption anyway, the British Empire was justified on the grounds that Britain was helping primitive peoples rise up the evolutionary tree. Conquered peoples were too uncivilized at the time of conquest to merit democratic rule, but at some undetermined point in the future they would have learned enough lessons from their colonial masters to earn gradually the right to control their destiny. Anti-colonialist critics in the colonies and socialist critics within Britain had another view of why the politically and economically powerful of the Mother Country had fought so hard to conquer and maintain control over colonies. Their view was best expressed in a speech by an outspoken imperialist and anti-socialist Cabinet Minister, Sir William Joynson-Hicks. "Jix," who later became Viscount Brentford, told the House of Commons:

> We did not conquer India for the benefit of the Indians. I know it is said at missionary meetings that we conquered it to raise the level of the Indians. That

[10] Betty Miller Unterberger, *America's Siberian Expedition, 1918-1920* (Durham, North Carolina: Duke University Press, 1956), p. 41 n. 9.

> is cant. We conquered India as the outlet for the
> goods of Great Britain. We conquered India by the
> sword and by the sword we should hold it.
> ("Shame.") Call shame if you like. I am stating the
> facts.. but I am not such an hypocrite as to say we
> hold India for the Indians. We hold it as the finest
> outlet for British goods in general, and for Lancashire
> cotton goods in particular.[11]

At least before the Bolsheviks came to power, Britain did not believe the Russians were much more ready for democratic rule than the Indians. The leaders of the short-lived February 1917 revolution proclaimed their intention to make Russia a democracy for the first time in its history. While publicly the British praised this goal, privately they gave their backing to the military strongman General Kornilov who was attempting to establish a military dictatorship as an alternative to the government of A.F. Kerensky. Kerensky's government was ineffectual, beset at once by war-weary workers and soldiers, susceptible to Bolshevik influence, and by hangers-on of the Czarist regime. The Allies were more interested in extinguishing the threat of communism than they were interested in promoting democracy. Neville Chamberlain, still a year away from his entry into Parliament and seven months before the Bolshevik revolution, wrote in his diary on 22 April 1917: "This Russian revolution which by a grim sort of irony is received everywhere with shouts of approval by our people as though it were going to win the war for us, is fomenting in all the unsteady brains of the world."[12] So much for the British elite's reaction to the possibility of a parliamentary regime in Moscow!

Yet, once the Bolsheviks were in power, their dismissiveness towards the parliamentary system of government was used by Allied governments to justify military interference in Russian affairs. Again, however, the Allies did not give their support to democratic opponents of the Bolsheviks. Instead they intervened militarily in a vain attempt to make Admiral Kolchak, another aspirant to the position of military dictator over the Russian people, the Russian ruler. They recognized that Kolchak, who established a government-in-waiting in Omsk, Siberia, lacked popular support and indeed they were aware, despite their public

[11] Ronald Blythe, *The Age of Illusion* (Oxford: Oxford University Press, 1983), p. 27.
[12] Keith Feiling, *The Life of Neville Chamberlain* (London: Macmillan, 1946), pp. 79-80.

statements to the contrary, that the Bolshevik regime enjoyed mass confidence. As the British ambassador to Russia, Sir George Buchanan, observed on his return to Britain in January 1918, "Bolshevist doctrines are without doubt spreading throughout the whole of Russia, and they appeal very specially to those who have nothing to lose."[13] By contrast, as General William S. Graves, the commander of U.S. troops in Siberia, admitted, "the Koltchak adherents..could not have existed away from the railroads." Indeed, "at no time while I was in Siberia was there enough popular support behind Koltchak in Eastern Siberia for him, or the people supporting him, to have lasted one month if all Allied support had been removed."[14]

Ultimately, lack of support from the Russian people for their would-be liberators from the communist menace defeated the Allied cause. The reactionaries or "White armies," as they were labelled to distinguish them from the Red Army created by the Russian government, also had to cope with the hostility of the people of the Allied countries. Within Britain, France, the United States, Canada and other countries, many workers supported the Bolsheviks. Only a minority wished to emulate the Russian example completely but many more welcomed the accession to power of a government which claimed to make its first priority the welfare of ordinary people. From the beginning there was popular opposition in the Allied countries to their governments' plans to send troops and munitions to help overthrow the Bolsheviks. The Allies, faced with mutinies by their troops and strikes by longshoremen and other workers, could not continue the unpopular war against the new Russian government. One by one, they were soon forced to withdraw their own troops and content themselves with providing arms, money and advice to the aspiring military dictators. Winston Churchill summed up well the difficulties faced by the alliance of Russian and Allied reactionaries as they fought desperately to restore older notions of the best social order. Describing the complicated battle for the Ukraine, which involved Allied armed forces alongside several competing Ukrainian military dictators, Churchill wrote:

> The foreign occupation offended the inhabitants; the Bolshevists profited by their discontents. Their

---

[13] Coates and Coates, *Armed Intervention in Russia* , p. 45.
[14] William S. Graves, *America's Siberian Adventure*, p. 157.

> propaganda, incongruously patriotic and Communist,
> spread far and wide through the Ukraine.
>
> The French troops were themselves affected by the
> Communist propaganda, and practically the whole of
> the fleet mutinied.[15]

A variety of despots in different regions of Russia and the Russian Empire received aid from nations whose rulers were desperate to nip the socialist project in the bud. While the combined might of these armies failed to remove the Bolsheviks, there is little doubt that the slaughter by the White armies profoundly influenced developments in the fledgling Communist state. Tensions within Bolshevik thought between firm party control over national life and popular control over the organs of the state were decided decisively in favour of the former. The military and industrial discipline required to fend off several armies, aided by anti-Communist foreigners, and yet keep the population fed wrecked the utopian hopes of many of the early Communists. Stalin's rise to power as a ruthless autocrat owed a great deal to Western efforts to prevent self-determination by the Russian people.

Such efforts to derail the revolution were the product of horror at the prospect of a "proletarian" government which aimed to eliminate the privileges of the well-to-do. Much as the French Revolution inspired horror and disgust among all the crowned heads of Europe and provoked foreign intervention to extirpate a cancer that threatened to destroy a healthy body based upon wealth and privilege, the Russian Revolution was greeted by elites everywhere as an outrage.

****

The passage of time would not temper this outrage. The view that the Communists of Russia were a plague rather than a government became a firm conviction of the elites of the Western countries and caused them to welcome fascism and Nazism in the countries most exposed to social unrest as suitable methods of restoring the capitalist body to its earlier good health.

---

[15] Winston Churchill, *The World Crisis*, Volume 5 (New York: Charles Scribner's Sons, 1957; orig. pub. 1929 under the title *The Aftermath*), p. 169.

Events quickly conspired to demonstrate that the Bolshevik Revolution would provide inspiration to oppressed groups within other countries, to the horror of the establishment. In Germany, as the war ended, the Soviet model was copied by workers and soldiers in Berlin and other cities who attempted to establish a workers' authority over industry and the state. Bloodily suppressed by the military with the blessings of the interim government of the country controlled by the Social Democrats, the soviet movement in Germany demonstrated nonetheless that a large section of the working class was prepared to follow revolutionary leadership. They had ignored the calls for patience and evolution towards socialism within a parliamentary framework from a Social Democrat leadership that had joined the bourgeois and aristocratic forces to wage World War One. In 1920 in Hungary a short-lived Soviet revolution installed the Communists under Bela Kun in power. Kun's government, like the Russian Soviet government, carried out land reforms at the expense of the aristocracy. Roumanian military intervention restored the power and privileges of the aristocrats.

Most troubling of all to the aristocrats and the bourgeoisie was the creation in 1919 of the Comintern or Third International in Moscow. The Second International, grouping the social democratic parties of various countries, had been troubling enough. Its left-wing elements had successfully sponsored a resolution in 1907 calling on proletarians to oppose wars between rival groups of national capitalists. In practice, however, the Social Democratic parliamentary and trade union leadership in European countries proved too enmeshed in the existing political and economic system to pose a threat to the established order when war was declared. Collaboration became the order of the day and revolutionaries and pacifists alike became alienated from the social democratic leadership.

Now however a new international was being formed that declared its allegiance not only to an abstract socialist order as the Second International had done but to Bolshevik Russia as well. The early Soviet leadership, beginning with V.I. Lenin, believed that socialism would not prosper in Russia if the backward, peasant nation remained encircled by hostile capitalist nations. Lenin looked to revolution in the west as the salvation for the workers of all countries but particularly for the Russian people, their soviet system made fragile by the relentless military attack by Russian reactionaries and their foreign allies. The creation of Communist parties in the Western countries, usually through breakaways from the Social Democrats, gave every country a Soviet-model party dedicated, at least formally, to a revolutionary seizure of power when the opportunity presented itself. In practice, most of these parties, within a few years, settled into a routine of parliamentarianism, stout and often mindless defences of all things Russian, and sectarian rhetoric that limited their ability to win new converts. The Social Democrats of 1914 had demonstrated more allegiance to nation than class and therefore the Communists regarded willingness to support the Soviet Union as a litmus test of proletarian internationalism. Unfortunately for them, in the Stalin years, this largely meant renouncing independent thought and adopting unthinkingly support for Soviet policies. Arguably, these parties would have been more effective had their autonomy and their propaganda not been so circumscribed by the shifting needs of Soviet foreign policy. Nonetheless, their very existence and their close links with the Soviet government and Soviet Communist Party made the Comintern members appear a grave threat to the European elites.

Unsurprisingly, the established politicians of the Right and big industrialists responded with fear to the development of the Communist parties and their activities within trade unions. Rather than looking to reforms within the capitalist system that might blunt the Communist revolutionary appeal, the elites became more hostile than ever to notions of democracy. The idea that nationalist strongmen, using a combination of brute force and demagogy, could rescue existing property and status relations spread quickly. This despite the fact that Communists never came close to winning an electoral majority in any country. Ironically, the fear and loathing of the Communists only increased in the late 1930s, when, following the Comintern's turn away from ultra-leftism, Communists were urged to form "popular fronts" with all anti-fascist forces. Though the Communists in this phase abandoned their previous goal of a violent revolution, their improved electoral performances and their importance to the survival of centre-left coalitions such as those formed in Spain and France in 1936 caused the rich generally to reject parliamentary democracy. After all, it was not simply the Communists' espousal of violence as a tactic to which the elites had objected; it was the

Communist programme of redistribution of wealth and power which was their true horror.

A constant theme in conservatives' assessments of Bolshevism after 1917 was that it was the worst political regime possible. Ultimately that would lead to the view that the replacement of parliamentary democracy by military rule or by fascism was justified if there was a sufficient reason to fear the outbreak of Bolshevism. And as noted below the elites seemed to find the Bolshevik threat everywhere. Their view that the masses were potentially irrational and violent allowed them to see the Bolshevik threat as one that could only be dealt with through a show of force against the "mob."

Robert Lansing, the American Secretary of State, typified this attitude of implacable hostility to the Bolsheviks. As World War One drew to a close and revolution in defeated Germany threatened, Lansing wrote privately of Bolshevism:

> Its appeal is to the unintelligent and brutish element of mankind to take from the intellectual and successful their rights and possessions and to reduce them to a state of slavery...

> Bolshevism is the most hideous and monstrous thing that the human mind has ever conceived....It is worse, far worse, than a Prussianized Germany, and would mean an ever greater menace to human liberty.[16]

There was a post-war Red Scare in the United States that included raids on various organizations and arrests of over 4000 individuals ordered by Attorney-General Mitchell Palmer, a campaign of state terror against the remnants of the Industrial Workers of the World, and extensive censorship of radical literature. Socialist leaders such as Eugene V. Debs, jailed during the war for their anti-war activity, languished in prison for several years afterward, and the lone socialist who managed to get elected to Congress in 1918 despite state repression of the Socialist Party was not allowed to take his House of Representatives seat by his fellow congressmen.

Socialist ideology however had a relatively weak grip on the American working class. In Europe, where socialist ideas had

[16] John M. Thompson, *Russia, Bolshevism and the Versailles Peace* (Princeton: Princeton University Press, 1966), p. 15.

become popular before World War One, the elites were terrified at the continuing spread of revolutionary ideas in the wake of the Bolshevik revolution. Like Lansing in America, they perceived the common people as stupid brutes and feared that Bolshevism would spread on a tide of resentment against class privileges they or their ancestors had earned as a reward for their intelligence and achievements. The American statesman Sumner Welles would later recall that in postwar Europe, "Governments and the wealthier classes saw the spectre of Bolshevism in every sign of unrest, political or social."[17] He likened the "panic of hysteria" that was overtaking the well-off of both Europe and North America to the hysteria that gripped their forbears after the American and French revolutions at the close of the eighteenth century.

In Britain, there was a long history of the popular classes demanding and gradually winning more civil rights, including the suffrage. But there was an equally long history of the ruling classes resisting demands for greater equality and using state violence to frustrate popular pressures for change. From the bloody suppression of Wat Tyler's peasant revolt in 1381 to Home Secretary Winston Churchill's employment of 50,000 troops to suppress a rail strike in 1919, the leaders of England had demonstrated that there were limits to the demands from below that they would concede. Always there seemed to be a sense of apocalypse in their reactions. So, for example, the moderate Yorkshire reformer, Reverend Christopher Wyvill, could proclaim in 1792, as he reflected on the American and French revolutions, that popular suffrage meant that "private property and public liberty" would be placed "at the mercy of a lawless and furious rabble." He believed that a few popular elections would create such chaos that "the Nation" (presumably an entity rather smaller than the entire population within it) would demand "the protection of Despotic Power."[18]

"The Nation" was not happy with the restiveness of British workers in the twenties and thirties. Stanley Baldwin, prime minister on three separate occasions in the twenties and thirties, commented at one point: "I doubt if we can go on like this: we shall have to limit the franchise."[19] Winston Churchill went

[17] Sumner Welles, *The Time for Decision* (New York: Harpe and Brothers, 1944), p. 312.
[18] E.P. Thompson, *The Making of the English Working Class* (Harmondsworth, England: Penguin, 1968), pp. 26-7.

37

further, claiming in October 1932 that "elections, even in the most educated democracies are regarded as a misfortune and as a disturbance of social, moral and economic progress." He was unsurprisingly unprepared to extend such a nuisance to the "untutored races of India."[20]

It was the short-lived and peaceful General Strike of 1926 that particularly sowed fear on the part of the ruling classes. The courts ruled the strike illegal and jailed the leaders; the rank-and-file then obediently obeyed back-to-work orders. But the defiance that preceded this retreat left its mark on a paranoid elite.

Neville Chamberlain wrote that "constitutional government is fighting for its life." If the strikers won a victory, "it would be the revolution for the nominal leaders would be whirled away in an instant."[21] Lady Diana Manners "could hear the tumbrels rolling and heads sneezing into the baskets." Her husband, Duff Cooper, MP, one of the more moderate Conservatives, answered his wife's worrying inquiries about when they could honourably exit the country: "not till the massacres begin."[22] Winston Churchill, then Chancellor, proposed asking territorial battalions, particularly in London, to volunteer as auxiliary police. They would be generously paid. When Home Secretary Sir William Joynson-Hicks questioned how this proposal was to be funded, Churchill said simply that the Exchequer would pay. "If we start arguing about petty details, we will have a tired-out police force, a dissipated army and bloody revolution."[23]

The advent of the dictators was greeted as a breath of fresh air by business interests, the conservative political elite and the reactionary elements of the Roman Catholic Church. Sumner Welles, seasoned American ambassador and Undersecretary of State in the Roosevelt administration beginning in 1937, recollected in 1944 that the major powers, "and in particular

[19] Margaret George, *The Hollow Men* (London: Leslie Frewin Publishers, 1967), p. 66.
[20] Robert Rhode James, *Churchill: A Study in Failure* (New York: World Publishing Company, 1970), p. 236. The generally anti-democratic cast of Churchill's thought during his political career is particularly evident throughout Clive Ponting, *Churchill* (London: Sinclair-Stevenson, 1994).
[21] Robert Rhode James, *Churchill*, p.46
[22] *Ibid.*, p. 46.
[23] Baron Hastings Lionel Ismay, *The Memoirs of General Ismay* (London: Heinemann, 1960), p. 57.

Great Britain" were delighted to see the Fascists triumphant in Italy in 1922. Mussolini's victory put that country in "hands that would ruthlessly root out all signs of Communism."[24]

British Foreign Secretary Austen Chamberlain commented in November 1925, with reference to the Fascist seizure of power from democratically-elected authorities, "if I ever had to choose in my own country between anarchy and dictatorship, I expect I should be on the side of the dictator." Winston Churchill went even further in his praise of the Italian Fascists, claiming in 1927 that their "triumphant struggle against the bestial appetites and passions of Leninism...rendered a service to the whole world." Italy had "provided the necessary antidote to the Russian poison." It was an antidote that others could apply to deal with the socialist disease. "Hereafter no great nation will go unprovided with an ultimate means of protection against the cancerous growth of Bolshevism."[25]

Even after the Second World War, a few of the elite of the pre-war period retained their affection for Mussolini and his Fascist takeover of Italy. Viscount L.S. Amery, who had been Colonial Secretary from 1924 to 1929 and served as Secretary of State for India under Churchill, was still admonishing Mussolini's critics in the 1950s. They focused too much on Mussolini's megalomania, he argued, and ignored the positive aspects of a fascist regime. Justifying the support of British imperialists like himself for Mussolini in the inter-war period, he wrote in 1955:

> We naturally now think mostly of the darker, repressive and corrupt aspects of the Fascist regime and of the insensate ambition and vanity which led Mussolini to drag an unwilling people into a disastrous war. But, even after allowing for a certain amount of eyewash and propaganda, there was undoubtedly a good deal being done by him to improve the... physical energy of the Italian people. ...As for the functional basis of political representation it may well have a future, here and elsewhere, not as a substitute, but as a complement and corrective to purely arithmetical democracy.[26]

[24] Sumner Welles, *The Time for Decision*, pp. 28-29.
[25] Writes Churchill biographer Clive Ponting: "Churchill was a great admirer of Mussolini...He welcomed both Mussolini's anti-Communism and his authoritarian way of organising and disciplining the Italians." *Churchill*, p. 350.

Since protection of property and privilege was their real goal – the constant criticisms of lack of democracy in revolutionary Russia were just so much hypocrisy –, conservative forces were all too willing to jettison the concessions they had made to the masses over the years in order to preserve social peace. More and more, authoritarian solutions were embraced. In this context, the embrace of Italian Fascism by the ruling elites, while disgusting in retrospect, seems to have been inevitable. It was, as we see in the next chapter, just as inevitable that Hitler, along with lesser fascist lights such as Franco and Salazar, would be similarly embraced.

[26] L. S. Amery, *My Political Life* (London: Hutchinson, 1955), p. 243.

CHAPTER THREE

HEIL TO THE DICTATORS!

> In a very short time, perhaps in a year or two, the
> Conservative elements in this country will be looking
> to Germany as the bulwark against Communism in
> Europe. She is planted right in the centre of
> Europe...only two or three years ago a very
> distinguished German statesman said to me: 'I am not
> afraid of Nazism, but of Communism' – and if
> Germany is seized by the Communists, Europe will
> follow...Do not let us be in a hurry to condemn
> Germany. We shall be welcoming Germany as our
> friend.[1]

This statement was made in the British House of Commons on
28 November 1934. At that time Hitler had consolidated his
power in Germany, closed the country's Parliament, arrested or
murdered his political opponents, proclaimed laws restricting the
civil liberties of Jews and other non-Germanic minorities, and
begun rearming Germany in violation of the Versailles Treaty.
One would expect then that the speaker was a far-right
Conservative with Nazi connections. In fact, it was Lloyd
George, the former Liberal prime minister who had played an
important role in the creation of the early British welfare state
and led his country's war effort against Germany during much of
World War One.

Lloyd George's readiness to welcome Hitler's Germany as a
friend demonstrates the extent to which anti-Communist hysteria
induced even the more liberal elements of the British
establishment to embrace pro-capitalist dictators.
Unsurprisingly, the Conservative-dominated National
government was pleased with Lloyd George's remarks, though it
could not, with impunity, publicly endorse the thuggish Nazi
regime as this elderly politician felt he could. Privately however
John Simon, the Secretary of State for Foreign Affairs, lauded
Lloyd George to Cabinet colleagues.[2]

This chapter demonstrates that in the 1930s the Western elites,
for the most part, were even more obsessed with the Communist
danger than they were in the 1920s. Having already embraced

---

[1] *British House of Commons*, 1934, Vol. 295, columns 905-922.
[2] *Documents on British Foreign Policy*, Series 2, Vol. 12, Doc. 235, p. 273.

Italian Fascism as an "antidote" to Communism, they were prepared to swallow pills even more bitter to ward off the Communist virus. Hitler's Nazism was welcomed not only because it would ward off the Communist disease in Germany but because it could potentially destroy the Communist germ in the Soviet Union where it had taken control of the entire body politic.

By the time Hitler seized power, the view had become widespread among the elite that democracy was a danger to their interests. In September, 1933, still early in Hitler's reign, Lloyd George mused on what regime would follow the overthrow of Hitler should foreign powers decide to remove him from office. "Not a Conservative, Socialist or Liberal regime, but extreme Communism," he warned. A German Communist regime would prove far more formidable than the existing Soviet regime because "the Germans would know how to run their Communism effectively."[3] As Hitler flagrantly violated the Versailles Treaty and created a vicious police state, the British ruling class, following Lloyd George's line of thought, took the position that he represented their best hope under current circumstances. War with Hitler could only bring Communism to power in Germany and eventually to all of Europe.

It was not Hitler alone among dictators and imperialists whom the establishment welcomed. As we shall see, Mussolini's Italy, the aggressively imperialist Japanese government and the Franco dictatorship in Spain which overthrew a democratically-elected regime received the endorsement of the British government. In the case of Japan, efforts were made to strike a non-aggression pact that would provide Japan with a "free hand" in the Far East. The proposed pact contained all the ingredients that following chapters demonstrate guided British policy with regards to the Nazis and the free hand in eastern Europe.

Harold Ickes, Secretary of the Interior in Roosevelt's Cabinet, perhaps expressed best the behaviour of the British elite in the 1930s in his diary in early 1939. Reporting President Roosevelt's words, Ickes wrote: "The wealthy class in England is so afraid of communism, which has constituted no threat at all in England, that they have thrown themselves into the arms of Nazism and now they don't know which way to turn."[4] Hitler

[3] Frederick L. Schuman. *Europe on the Eve* (New York: Alfred A. Knopf, 1942), p. 340.

understood well the fears of the establishment in Britain and other countries. His own interests lay in the areas of imperial conquests and in the creation of racial hierarchies; the battle between socialism and capitalism, *per se*, was of little interest to him. But he recognized that the capitalists and aristocrats of his own country were only willing to leave him in power to pursue his Nazi programme if he, in turn, protected their interests.

Similarly, untempered anti-Bolshevism, Hitler recognized, would win him the support of the privileged classes of other European countries. He confided to one of his associates: "I've got to play ball with capitalism and keep the Versailles powers in line by holding aloft the bogey of Bolshevism – make them believe that a nazi Germany is the last bulwark against the Red flood."[5] The capitalists, he believed, would accept his right to seize the Ukraine, among other things, if they felt forced to choose between him and Stalin. So, as he illegally rearmed his country, Hitler lulled the Versailles powers to sleep by singing over and over again his lullaby about how the Nazis had stanched the Communist poison in Germany and were preparing to do the same elsewhere. "By taking upon herself this struggle against Bolshevism Germany is but fulfilling, as so often before in her history, a European mission," he intoned on many an occasion.[6]

The view that the Nazis, however distasteful they might seem in certain respects, were the salvation of the existing social order, was widespread among the elites. Stanley Baldwin, British prime minister in the early Hitler period, echoed Lloyd George's view that there was no alternative to the Nazis. Cabinet minutes record his rejection of French suggestions that force be used against Germany to punish Hitler for his reoccupation of the Rhineland in 1936. The reoccupation violated the Locarno agreement and the Covenant of the League of Nations. But enforcement of these agreements, in Baldwin's opinion, could only lead to war. With Russian aid the French might defeat Germany and rid Europe of the Nazis. But what of it? "It would probably result in Germany going Bolshevik" and was therefore unthinkable.[7] It would also, given the strong Communist

[4] *The Secret Diary of Harold Ickes*, Volume 3 (New York: Simon and Schuster, 1954), p. 571.
[5] G. W. Ludecke, *I Knew Hitler* (London: Jarrolds Publishers, 1938), p. 422.
[6] *The Speeches of Adolph Hitler* (Oxford: Oxford University Press, 1942), p. 668.
[7] British Cabinet Minutes, 23/81, March 11, 1936, p. 292.

movement in France, likely lead to a victory for communism in France, worried Harold Nicolson, a "National Labour" MP (Nicolson was part of the minority of supporters of the "National" government who was not a Conservative).[8]

Robert Coulondre, French ambassador to Moscow, shared the common establishment view that support for Nazi Germany was the only way to prevent France from becoming a Communist state. If the rest of Europe made war on Germany, France was a loser no matter the outcome of the war. "Vanquished, she was nazified; victorious, she had, especially following the destruction of the German power, to sustain the crushing weight of the Slavic world, armed with the communist flame-throwers."[9] Coulondre was hardly alone among the official and business classes in France in opposing the anti-Nazi position that the Popular Front government, elected in 1936, embodied. The French journalist Genevieve Tabouis wrote of a meeting in March 1936 with a "big industrialist," a family friend. He told her: "Everything is better than war, since any war in Europe now would mean the end of our capitalist system, and then, where would we go?"[10] The Popular Front in tatters and the traditional ruling group restored, Tabouis had occasion to interview Georges Bonnet, the foreign minister, also a family friend, in September 1938. Bonnet, a man unknown to lose his composure, became very emotional when Tabouis suggested that France ought not to accept the cession of the Sudetenland to Germany. Warfare must be avoided at all costs, he insisted, because if there were a war, he was sure that there would be revolution in France. The prospect of revolution would be so unnerving for him that he would throw himself into the Seine at the first sign of war, he told Tabouis.[11]

The view that thuggish dictators like Hitler were all that protected Europe from an imminent triumph of Communism caused the Versailles powers and especially Great Britain to ignore – indeed, as the next chapter argues, to encourage – Germany's rearmament and expansionist objectives. It led to the disastrous policy of giving Germany a "free hand" in Europe. So

---

[8] Harold Nicolson, *Diaries and Letters, 1930-1939* (New York: Athenaeum, 1968), pp. 249-250.
[9] Our translation of Robert Coulondre, *De Staline à Hitler: Souvenirs de Deux Ambassades, 1936-1939* (Paris: Hachette,1950),p.21.
[10] Our translation of Genevieve Tabouis, *Ils l'ont appelé Cassandre* (New York: Éditions de la Maison de France, 1942), p. 266.
[11] *Ibid.*, p. 342.

convinced were the privileged of England that the private property system was the essence of "civilization" that they regarded Hitler as an ally in preserving civilization from the Bolsheviks. Neville Chamberlain could write on 29 September 1938 to Hitler, the man who was destroying the integrity of the Czechoslovak state: "I cannot believe that you will take the responsibility of starting a world war, which may end civilization, for the sake of a few days delay in settling this long standing problem."[12]

The view that another European war would likely lead to a generalized social revolution on that continent was general among the well-to-do. Oliver Harvey, secretary to Neville Chamberlain's Foreign Minister Lord Halifax, reported on a conversation that he had had with Lord Strang, an important government official.

> Strang and I agree that the real opposition to rearming comes from the rich classes in the Party who fear taxation and believe Nazis on the whole are more conservative than Communists and Socialists: any war, whether we win or not, would destroy the rich idle classes and so they are for peace at any price. P.M. is a man of iron will, obstinate, unimaginative, with intense narrow vision, a man of pre-war outlook who sees no reason for drastic social changes. Yet we are on the verge of a social revolution.[13]

"Peace at any price," however, distorts the viewpoint of the "rich idle classes" of Britain. They were not counselling a complete disengagement from the world. Their desire to maintain the British Empire and to stamp out socialism everywhere made such detachment impossible. The elite's reaction to the Spanish Civil War and to Japanese expansionism demonstrates that peace as such was not their goal.

In the Spanish Civil War, the western democracies pointedly took the side of the fascists rather than the democratic forces. As Claude Bowers, American ambassador to Spain, recalled with disgust in 1954: "I prefer to think we shall not return to the shoddy days just before the war when it was popular in high circles to believe that to oppose communism one must follow the

[12] Keith Feiling, *The Life of Neville Chamberlain* (London: Macmillan, 1946), p. 372.
[13] *The Diplomatic Diaries of Oliver Harvey* (London: Collins, 1958), p. 222.

Fascist line."[14] Yet the government whose overthrow "high circles" sought was both elected and non-communist. A broad coalition of left-wing and centrist forces had won a modest victory in national elections in Spain despite the jailing of many of its leaders by the authorities and the loud opposition of the press and the Roman Catholic Church. The Communist Party had participated in the coalition but it won only a small number of seats and was given no Cabinet posts in a government initially dominated by the Socialist Party and the Republican Party, a party that was not anti-capitalist but which was hated by the Church because it took a firm line in favour of secularization of Spanish society. Only after the Civil War began were the Communists included in the Cabinet – they received two portfolios out of thirteen with the Socialists, who had the largest number of parliamentary seats, holding six.

The new democratically-elected government had barely taken office when conservative forces decided to overthrow it. Military officers with the support of the Church, landowners, and big business gave their support to a revolt led by General Francisco Franco. Franco announced his intention to end democracy in Spain and install a government based on Fascist principles. Supporters of the republican government armed to resist the Francoists and sought foreign support and arms to balance the armed aid that Franco had received from Hitler and Mussolini to begin his revolt against the elected government. The Soviet Union, concerned no doubt more with containing fascism than with protecting "bourgeois democracy," weighed in on the republican side.

The Western democracies had been hostile to the new government of Spain from the time of its election. Though the government was moderate, its election had raised the expectations of average Spaniards. The peasantry demanded land reform while the workers called for civil rights and legal protection of their unions. Huge demonstrations by the people in support of their demands created fears among the Spanish "rich idle classes" that the left-wing government would be impelled to make broader and swifter changes than it had promised. The moguls of the Western press, quick to find threats to the rule of their class in demands from below, painted a picture of a society in chaos. Stories of mob violence became regular fare in the

[14] Claude G. Bowers, *My Mission to Spain* (New York: Simon and Schuster, 1954), p. v.

newspapers of the United States and Great Britain.[15] Bowers, able to travel the country to check the accuracy of such reports, determined that they were largely fabrications or wild exaggerations.[16]

Such stories however became an excuse to support German and Italian intervention on behalf of the Fascists under the guise of non-interventionism. Anthony Eden had initially joined the rest of the British Cabinet in viewing benignly the intervention by the fascist powers in Spain. Indeed, as late as November 1936, he maintained in the House of Commons that the intervention by Germany and Italy in the conflict was less serious than the intervention of other nations, a less than subtle reference to the Soviets.[17] He knew better.[18] Alarmed at the implications of allowing the dictators to have their way in Spain, he proposed at a Cabinet meeting on 4 January 1937 that the British Navy should take an active part in preventing volunteers and arms from reaching Spain. But Home Secretary Sir Samuel Hoare spoke for the Cabinet majority in rejecting Eden's proposal. The course of action proposed by Eden, he suggested, would mean that "as a nation we were trying to stop General Franco from winning."[19]

Britain and France together were certainly in a position militarily to fend off Hitler's and Mussolini's assistance to the Spanish fascists. Their naval might easily outstripped that of the fascist dictators and could have been used to blockade outside intervention. The fascist air forces posed no threat at the time. Liddell Hart, who, like Eden, fought a futile battle to convince the Cabinet of the danger of allowing foreign fascists to determine Spain's fate, was told by Cabinet members that any British intervention could lead to war with Italy and Germany. But Hart recognized that because of the strategic position of Britain and France in the western Mediterranean, "it was ideal ground strategically to challenge the dictators' aggressive progress, and produce a sobering check – and the German

[15] Bowers, *My Mission to Spain*, p. 200; *The Memoirs of Captain Liddell Hart* (London: Cassell, 1965), p. 129.
[16] Bowers, *My Mission to Spain*, p. 200.
[17] *DBFP*, Series 2, Volume 17, Document 395, Note 1, p. 578.
[18] The civil servants most familiar with Spain certainly believed that Eden must know he was not telling the truth about the Spanish situation.
    DBFP, Series 2, Volume 17, Document 406.
[19] Telford Taylor, *Munich: The Price of Peace* (New York: Doubleday, 1979), p. 544. The author's source is British Cabinet Minutes, 23/87.

archives captured in 1945 have shown that Hitler, on the same calculations, would not have ventured to risk a fight over Spain."[20] Hart's credentials on military matters were impeccable. He had served over the years as military advisor to Lloyd George, Anthony Eden, Winston Churchill and Sir Leslie Hore-Belisha. Saddened that so many of the leading lights of his society "desired the rebels' success," Hart could only conclude that : "Class sentiment and property sense would seem to have blinded their strategic sense."[21]

Hart would later indicate that he kept the government informed of the behaviour of the fighters on both sides of the conflict. He made it clear that the Franco side was responsible for atrocities "directed by the military leaders in pursuance of a deliberate policy of exterminating opponents and stifling resistance to their advance by establishing a reign of terror in the places they occupied." By contrast, the republican government respected civilized norms in dealing with opponents though it was sometimes unable to stop massacres by "frenzied mobs" eager for revenge against Fascist atrocities.[22] Hart was amazed at the frankness of Francoist envoys in Britain who "gloated" over their savage treatment of opponents and potential opponents.

Knowledge of Francoist atrocities however did not move government officials, fixated as they were on the phantom communist threat in Spain and indeed on the possibility that this threat might spread to Spain's neighbour France which had elected a similar centre-left coalition just months after the Spanish election. Orme Sargent, Assistant Under-Secretary in the Foreign Office, claimed the British should remain neutral in the Spanish war because it was "a conflict between Fascism and Communism." "Both systems are almost equally abhorrent" to a parliamentary democracy, he wrote. He then added his fears that the Popular Front government of France – whose programme the Communists in the French parliament supported though the Communists had declined seats at the Cabinet table – might prove unable to resist Communist pressures, "both domestic and Muscovite." Then, seemingly forgetting his commitment to democracy, he added that Britain should take measures that might help to remove the Popular Front government from office

[20] *The Memoirs of Captain Liddell Hart*, pp. 129-130.
[21] D.N. Pritt, *Must the War Spread?*(Harmondsworth, Middlesex: Penguin, 1940), p. 13.
[22] *The Memoirs of Captain Liddell Hart*, Vol.2, pp. 128-9

"even though this might involve at a certain stage something like interference in the internal affairs of France."[23]

Sargent indeed was not neutral in the Spanish conflict, a conflict that was, in fact, between parliamentary democracy and Fascism rather than Communism and Fascism. Seized by the Communist bogeyman, he made one of Britain's aims in the Spanish conflict "the importance of our preventing France by hook or by crook from 'going Bolshevik' under the influence of the Spanish civil war." Excusing German and Italian interference in the Spanish conflict, Sargent suggested that it was their fear of Communism in France – that is a fear matching his own – that motivated their cooperation to defeat the Spanish republicans. He did not believe that Britain should take action to ward off their appetites for both unwarranted interference in the internal affairs of other nations and for territorial conquests. Rather Sargent argued that had Italy not been made to feel isolated by European nations after its illegal seizure of Abysinnia (Ethiopia), it would be more inclined to bend to European opinion generally on foreign policy matters.[24]

The majority of the British establishment supported Franco in 1936. Even men like Winston Churchill, Anthony Eden and Harold Nicolson, who would later prove formidable foes of Hitler, were sufficiently misled by the Communist bogeyman to support Franco and his foreign friends, at least in the early stages of the conflict. "Whitehall circles," as Liddell Hart noted, "were very largely pro-Franco" with the Admiralty particularly fond of the dictator.[25] Robert Vansittart, Permanent Under-Secretary in the Foreign Office and no lover himself of fascists, had to tell the French Foreign Minister that he could not expect British aid in suppressing the foreign fascist intervention in Spain. His official record of his comments in September 1936 included the comment: "M. Blum [Leon Blum, the French prime minister during the short-lived Popular Front government] must remember as I had told him in Paris, that the British government was upheld by a very large Conservative majority, who were never prepared, and now probably less than ever, to make much sacrifice for red eyes."[26] That Communism was not at issue in Spain made little difference to the analysis made by Britain's

[23] *DBFP*, Series 2, Vol. 17, Document 84, p. 90.
[24] *Ibid.*
[25] *The Memoirs of Captain Liddell Hart*, Vol 2, p. 130.
[26] *DBFP*, Second Series, Volume 17, Appendix 1, p. 773.

"idle rich." Their increasing fears of the anger of the deprived classes made them see a Communist threat everywhere that demands for social justice appeared. Unwilling to see such demands appeased, they threw their lot in with Fascists who promised to protect the privileges of the propertied and to deal brutally with members of the subordinate classes who showed insufficient respect for their traditional betters.

Unsurprisingly then, when Italian and German intervention in Spain were discussed early in the war, the British Cabinet concluded that the Foreign Office "should in the light of the discussion adopt a policy of improving relations with Italy." During the discussion, Hoare, Chamberlain and Halifax, among others, spoke to the need to excuse Italy's activities in Spain. The Colonial Secretary, W.G.A. Ormsby-Gore, suggested that too great a desire to please France "had prevented us getting on terms with the dictator powers."[27]

That would soon be corrected. Vansittart's candid comments revealed part of a strategy to induce France to join Britain in refusing to intervene to help the republicans in Spain or in other words to leave the field to Hitler and Mussolini. Liddell Hart claims that Britain, on 8 August 1936, openly threatened to pull out from the Locarno agreements if France helped the republicans. This would remove Britain's obligation to come to France's assistance in case of a Franco-German war.[28] What did the British government think would be the result of condoning Italian intervention on the part of the Spanish fascists while France was restrained from responding to requests for aid from the legitimate government of Spain? As Anthony Eden admitted in a memorandum in December 1936: " What was anticipated in August was that General Franco would make himself master of Spain largely as a consequence of help received from Italy."[29]

Publicly, the British pretended to be concerned about foreign intervention in Spain. The League of Nations established a Non-Intervention Committee consisting of the major European powers early in the Spanish conflict. But it was a farce, a good example of language being used to cloak the truth. For in truth the Non-Intervention Committee was a smokescreen behind which the fascists could pretend to support non-intervention

[27] Telford Taylor, *Munich: The Price of Peace*, p. 544.
[28] *The Memoirs of Captain Liddell Hart*, Volume 2, p. 128.
[29] *DBFP*, Series 2, Vol. 17, Doc. 471, p. 678.

while they intervened at will. Lord Halifax cynically reported that though the committee's work did nothing to prevent the movement of men or materials into Spain, it was a success.

> What, however, it did was to keep such intervention as there was entirely non-official, to be denied or at least deprecated by the responsible spokesman of the nation concerned, so that there was neither need nor occasion for any action by Governments to support their nationals. After making every allowance for the unreality, make-believe and discredit that came to attach to the Non-intervention Committee, I think this device for lowering the temperature caused by the Spanish fever justified itself.[30]

This was tantamount to an admission that Britain was concerned only with form and not substance on this issue of non-intervention. So long as Hitler and Mussolini claimed not to be intervening, Britain was prepared to allow them to escalate their intervention in Spain, using the so-called Non-intervention Committee as a cover for their illegal actions.

The United States joined Britain in refusing to defend the elected Spanish government against the Fascists who wished to overthrow it violently and illegally. In early 1937 President Roosevelt placed a strict embargo on the shipment of materials to Spain that might be used for military purposes. Too late, by early 1939, Roosevelt recognized that he had made a fatal error. He confided to Harold Ickes that "this embargo controverted old American principles and invalidated established international law." Instead he should have simply forbidden the use of American vessels to carry shipments of munitions to Spain. "Realistically," concluded Ickes, "neutrality in this instance was lining up with Franco, and lining up with Franco has meant the destruction of Democratic Spain." The impetus that the fascist victory in Spain had given to Hitler's and Mussolini's preparations for war meant that democracy everywhere was under foreign threat.[31]

***

But for the dominant element of the British government and elites more generally, protection of property and privilege, not

---

[30] *Ibid.*, p. 541.
[31] Ickes, Volume 2, pp. 569-570.

democracy, was the issue. To defend their privileges and their imperial possessions, they were prepared not only to sacrifice democracy but the territorial integrity of nations in conflict with the fascists. The attitudes of Chamberlain and his associates to Japanese expansionism demonstrate well the priorities of the "rich idle classes" as they searched everywhere for allies in their mortal – if largely paranoid – combat with Communism.

The Japanese invasion of Manchuria in 1931 highlighted the aggressive expansionism of the Japanese government. The League of Nations denounced the Japanese takeover of this important industrial province of China. The League Covenant forbade foreign aggression against sovereign nations for the purpose of seizing territory. A Nine-Power Agreement that included the European powers, the United States and Japan itself guaranteed Chinese territorial integrity. Heedless of League criticism, backed up only with sanctions that the major powers ignored, Japan changed the name of Manchuria to Manchukuo and imposed a puppet government.

Britain was among the nations that ignored the sanctions meant to pressure Japan to obey the League covenant. The British government was at best indifferent to the fate of Manchuria and at worst supportive of Japan's conquest. Winston Churchill declared in 1933 that Britain had refused to support China over Japan because its interests and indeed world interests required that "law and order should be established in the northern part of China."[32] Britain's main concern regarding Japan was that it be prevented from seizing British colonial possessions in the Orient. Important members of the Cabinet believed that this could best be accomplished by creating an alliance with Japan in the region. Neville Chamberlain, then Chancellor of the Exchequer, was the main proponent of such an alliance and, among those he convinced to support his position was Sir John Simon, Minister of Foreign Affairs.

Ultimately the government rejected Chamberlain's plan. But it is worth examining in some detail because, in its motivation and in its details, it became the prototype for the arrangement Chamberlain would make with Hitler a few short years later when he became prime minister of Britain.

[32] G. Salvemini, *Prelude to World War Two* (London: Victor Gollancz, 1953), p. 125.

Essentially Chamberlain proposed a free hand for Japan in the Far East outside of territories controlled by Britain, though, of course, aware of diplomatic niceties, he always rejected the phrase "free hand." While he argued that this would result in trade advantages for Britain, he made little attempt to disguise his underlying motivation: the encouragement of Japanese aggression on the Soviet Union's eastern borders. Maintaining the obsession with destroying Communist rule that he had held since the Bolshevik Revolution, Chamberlain was quick to see the possibilities in encouraging the militaristic Japanese state to grab chunks of the Soviet Union for itself.

On 1 September 1934 Chamberlain addressed a personal and confidential letter to Sir John Simon, Minister of State for External Affairs, proposing a non-aggression pact between Britain and Japan. Significantly for someone who would soon lead the pack in England of those proclaiming that Hitler stood for peace, Chamberlain argued that Germany threatened the rest of Europe and much of Europe's focus had to be on dealing with that threat. There was no room for confrontation in the Orient that would blunt England's ability to participate fully in staving off the German military threat.

Setting the framework for his proposal, Chamberlain wrote: "I suggest that the paramount consideration in this matter to which everything else, home politics, economy, or desire for disarmament must be subjected is the safety, first of this country and then of the British Empire."[33] The safety of Britain and its empire, he noted, were not affected by the Japanese takeover of Manchuria which "is actually likely to benefit British exporters." Indeed the language Chamberlain used to describe Japanese expansionism attested to the limited importance he placed upon League principles of sanctity of agreed-upon borders and collective action to punish aggressors.

After noting that Japan was "unpopular in Europe" because of her defiance of the League and "her aggressive export policy," he concluded: "Yet it is at least arguable that the Manchukuo affair, except insofar as it served to discredit the League, has not hitherto harmed us and, so long as the open door is maintained, is actually likely to benefit British exporters."

---

[33] *Documents on British Foreign Policy*, 2nd Series, Vol. 13, Doc. 14.

The interests of Britain and the British Empire dictate to Chamberlain a particular perception of events. The Manchurian invasion becomes the "Manchukuo affair," implying an event of little consequence and accepting as a given the conqueror's acquisition, including his renaming of the conquered territory. The League, rather than the violator of the League covenant, is said to be discredited (we shall see later on that Chamberlain, by this point, was privately expressing complete contempt for the League). Throughout his note, Chamberlain persists in using language that belittles the importance of Japanese aggression. Another of his euphemisms for the invasion of Manchuria is "the Japanese action in Manchukuo;" his only admission of Japanese aggressiveness is a reference to "her aggressive export policy." Unsurprisingly, after describing events in this manner, Chamberlain can counsel that "whatever difficulties and objections there may be in exploratory discussions with Japan just now they are not so serious as to outweigh the immense advantages which would accrue from a satisfactory outcome."

A "satisfactory outcome" from Chamberlain's point of view would be a ten-year Non-Aggression Pact with Japan that would leave the Japanese free to pursue their territorial ambitions so long as they left British possessions alone. Those territorial ambitions, he noted, were threatened by the Soviet Union and there is a strong undertone to Chamberlain's note that suggests he believed a British-Japanese pact would encourage Japan to come to blows with the Soviets.

Chamberlain observes that Japan has "anxieties about the Soviet Government" and is clear about the source of such "anxieties": the Soviet Union is "the only Power which really menaces their present acquisitions or their future ambitions." Though some may suggest that the military influence over the Japanese government will impede the government from signing a peace treaty with Britain, "With Russia on their flank it seems to me that Japan would gladly see any accession of security in other directions."

Interestingly, while Japan's invasion of a sovereign nation and gobbling up of its most productive industrial province constitutes an "action" or an "affair," the Soviet Union's mere existence on the border of territories the Japanese have illegally acquired constitutes a "menace." Britain and Europe more generally, Chamberlain admits, do not "menace" Japan's spoils of war present or future. Why then should Japan wish to sign a peace pact with Britain? The answer is that Britain would guarantee not to interfere with the "future ambitions" of Japan, much less its "present acquisitions" provided it left Britain's colonies alone. Japan would have a free hand to grab territory, needing to fear only the Soviet Union as a menace to its territorial ambitions.

Chamberlain recognized that there would be American objections to "appeasement" of the Japanese that went this far. But he encouraged Simon not to be "browbeaten" by the Americans where British interests were at stake. In any case, the Americans would have to present "really solid" reasons for opposing a pact; "the objection could not be merely to our agreeing not to settle differences by force."

In other words, Britain would retain the right in international bodies to express disappointment as Japan used force to satisfy her "future ambitions" but would renounce in advance the use of force in response. Since, as Chamberlain admitted, Japan had already proved impervious to peaceful international pressures, Britain would, to all intents and purposes, be giving Japan a free hand in Asia outside of British-occupied areas. He did not, of course, use the phrase "free hand," which has an odious reputation in international dealings. But he was advocating the substance of a free hand. John Simon certainly understood. While sympathetic with Chamberlain's objectives, he objected to Chamberlain's draft on the grounds that it was too obviously a free hand that was being advocated. His solution was to work with Chamberlain to redraft Chamberlain's memorandum to Cabinet to state explicitly that the policy being suggested did not mean the granting of a free hand to Japan in the Far East. Otherwise however the memorandum remained essentially unchanged from Chamberlain's first draft.

Chamberlain was not especially candid on this occasion about his obsession with the destruction of the Soviet Union. But his rhetoric disguises thinly his hopes that the Japanese would end up at war with the Soviets, secure in their knowledge that they could prosecute wars over territory with the Soviets without fear of being attacked "in other directions."

Experts on foreign policy with a broader view of British interests than simply finding opportunities to eradicate a

55

Communist government, disagreed with Chamberlain's proposal. C. W. Orde, head of the Far Eastern Department of the Department of Foreign Affairs, noted that a British-Japanese pact "will surely bring nearer the day when she will attack Russia." This could only be music to Chamberlain's ears. But Orde added that after attacking Russia, Japan, "after a pause," would "proceed against the East Indies."[34] So a policy that was supposed to protect the British Empire would in fact prove to be its undoing in Asia.

It would also, argued Orde, undermine Britain's relations with China. Japan had already torn up the Nine Power Treaty which guaranteed China's territorial integrity. Chamberlain was proposing that a new treaty guaranteeing China against further violations of its territory could be explored. But, in the context of an Anglo-Japanese treaty that excluded the use of force when "differences" occurred between the two signing partners, "would a new treaty protecting China against further aggression look like anything but mockery?"

Orde observed that there was yet a more important reason not to strengthen Japan by signing a non-aggression pact. Agreeing with Chamberlain that the chief threat to British security came from Germany, he pointed out that Russia had to "be sufficiently strong to be a potential check on Germany." If Russia faced alone an aggressive Japan, its ability to deal militarily with an aggressive Germany at the same time was considerably weakened. But Orde had a world view that was not clouded by an obsession with obliterating Communism.

Chamberlain, presumably because of his obsession with weakening and eventually destroying the Soviet Union, rejected Orde's arguments. So did Simon. In their joint memorandum, they described Japan's violation of the treaty protecting Chinese sovereignty over its territories as "largely past history." Of course, with the Japanese invasion of China having occurred only three years earlier, this reflected a rather swift capitulation to one country's illegal and unprompted seizure of lands from another.

Ignoring both their treaty obligations to China and Britain's larger obligations under the League Covenant, Chamberlain and Simon ceded "Manchukuo" to the conquerors. "The important

---

[34] *DBFP*, 2nd Series, Vol. 13, Document 15, p. 31.

thing, both for China and ourselves," they stated, "is that Japanese aggression and penetration should not pass the Great Wall and invade or monopolize China proper."[35]

Of course, neither minister had permission from the Chinese government to speak on its behalf. China's position remained indeed that the territories seized by Japan WERE part of "China proper." The Great Wall as a boundary, whatever Chamberlain and Simon believed, had no meaning in international law. Clearly, their desire for a treaty with Japan exceeded their desire to respect international law.

Orde and Chamberlain agreed that an Anglo-Japanese treaty would encourage Japanese aggression against the Soviets. But while Orde deplored any action that would weaken Russia's ability to stand up to Germany, Chamberlain sought only to insure that Britain would not be placed in a position of having to defend the Soviets against aggression by Japan. Using his peculiar logic in all matters related to the Soviet Union, he noted that, in theory, since the Soviets were now League members and Japan had been forced out of the League, a war between these two countries would create "anxiety" for Britain as a League member. But, wrote Chamberlain and Simon, "the creation of especially friendly relations between ourselves and Japan would help to correct the balance and to maintain the neutral attitude which we beyond question would have to adopt."[36] But what "balance" would there be in Britain's foreign relations if it adopted a non-aggression pact with a League outcast while recognizing no obligations to a League member threatened by that outcast nation? How could Britain maintain a "neutral attitude" if it announced in advance that it had no intention of intervening if Japan violated Soviet territory?

In the end, the British government did not conclude a peace treaty with Japan. Nor did it change its position of *de facto* acceptance of Japanese sovereignty over Manchuria. It would seem that the desire not to offend the League, the United States and China itself rather than a real desire to limit Japanese expansionism motivated state policies.[37] When Chamberlain

[35] *DBFP*, 2nd Series, Vol. 13, Document 29, p. 61.
[36] *Ibid.*, p. 65.
[37] In other words, Orde's logic did not prevail over Chamberlain's. Britain remained more concerned with observing the forms of opposition to the Japanese takeover of Manchuria than with fulfilling the spirit of its international obligations to protect Chinese territorial integrity.

became prime minister in 1937, he proved willing to countenance this state of affairs rather than negotiate a formal agreement with Japan to give the latter a "free hand" outside British possessions in Asia. In the case of Germany, however, he proved, as we will see, willing to apply the logic that he had used in 1934 regarding Japan.

***

The desire to come to terms with Japan indicated a cavalier disregard for Britain's responsibilities as a member of the League of Nations. Like the government's attitude in the Spanish "civil" conflict, it demonstrated indifference and indeed contempt for the League and the policy of collective security that provided its *raison d'être*. The cynical gap between the foreign policy announced for public consumption and the real foreign policy practised by the government had a purpose. It was important to convince the public that the government was not condoning tyranny while letting the tyrants know that the opposite was true. The government's conduct in the League of Nations exemplified this strategy. The objective of the League, when it was created in 1919, was to provide collective security to nations. The League covenant threatened collective reprisals against aggressors and Britain, as a member nation, was sworn to uphold League principles.

Publicly the leading political figures claimed to do so. So, for example, on 12 September 1935, in the run-up to a British general election, Foreign Secretary Samuel Hoare addressed the League and assured its members of the unswerving support of the British government. Speaking in the context of the League's discussions about how to punish Italy for its occupation of Abyssinia (Ethiopia), Hoare specifically mentioned "the obligation to take collective action to bring war to an end in the event of any resort to war in disregard of the Covenant obligations."[38]

Yet, a day earlier Hoare had reached agreement with his French counterpart Pierre Laval to avoid, if possible, provoking Mussolini into open hostility. The two countries would apply 'cautiously and in stages' any collectively determined economic pressures against Italy.[39] Hoare had been convinced that Italy

[38] The full text of the speech is found in *DBFP*, 2nd Series, Vol. 14, Appendix 4, pp. 784-790.

was in no mood for compromise and, despite what he said in the League assembly, was unwilling to push Italy too far. In December 1935 the Hoare-Laval agreement was leaked and the popular outcry forced Hoare's resignation.

Yet Hoare's speech to the League was approved by his senior colleagues who had opposed a tougher response in practice to Italy.[40] Eden, the Junior Foreign Minister, claimed later to have "remained puzzled that Ministers should have supported such firm language, particularly in view of their refusal to allow me to give warning to Laval earlier of our intention to fulfil the Covenant."[41] Hoare, in hindsight, would admit cautiously that his "revivalist appeal" might be viewed as having been no more than a bluff but added: "it was a moment when bluff was not only legitimate but inescapable."[42] Eden's response: "Never for an instant was a hint dropped that the speech was intended to bluff Mussolini into surrender."[43]

If Hoare was simply lying, Eden was at least guilty of disingenuousness in claiming to have been "puzzled" by the ministers' firm language. As Eden would have known, most of the British elite had never been happy with the League covenant and until the Hoare-Laval agreement revealed their hypocrisy regarding the international body, few had ventured a public comment critical of the League. It was too important to convince public opinion that Britain was actively participating to achieve collective security. Privately however the British leaders had contempt for the League. So did the French leaders.

This was hardly surprising. Britain and France were imperialist powers that denied self-determination to the people of their vast colonial empires. Their attitude to a League whose purpose was to protect national entities from aggression reflected their imperialist assumptions. So, for example, when the League gave a Conference of Ambassadors the power to determine Albania's borders in 1921, it was predictable that the British and the French teamed up with the Italians to make Albania effectively an Italian protectorate. This action by the League would give Mussolini's Fascists, who seized power the following year, the

[39] Lord Templewood, *Nine Troubled Years* (London: Collins, 1954), pp. 167-8.
[40] Anthony Eden, *Facing the Dictators* (London: Cassell, 1962), p. 261.
[41] *Ibid.*
[42] Lord Templewood, *Nine Troubled Years* , p. 166
[43] Anthony Eden, *Facing the Dictators,* p. 261.

excuse they required to gradually erode Albanian independence and in 1939 to annex the country "by typical Fascist methods of treachery and violence."[44]

Throughout the 1920s the British, while proclaiming publicly that the League covenant was central to their foreign policy, made clear in their statements in the League and their responses to various incidents that they were unprepared to abide by League principles or decisions where these did not suit them. F. P. Walters, a British citizen who was Deputy Secretary General of the League of Nations, notes with regards to Austen Chamberlain, the British representative in the League assembly, that he was always "on the side of restriction." Explains Walters: "The League to him was a part of the diplomatic system, to be used or not according as convenience may dictate."[45]

Convenience did not dictate effective use of the League after Japan invaded Manchuria. Chamberlain's view on the subject, expressed in the British Parliament, was that the "moral authority" of the League would be greater if it did not use force to achieve its objectives.[46] A more honest version of British thinking on the issue was expressed privately by Winston Churchill. He did not believe that either force or "moral authority" should be used to get Japan out of Manchuria. Rather he saw Japan as an "ancient state with the highest sense of national honour and patriotism" which was confronted with "the dark menace of Soviet Russia" and "the Chaos of China."[47]

Neville Chamberlain, publicly a strong supporter of the League, agreed with Churchill's assessment of Japan's actions. He was furious with the League of Nations because most of its members wanted to apply sanctions to Japan. Referring to the League of Nations Union, a British organization devoted to the defence of the League's Covenant and principles and to collective security, he said: "The kind of person which is really enthusiastic about the League is almost invariably a crank and a Liberal, and as such will always pursue the impracticable and obstruct all practical means of obtaining the object in view."[48]

[44] F. P. Walters. *A History of the League of Nations* (London: Oxford University Press, 1960), p. 161.
[45] *Ibid.*, p. 339
[46] Martin Gilbert, *Britain and Germany Between the Wars* (New York: Barnes and Noble, 1964), p. 27.
[47] *Ibid.*, p. 27.

Chamberlain was as contemptuous of League attempts to dislodge Italy from Abyssinia as attempts to force Japan out of Manchuria. Leo Amery would recall that Chamberlain, like Hoare, wanted only a public show of solidarity with the League after the Italian seizure of Ethiopia. Britain would apply mild economic sanctions which it could lift once it became clear they were having no effect. Since France was unwilling to apply sanctions, Britain would be able to claim that it had wanted to make sanctions effective but that unfortunately the necessary degree of international support for this policy did not exist.[49]

Yet Chamberlain would say during the election of 1935 that "the choice before us is whether we shall make one last effort at Geneva for peace and security or whether by a cowardly surrender we shall break our promise and hold ourselves up to the shame of our children and their children's children."[50] Amery's comment: "After the frank cynicism of his talk to me only a few days before I thought the unctuous rectitude of this effort a bit thick."[51]

Less than a year later Chamberlain's public position on sanctions changed. The election of the Popular Front government in France led by Leon Blum meant the removal from office of the politicians led by Laval who had favoured an understanding with Fascist Italy that included its right to remain in possession of Ethiopia. Chamberlain addressed the 1900 Club on 10 June 1936 and described the view that it was still possible to regain Ethiopia's independence "the very midsummer of madness." "Nations cannot be relied upon to proceed to the last extremity unless their vital interests are threatened," he argued, presumably forgetting about his children and his children's children. With some vagueness he suggested that the League should be exploring ways of "localizing the danger spots of the world" through the creation of regional blocs with vital interests in particular areas. Only the members of a particular bloc, rather than all League members, would guarantee the security of nations within "danger zones."[52]

---

[48] Keith Middlemas, *The Strategy of Appeasement* (Chicago: Quadrangle Books, 1972), p. 100.
[49] Leo Amery, *My Political Life* (London: Hutchinson, 1955), p. 174.
[50] Martin Gilbert, *Britain and Germany Between the Wars*, p. 34.
[51] Leo Amery, *My Political Life*, p. 175.
[52] Keith Feiling, *The Life of Neville Chamberlain*, p. 296.

Chamberlain, on behalf of the government, was dashing the hopes of those who believed that the change in government in France would translate into a collective effort to force Mussolini out of Ethiopia through a rigorous application of sanctions. In fact, there had never been any willingness on Britain's part to enforce sanctions and Hoare, though sacked over the Hoare-Laval agreement, was in step with the government as a whole.

Britain had joined forty-nine other states in the League in supporting sanctions against Italy in October 1935. Only Austria and Hungary, among League members, had opposed this move. Yet Eden, who was in Geneva for the League meetings, reveals that his government cautioned him not to take too much initiative in the discussions on sanctions. Eden believed that sanctions could force an Italian retreat because the United States, which had only embargoed war material to Italy, was willing to consider a "wider definition of munitions of war, if and when the League did so."[53]

But his government had other ideas despite its public stance in favour of the League and sanctions. It had created an Inter-Departmental Committee on British interests in Ethiopia once it learned of Italy's plans to seize the country. That committee issued its report – the Maffey report – on 18 June 1935 and concluded that Ethiopia's fate was of neither economic nor strategic interest to Britain.[54] Collective security, the purpose of the League, obviously was of little moment to the British government. Rather than asking whether Italy's aggression violated the interests of collective security, the government was only interested in whether British "vital interests" were at stake. Having decided that they were not, maintaining Mussolini's friendship and avoiding a military encounter became its real aims though publicly the charade of support for the League position on Ethiopia would last for a year.

The government, much to Eden's chagrin – or at least his retrospective chagrin – embargoed arms not only to Italy, which was producing its own arms, but also to the government of Ethiopia.[55] It was the latter government that required military assistance and Britain's interdiction of arms to both parties was

---

[53] Anthony Eden, *Facing the Dictators*, pp. 281, 283.
[54] *DBFP*, 2nd Series, Vol. 14, Appendix 2, pp. 743-777.
[55] Anthony Eden, *Facing the Dictators*, pp. 289-290.

a demonstration of support for Italy under the guise of implementing sanctions against Italy. One Foreign Affairs official thought this measure was so perverse that he noted that lifting the embargo altogether might prove somewhat more beneficial to Abyssinia than Italy.[56]

Interestingly, Hoare and others tried to defend their support of inaction in the face of Italian aggression by claiming that Britain was militarily unprepared to deal with Mussolini.[57] The Navy did not agree. Admiral Lord Cunningham, in his autobiography, claims that the Mediterranean Fleet was prepared and ready to stop Mussolini if the orders came, but they never did. "The mere closing of the Suez Canal to his transports which were then streaming through with troops and stores would effectually have cut off his armies concentrating in Eritrea and elsewhere." The Fleet's morale was high and they had little doubt that they could easily defend against the Italian Navy.[58]

The election long past and the opportunity to hide behind France's unwillingness to apply sanctions lost, the British government moved quickly in June 1936 to distance itself from any suggestion of support for military or economic retaliation against the Italian aggressor. Chamberlain's speech on 10 June was followed by a firm statement on 18 June by Home Secretary John Simon against British naval involvement to bring Italy to heel.[59] Prime Minister Baldwin on 20 June went further still announcing that Britain was dropping its economic sanctions against Italy because they were ineffective. Ignoring the principle of collective action that underpinned the League of Nations, he said that there was no point in the sanction strategy "even if all nations desire it."[60]

Britain had walked away on the League and its principles. It played an important role in making the League a paper tiger unable to protect anyone. Neville Chamberlain spoke of the

---

[56] *DBFP*, 2nd Series, Vol. 14, Appendix 3, p. 783: R.I.Campbell, Foreign Office, 9 August 1935.
[57] For example, Hoare claimed "militarily we are so totally unprepared either for meeting some mad-dog act or for involving ourselves in war." Record by Hoare of his conversation with Liberal Leader Herbert Samuel, 28 August 1935 *DBFP*, 2nd series, Vol. 14, Document No. 477, p. 516.
[58] Viscount Cunningham of Hyndhope, *A Sailor's Odyssey* (New York: Dutton and Company, 1951), p. 173.
[59] Frederick L. Schuman, *Europe on the Eve*, 1942), p. 233.
[60] *Ibid.*

effect while ignoring the cause when he addressed the House of Commons on 22 February 1938:

> If I am right, as I am confident I am, in saying that the League as constituted today is unable to provide collective security for anybody, then I say we must try not to delude small weak nations into thinking that they will be protected by the League against aggression – and acting accordingly when we know nothing of the kind can be expected.[61]

The nation that threatened "collective security" the most by 1938 was Germany. The message that such a public statement from the leader of Britain gave to Germany is obvious: Britain would do nothing to protect small nations against whom Germany might commit aggression. Chapter Four examines how a nation supposedly disarmed after World War One became a menace without significant attempts by other countries to prevent its military resurgence.

---

[61] Telford Taylor, *Munich, The Price of Peace*, 1979), p. 497

CHAPTER FOUR

LETTING HITLER REARM:
EVOLUTION OF THE FREE HAND
(FROM 1933 TO THE NAZI OCCUPATION OF THE
RHINELAND)

At first, however, the major powers, and in particular Great Britain, breathed a sigh of relief. From their standpoint Italy had become quiet and orderly. It was in hands that would ruthlessly root out all signs of Communism.

Business interests in every one of the democracies of Western Europe and of the New World welcomed Hitlerism as a barrier to the expansion of Communism. They saw in it an assurance that order and authority in Germany would safeguard big business interests there. Among the more reactionary elements of the Church, there was a paean of praise.

In the case of Hitler, as in the case of Mussolini, the greedy, the Tories and the shortsighted heralded his rise to power with enthusiasm. I can remember one American Ambassador who publicly applauded Mussolini as the harbinger of a new era of glory, not only for the Italian people but for the rest of the civilized world as well.
                                        -Sumner Welles, 1944[1]

The British Cabinet was aware from the earliest days of Hitler's regime that he intended to undertake a vast rearmament programme and engage in wars of conquest. France was also aware of Hitler's intentions and was far more alarmed than Britain. The French had bitter memories of German occupation during World War One and earlier conflicts. They were concerned about the continued claims by influential Germans to portions of French territory. For most French politicians the enforcement of provisions of the Versailles Treaty that forbade German rearmament were a requirement of national security. If necessary, France believed, Britain and France should make use of the provisions of the treaty that allowed them to use force to prevent German rearmament beyond the small army allowed

[1] Sumner Welles, *The Time for Decision* (New York: Harpe and Brothers Publishers, 1944), p. 312. Welles, a close friend of President Roosevelt's, had a long diplomatic career and served as Undersecretary of State during part of Roosevelt's presidency.

under the peace treaty. But Britain resisted all such pressures. As this chapter demonstrates, the concern of the British government became not to thwart German rearmament but to minimize public knowledge and anxiety about the extent and threat of this rearmament. The leading politicians chose cynically to reassure their own electorate and foreign governments of the Nazis' peaceful objectives. An obsession with encouraging Hitler's stated plans to destroy the Soviet Union to the exclusion of most other considerations informed British policy towards the Nazi state almost from day one.

The Allied powers and particularly Britain had helped to sow the seeds of the virulent nationalism represented by the Nazis. After Germany surrendered, the Allies had the power to break the back of German militarism by favouring democratic forces anxious to punish the armaments manufacturers, bankers and military leaders who had led their country and all of Europe into a devastating war. But, alarmed by Bolshevism and fearing the spread of social revolution into their own countries, they chose to leave the social structure unchanged. Extreme right-wing military groupings such as the Free Corps were left in place to attack Communists.[2] The British Ambassador to Germany from 1923 to 1925, Lord D'Abernon, stressed the need to enlist Germany in a European-wide alliance against Communism.[3]

The Versailles agreement allowed the ruling classes in Germany to retain their old powers but reduced their ability to make war. They would have an army of 100,000, that is an army sufficient to put down unrest at home but insufficient to threaten neighbours such as France. They would however have no navy and no air force. Enforcement of such an agreement would require vigilance on the part of the Allies. Those sections of German society that had led the country to war in the first place were anxious for revenge and still determined to win more territory for Germany not to mention to regain territory lost at Versailles.

In Britain, well before Hitler came to power, a large section of establishment opinion held that Germany, if allowed to rearm, would menace its eastern rather than its western neighbours. The

[2] J.W. Wheeler-Bennett, *The Nemesis of Power* (London: Macmillan, 1967), pp. 36, 43.
[3] *Lord D'Abernon's Diary*, Volume 1 (London: Hodder and Stoughton, 1929), pp. 213-14.

ink was hardly dry on the Versailles Treaty when former prime minister Arthur Balfour, Foreign Secretary when Versailles was signed, made clear his government's rejection of the spirit of the agreement. In particular, he rejected France's tough position that Versailles ought to be enforced to the letter and Germany prevented from ever remilitarizing the Rhineland. The French, noted Balfour, believed that the defeated Germans would before long develop a desire for vengeance, rearm, and invade France once again, this time succeeding in conquering their enemy.

Balfour rejected this prophetic perspective. France had been invaded by Prussia in 1870 and by Germany during World War One. The English, by contrast, still believed their island was impregnable, their Navy providing a measure of security that no branch of the armed forces could provide for France. Deluded into a false sense of national security, the British elite, unlike the French elite, could afford a fixation on the Communist threat, real or imagined, to their class rule. The potential German role in eliminating revolutionary Russia prevented their acceptance of the rational calculation of the French government that Germany, not Russia, posed a threat to the security of Europe. Balfour, while not absolutely dismissive of French fears, expected that "if there is a renewal of German world politics, it is towards the East rather than towards the West that her ambitions will probably be directed."[4] He therefore thought that even the temporary French occupation of the Rhineland was counterproductive since it would cause German militarists to look westwards in search of lost territory rather than look eastwards.

Indeed if the French had not been insistent on disarming a nation that had fought on its territory, leaving a heavy toll of death and destruction, Britain might not have been a party at all to German disarmament. Lord Milner, the British Secretary of War, had proposed in 1918 a negotiated peace with Germany that granted the defeated country territorial concessions within the Russian Empire as compensation for the loss of her colonies. He resisted the call for German demobilization on the grounds that German troops would be needed in the fight against Bolshevism.[5]

---

[4] Blanche E. C. Dugdale, *Arthur James Balfour* (Westport, Connecticut: Greenwood Press, 1970: first published London: Hutchinson, 1936), p. 277.
[5] John M. Thompson, *Russia, Bolshevism, and the Versailles Peace* (Princeton: Princeton University Press, 1966), p. 25.

German officials recognized Britain's obsession with Communism and used it as a lever to prevent an over-scrupulous British enforcement of the Versailles agreement. In 1920 Dr. Simons, the German Minister for Foreign Affairs, and General Hoffmann[6] both advised an appreciative D'Abernon that their country would like to be part of a crusade against the Soviet Union. Simons suggested that it was Germany rather than Poland that was the bulwark against Bolshevism.[7] Such propaganda worked its effect not only on the gullible D'Abernon but even on Winston Churchill who, in 1925, let friends know that he believed German aggression on its eastern neighbours was acceptable.[8]

Well before the Nazi takeover, the British government, despite French, Polish, Belgian and sometimes Italian objections, had adopted a *de facto* policy of turning a blind eye to German violations of the Versailles agreement and suppressing public knowledge of these violations. Robert Vansittart, Permanent Under-Secretary for Foreign Affairs since 1930, watched with dismay as the Disarmament Commission reports went unpublished. They revealed that armaments factories remained in operation and war materials had not been destroyed. While the British public was told that Germany was no longer a military threat, a military infrastructure that would prove very beneficial to Nazi war aims was being put into place.[9]

The Nazis formed a coalition government in Germany on 30 January 1933 with Hitler as chancellor and then manoeuvred to take absolute power in the country after the burning of the Reichstag the next month. The British Cabinet heard from reliable and conservative sources that year that Hitler remained as warlike and maniacal as he had been when he wrote *Mein Kampf* ten years earlier. Only concerted and tough action by European states could nip in the bud his plans to create a military machine whose goal would be domination of all of Europe and eventually the whole world.

---

[6] Lt.-General Wilhelm Hoffmann served on the Russian front on the staff of Marshal von Hindenburg.
[7] *Lord D'Abernon's Diary*, Vol. 1 p. 78 and Vol. 2 p. 178.
[8] Correlli Barnett, *The Collapse of British Power* (London: Eyre Methuen, 1972), pp. 329-330.
[9] Robert Vansittart, *The Mist Procession: The Autobiography of Lord Vansittart* (London: Heinemann, 1958), pp. 276, 341.

Sir H. Rumbold, British ambassador to Berlin, sent Foreign Secretary John Simon a report on 26 April 1933 that left no doubt about both the warlike intentions of the Nazis and the manipulations they were using to hide their real aims. "The only programme, which the Government appear to possess may be described as the revival of militarism and the stamping out of pacifism," he wrote.[10]

Rumbold warned that the new German government's "protestations of peaceful intent" were purely expedient, meant "to lull the outer world into a sense of security." While the Nazis would continue to talk peace for foreign consumption, the real philosophy of the government, revealed in Nazi leaders' speeches, was militaristic in the extreme. Hitler, he noted, believed that the nation must define itself as a "community of fighters." A nation or a race that ceased to fight would perish. "Pacifism is the deadliest sin, for pacifism means the surrender of the race in the fight for existence...Only brute force can ensure the survival of the race."

Like others who had observed the Nazis before they came to power and in their early days of power, Rumbold had faint hope that the Nazis would become more moderate with time. But he feared that this ruthless, manipulative government might manage to "lull their adversaries into such a state of coma that they will allow themselves to be engaged one by one." His conclusion was that Germany's neighbours had "reason to be vigilant" and might have to act soon if they wished to prevent Hitler from making war on other nations.

Yet, for the obsessive anti-Communists of the British government, there was solace, however unintended, in the diplomat's summary of events in Germany. While Hitler was mainly interested in European expansion, he believed "the new Germany must look for expansion to Russia and especially the Baltic states." He was not interested in allying with Russia in a war against the West since he believed the aim of the Soviets was "the triumph of international Judaism."

Rumbold was one of many sources the Cabinet could draw upon to recognize the dangerous character of Hitler's aims. Robert Vansittart, still the Permanent Under-Secretary for Foreign

[10] *Documents on British Foreign Policy*, Series 2, Volume 5, Document 36, pp. 47-55.

Affairs in Britain during the early Hitler years, made certain that the Cabinet had at its disposal the views of experts who recognized the dangers posed by the Nazis. On 16 May 1933, for example, Vansittart circulated to the entire Cabinet a report prepared by Brigadier General A.C. Temperley, a British member on the Disarmament Commission. The Disarmament Commission involved Britain, France, Germany, the United States and other powers in a largely futile effort to find ways of creating a lasting peace in Europe and easing the financial burdens of reparations on Germany that had contributed to the weakness of the economy of the World War One loser.

Temperley wrote of the "delirium of reawakened nationalism and of the most blatant and dangerous militarism" in Hitler's Germany.[11] Though the Nazi government was new in office, it had already violated the peace treaty in many ways. About 75,000 members of the Nazis' bully-boy Storm detachments had been incorporated into the police and were receiving military training. "The incorporation of these groups in the police is, of course, a flagrant violation of the peace Treaty." A National Labour Corps, with about 250,000 members, was also receiving military training. Meanwhile, firms forbidden by the treaty from producing armaments were doing so secretly and the government was preparing to reopen eight former government arsenals.

Temperley, as a military man, was blunter than Rumbold about the options facing the nations of Europe in the face of a belligerent German government that was rearming secretly and rapidly with no regard to Versailles.

> France, the United States and ourselves should address a stern warning to Germany that there can be no disarmament, no equality of status and no relaxation of the Treaty of Versailles unless a complete reversion of present military preparations and tendencies takes place in Germany. Admittedly this will provoke a crisis and the danger of war will be brought appreciably nearer. We should have to say that we shall insist upon the enforcement of the Treaty of Versailles, and in this insistence, with its hint of force in the background, presumably the United States would not join. But Germany knows that she cannot fight at present and we must call her

[11] *DBFP*, Series 2, Volume 5, Document 127, pp. 213-217.

bluff. She is powerless before the French army and our fleet. Hitler, for all his bombast, must give way. If such a step seems too forceful, the only alternative is to carry out some minimum measure of disarmament and to allow things to drift for another five years, by which time, unless there is a change of heart in Germany, war seems inevitable...There is a mad dog abroad once more and we must resolutely combine either to ensure its destruction or at least its confinement until the disease has run its course.

Vansittart, over the next several years, would reiterate vainly to Cabinet Temperley's warnings about the Nazis' ultimate goals and the need for united action by France and Britain to prevent German rearmament. Alarmed by the refrain within Cabinet and the establishment generally that Hitler had saved Germany from communism, Vansittart, in a memorandum in August 1933, suggested that many had been "gulled by German propaganda as to the fictitious 'dangers' from which Hitlerism saved a Germany that required no saving."[12]

But proofs of Hitler's duplicity provided by its own professional foreign service did not shake the Cabinet's unwillingness to confront this self-proclaimed protector of the rights of capital and of property. Unsurprisingly then, French proofs provided to the British of Nazi violations of the Peace Treaty were also rebuffed. Joseph Paul-Boncour, the French Foreign Minister, visiting John Simon, his British counterpart in December 1933, was astounded by Simon's claim that there was no substantiation of charges that Germany had indeed violated the Versailles Treaty.[13]

Simon, of course, was lying. Quite apart from whatever the French revealed to him, his government had "secret information that the Germans are rearming," as a Foreign Office official put it in a memorandum on 29 May 1933. The official, Allen Leper, put it to the government that "if we have certain secret information that the Germans are rearming, it is a safe guess that the French have a great deal more." He suggested sensibly that France and Britain confront Germany with its perfidy in the Disarmament Commission and end the disarmament talks. But this, of course, would mean publicly challenging Nazi Germany and joining with the French to destabilize the Nazi regime.[14] As

[12] *DBFP*, Series 2, Volume 5, Document 371, pp. 547-560.
[13] *DBFP*, Series 2, Volume 6, Document 144, pp. 216-225.

we shall see, such advice did not appeal to the British "National" government dominated by the Conservative party.

The British government was aware in far more than general terms of the extent of German rearmament. A memorandum in March 1934, for example, noted that Germany had assembled a fleet of 600 military aeroplanes and had facilities to quickly increase that number. "She can already immediately mobilize an army three times as great as that authorized by the Treaty."[15] No wonder then that the British government was concerned about French calls for an investigation into German rearmament. It was well aware, as it admitted privately, that the French were right. Concerned to prevent a rift with France over Germany, the British government however was not prepared to join France in insisting that Versailles be respected.[16]

Respected statesmen had begun to argue publicly that the supposed Soviet danger justified German rearmament. The young John F. Kennedy, who could just as easily have been writing about his father as the British elite, noted in 1940:

> ...during this period, the fear of Communism, not of Nazism, was the great British bogey. Germany, under Hitler, with its early program of vigorous opposition to Communism, was looked on as a bulwark against the spread of the doctrine through Europe. Sir Arthur Balfour, in speaking of the Russian danger, said, 'One of the greatest menaces to peace today is the totally unarmed condition of Germany.'[17]

Balfour had made this statement in 1933, the first year of Hitler's accession to power. A similar view was expressed by Foreign Minister John Simon in an address to Parliament on 6 February 1934. Simon proclaimed that "Germany's claim to equality of rights in the matter of armaments cannot be resisted, and ought not to be resisted."[18]

Indeed by June 1934, Stanley Baldwin, Lord President and the effective leader of the government,[19] began tentatively to support

[14] *DBFP*, Series 2, Volume 5, Doc. 179, pp. 282-285.
[15] *DBFP*, Series 2, Vol. 6, Doc. 363, pp. 574-582.
[16] *DBFP*, Series 2, Vol. 6, Doc. 264, pp. 395-398.
[17] John F. Kennedy, *Why England Slept* (New York: Wilfred Funk, 1940), p. 55.
[18] *Ibid.*, p. 67.
[19] Baldwin became prime minister in June 1935. But, as leader of the

publicly Germany's right to a degree of rearming that went beyond the peace treaty. Versailles undid the German *Luftwaffe* but Baldwin argued in the House of Commons that this was an unfair provision. Virtually inviting Germany to rearm and to establish anew its air force, he told parliamentarians that "the moment she feels free to rearm" Germany would look to her air defences. "She has every argument in her favour, from her defenceless position in the air, to try to make herself secure."[20]

Baldwin was disingenuous in implying that Germany's actions were purely defensive. His government had been warned by the British Chiefs of Staff in October 1933 that German rearmament was proceeding rapidly and would make Germany within a few years a "formidable military power."[21] Anthony Eden, then the Junior Minister at the Foreign Office, would later admit: "By November 1933 we knew that Hitler was starting to build military aircraft in quantity and that paramilitary organizations were being equipped and trained. In a few years Nazi Germany would be an armed menace."[22]

But an "armed menace" to whom? The report of the Chiefs of Staff that alerted the government to Germany's rapid rearmament suggested that Germany's objective was a "revision of frontiers in the East." While Eden indicates with hindsight that the Foreign Office did not believe that Germany would restrict its military objectives to the East, the Chiefs of Staff and much of the government appear to have thought otherwise. Hitler, aware of their anti-Communist obsession, encouraged their delusion. Meeting with the British Ambassador to Germany, Sir Eric Phipps, on 24 October 1933, the German dictator confided that his country sought to expand in Eastern Europe. That should have been met with an immediate and stern warning from Britain that Germany would face immediate consequences if it violated the frontiers agreed upon at Versailles. But, as Eden comments, Hitler's "threat" was

Conservative party, which held most of the ministries in Ramsay MacDonald's National government, he was the *de facto* leader of the government for the four years before he became the official prime minister. MacDonald, the renegade Labourite, apart from having few party supporters in the Commons, was ill for several years before he resigned as prime minister and served mainly as a figurehead for what amounted to a Conservative government.
[20] Gaetano Salvemini, *Prelude to World War Two* (London: Victor Gollancz, 1953), p. 165.
[21] Barnett, *The Collapse of British Power*, p. 344.
[22] Anthony Eden, *Facing the Dictators* (London: Cassell, 1962), pp. 47-48.

"calculated to reassure those who believed, wrongly in my opinion, that Hitler's ambitions could be tolerated if diverted that way."[23]

"Hitler's ambitions could be tolerated if diverted that way" even though it would mean that the frontiers and even the existence of various Eastern European states would be violated. Clearly this was to be accepted because Hitler could only lead the crusade against the Soviet Union that he claimed to crave if allowed to operate freely in countries that separated Germany from the Communist power. Instead of an immediate reply to Hitler, the British government dithered for six weeks and then decided not to respond at all. When Phipps met Hitler again on 8 December, he did not raise the matter of Germany's expressed intentions to expand eastwards. Indeed Hitler had made his intentions equally clear to the Americans and the Italians who also made no efforts to discourage his expansionist aims.

Phipps was not happy with the role he was required to play. Like his predecessor, Rumbold, he recognized the urgency of tough international action against the Nazis. On 31 January 1934 he sent a blunt report to John Simon.[24] "Nothing had so enhanced the prestige of Herr Hitler in Germany as the behaviour of the ex-Allies since he took office." Moderate voices in Germany had warned that the country courted invasion or at least strong economic retaliation if it left the League and violated the Versailles agreement. But they were being proven wrong. Hitler's policy was "simple and straightforward," noted Phipps. "If his neighbours allow him, he will become strong by the simplest and most direct methods." Only a united and tough-minded response by the Western powers would cause Hitler to lose the public and elite support that he depended upon for his militaristic policies. Echoing Temperley, Phipps warned Simon that Germany is "still sufficiently conscious of her weakness and isolation to be brought to a halt by a united front abroad, though the time is not far distant when even a threat of force will prove ineffective."

Silences play an important role in diplomatic relations. Hitler had every reason to believe at the end of 1933 that the Western powers generally had given him a free hand to do as he pleased in eastern Europe. He had been explicit about his intentions to

[23] *Ibid.*, p. 48.
[24] *DBFP*, Series 2, Vol. 6, Doc. 241, pp. 362-366.

grab territory to Germany's east. The road to Munich had thus begun to be paved by the end of the Nazi leader's first year in power.

The British leaders shared a common excuse in later years as to why the government did little to stop Hitler while German rearmament was still inadequate to face a British-French alliance. The British public, they argued, still weary of war after the exhausting experience of World War One, would not allow it to do more. But the British government did everything in its power to suppress information that might make the British public aware of the danger that Hitler represented to Western democracy.

In the first place, information about the extent to which Versailles had already been violated continued to be suppressed. As far as the public knew, the Germany which Hitler took over was militarily too weak to pose a threat to any nation. Nor was the public to learn early about Hitler's measures to aggressively add to Germany's armed forces and its stock of weaponry. Attempts by other nations to have an investigation of German compliance with Versailles were rebuffed. The Premier of Belgium told his country's Senate on 6 March 1934 that Britain along with Fascist Italy "would refuse to order an investigation" and that this guaranteed that Germany would refuse to allow one.[25]

Yet that month the German military budget was published and showed an increase from 78 million marks to 210 for the air forces and from 344.9 to 574.5 for the land forces. John Simon however told the Commons that there was no cause for concern. The French and Soviet foreign ministers called for the Disarmament Conference to discuss measures to strengthen collective security. Simon disagreed.[26] One month earlier the Defence Requirements Sub-Committee of the Committee of Imperial Defence had suggested that if the Disarmament Conference broke down, Britain's choices were collective security and/or a massive British rearmament programme.

In practice, however, the Cabinet, while authorizing a modest rearmament programme, rejected both alternatives in favour of

---

[25] Frederick L. Schuman, *Europe on the Eve* (New York: Alfred A. Knopf, 1942), p. 51.
[26] *Ibid.*, pp. 51-52.

trusting Hitler. Having rejected earlier European calls for investigation of German violations of Versailles, Britain rejected a similar American plan in February 1935 and rejected suggestions that violations be publicized.[27]

Nonetheless, the scale of German rearmament made it inevitable that, despite the government's tactics, news reports would gradually make the public aware that Germany was once again becoming a potential military threat to the rest of Europe. It was at this point that statements like Baldwin's, mentioned above, which defended this rearmament and made it sound benign, began to appear.

The government was particularly pleased when Lloyd George asked the Commons on 28 November 1934 not to condemn Germany for its rearmament. Echoing his earlier defences of Nazi Germany, the man who was prime minister at the time Versailles was negotiated was now prepared to ignore the treaty because Germany was necessary as a bulwark against communism.[28] John Simon, still the Foreign Secretary, informed the Cabinet committee on German rearmament of how pleased he was with Lloyd George's speech. "We ought, I think, to make much of the growth of British opinion in favour of this course," he argued, adding that, "from this point of view," George's comments were "extremely useful."[29] In short, the government was not helpless before a public opinion that argued for ignoring Germany's belligerent behaviour. Rather it was actively shaping that opinion and then pretending to defer to *vox populi*.

The Cabinet minutes for 21 November 1934 nicely sum up the government's policy regarding Germany as "our policy of ignoring Germany's action in regard to rearmament." The Cabinet meeting that day considered whether the government should abandon this policy and join with the other Versailles powers to expose German violations of the treaty. Government sources indicated that Hitler feared such a turn of events. "If such action were taken now, Hitler's prestige might be affected," noted the Cabinet minutes.[30]

---

[27] *Ibid.*, p. 53.
[28] *Ibid.*, p. 340.
[29] *DBFP*, Series 2, Volume 12, Document 235, p. 273.
[30] Barnett, *The Collapse of British Power*, p. 398.

But, despite growing concerns about the scale of German rearmament, Cabinet agreed to do no more than establish a committee to study the extent of Nazi rearmament and an appropriate response of Britain and the Allies. This committee, however, appeared to be more concerned with dealing with Hitler's critics than with Hitler himself. John Simon was filled with dread that France might make a formal declaration that Germany had violated Versailles. Since Britain would be publicly embarrassed if France took such a step, Simon believed it was crucial to continue to make France aware of its objections to such a course. His task, he believed, was to persuade France that Germany's resolve to rearm was unstoppable. It was necessary to come to agreement with Germany while it remained weak rather than wait until its military might made agreement impossible. But he left unstated why France and England could not simply use tough diplomacy with the threat of military action in the foreground to stop Germany while it remained far weaker than its World War One adversaries.[31]

As the evidence in Chapter 3 suggested, the British leaders believed a war with Germany was unthinkable not because of the military consequences but because of the political consequences. The Communist bogeyman was at base the bugaboo of the British ruling classes. On the one hand, as we have seen, there was the illusion that Nazi Germany represented the best hope of military destruction of the Soviet Union. The Allies, having been forced by public opinion to abandon their military crusade against the Communist state after World War One, had no hopes of leading another attack in the 1930s. Hitler, who had no electorate to face, was promising to do it for them. On the other hand, even if Hitler failed to deal with the 'Soviet menace' and simply became a bully-boy to his neighbours, the Communist haters could not bring themselves to see him as an evil who ought to be removed or neutralized. An Allied war against Germany, they argued, if it removed Hitler from power, would hand Germany over to the Communists. Never mind that the Communists' largest-ever vote was in the range of 14 percent of the electorate. Worse, memories of the social unrest that followed World War One convinced the "appeasers" that all of Europe might go Communist after a war against Germany. So, from this point of view, a victory against Hitler would, in reality, be a defeat. Unwilling to embrace a sufficient programme of reform to dampen enthusiasm for Communism, most of the

[31] *Ibid.*, Chapter 5, *Covenants Without Swords.*

British elite convinced itself that, as Lloyd George argued, the Nazis were best viewed first and foremost as a bulwark against Communism.

The message that Britain wished to convey to France was nicely summed up in the Cabinet minutes for 3 November 1936. "The PM thought that at some stage it would be necessary to point out to the French that...they might succeed in crushing Germany with the aid of Russia, but it would probably result in Germany going Bolshevik."[32]

Nonetheless, two years earlier, John Simon, wishing to calm the fears of the French, had maintained that Britain would draw the line at German reoccupation of the demilitarized zone of the Rhineland. Events would prove that his government's resolve in this area was more apparent than real. No doubt, "our policy of ignoring Germany's action in regard to rearmament" encouraged Hitler to believe that the Allies would also ignore further policies of rearmament, including military occupation of the Rhineland.

On 9 March 1935 Hitler made public the existence of a German military air force. On 16 March 1935, Germany re-established compulsory military service and Hitler formally denounced Part v of the Versailles Treaty which restricted German rearmament. Five days later Hitler made a speech in which he purported to define National Socialism. The speech featured a ringing defence of private property and a stinging rebuke to Bolshevik ideology. National Socialism, intoned Hitler, whose whole programme was predicated on a notion of international domination by superior military force, was "a doctrine which applies exclusively to the German people" while Bolshevism stressed its "international mission."[33]

Neville Chamberlain, then Chancellor of the Exchequer and an apologist for Nazi Germany's supposedly peaceful intentions, claimed the speech "has made my position much easier." While Chamberlain had supported a degree of expansion of Britain's air force, he had opposed more ambitious programmes – "panicky and wasteful," in his words, – that assumed an imminent German threat to western Europe to which Britain

[32] *CAB* 23/81 11 March 1936.
[33] Norman H. Baynes, ed., *The Speeches of Adolf Hitler*, Volume 2 (London: Oxford University Press, 1942), pp. 669-670.

would have to respond. This despite the fact that a year earlier in the Cabinet debate on the proper British attitude to Japan he had readily admitted the overwhelming significance that the German threat should play in the determination of foreign and defence policies. Chamberlain was not unaware of Hitler's foreign-policy objectives in his speech. "It is clear that Hitler laid himself out to catch British public opinion and, if possible, to drive a wedge between us and France," wrote Chamberlain. His conclusion, nonetheless, was that "the general effect is pacific, and to that extent good."[34]

As we have seen, the British government, while perhaps pleased that Hitler was trying to sound "pacific," were well-informed that he was rearming to a point that was hardly compatible with pacific intentions. He had made clear in 1933 to the British his desire to expand eastwards and they had informally given him a free hand by refusing to expose his belligerent objectives or to challenge them. A more formal endorsement of Hitler's foreign policy objectives was on its way.

France, still fearing that German rearmament meant an eventual attack on French territory, wanted the Allies to take a firmer stance. In order to calm France, Britain agreed to a meeting of the two countries along with Italy at Stresa in April 1935 to consider measures that might be taken against Germany. But, with Britain unwilling to provoke Hitler in any way, only words came out of this conference. The three powers denounced Germany's unilateral action and confirmed that Part V of Versailles was still in full force.

Just before Stresa, Simon, as Secretary of Foreign Affairs, and Eden, his junior minister, visited Hitler and Foreign Office documents indicate that Simon used the occasion to reassure Hitler that Stresa would be a harmless conference. Though the meeting with Hitler occurred just days after Hitler's announcement of a major rearmament effort, Simon assured the dictator that the British people understood "the determined efforts on the part of Germany to rehabilitate herself in the moral spheres and in other spheres." He did allow that "a series of acts" by Germany had "disturbed" public opinion but added that he did not wish to discuss "whether these acts were justified or not." While Stresa's purpose was to reassert the post-war

---

[34] Keith Feiling, *The Life of Neville Chamberlain* (London: Macmillan, 1946), entry of 26 May 1935, p. 289.

balance of power determined at Versailles, Simon told Hitler that the British people "were anxious to see if they could find some basis of co-operation with Germany on a footing of real equality."[35]

Stresa was meant to appease France. In reality, British government perspectives on the aims of German rearmament had not altered. John Simon's diary and notes during the meetings at Stresa are dismissive of common-front efforts at that time to confront Germany. Stresa is lumped in with other public denunciations of German behaviour as "empty and futile protests." He reconfirms the view that Germany has no designs on the west. If Germany acts, "it is surely better that she act in the East. That will at worst occupy her energies for a long time."[36]

Yet Simon still thought that the Versailles partners in certain circumstances must be prepared to act in concert. Their unity must be preserved because a common-front approach will be "our only security if Germany turns nasty." Clearly he did not believe that German assaults eastwards constituted nastiness. Indeed such German belligerence would "occupy her energies for a long time," that is it would insure that Germany had no armed forces available for any adventures in the west. The only country in the east that could occupy German military energies for any length of time was the Soviet Union. It is rather clear that Simon hoped that the Germans would defeat the Soviets since his worst-case scenario is that the Germans would be bogged down in their eastern adventures; presumably his "at best" would be the slaying of the Soviet Communist dragon by the German Nazi defenders of capitalism.

Britain revealed publicly its insincerity at Stresa just two months afterwards. The announcement in June 1935 of an Anglo-German Naval Treaty shocked France and Italy, and demonstrated the favourable attitudes towards Nazi Germany that prevailed in the British government. The Treaty allowed Germany to build her navy up to 35 percent of the strength of the British Navy. This was a clear and unilateral violation of the Versailles agreement that Britain claimed to uphold. By signing this agreement, Britain implicitly recognized that Germany was

[35] *DBFP*, 2nd series, Document 651, p. 703.
[36] L.R. Pratt, *East of Malta, West of Suez* (Cambridge: Cambridge University Press, 1975), p. 20.

no longer bound by the Versailles military clauses. An important victory from Nazi Germany's point of view was that while the Anglo-German Naval Treaty set naval limits, it placed no restrictions whatsoever on Germany's land forces.

The treaty allowed Germany to build her submarine force up to half of Britain's and left open the possibility of ultimate parity in submarines. In any event, the 35 percent figure understates the advantages Germany achieved by this treaty. Germany, unlike Britain, did not have to defend sea communication lines within an empire. It could concentrate its navy in the Baltic, easily becoming the dominant naval power in that sea. Moreover, since the German ships would be newly constructed, many of the naval ships that constituted the magic 35 percent would be of better quality than the often archaic battleships of the British Navy. Such a unilateral abandonment of Versailles also constituted an abandonment of Simon's notions that the Allies had to maintain a common front in case Germany turned "nasty." Faith in Hitler had reached a point where only attacks on eastern neighbours and the Soviet Union could be contemplated while real nastiness – such as an attack on Belgium or France – was dismissed.

Unsurprisingly Germany regarded the Anglo-German Naval Agreement as British support for a free hand to Germany in central and eastern Europe in return for an agreement not to challenge the *status quo* in the British Empire or Western Europe. France and Italy were outraged at Britain's craven acceptance of an agreement that gave away so much to Germany without consultation with Britain's allies. Donald Cameron Watt sums up the reactions of the various nations as follows. Note however his implausible claim regarding the British attitude to the agreement.

> ...Joachim von Ribbentrop confronted the British at the opening meeting with a blunt alternative: either an agreement with Germany which fixed German naval strength at 35 per cent of that of Britain or an end to the talks. The British Cabinet accepted, not realizing or even discussing the diplomatic consequences of their action in Europe. For Hitler the subsequent Anglo-German Naval Agreement represented the concentration of German strength on dominion in Central and Eastern Europe and an act of demonstrative disassociation by Britain from any

81

resistance to these plans. It was a voluntary sacrifice of any plans to challenge Britain on the world's oceans, plans which he believed had condemned imperial Germany to British hostility and defeat. To France the signature of the agreement on the 120th anniversary of her defeat at Waterloo at the hands of Wellington and Blucher was a deliberate insult. To Mussolini it was an act of hypocrisy which made him the more determined to snatch at empire in Abyssinia.[37]

Watt does not appear to feel the need to explain how an agreement, which Germany, Italy and France all saw as the granting of a free hand to Germany in central and eastern Europe could be seen with equanimity by the British Cabinet. His claim that they did not realize the diplomatic consequences of their actions is not only incredible but an insult to the members of the British government who were as able as the members of any government to determine how other nations would view their actions. That they did not discuss these consequences is hardly surprising. They were determined to have their agreement with Germany and they had discussed in the past the need to grant Germany a free hand in the east. What exactly does Watt think they still had to discuss?

Those in the know were aware without discussion that Hitler's interpretation of the Anglo-German Naval Agreement was also that of the British Cabinet. The conclusion of the Agreement and the general tenor of Cabinet discussions about relations with Germany convinced Robert Vansittart that his political masters were committed to a dangerous course that amounted to giving Germany a free hand in eastern Europe. Indeed throughout 1935 the government sought what it called a "general agreement with Germany" that would guarantee France against a German attack but leave Germany a free hand in eastern Europe.[38] Vansittart was worried enough about the direction of events to risk his civil service career by informing King George V of his concerns.

---

[37] Donald Cameron Watt, *How War Came: The Immediate Origins of the Second World War 1938-1939* (London: Heinemann, 1989), p. 22.

[38] Orme Sargent, Assistant Under Secretary in the Foreign Office, noted: "The proposed `General Statement` with Germany, and the proposed Air Agreement for Western Europe are both intended to afford France the security which she is looking for." Memo by O. Sargent, 7 February 1935, *DBFP* 2nd Series, Volume 12, Document 428.

At the king's request, the Permanent Under-Secretary of State for Foreign Affairs sent a letter on 7 November 1935 to Lord Wigram, the king's secretary. Though he was careful to accuse no individual of committing or contemplating treason, his message was clear, even desperate:

> ...Any attempt at giving Germany a free hand to annex other people's property in central or eastern Europe is both absolutely immoral and completely contrary to all the principles of the League which form the backbone of the policy of this country. Any British government that attempted to do such a deal would almost certainly be brought down in ignominy – and deservedly...

> Any suggestion that a British Government contemplated leaving, let alone inviting, Germany to satisfy her land hunger at Russia's expense would quite infallibly split this country from top to bottom, and split it just as deeply and disastrously as France is now split, though on rather different lines. This is an undoubted fact, whatever we may think of it, and I hope it will always be in the mind of our political folks.[39]

Vansittart was obviously not wasting the King's time with a letter about hypothetical actions which "any British government" might take. Nor could he have been concerned about the Opposition becoming the government and supporting a free hand to the Nazis in central and eastern Europe. The Labour Party was strongly anti-fascist and the Liberals outside the National government fold were a rump. As for the small group of dissident Conservatives among whom Winston Churchill figured prominently, they were more in tune with Vansittart's beliefs than the governing Conservatives within the National government that also included right-wing defectors from Labour and the Liberals. It was, in fact, clear that the British government which Vansittart believed might consent to invite Germany to invade Russia was the government that he was serving at the time.

Vansittart would continue the following year to fear that the government, still following collaborationist policies with Hitler, would fail not only to reverse those policies but go further to formally cede eastern Europe to Hitler. Harold Nicolson, the

[39] Ian Colvin, *Vansittart in Office* (London: Victor Gollancz, 1965), p. 51.

former National Labour MP, wrote in his diary on 28 April 1936 of having lunch with Vansittart and being told that "we have no right to buy Germany off for a generation by offering her a free hand against the Slav countries." This would prove only the first step towards German domination in Europe and indeed the world. A Germany with hegemony over continental Europe would not resist the opportunity to fall upon Britain and the British Empire and the result would be "the end of the British Empire."[40] Vansittart's letter to the King suggested that he believed there were other moral principles involved in combating Hitler besides preserving the British Empire but no doubt he hoped that conservative politicians could be dissuaded from their anti-Communist obsession if he emphasized the threat that Germany ultimately represented to their cherished Empire.

But even from within the Foreign Affairs ministry the proponents of the free hand were receiving advice that encouraged their strategy. While Vansittart rejected on moral grounds the notion of inviting Germany to attack the Soviet Union and on prudential grounds the idea that a well-armed Nazi Germany posed only a threat to countries east of Germany, his Assistant Under Secretary had somewhat different views. Orme Sargent had been asked to assess France's proposed military pact with the Soviets, a pact the French wanted because they believed that their best protection against a successful German attack was an alliance that would insure that the Germans could not concentrate all their forces on one front. An attack on France would bring Russia into the fray and vice versa.

Sargent, writing on 7 February 1935, opposed such a pact and suggested that France was playing into Soviet hands by considering it. The Soviets, he noted, feared that Germany, as well as Poland, had designs on their territory. Menaced by an expansionist Germany in Europe and an expansionist Japan in Asia, the Soviets wanted an ally in Europe that could help them fend off a German attack on the Soviets' western frontiers. France was the logical candidate because the Soviets could offer France a guarantee of her own territory from German designs. Should Germany attack France, it would be faced with retaliation by the Soviet Union and therefore a battle on two fronts. Britain's aim therefore, from Sargent's perspective, must be to provide France with means other than a Franco-Soviet

[40] Harold Nicolson, *Diaries and Letters 1930-39*, (London: Collins, 1967), p. 259.

alliance of achieving a sense of security with respect to Germany. "The proposed 'General Settlement' with Germany, and the proposed Air Agreement for Western Europe are both intended to afford France the security which she is looking for."[41]

Russia, suggested Sargent, would try to cajole France into a treaty by threatening to come to terms with Nazi Germany if it could make no headway with France. An aggressive Soviet-German alliance would leave France at the mercy of Germany. But, reasoned Sargent, this was "bluff" because there was no possibility that Hitler would come to terms with the Communist power. Nazism, he noted, had two fundamental principles: total opposition to Jews and total opposition to Communists. Rather unprophetically, he suggested that Hitler could not make a deal with the Soviet Communists without destroying the *raison d'être* of the Nazi regime.

Sargent concluded by emphasizing that the Soviets were right to fear Germany. "The need of expansion will force Germany towards the East as being the only field open to her, and as long as the Bolshevist regime exists in Russia it is impossible for this expansion to take merely the form of peaceful penetration." Clearly then, the General Agreement with Germany, meant to insure security for France, would do so at Soviet expense. Such a position, while "immoral" to Vansittart, was supported by Sargent, who confirmed that it was the position of the government.

But while Britain continued efforts to win support for the General Agreement, France's determination to proceed with the pact with the Soviets proved a setback to these efforts. On 2 May 1935 the two powers signed a pact of mutual assistance. On 16 May 1935 a similar pact was signed by the Soviet Union with Czechoslovakia.

The Anglo-German Naval Accord in June demonstrated that Britain was moving in a different direction. It was universally understood that the accord would give Germany dominance in the Baltic. The Admiralty informed the Foreign Office that this was of no consequence to Britain. "Vital British interests," concluded the Admiralty, would not be affected by Germany

---

[41] Memo by O. Sargent, 7 February 1935, *DBFP Second Series, Vol. 12*, Doc. 428.

ignoring Articles 195 and 196 of Versailles which forbade German fortifications on the Baltic and North Sea coasts. Britain's main interest in the Baltic was trade and "this trade is not vital." The Lord Commissioners of the Admiralty assumed that the danger of a British-German war loomed only if German actions forced Britain to recognize its responsibilities in western Europe under the Locarno agreement and the proposed Air Pact for Western Europe. "It is, and presumably will continue to be, no part of our policy to enter into commitments in respect of Eastern European affairs."[42]

The Admiralty recognized explicitly that, as a result of the treaty, Germany was likely to control and possibly close the entrance to the Baltic. Sweden, Poland, Lithuania, Estonia, Latvia, Finland, and the Soviet Union would all be affected by such action on Germany's part. The security of these countries, it seems, was not vital to "British interests." Indeed Lord Gladwyn of the Foreign Office would recall in his memoirs many years later his own understanding that the thrust of British foreign policy at this time was to cede to Germany the right of control over territories to its east. Without attempting to deny his own role as an 'appeaser' of Germany, Gladwyn noted that Britain sought a common front of the "four great European powers" – Britain, France, Germany and Italy. In other words it was a front which included expansion-minded Germany but excluded the Communist giant, the Soviet Union. If Germany proved intractable, the thinking went, Italy should be offered special concessions that would prevent her allying with Germany. Interestingly, Gladwyn referred to the potential four-power alliance as the "Stresa Front." Stresa, as we have seen, was presented publicly by the British government as an effort to demonstrate the willingness by Britain, France, and Italy to curb German expansionism. Gladwyn's phrase suggests the extent to which this was a charade. Suddenly, Germany, the country against whom Stresa was supposed to be directed, was a member of the "Front." Against whom then was the Front united?

Gladwyn admits candidly that he had decided before March 1936 when Germany reoccupied the Rhineland that Germany could not be prevented from re-occupying the Rhineland, conquering Austria and dominating southeastern Europe. "She would be bound one day to seek further 'outlets' in the Ukraine,

---

[42] *DBFP*, Series 2, Volume 13, Document 411, p. 522, July 12, 1935.

in other words that she would eventually come up against the Soviet Union, in which case the West would do what it seemed in its best interests to do, having by that time accumulated heavy armaments, more especially in the air." Perhaps thinking of the sensitivities of his readers in 1972, Gladwyn adds: "The policy may appear to be immoral to some."[43] As we have seen, it appeared immoral to Vansittart. But this anti-Soviet policy would remain the policy of the government until well into 1939 and arguably, as we see in Chapters 8 and 9, until the fall of the Chamberlain government in May 1940.

John Simon, as we have seen, in late 1934 and early 1935, while anxious to come to terms with Germany on the basis that Germany was to look eastwards and leave the west alone, thought two conditions were necessary to insure that Germany was kept under control. The first, mentioned in his April 1935 notes, was that the remaining three European powers acted in concert. The June 1935 Anglo-German Naval Accord removed that condition. The second, mentioned in his discussions with France, was to keep Germany from remilitarizing the Rhineland. In March 1936, however, as Germany reoccupied the Rhineland, that condition evaporated as well.

The Versailles Peace Treaty demilitarized the Rhineland, forbidding remilitarization by Germany. The Locarno Treaty negotiated by the European powers with Germany maintained the demilitarized status of the Rhineland, stipulating that minor violations should be reported to the League of Nations for appropriate action. France was given the right to consider flagrant violations as an act of aggression against herself and to react militarily without having to wait for a League verdict. Britain was obligated to assist France.

In his early years in office, Hitler, while condemning the Versailles Treaty because it had been imposed on a defeated Germany, claimed he would respect Locarno because Germany had freely negotiated its terms. He specifically pledged to respect the demilitarized status of the Rhineland.

The French government was divided as to how to deal with resurgent Germany after it violated Locarno and occupied the Rhineland. A Cabinet majority wanted to force the issue with

---

[43] *The Memoirs of Lord Gladwyn* (London: Weidenfeld and Nicolson, 1972), p. 54.

the Nazis, demanding they withdraw or face being thrown out by the combined forces of Britain and France. German rearmament had not proceeded far enough for Hitler to withstand the armed forces of the Allies. But there was a significant element in the French government and establishment, as we note below, who opposed a belligerent response to Hitler on the grounds that Hitler was Europe's best protector of elite interests against threats of social revolution. For the forces within France that demanded a tough response to Germany to prevail, British support was essential. But it was not forthcoming. Indeed the British, afraid of the consequences for social stability in Germany – that is, the famous Communist threat –, were insistent that France not assert its rights under Locarno. It is important to note that it was recognized at the time that France easily could have defeated Germany in any military confrontation.

The British Cabinet minutes note Prime Minister Baldwin's strong stance against France's request that Locarno be invoked and his stark reasoning about why Germany must be left to do as it wished in the Rhineland.

> The Prime Minister thought at some stage it would be necessary to point out to the French that the action they propose would not result only in letting loose another great war in Europe. They might succeed in crushing Germany with the aid of Russia, but it would probably result in Germany going Bolshevik.[44]

Harold Nicolson, the National Labour MP who would be Minister of Information in Winston Churchill's wartime government, had even direr predictions to make about the impact of France and Britain responding militarily to Germany's violation of Locarno. "Naturally we shall win and enter Berlin," he wrote in his diary a few days after German reoccupation of the Rhineland. "But what is the good of that? It would only mean communism in Germany and France."[45]

France and Britain ultimately did not react to German reoccupation of the Rhineland. Nor were official circles in France prepared, as Britain seemed to fear, to draw the Soviets into the fray though the latter were willing, as they had been

[44] *CAB* 23/81, 11 March 1936, p. 292.
[45] Harold Nicolson, *Diaries and Letters 1930-1939* , p. 250.

since 1934, to join any common front meant to deter Germany's expansionist objectives. The message to the smaller nations of Europe was clear. Neither Britain nor France could be counted on to live up to their treaty military obligations. Germany would be allowed to do pretty much as it wished without reprisals from the great powers who were pledged to constrain her aggressive capabilities. Countries that were vulnerable to German attack would have to come to terms with the Nazi dictatorship if they wished to avoid invasion. Events in the months and years following the occupation of the Rhineland would reinforce such a perspective.

***

It ought to be emphasized that the notion that Hitler was a potential saviour of propertied elites against the threat of socialist revolution was not restricted to the British Cabinet. In earlier chapters we have noted that the establishment in Britain and other countries felt menaced by the Russian Revolution and reacted with relief to the seizures of power in Italy, Spain and Portugal by Fascist dictators who, whatever else they espoused, were vigorous defenders of the rights of capital and of property-holders. That was also their reaction to Hitler's coming to power and, as we have seen, Hitler was well aware that he could win a great deal of support from the establishment across Europe by underlining his anti-communist and pro-capitalist credentials. Hitler's militaristic objectives did little to undermine the good opinion that the elites in Britain and France held of him and his Nazi programmes.

Among the political elite, it was clear that the Baldwin government spoke for the vast majority of the elected members of the National government. Baldwin, Chamberlain, Simon and company were not a small cabal of ministers manipulating their fellow Cabinet and caucus members to support a policy of encouraging German aggression in the direction of the Soviet Union. Harold Nicolson was blunt about the opinions of government supporters in his diary entry for 16 June 1936. He described the poor reception that Winston Churchill received at the Foreign Affairs Committee that day. Churchill shared with his fellow Conservatives the view that defence of the British Empire and the Rhine frontier must be Britain's chief objectives in assessing the right course to take in responding to German belligerence. As Nicolson put it, "what we have got to ask ourselves is whether that task would in the end be facilitated by our telling Germany that she could take what she liked in the East."[46] That was, as Nicolson recognized, implicitly the message the British government was conveying to Hitler though it always denied that this was the case. Churchill warned the Foreign Affairs Committee that a German conquest of most of the Soviet Union would mean a Germany powerful enough to menace the security of Britain's World War One allies and the British Empire itself. Nicolson noted the response: "the general impression left was that the majority of the National Party are at heart anti-League and anti-Russian and that what they would really like would be a form of agreement with Germany and possibly Italy by which we could purchase peace at the expense of the smaller states."[47]

There is considerable evidence that Nicolson was correct. For example, just a few weeks earlier, Stuart Russell, a Conservative MP, argued: "To go to war with Germany because war broke out in Eastern Europe would be sheer distaste to this country." He demanded an immediate end to the "far-reaching commitments" of the League of Nations and the removal of clauses calling for coercion against aggressors from the League covenant.[48] Conservative MP Sir Henry ("Chips") Channon was even more callous and willing to invoke the elite's dream of letting Hitler destroy Communism for them. Wrote Nicolson in his diary on 20 September 1936:

> The Channons...think that we should let gallant little Germany glut her fill of the reds in the East and keep decadent France quiet while she does so. Otherwise we shall have not only reds in the West but bombs in London...Chips says we have no right to criticize a form of government or thought in another country.[49]

Lord Lothian (Philip Kerr) serves as an example of non-government elite opinion in Britain. Because he held no public office in the early Nazi period, he could afford to be more direct in the expression of his pro-Hitler views than could members of the government. Lothian had served as secretary to Lloyd George for five years. He played an important role in formulating the terms of the Versailles Peace Treaty. Among

[46] *Ibid.*
[47] *Ibid,* p. 269.
[48] Gaetano Salvemini, *Prelude to World War Two,* p. 505.
[49] Harold Nicolson, *Diaries and Letters 1930-1939,* p. 273

other distinctions, he had been secretary to the trustees of Sir Cecil Rhodes who determined the rules for recipients of Rhodes scholarships, first editor of the influential journal, *The Round Table*, and under-secretary for India. The government made use of him on several occasions to convey and receive communications with Nazi Germany. In August 1939, just before the outbreak of war between Britain and Germany, this long-time 'appeaser' was named British ambassador to the United States by the government of Neville Chamberlain.

Lothian offered his advice to the British Cabinet throughout the early Hitler period and it was well received as his appointment by Chamberlain in 1939 suggests. While initially unwilling to see the boundaries determined at Versailles tampered with or to sanction German, Japanese or Italian aggression, his position by 1935 was quite opposite. Japan and Germany, he wrote an American friend, were "entitled" to a degree of territorial expansion "because of their power and traditions." "The oceanic democracies," he argued, should be sufficiently strong militarily to deter Germany from threatening "their own liberty" and no more. That was the only course to follow "unless we are prepared to stand in the way of her course in the East, which this country certainly is not."[50] In a letter to Anthony Eden in June 1936, Lothian again suggested that German demands for relatively unrestricted remilitarization and for more territory were a matter of "justice" and entitlement. "Germany must have the position in Europe and the world to which she is entitled by her history, her civilization and her power," wrote Lord Lothian. He denounced France and Russia for trying to prevent Germany from obtaining "adjustments" by "maintaining an overwhelming military alliance against her."[51]

Justice in Lothian's view did not suggest a defence of the right of self-determination of Germany's eastern neighbours. In an address at Chatham House on 2 April 1936, he stated clearly: "Let us make it clear therefore that we would not go to war simply to maintain the status quo or to prevent German predominance in Eastern Europe."[52] Indeed, he believed that a war against the German, Japanese and Italian dictatorships

[50] J. R. M. Butler, *Lord Lothian* (New York: Macmillan and Company, 1960). p. 209.
[51] *Ibid.*, pp. 354-355.
[52] *Ibid.*, p. 214.

91

would destroy the British Empire. To prevent such an eventuality, he called for cooperation between Britain and the United States to police respectively the Atlantic and Pacific oceans so as to keep the dictatorships from threatening the major democracies. A clear line had to be drawn between British responsibilities for western Europe, mainly France and Belgium, and for its own empire with its responsibilities elsewhere in the world. These for Lothian simply did not exist. Indeed, in line with elite opinion generally, Lothian believed that a war to stop Germany from aggressing upon its eastern neighbours was "madness" because "another world war will reduce the whole world to communism or fascism."[53] Again, we have the conservative conviction of the period that their social order would fall victim to a war win or lose. If the democracies won, the sacrifices required of the people in these countries so soon after the slaughter of World War One would turn them away from their current leaders towards their socialist opponents.

Fear of communism and hopes of destroying the Soviet Union pervaded elite thinking about how to respond to the Nazi takeover in Germany. Again and again "democracy" was equated in a self-interested way with capitalism and dictatorship with socialism even as the elites extolled the fascist dictatorships as bulwarks against communism. An example of the discourse that conflated pro-capitalist Nazi Germany with "democracy" is found in the influential *Fortnightly Review* in 1934. L. Lawton began from the familiar elite viewpoint that "Hitler at present looks to the East only" – his purpose in looking that way was not mentioned but understood by his readers to be for expansion. He then suggested that a German-Polish compromise "at the expense of others" could detach Ukraine from Russia and make it part of western Europe. "With Ukraine as part of a democratic federated system," Britain would find a Europe more congenial than it currently did. Lawton did not pretend to explain to his readers how or why Germany and Poland, both dictatorships, were to turn Ukraine into a democracy after forcibly detaching it from the Soviet Union. But for readers whose interest was to crush social revolutionary movements and countries, the precise meanings of democracy and dictatorship were irrelevant.[54]

---

[53] *Ibid.*, p. 224.
[54] Frederick Schuman, *Europe on the Eve*, p. 340.

Readers of journals of opinion of this period in Britain were bombarded with commentaries by members of the elite, including former government ministers and key civil servants, that sounded similar refrains. Hitler was a threat only to countries to Germany's east; Britain had no business protecting Russia or the countries that Germany might march through to invade the Soviet Union; Hitler, while no democrat, had saved Germany from Communism and deserved some understanding on the part of other European countries; any war with Hitler and the other dictators would only benefit the causes of socialism and communism to the detriment of the privileges of the ruling classes.

True, Britain was a member of the League of Nations. But Lothian believed that it should "abandon the universal automatic commitment to take sanctions under Articles X and XVI of the Covenant."[55] Significantly, Lothian expressed his views of the League and of Britain's limited responsibility to protect nations from aggression in a letter to Neville Chamberlain in June 1936 and received a reply indicating the latter's substantial agreement with his views.[56]

The letter to Chamberlain expressed the fear that anti-German forces wanted a war in the short term "before Germany is fully rearmed" and noted that only British resolve not to join the anti-German side could maintain the peace. But the peace envisioned by Lothian, like the peace envisioned by the government, was simply peace in western Europe. War in the east was Germany's prerogative. His view of the proper British strategy is perhaps best summed up in this part of the letter:

> ...provided our complete disinterestment in Eastern Europe is combined with the Locarno guarantee against unprovoked aggression against the frontiers and soil of France and Belgium, the German General Staff, in the event of another European war, will probably reverse the Schlieffen plan and strike Eastwards first while remaining on the defensive in the West. It may be difficult to keep out of another European war to its end, but there is all the difference between automatic commitment to go to war on one side when somebody else presses the button and a free hand.[57]

[55] *Ibid.,* p. 354.
[56] *Ibid.,* pp. 215, 354-355

Lothian was hardly alone among important figures of the World War One period to encourage the political leaders of the 1930s to cooperate with Hitler and to desist from deterring his aggressive intentions towards the nations east of Germany. We have already seen the pro-Hitler sentiments of Lloyd George. Leo Amery was a journalist who had been junior minister at the Colonial Office and the Admiralty during the Lloyd George prime ministership and later served from 1924 to 1929 as Colonial Secretary. Out of office during the 1930s, he joined Lothian and others in calling publicly for non-interference by Britain in Germany's rearmament programme, and for abandonment of League of Nations' clauses that required collective retaliation against aggressor nations. Like Chamberlain, whose anti-Sovietism caused him to champion not only German claims on the Soviet Union but Japanese claims as well, Amery argued that "it would be no concern of ours...to prevent Japanese expansion in eastern Siberia."[58]

Views such as Amery's and Lothian's, given a great deal of exposure in the British press, added to government assurances of Germany's pacific intent, were intended to limit the growth of sentiment in Britain for a strict interpretation of Versailles. *The Times*, leading newspaper of the elite, supported the policy of allowing Germany to rearm and making clear that Britain had no responsibility to protect eastern Europe from German aggression, Versailles notwithstanding.[59] Indeed it was unwilling to give space to those who might have another viewpoint. Liddell Hart, who wanted Britain to take a tougher line with Hitler, complained to assistant editor Robert Barrington-Ward about editorial tampering with his commentaries. For example, in November 1936, Hart had written a leader for *The Times*, only to find that without his authorization the editor had added passages to the piece with which Hart did not agree. He was

[57] *Ibid.*, p. 355.
[58] Frederick Schuman, *Europe on the Eve*, pp. 340-1.
[59] *The Times* was edited from 1912 to 1919 and again from 1922 to 1941 by Geoffrey Dawson, an ultra-imperialist and anti-democrat who was fiercely loyal to the Conservative leadership and happy to follow their line on Nazi Germany uncritically in his newspaper. Dawson was also a close associate of the wealthy Astors who were supporters of harmonious relations between Britain and Nazi Germany. J.J. Astor, brother of Lord Astor, was part-owner of *The Times* while Lord Astor owned the Sunday *Observer*, another mouthpiece for appeasement.
   Margaret George, *The Warped Vision: British Foreign Policy, 1933-1939* (Pittsburgh: University of Pittsburgh Press, 1965), pp. 136, 140-146.

"particularly perturbed" to read an added sentence that suggested Britain regarded the creation of "antagonistic blocs" as a deterrent to peace, followed by an equally unauthorized statement that Britain committed itself only to resisting "unprovoked aggression in Western Europe." The latter statement added that Britain might have to rethink even its blanket Western European commitment.[60]

Hart wrote Barrington-Ward to suggest that *The Times* seemed to be implying that it wished to give Germany a "free hand" in eastern Europe. When Barrington-Ward resisted such an interpretation, Hart replied to note that the leader demonstrated so predominant a concern with western Europe "to the comparative disregard of what happens elsewhere" as to make it possible that "others, especially the Germans, might read it still more definitely in this way." Barrrington-Ward responded ambiguously but in a manner that Hart could only interpret as confirming his right to be concerned about the message *Times* editorials might convey abroad.

> Aggression in the Mediterranean or in Western Europe will immediately encounter determined military resistance. As to aggression elsewhere, we are not prepared to say in advance precisely what we will do but the aggressor can take it as certain that he will encounter our resistance in some form.[61]

Barrington-Ward, then, proposed a policy of letting Germany know that there would be "some form" of British response to aggression anywhere though only if the aggression were against a small band of countries would that response necessarily be war. This conformed to the general approach taken by the British government and elite: let Hitler know that Britain would not tolerate an attack westwards but be ambiguous and non-committal regarding an attack eastwards. It allowed leading figures to deny, as Barrington-Ward did to Hart, that Britain regarded a free hand to Germany in the east as acceptable, at the same time giving Germany many clues that if it attacked countries to Germany's east, the British "resistance in some form" would not be particularly fearsome.

---

[60] *The Memoirs of Captain Liddell Hart*, Volume 2 (London: Cassell, 1965), p. 130.
[61] *Ibid.*, Volume 2, p. 131.

If Barrington-Ward was less than candid with Hart, Field-Marshal Sir John Dill, Director of Military Operations and Intelligence, proved quite frank with Hart in expressing his views and the views of the elite generally. Hart recalled of his meeting with Dill in March 1935: "He clearly disliked the idea that we might be on the side of Russia, in a French-Italian-Russian Bloc against a German-Japanese bloc. Could we not let Germany expand Eastwards at Russia's expense?"[62]

Lord Strabolgi, a Labour peer, recognized that despite the public disclaimers otherwise, the largest element of the political elite of Britain had thrown in their lot with Germany against the Soviet Union. They could not convince public opinion that such a course was moral or prudent and so they pretended that their real goal was peace rather than support for aggression. His conclusion, expressed in a House of Lords debate in April 1936, is important because it demonstrates the way in which the British leaders let Hitler know that he could plan for an attack eastwards with impunity while publicly denying that they were doing any such thing.

> I find a tendency in many influential quarters to clear the field, if I may express it, for a German attack on Russia. It is called by other names of course. "Limiting the risks of membership of the League of Nations" is one of the phrases used. "We must not entangle" is another..Lord Halifax...said we must limit our commitment in the West, and that French obligations must not involve us in trouble in the East, or words to that effect...I find suggestions in many quarters, from important people, to the effect that Russia must be left to her fate and Germany must perhaps be compensated in Europe in that way.[63]

How general was support for fascism and for Hitler among the British elite? Some historians have tried to minimize its importance, denying, for example, that the weekend guests of the wealthy Astors at Cliveden formed a "set" that plotted British support for Hitler as left-wing commentators charged.[64]

[62] *Ibid.*, p. 291.
[63] *The Parliamentary Debates, House of Lords*, Volume 100, Col. 574, 8 April 1936.
[64] Paul Addison, *The Road to 1945: British Politics and the Second World War* (London: Quartet, 1977), pp. 132-3. Addison tries to ridicule the notion of the Cliveden set by reference to two outlandish rumours about the Astors

But, as Margaret George, a perceptive analyst of British foreign policy in the 1930s argues, "controversy about the existence or nonexistence of a 'Cliveden Set' seems decidedly pointless." It is a red herring whether the elite who gathered at the Astors were plotting or merely chatting. What is important are the views that these powerful individuals shared, views which shaped government policy without any need for a conspiracy. Writes George:

> Certainly there was, from the mid 1930s, a group of intimate friends, wealthy and influential people, meeting socially at that estate or the city, their consuming interest, in conversation as in occupation, the burning political questions and the critical foreign events of the decade; their views on these matters were uniformly pro-German; that is to say, Cliveden regulars, members of the aristocracy, and the upper-middle classes unhesitatingly chose, in the ideological polarization of the 1930s, the anti-Communist side – that side manned with obliging zeal by the Fascists. But the Cliveden Set, with its shifting personnel, had no monopoly on enthusiasm for Fascism; they were one circle among many, all of them made up of people of similar social status and public prestige.[65]

***

In France, of course, fear of a resurgent Germany had led to mutual assistance pacts with the Soviets and the Czechs. The French government implored Britain to take a tougher line on German rearmament and to join with France in giving Germany stern warnings that violations of the Versailles Treaty, the League of Nations covenant, and the Locarno agreement would result in military retaliation. But French elite opinion was sharply divided. While memories of World War One caused some politicians and businessmen to believe that a 'devil's pact' with the Soviet Union was a necessary risk, others shared the British elite's obsession with Communism as an evil greater than

spread during the war. These simply beg the key questions of the Astors' views, and their influence on the leading politicians. "By exaggerating a grain of truth [journalist] Cockburn brilliantly symbolized the thesis that the wealthy classes were plotting to sell the pass of democracy to Hitler, in return for protection against communism." This type of pooh-poohing, as opposed to careful argument, is typical of defences of the British elite of the 1930s by conservative British historians.
[65] Margaret George, *The Warped Vision*, pp. 136-137.

any other. For them, neither German militarism nor Nazism represented as great a threat to their privileges as the Marxist philosophy. The growing strength of the French Communist party, the militancy of trade unionists, and even the electoral popularity of the non-revolutionary French Socialist party alarmed many members of the "rich idle classes" of France. They joined the British elite in welcoming the fascist dictators who seized power in Italy, Spain and Portugal and regarded Hitler in a similar light. The importance of this pro-Hitler elite in France, aided and abetted by the near-unanimity of the British elite in supporting their position, greatly weakened the position of anti-fascist and anti-German forces in French governments. The Nazis could take comfort in the fact that while French governments appeared more belligerent than British governments in opposing Nazi objectives, they could not speak for important sections of the political, military, or business establishments. There was therefore no likelihood of a French-led resistance to German rearmament or aggression, particularly aggression eastwards.

In Chapter 3 we noted the candid comments made by a French industrialist to journalist Genevieve Tabouis about why he refused to consider the possibility of a war in which France united with other countries against Germany. Robert Coulondre, French Ambassador first to Moscow and then Berlin in the 1930s, had little doubt that the Nazis, as defenders of private property, had more support among the French elite than the Soviet Communists. The former represented "civilization" while the latter represented "the forces of destruction of world revolution." In Coulondre's words: "National Socialism presents itself, in Europe, as the champion of civilization against the forces of destruction of world revolution. Here is what will not facilitate the grouping of French opinion for the alliance with the Soviets."[66] In other words, elite opinion favoured the view that an ideological alliance with Nazi Germany against the Soviets made more sense than a strategic alliance with the Soviet Union against a militaristic, and expansion-minded Nazi Germany. As we shall see in subsequent chapters, Coulondre proved correct. While France signed a mutual assistance pact with the Soviets in 1935, an important section of the elite preferred an alliance with the Nazis to an alliance with a Communist regime.

[66] *Ibid.*, p. 42.

But it was in Britain, not France, that elite opinion in favour of an arrangement with Hitler and against Stalin was sufficiently united that the move from an informal "free hand" to Germany in the east to a formal, though secret, arrangement would be made. The next chapter details the coming of that agreement.

CHAPTER FIVE

PREPARING FOR A FORMAL DEAL:
FROM THE RHINELAND TO THE ABANDONMENT OF
CZECHOSLOVAKIA

When Hitler marched military forces into the Rhineland in March 1936, he could not know for certain that Britain and France would not react. These two countries still easily outdistanced Germany militarily and could have forced Germany into a humiliating retreat which probably would have resulted in the military removing the Nazis from power. But Hitler had good grounds for believing that Britain would fail to react and would pressure France to do the same. He was aware from his foreign office and intelligence staffs that his emphasis on the anti-communism of Nazism had won him admiration within the British ruling class and a large measure of support for a "free hand" for Germany within eastern Europe. While the British leaders assured the public in their country that they were committed to collective security, their private statements and correspondence and even the undertone of their public statements suggested otherwise. So did their actions. They did nothing about Germany's rearmament and Hitler's Naval Agreement with Britain hammered the last nail in the coffin of the Versailles Treaty.

The lack of reaction to his occupation of the Rhineland emboldened Hitler. He continued his rearmament, actively involved his country in Franco's war against the republic in Spain, and began putting pressures on Austria and Czechoslovakia. In every case he was testing the limits of British and French tolerance for Nazi aggression. He was not however simply being adventurist. The British leadership, well before Chamberlain met with Hitler in a series of meetings in fall 1938, gave Hitler many hints that they would not oppose his ambitions. This chapter traces the events of the two years preceding Chamberlain's granting of a formal "free hand" to Hitler in central and eastern Europe. Anxious to insure that Germany's aggressions were directed eastwards rather than westwards, Chamberlain informally conceded the countries to Germany's east to the Nazis. His government's goal was to try to find ways of insuring that the Germans got their way without

101

having to use military force since Nazi invasions would offend British public opinion. Cabinet policy towards Nazi Germany both before and after Chamberlain's accession to power was governed by two considerations: first, the desire to prevent a war on western European soil that might have social revolution as a byproduct, and secondly, to let Nazi Germany attempt to destroy the Communist Soviet Union. Though Germany's military power grew and her aggressive behaviour towards neighbours increased, the main lines of British policy did not budge.

Stanley Baldwin, in his last days in office as prime minister, had been prepared to meet with Hitler and to demonstrate Britain's willingness to find common ground with the fascist state. But there was sufficient uneasiness in the government to forestall such a meeting.

Most of the British establishment was prepared to excuse the violation of the Treaty of Locarno represented by the remilitarization of the Rhineland. In tune with much of official British thinking about Nazi Germany, the elite appeared angrier with those who called for enforcement of treaties that Germany had violated than with Germany itself. In this case, that meant France. Journalist Violet Markham, for example, writing Baldwin's confidant and advisor Tom Jones, lambasted France for having exulted in the military guarantees provided by Locarno. France had done this during discussions in London about how to react to Germany's provocative actions. Reflecting the usual obsession with the Soviets and the paranoid establishment notion that the Labour party was in cahoots with Communism, she commented: "...because of the Soviet Pact with France the whole Labour Party has swung over on to the French side and Russia is coming out on top in a most disgusting way."[1]

Jones heard similar views expressed in a meeting of Conservative backbenchers. Though an initial meeting attended by the infrequent attendee Winston Churchill along with veteran Austen Chamberlain was pro-French, a second meeting had a "majority of perhaps 5 to 4 for Germany." Noted Jones in a letter in April 1936: "Part of the opposition to France is influenced by the fear of our being drawn in on the side of Russia."[2]

[1] Thomas Jones, *A Diary with Letters 1931-1950* (London: Oxford University Press, 1954), p. 184. Markham wrote Jones on 22 March 1936.

A month later Jones was working actively to arrange a Baldwin-Hitler meeting. He met with Hitler's Foreign Minister Joachim von Ribbentrop and said of this pseudo-aristocratic figure: "He talks English very well and I'm sure does not want war in the West."[3] As we have seen in Chapter Four, this formulation meant that as long as Hitler sought war only in the east, he should not be opposed. Jones, like much of the elite, wanted a clear understanding between Imperial Britain and Nazi Germany. He advised Baldwin on several occasions that "conciliation" between the other western powers and Germany required that Germany not be put in the dock and plied with questions "as if she were a criminal."[4] He joined Hitler sympathizers among the elite in encouraging Baldwin to remove Ambassador Phipps from Berlin. Phipps remained completely unsympathetic with advocates of "conciliation," spending much of his time documenting for the British government the extent of German rearmament and the sinister character of Hitler's true aims.

Von Ribbentrop, well aware of Phipps' hostility, used Jones as a conduit to invite Baldwin to meet with Hitler. Jones met Hitler on 17 May 1936 and, as he indicated in his diary, informed the dictator that Baldwin had confided to him that his aims after the 1935 election included measures "to get alongside Germany." After his visit with Hitler, Jones spent several days at Chequers as Baldwin's guest and recommended that he replace Phipps as ambassador with someone able "to enter with sympathetic interest into Hitler's aspirations." He also conveyed his support for a "secret visit" of the British prime minister with Hitler. Further, presumably in "sympathetic interest into Hitler's aspirations," he counselled that if Austria fell "into the lap of Germany," Britain should not impose sanctions and should make its intentions in this regard "crystal clear" in advance to France. Jones advocated that Lord Halifax, whose sympathies for an understanding with Hitler were known, be sent to Germany to prepare the ground for a Baldwin-Hitler meeting.[5]

---

[2] *Ibid.*, p. 185.
[3] *Ibid.*, p. 186.
[4] *Ibid.*, p. 193. Jones was specifically referring to a communication from Britain to Germany after the German march into the Rhineland in which Britain, attempting to assuage public anger against the government's do-nothing response, demanded German answers to a score of questions
[5] *Ibid.*, pp. 193, 197, 200, 208.

On 23 May, 1936, while still a guest at Chequers, Jones summed up in a letter his meetings with Hitler and Baldwin. The former, he recounted, was asking "for an alliance with us to form a bulwark against the spread of Communism." Baldwin was "not indisposed to attempt this as a final effort before he resigns after the Coronation next year, to make way for Neville Chamberlain."[6]

Jones met von Ribbentrop again to discuss the logistics of a Hitler-Baldwin meeting and tried to steer the whole question of such a summit meeting away from the Foreign Office where Vansittart and others remained staunchly opposed to collaboration with Hitler. But on 16 June Anthony Eden, the Foreign Secretary, informed Jones that he strongly objected to the proposed meeting and preparations stopped. Two years later however the ground for such a meeting would be more fertile. The Baldwin government, in its last days, replaced Phipps as ambassador to Germany with the shamelessly pro-Nazi Sir Nevile Henderson. Halifax had replaced Eden as Foreign Secretary in February 1938. And Chamberlain had succeeded Baldwin to the prime ministership.

***

Chamberlain had been an important player in the Cabinet throughout the Ramsay Macdonald and Stanley Baldwin years. Chancellor of the Exchequer from 1931 to 1937, he was reasonably accurate when he wrote privately in March 1935 that "I have become a sort of acting PM."[7] Baldwin's chosen successor, he had been one of the key Cabinet members calling for a conciliatory policy towards Nazi Germany. As Chancellor, he has to bear much of the blame for the government's failure to allocate sufficient funds to maintain Britain's military strength relative to Germany. His firm refusals to the ministries responsible for rearmament for the large appropriations they desired were predicated on his benign view of Hitler and the Nazis. Like Baldwin, he believed that Hitler looked only eastwards for conquests and that he represented a threat to the Bolsheviks of Russia but no threat to the Western democracies. Hitler's intervention in Spain made no dent on this viewpoint.

---

[6] *Ibid.*, p. 215.
[7] Keith Middlemas, *The Strategy of Appeasement* (Chicago: Quadrangle Books, 1972), p. 51.

Chamberlain had actively involved himself in foreign policy matters before becoming prime minister in May 1937. Hoare consulted him, for example, receiving his approval before delivering his hypocritical defence of the League of Nations at Geneva. He felt secure enough to intrude on Eden's domain with his "midsummer madness" speech that urged an end to League sanctions against Italy.

As prime minister Chamberlain moved quickly to assemble a foreign-policy team that reflected his pro-Germany position. He promoted Vansittart to a ceremonial post that gave him less influence over foreign affairs and appointed in his stead as Permanent Under-Secretary for Foreign Affairs, Sir Alexander Cadogan, who shared his own perspectives on European affairs. Largely circumventing Eden's authority as Foreign Secretary, Chamberlain made Eden believe, as we note later in the chapter, that he had no choice but to resign from Cabinet. His replacement, as noted above, was Lord Halifax, who shared his own desire for an "understanding" with an unhumbled Nazi Germany. The pro-Nazi Nevile Henderson, appointed by Baldwin, remained Britain's ambassador in Berlin. With Phipps, Vansittart and Eden largely out of the picture, Chamberlain was certain to get the kind of advice he wished to receive.

Before taking office in Berlin, Henderson met Chamberlain who was Prime Minister designate and just two months away from assuming that office. He was delighted to find that their views were parallel. Wrote Henderson of their conversation and its impact upon his duties as ambassador: "...to the last and bitter end I followed the general line which he set me, all the more easily and faithfully since it corresponded so closely with my private conception of the service which I could best render in Germany to my own country." Once the war had started, he claimed retrospectively that he indicated to Chamberlain that, "while doing my utmost to work as sympathetically as possible with the Nazis, it was essential that British rearmament should be relentlessly pursued."[8] If Henderson truly gave this advice, it was perhaps the only advice from the ambassador to Berlin that Chamberlain ignored.

Henderson's diametrically opposed views to Phipps's were revealed in a report dated 10 May 1937 and included in a letter

---

[8] Sir Nevile Henderson, *Failure of a Mission* (New York: Putnam's Sons, 1940), pp. 7, 8.

to the Foreign Office dated 20 July 1937. While it gave lip service to such goals as morality, peace and commitment to the League of Nations, the report was generally a sterling defence of the aims of the Nazi regime and a racist defence of Germans against Slavs. Wrote the British ambassador:

> To put it bluntly, Eastern Europe emphatically is neither definitely settled for all time nor is it a vital British interest and the German is certainly more civilized than the Slav, and in the end, if properly handled, also less potentially dangerous to British interests – One might even go so far as to assert that it is not even just to endeavour to prevent Germany from completing her unity or from being prepared for war against the Slav provided her preparations are such as to reassure the British Empire that they are not simultaneously designed against it.[9]

Henderson wanted to achieve an understanding with Germany that would include France. That country should be induced to enter upon such an understanding by Britain convincing her "that she must and can rely only on us to guarantee her security as part of an understanding with Germany." As a last resort, if France proved intractable, the alternative had to be "a direct Anglo-German understanding based on French security and integrity but including some guarantee of neutrality in the event of a Russo-German conflict."

Yet Henderson was neither unaware of nor opposed to Germany's aims. Echoing Phipps's "valedictory dispatch," he listed as the key aims: the absorption of Austria and other German-speaking areas; expansion in the East; and the recovery of colonies. "In themselves none of these aims need injure purely British national interest," he concluded callously. He claimed to remain supportive of the view that the "national independence and integrity" of Germany's neighbours was to be safeguarded. He also claimed to believe that the British government could not object to a "political and economic predominance which the German armies and German industry and population will in any case ensure of their own volition." How these two contradictory positions could be squared Henderson did not say. His overall position expressed on this and other occasions was that the racially superior Germans had, in any case, a right to dominate their Slavic neighbours. He was

[9]   *DBFP*, 2nd Series, Vol. 19, p. 98.

hardly likely to put the "national independence and integrity" of small nations ahead of Germany's need for "political and economic preponderance."

Henderson, wanting to let the Germans know that he would take a rather different line from Phipps, asked for and received Chamberlain's permission to be "slightly indiscreet" in his early months in Berlin.[10] He committed his 'indiscretion' in a speech to the Anglo-German Association on 1 June 1937. In his speech, he said:

> In England...far too many people have an entirely erroneous conception of what the National-Socialist regime really stands for. Otherwise they would lay less stress on Nazi dictatorship and much more emphasis on the great social experiment which is being tried out in this country. Not only would they criticize less, but they might learn some useful lessons.[11]

So the new official British position on Germany, as reported by its ambassador, was that popular opinion – "far too many people" – in Britain was wrong to be appalled by Nazi dictatorship. Democracy as such was not the issue; rather the character of the "social experiment" was the issue. Henderson, like most of the British ruling class, preferred the Nazi experimentation to Bolshevism because the former did not threaten their property and privileges.

But coming to terms with the Nazis remained a problem. Nevile Henderson of course forcefully advocated the "free hand in the East" solution that had seemed so attractive to much of the elite from the start of the Nazi regime. His statement on the need for British and French "neutrality" in the case of a Russo-German war was one formulation of this solution. On 5 July 1937 he wrote Eden that Germany was not opposed to Franco-British cooperation but to the possibility that Britain would enter the "French system of alliances in Central and Eastern Europe." Indeed the Nazis hoped to convince France or its eastern allies to sever these alliances. Dealings with Germany on the "colonial question," felt Henderson, could not begin "until the first objective of 'a free hand in the East' is attained." He was confident that if Britain and France were prepared to concede a

[10] Nevile Henderson, *Failure of a Mission*, p. 8.
[11] *DBFP*, Series 2, Volume 18, Document 568, p. 841.

'free hand' to Germany in eastern and central Europe that Germany would sign and likely live up to a non-intervention agreement with the other two nations "which would be limited to the West."

Then colonial questions could be dealt with. Germany was demanding the return of her pre-war colonies mandated by the Versailles Treaty to various Allies. Britain was reluctant to accede to this demand but Henderson and others believed that Germany would prove conciliatory on this question if allowed to have its "free hand" in eastern and central Europe.[12] In general, British policy on the "colonial question" was that colonies should be given over to the racist Nazi regime but that these colonies should come from Portugal, France and Belgium and not from the British Empire.[13]

Britain repeatedly assured Germany that it would not oppose that country's aspirations in the east so long as they were achieved peacefully. But the Cabinet was aware that such aspirations could only be achieved through violence. In February 1937, the Cabinet affirmed a report from the Committee of Imperial Defence (C.I.D.) which reached this conclusion.[14] It had indeed been obvious from the beginning of the Nazi regime that notions of the countries of central and eastern Europe simply subordinating themselves to Hitler without military conquest made little sense. The Pollyanna approach in which a "free hand in eastern Europe" was advocated at the same time as German violence to achieve dominance in the region was rejected was completely disingenuous. The British leaders only pretended that Germany's furious and illegal rearmament, its provocative violation of Locarno, and the growing belligerence with which it demanded both colonies and a free hand in the east did not mean that Germany actually was planning aggression. As we have seen clearly in Chapter 4, the elite was at best indifferent and at worst actively behind Germany's eastward expansion plans, the one hope of dismantling the Soviet Union.

Fear however grew that the policy of allowing Germany to rearm with impunity might backfire on Britain. Britain had failed to commit sufficient funds to modernize its defences to meet the Nazi German threat that had been recognized, however

[12] *DBFP*, Series 2, Vol. 19, Doc. 16, p. 31.
[13] *DBFP*, Series 2, Vol. 18, Doc. 473, p. 719.
[14] *DBFP*, Series 2, Vol. 18, pp. 965-987.

begrudgingly, from Hitler's accession to power. The Chief of Staff Subcommittee of the C.I.D. recognized in November 1937 how quickly the balance of forces between Germany, on the one hand, and Britain and France, on the other, was changing. At that point France was still capable on its own of mobilizing as many army divisions as Germany. But "by 1939 this will no longer be the case." Germany's air force would also be more powerful in 1939. But the subcommittee feared that even in 1938, Germany might risk air attacks if she were to "become aware of our deficiencies in modern bomber aircraft and the backward state of our air defence measures and the industrial weakness of France."[15]

Reports from Germany indicated her awareness that time worked for her. While the Nazi state rearmed massively, the slower pace of rearmament in Britain and France that produced the deplorable state the subcommittee described meant that Germany had less and less to fear a war. In 1933, when Hitler took power, either France or Poland on their own could have won a war with Germany, the violations of the Versailles Treaty to that point, while noticeable, not having returned her to her former position as a military force to be reckoned with. Germany's ability to show restraint in foreign affairs while she rearmed was however limited by Hitler's impatience. He feared that with advancing age his ability to lead would fade. He also feared that he might be assassinated before he had achieved his dream of a greater Germany dominant in world affairs.

Hitler proved less interested in meeting with the British leaders in 1937 than he had been in 1936. As Germany's military power increased, there was less and less likelihood that the Western powers could prevent her from having her way with central and eastern Europe. The nuances in public statements by the British government suggested that Britain did not really much care what Germany did to her east. So Hitler, in a sense, needed a formal "free hand" less than when Germany's military strength was weaker. A British invitation to German Foreign Minister Baron von Neurath to visit led to several German calls for a delay before it was eventually declined. Lord Halifax met Hitler when he was invited to a hunting exhibition in the country but only after efforts on Britain's part to have such a meeting take place.[16] It was at this point that Chamberlain became determined

[15] *DBFP*, Series 2, Vol. 19, Doc. 316, p. 512.
[16] *DBFP*, Series 2, Vol. 19, Doc. 264, p. 433; Doc. 283, p. 459; Doc. 284, p.

that there should be a more formal understanding with Germany, one that would give Germany both a free hand and colonies in exchange for restraint in the exercise of that free hand and firm promises to leave Western countries alone.

Lord Lothian, a close associate of Chamberlain and a man mistrusted by the Foreign Office, visited Hitler on 3 May 1937, with the Germans informed that he was "in a different category" from other unofficial visitors.[17] While other such visitors' views were to be disregarded, this was not to apply to Lothian. Hitler focused on Germany's desire to restore her former empire. Lothian, informing him that outside perhaps of west Africa, this could not be easily accomplished, suggested "there was no reason why Germany should not extend her influence economically in Central and Eastern Europe."[18] If Germany guaranteed the countries in these regions their national sovereignty, there was no reason why they would not prove more amenable to trade. "In that way Germany would have at her disposal a trade area like that of the British Empire, and the raw material problem would cease to exist."

Of course, Lothian was aware that the British Empire, however it might recognize the national identities of conquered peoples, had been established through violence and was maintained by force. He implied to Hitler that Britain would not necessarily expect Germany to be less violent in establishing for itself an economic empire. "There were only certain definite things for which the British Empire would have recourse to war. These were the defence of the Empire, the defence of the Low Countries or France against unprovoked aggression, the defence of British shipping." Further, "the British people would not fight for the League or hazy ideas, or for Abyssinia or anything else that did not directly concern them."

Vansittart, then in his last days as Permanent Undersecretary for Foreign Affairs, described Lothian as an amateur. Having long fought the fascination of the Chamberlains and Lothians with

---

460; Doc. 298, p. 476; Doc. 310, p. 492.

[17] The Germans had been advised to give little importance to what unofficial visitors told them but that this did not apply in Lothian's case. *DBFP*, Series 2, Vol. 18, Doc. 480, p. 727.

[18] *Ibid.*, p. 729. This opinion, while in tune with Chamberlain's thinking, had no support in the Foreign Office which wanted Britain to help central Europe resist German economic infiltration.

the "free hand" solution to Anglo-German relations, he now countered Lothian's recommendations by writing prophetically:

> It means to be quite precise, the conquest of Austria and Czechoslovakia & the reconquest of Danzig and Memel; followed by the reduction of the other states to the condition of satellites – military satellites – when required.
>
> This is a quite clear and comprehensible programme, but it is quite incompatible with our interests. We fought the last war largely to prevent this.
>
> If HMG fell in with this, they wd be going dead against the democratic tide; and the effect on the US wd be catastrophic. I doubt if we shd ever recover.[19]

Meanwhile, Cabinet discussions had occurred on the question of handing colonies to Germany. Some members of the Cabinet Committee on Foreign Policy questioned the morality of handing over colonies to the Nazi state. Chamberlain, at the time just a month away from becoming prime minister, sidestepped the issue by claiming that Germany had demonstrated a reasonable record towards colonial peoples as an imperial power.[20] In fact, Germany had responded to an uprising in South West Africa at the turn of the century by wiping out a large section of the population. But even had Germany's colonial record been spotless, what of it? Germany did not have a Nazi regime in its colonial past and Chamberlain's references to the colonial record were clearly an attempt to by-pass the issue of the morality of subordinating non-white peoples to a regime whose underlying philosophy was racist in the extreme. Hitler's miserable treatment of the Jews was well known and, in the Nazi racial hierarchy, blacks were below Jews. The Cabinet, anxious to placate Hitler, accepted Chamberlain's perspective. Anthony Eden would write Henderson a few months afterwards that he should let Hitler and his foreign minister know that Britain was prepared to consider German administration of part of Africa even though British public opinion was against this. All European powers with control over portions of African territory would be expected to make "stipulations for the welfare and progress of the natives." Eden knew perfectly well that this request of an ultra-racist dictatorship was hypocrisy, about as

[19] *DBFP*, Series 2, Vol 18, Doc.480 (enclosure), p. 731.
[20] *DBFP*, Series 2, Vol. 18, Doc. 379, p. 579.

useful as asking a bird-eating cat to administer a bird-feeder with due care for feathered visitors.

Halifax, after visiting Hitler, believed that handing over colonies to Hitler might make him more amenable to using means short of war to meet German objectives in central and eastern Europe.[21] The idea was to mollify anti-Nazi public opinion in Britain and keep France happy enough that it did not go to war as a consequence of its commitments to Russia and Czechoslovakia. In the early Nazi years the leading members of the British elite had not been too concerned about how Hitler achieved his objectives in the east and indeed wanted him to attack the Soviet Union. As Lothian revealed, they still were unprepared to actually attack Hitler if he limited his aggression to the east. But with France and public opinion to deal with, it seemed increasingly important to convince Hitler that he could reach his objectives without having to resort to invasions.

Nevile Henderson, always the cheerful supporter of an understanding with Hitler, provided the phrase that would allow the Cabinet to make intimidation appear benign. Describing in November 1937 Nazi attempts to convince Austria that union with Nazi Germany was inevitable, he referred to the Germans' "beaver-like activities" that were causing the Austrian government's "dam to crumble away."[22] Halifax and Chamberlain picked up on this expression. Notes of a Cabinet meeting shortly thereafter indicate Halifax "would expect a beaver-like persistence in pressing their [German] aims in Central Europe but not in a form to give others cause – or probably occasion – to interfere."[23] Chamberlain concurred: "There would be nothing to prevent the Germans from continuing what Lord Halifax called their 'beaver-like activities', but he would regard that as less harmful than (say) a military invasion of Austria."[24]

The real aims of the German beaver, however, were easy to discern for those not blinded, as Chamberlain, Henderson and others like-minded were by fears of social revolution and the Soviet Union. St. Clair Gainer, the British consul in Munich, wrote a report on 30 April 1937 that shed a great deal of light on

[21] *DBFP*, Series 2, Vol. 19, Doc. 336, p. 548.
[22] *DBFP*, Series 2, Vol. 19, Doc. 315, p. 500, 12 November 1937.
[23] *CAB*, 23/90, 24 November 1936, p. 166.
[24] *Ibid.*, p. 168.

Hitler's thinking at the time. General von Reichenau, who had dined with the dictator just three days earlier, had repeated many of Hitler's comments to Gainer at dinner the previous night. The Chancellor indicated that with the French government in disarray, he was confident that Germany's eastern frontiers could be revised. Should this be possible through peaceful means, well and good, but "if peaceful means should fail he would not hesitate to apply force." While Hitler would be happy to make a pact with the Western countries, he would not agree to any disarmament nor to any security arrangements concerning the eastern countries.[25]

The much-ignored and increasingly disillusioned Vansittart minuted on the report: "Here we have again – for the nth time – most ample evidence of Germany's intention to expand at the expense of her neighbours, by force if necessary. That is a policy of violence and robbery...What separates us is really a fundamental difference of conception, of morality. And that is the real answer to all the weak stomachs who would like us to be immoral because they prefer to be blind." Eden, equally a thorn in Chamberlain's side, added to the minute: "Most useful. Mr. Gainer should be thanked."

Nevile Henderson, while an unblushing sympathizer of the Nazis, sometimes provided information that simply confirmed the suspicions of the anti-Hitler forces in the government. For example, in July 1937, at Eden's request, he reported on his visit with Nazi Air Minister Herman Goering. He emphasized that Goering wanted an "Anglo-German understanding" but his report of Goering's comments made clear that this understanding would not involve a German abdication of the right to use force to achieve her aims in the east. Belligerently, Goering had commented that "Germany had to be militarily strong and now that she had abandoned all idea of expansion in the West...she had to look Eastward. The Slavs were her natural enemies."[26]

Eden had begun publicly to break however cautiously with the Chamberlain view of Anglo-German relations before he was forced out of the Cabinet in February 1938. In May 1937, addressing the delegates to the Imperial Conference, he admitted that Germany's flouting of the Treaty of Locarno by

[25] *DBFP*, Vol. 18, Doc. 466, p. 709.
[26] *DBFP*, 2nd Series, Vol. 19, Doc. 52, p. 93.

remilitarizing the Rhineland "was a serious blow to France."[27] While he tried to explain away Britain's failure to join with France to force Hitler to pull back,[28] his admission that the remilitarization of the Rhineland was not the minor event that the British government at the time had pretended was not what Neville Chamberlain would want to hear.

But it was not Eden and Vansittart who would decide how to deal with the "violence and robbery" of Hitler. Rather, Chamberlain and Halifax, the blind men with weak stomachs, from Vansittart's point of view, were in charge. They saw a beaver rather than a viper and spent a great deal of time trying to 'find out Germany's final aims'[29] despite the fact that, as Gainer's report indicated, those aims, known since 1933, were not changing.

***

There are two records of the Halifax-Hitler meeting of November 1937. One is a written account by Halifax[30] which was discussed by the Cabinet on 24 November 1937.[31] It mixes notes taken at the time of the meeting, and some afterthoughts and includes some editing of the original notes. The second and more detailed account was prepared by Dr. Paul Schmidt, the German interpreter present at the meeting. His minutes of the visit were found by the Soviet Union in their zone of occupation in Germany and their authenticity has not been challenged. At the Cabinet discussion of the meeting, Halifax himself relied to some extent on Schmidt's report.[32] A summary of its contents reveals the message that official Britain wished to convey to the Nazi leader at the end of 1937.

---

[27] *DBFP*, Vol. 18, Doc. 510, p. 763.

[28] He explained this failure in terms of a degree of frostiness in relations between France and Britain at the time. As we noted in Chapter 4, this is simply irrelevant as an explanation of Britain's behaviour at the time.

[29] In the later Baldwin years and early Chamberlain years the Cabinet seemed very concerned to decipher what Hitler meant when he stated on a number of occasions that Britain stood in the way of Germany attaining its aspirations. Wanting to reach an understanding with Hitler if at all possible, they sought to find out what Germany's aspirations were, and in what respects Britain stood in the way of their attainment. There is a voluminous British diplomatic correspondence on this issue. See, for instance , *DBFP*, Series 2, Vol. 18.

[30] *DBFP*, Series 2, Vol. 19, Doc. 336, p. 540.

[31] *DBFP*, Series 2, Vol. 19, Doc. 346, p. 571.

[32] *Ibid.*, p. 574.

Halifax began by repeating Henderson's 'indiscretion' and demonstrating that it was nothing of the kind in the eyes of the British government. The government of Britain, he noted, though not always the people, recognized "the great services the Führer had rendered in the rebuilding of Germany." Unlike the Anglican Church and the Labour Party and uninformed public opinion, the government appreciated that Hitler, "by destroying Communism in his country.. had barred its road to Western Europe, and that Germany therefore could rightly be regarded as a bulwark of the West against Bolshevism."[33]

Halifax indicated that Britain would like to reach an understanding with Germany and then follow that up with a four-power agreement that included France and Italy. The Soviet Union, significantly, was not required in official Britain's plans for maintaining peace in Europe.[34] He stressed that Britain had not stood in the way of Hitler's plans. It had, for example, not reacted to the remilitarization of the Rhineland. "He must once more stress, in the name of the British government, that no possibility of changing the existing situation must be precluded."[35] Halifax's making of such an open-ended statement ran contrary to the advice he received from Eden, whose days at the Foreign Office were numbered.[36]

While pleased with Halifax's message, Hitler suggested that "there were big obstacles to reasonable solutions especially in democratic countries." "The demagogic lines of the political parties" made it difficult for governments to negotiate such "reasonable solutions."[37] Halifax pointed out that the British government had negotiated the Naval Agreement despite opposition from the political parties. But Hitler's perception that leaders of democracies could not deliver on their promises would dog the continuing efforts of the Chamberlain government to achieve an overall settlement with Hitler with the free hand for Germany in eastern Europe as its centrepiece.

---

[33] *Documents and Materials Relating to the Eve of the Second World War*, Volume One (Salisbury, North Carolina: Documentary Publications, 1978), pp. 19-20.
[34] An earlier four-power treaty among these four countries, proposed by Italy in October 1932, had been signed in June 1933 but was never ratified.
[35] *Documents and Materials Relating to the Eve of the Second World War*, Volume One , p. 25.
[36] *DBFP*, Series 2, Vol. 19, Doc. 273, p. 447.
[37] *Documents and Materials Relating to the Eve of the Second World War* Volume One , p. 25.

After Halifax's meeting with Hitler, Chamberlain, Eden and Halifax met with French Prime Minister Camille Chautemps and Minister of Foreign Affairs Yvon Delbos. Chamberlain gave assurances, as British governments throughout the Hitler period had done, that Britain had not handed Germany a free hand in central or eastern Europe. Yet he made clear to the French leaders that Britain would not become entangled in a war on account of Czechoslovakia.[38]

The overall message of the Halifax visit to Hitler was that Britain was willing to recognize German domination over central and eastern Europe as long as it was achieved by the "beavering" methods which Henderson, Halifax and Chamberlain endorsed. Some members of the Foreign Office continued to denounce this approach, though without impact on the government. Lord Strang put the anti-collaborationist argument well in a note to Halifax on 13 February 1938:

> It would be unwise to assume too confidently that any considerable territorial change in Central and Eastern Europe...could in fact be effected without resort to force, that is to say without war or threat of war by the stronger Power...
>
> General settlements usually only follow wars; peace settlements...have limited objectives...dictated by the changing balance of forces. Germany is likely to use the existence of her military strength...as a diplomatic instrument for the attainment, by peace if possible, of those aims...There is, in fact, no stated limit to those aims; and the principles upon which Germany's foreign policy would be based have been set out with brutal clarity in *Mein Kampf*.[39]

The invasion and annexation of Austria would demonstrate the truth of Strang's words but would occasion no change in the British government's policies towards Germany. If anything, it appeared to intensify the demand by the militant anti-communists dressed up as peacemakers for a formal understanding with Hitler.

***

---

[38] *DBFP*, Series 2, Vol. 19, Doc. 354, p. 590.
[39] *DBFP*, Series 2, Vol. 19, Doc. 319, p. 517.

The Versailles Peace Treaty forbade the political unification (*Anschluss*) of Germany and Austria. The Allies wanted to reduce Germany's manpower potential and therefore the number of divisions she could put on the field should she once more rearm and prepare for war. Equally importantly, preventing *Anschluss* meant preventing Germany from obtaining borders with Italy, Yugoslavia and Hungary and from expanding its frontier with Czechoslovakia. *Anschluss* would make Czechoslovakia extremely difficult to defend.

There were further grounds for opposing Austrian annexation to Germany after the Nazis took power in the latter country. After 1933, supporters of civil rights recognized that a unification of Austria with Nazi Germany meant guaranteed repression for the large Jewish community of Austria and the huge Social Democratic Party of that country. Yet, by 1937, the British government maintained that it would not oppose *Anschluss* if it resulted from "beaver" activities by the German Nazis.

On 1 June 1937 Franz Von Papen, German Ambassador to Austria, reported to Hitler on a meeting that he had with Henderson concerning German-Austrian relations. "Sir Nevile...entirely agreed with the Führer that the first and greatest danger to the existence of Europe was Bolshevism, and all other viewpoints had to be subordinated to this point of view."[40] In this light, the British Ambassador to Berlin supported the *Anschluss*. When Von Papen indicated that this view contradicted the perspective of the British Ambassador in Vienna, Henderson, while asking that his contrary views not be conveyed to the Ambassador in Vienna, assured Von Papen that "my view will prevail in London." Germany, however, he hoped, would not rush to absorb Austria because Britain needed time "to correct the French standpoint" on this issue.

Even Eden was letting on to the Germans that Britain would not react to *Anschluss*. Meeting with Von Ribbentrop, German Ambassador to Britain in London in December 1937, he admitted that he had told the French that the fate of Austria was of greater concern to Italy than England. The British believed unification was inevitable but "wished, however, that a solution by force be avoided."[41]

---

[40] *Documents on German Foreign Policy*, Series D, Vol. 1, Doc. 228, p. 427.
[41] *DGFP*, Series D, Vol. 1, Doc. 50, p. 90.

Henderson, by this time, even by his own account, was beginning to use the Nazis' own rhetoric in his discussions with German officials meant to demonstrate his government's willingness to come to an understanding with Hitler. Summarizing a meeting with Ribbentrop in January 1938, the ambassador to Berlin mentioned that he had told the about-to-be German Foreign Minister that a war between the two countries would have a disastrous outcome no matter who won. Britain could lose its Empire, a possibility he found unbearable. Yet, "I would view with dismay another defeat of Germany which would merely serve the purposes of inferior races."[42] Henderson's sympathies with Nazi notions of a hierarchy of the races and his anti-Semitism were evident in a variety of his dispatches to London as well as in his conversations with Hitler. He referred to "Jewish fomenters of war" but his racism did not cost him his job.[43]

When the showdown between Germany and Austria finally arrived, Chamberlain demonstrated that Eden and Henderson were being frank with Germany about Britain's unconcern. On 12 February 1938, Austrian Chancellor Schussnigg met with Hitler in Berchtesgaden and was forced to capitulate. Chamberlain's description of the meeting to Parliament a few weeks later implied that two equal leaders had simply arrived at a joint agreement. He saw nothing sinister in this and concluded: "It appears hardly likely to insist that just because two statesmen have agreed on certain domestic changes in one of the two countries – changes desirable in the interest of relations between them – that one country renounced its independence in favour of the other."[44]

Chamberlain knew he was lying. On 19 February 1938, eleven days before he addressed Parliament, he wrote: "Schussnigg the Austrian Chancellor was suddenly summoned to Berchtesgaden, where he was outrageously bullied by Hitler and faced with a series of demands to which he was obliged to yield, since on this occasion Mussolini gave him no support."[45] This rather begged

---

[42] *DBFP*, Series 2, Vol. 19, Doc. 474, p. 821.

[43] Charles Bloch, *Le III e Reich et le monde* (Paris: Imprimerie Nationale, 1986), p. 251.

[44] William Manchester, *The Last Lion, Winston Spencer Churchill, Alone(1932-1940)* (Boston: Little, Brown and Company, 1988), p. 275.

[45] Keith Feiling, *The Life of Neville Chamberlain* (London: Macmillan, 1946), p. 337.

the question of why Britain on this occasion gave Austria no support.

It was at this time that Chamberlain carried out his housecleaning of those insufficiently willing to support his policies of cooperating with Hitler. Cadogan, who would replace Vansittart within a week, wrote in his diary on 15 February 1938: "I almost wish Germany would swallow Austria and get it over. She is probably going to do so anyhow – anyhow we can't stop her. What is all this fuss about?"[46] Such callousness squared well with Chamberlain's strategies for Anglo-German relations.

Eden resigned as Secretary of State for Foreign Affairs on 20 February and two days later Chamberlain told Parliament that small nations should not be "deluded" into believing that the League would protect them against aggression.[47] The extent to which the British government was unwilling to protect not only the treaties that it had already allowed Germany to violate but any notion of morality among nations was becoming increasingly public. With Halifax and Cadogan replacing Eden and Vansittart respectively, Chamberlain could expect to receive the pro-German advice he wanted. Another new appointment at this juncture was Rab Butler, a friend of Chamberlain's, to the position of Parliamentary Under Secretary of State in the Foreign Office. While Hitler bullied Schussnigg, Butler met with a German official at the Embassy in London and emphasized Britain's desire to work closely with Germany. He confided to the official his view that the Foreign Office had been dominated by individuals too much under French influence. Now with Vansittart gone, the balance within the Foreign Office should tilt away from "the French line."[48]

Henderson, the ambassador about as far away from the French line and as close to the German line as an official could get, met with Hitler and Ribbentrop, who had been named German Foreign Minister in February, on 3 May 1938. They discussed the granting of colonies then controlled by France, Belgium and Portugal to Germany. Such discussions, noted Henderson, must be kept top secret since it was important that these three countries be unaware of such plans until the last minute. It was

[46] David Dilks, *The Diaries of Sir Alexander Cadogan, O.M., 1938-1945* (London: Cassell, 1971), p. 47.
[47] *Debates of the House of Commons*, February 1938, col. 227.
[48] *DGFP*, Series D, Vol. 1, Doc. 128, p. 223.

suggested that the transfer of some colonies to Italy could also be considered.[49]

Henderson, while careful not to condemn in the slightest German aggression against Austria, made the usual suggestion that the British government's desire to collaborate more closely with Germany would be less likely to clash with public opinion if the Nazis were not too nasty in their dealings with the nations they wished to dominate. Hitler responded belligerently that "Germany would not tolerate any interference by third powers in the settlement of her relations with kindred countries or with countries having large German elements in their population."

Further, "if England continued to resist German attempts to achieve a just and reasonable settlement, then the time would come when one would have to fight." What resistance, one might reasonably have asked, had England offered to that point to Germany's aims? Just how much more accommodating could the British government be without openly declaring itself subordinate to Hitler and the Nazis? Yet Germany was threatening war. Hitler warned: "whoever proceeded by force against reason and justice would invite violence." The Nazis then were to be equated with "reason and justice."

Henderson did not take umbrage at such threats of war and the implication in Hitler's words that he was not open to compromise. His response was servile and emphasized Chamberlain's oneness of thought with Hitler's. "Chamberlain had himself assumed the leadership of the people, instead of being lead by them," he noted. "In history it was often most difficult to find two men who not only wanted the same thing, but also intended to carry it out at the same time." In response to Hitler's queries about criticisms made by the British ambassador in Vienna concerning Germany's behaviour towards Austria, Henderson was quick to repeat his earlier claims to von Ribbentrop that that ambassador did not speak for the British government. He made clear his personal support for the *Anschluss*.

The German government received confirmation from its attaché in London, Dr. Erich Kordt, of Henderson's statements regarding Chamberlain's attitude to Anglo-German relations. Kordt reported on a conversation he had with Sir Horace

[49] *DGFP*, Doc. 138.

Wilson, the leading Chamberlain advisor, on 10 March 1938, in which Wilson stressed that Chamberlain was determined to press on and obtain an agreement with Germany and Italy. This despite a growing campaign against him by Eden and by leftists as a betrayer of democracy. Wilson told Kordt that the British prime minister had been pleased by a statement by Hitler that Germany and Britain were "two pillars upon which the European social order could rest."[50] Again, there were the usual humble requests that Germany not be too obviously using force as it beavered away to make itself dominant in central and eastern Europe. But this report, like Henderson's comments, would have tipped Hitler off that Britain would not respond if Germany annexed Austria.

As it happened, Chamberlain and Halifax had just lunched with von Ribbentrop the day that they received word that Hitler had ordered Schussnigg to resign as chancellor and for the annexation of Austria to occur without holding the plebiscite on the issue already called by Schussnigg. Ribbentrop wrote that at the luncheon, Chamberlain had asked him to convey to the Führer that he earnestly wanted an understanding with Germany. Afterwards, telegrams arrived, informing Chamberlain and Halifax of events transpiring in Austria. Halifax was angry that Germany had threatened the chancellor and that it had cancelled the plebiscite though he soon regained his composure. Chamberlain never lost his. "Chamberlain again stated that personally he understood the situation" but added that British public opinion would be against Germany on this matter.[51]

Bowing with his public face to public opinion, Chamberlain did denounce Germany's use of violence to annex Austria when he addressed Parliament on 14 March. Under-Secretary Butler told the House that Britain had made strong representations to Germany including a request for the withdrawal of the German troops. The German Foreign Office was unaware of such representations. Britain had protested, but weakly.[52]

This was because Chamberlain did not want to have to wait too long before beginning formal negotiations with Hitler on the future of Europe. Ernst Woermann, who was in Hitler's circle of close advisors, along with Kordt, met with Under Secretary

---

[50] *DGFP*, Series D, Vol. 1, Doc. 148, pp. 271-2.
[51] *DGFP*, Series D, Vol. 1, Doc. 150, pp. 273-275.
[52] *DGFP*, Series D, Volume 1, Doc. 392, p. 606.

Butler after the Austrian annexation and reported Butler's view that Chamberlain remained as committed as ever to "the idea of a real understanding with Germany...the events in Austria had not altered this in any way."[53]

Butler, like Henderson, was both exceedingly sympathetic to the German Nazis and to their racial view of reality. He told Woermann that the people closest to Prime Minister Chamberlain "understood that Germany had to pursue her national aims in her own way." The two peoples of Germany and Britain "were of the same blood" and it was unthinkable that they should fight another war. Speaking obliquely of Czechoslovakia, Butler indicated that he was certain Germany would attain "her next goal." It was important, of course, that it do so in ways that did not create more problems with public opinion for the British government.

***

The British government was concerned about public opinion regarding Czechoslovakia but it was not concerned about Czechoslovakia itself. Once Germany had swallowed up Austria, it became obvious that it would next attempt to annex portions of Czechoslovakia if not the whole country. Chamberlain's government found itself walking a tightwire, attempting to placate at once the Nazi government of Germany and British public opinion which was against allowing Germany to become bullyboy to the small nations of Europe.

Cadogan, Chamberlain's chosen successor to Vansittart, saw his role as preventing British involvement in the inevitable showdown between Germany and Czechoslovakia. He was determined to stand up to those in the Foreign Office who agreed with Vansittart's position that Britain had to oppose German aggression. In his diary on 15 March 1938, he confided his view that a "death-struggle with Germany" was not in British interests. Aware of the Vansittart argument that to "stand aside" on Czechoslovakia as Britain had on Austria was "fatal" to British interests and stature, Cadogan wrote: "I'm inclined to think not." Reflecting the opinion of Nazi sympathizers in the British elite, he described Vansittart and his supporters, rather than Hitler, as "evil." "I shall have to fight Van, Sargent and all

---

[53] *DGFP*, Series D, Vol. 1, 750. pp. 1092-1093.

the forces of evil," concluded Chamberlain's man in the Foreign Office.[54]

In Cabinet that day Chamberlain dismissed the abandonment of Austria to the Germans: "At any rate the question was now out of the way." He admitted that Germany's use of force to get its way with Vienna would make "international appeasement much more difficult" but added ambivalently that it was important "to prevent an occurrence of similar events in Czechoslovakia."[55] The ambivalence was whether he wished to prevent Czechoslovakia being swallowed up or to prevent its sorry fate at the hands of the Nazis becoming a further setback to the achievement of "international appeasement."

Other statements by Cabinet members and Chamberlain as well as events in the following months clarify Chamberlain's meaning: Germany must have its way with Czechoslovakia but it must be the result of a larger agreement among Britain, Germany, France and Italy about how to distribute power among themselves in Europe and the world. In the meantime, France's mutual assistance pact with Czechoslovakia was a potential danger that could draw France, and therefore Britain, into war with Germany. Pressuring France to ignore its obligations under the pact became a key goal of the Chamberlain government.

At least one minister at the 12 March Cabinet meeting (Sir Leslie Hore-Belisha, Minister of War and the only Jew in Cabinet) believed the Austrian events demonstrated the need for greater rearmament by Britain. Halifax rejected this view, suggesting German attitudes to Britain had not changed.[56] He expanded on this perspective six days later at a meeting of the Foreign Affairs Committee. He did not wish to give Germany the impression that there was a plot, involving Britain, France and Russia to encircle Germany. He did not, he said, accept "the assumption that when Germany had secured the hegemony of central Europe, she would then pick a quarrel with ourselves."[57] Having rejected further rearmament just days ago, he admitted that Britain was "in certain respects...very unprepared" for battle. But instead of concluding that rearmament was vital, he

---

[54] David Dilks, *The Diaries of Sir Alexander Cadogan* , p. 63.
[55] Ian Colvin, *The Chamberlain Cabinet* (London: Victor Gollancz, 1971), pp. 105-106.
[56] *Ibid.*, p. 107
[57] *Ibid.*, p. 109.

argued instead that what was necessary was to make clear to France that Britain would not provide it with military assistance if it chose to follow through on its treaty obligations to Czechoslovakia after a German attack on the latter.

Interestingly, Halifax did not talk about "if" Germany secured hegemony over central Europe, he spoke of "when." From the point of view of the man responsible for leading the process of making foreign policy for Britain, there was no question of resisting German control over the region. Other Cabinet ministers were even more explicit about what this meant for British policy regarding German threats to Czechoslovakia. Sir Thomas Inskip, Minister for the Co-ordination of Defence, told the same meeting that Britain had no reason to get involved in maintaining Czechoslovakia's existence.[58]

Later that month the Chiefs of Staff reported on "Military Implications of German Aggression Against Czechoslovakia." Chamberlain had provided the military leaders with several scenarios. All had in common a neutral Soviet Union, an interesting assumption since the Soviets, like France, had a mutual assistance pact with Czechoslovakia and had been pressing since 1934 for a united front with Western countries to confront Nazi Germany.[59]

The Chiefs' report affirmed that Germany was unlikely to succeed in piercing the French Maginot line of defence. In consequence, the report said, Germany might try to deliver a knockout blow to Britain by intensive air bombing. Britain's air defences remained weak and such a tactic might therefore succeed in forcing Britain out of the war.

Chamberlain's exclusion of the possibility of Soviet participation was calculated to draw a pessimistic appraisal from the chiefs of staff. Such pessimism was also inevitable because for years the chiefs had been requesting far larger appropriations for rearmament with no success. They had suffered a rebuff just weeks earlier "by the Chamberlain-Simon-Inskip combination." To argue now that Britain was ready to respond to German aggression in central Europe would have undermined their case for larger appropriations.[60] Interestingly, Air Chief Marshall Sir

[58] *Ibid.*, p. 108.
[59] Telford Taylor, *Munich: The Price of Peace* (New York: Doubleday, 1979), pp. 629-630.

Hugh Dowding presented a brighter report of the British Air Force.[61] But the minority report by Dowding, who headed the RAF Fighter Command and would lead it during the Battle of Britain, was not presented to Cabinet.

The Cabinet, faced with such a gloomy report, concluded that Britain could not agree to any commitments related to the protection of Czechoslovakia against aggression. But it remained opposed to increasing armaments expenditures. Chamberlain's attitude to the bombing scare varied, in any event, with the issue in question. When he wanted to restrict military appropriations, he would put himself on record as not believing in the possibility of a bombing knockout against Britain. When he had to take a position on committing Britain to prevent German aggression, he took the opposite point of view.

On 17 March 1938 the Soviet government proposed that a conference be held to study the situation resulting from the annexation of Austria and discuss means to resist further aggression. The proposal, which indicated willingness to participate in such a conference either under League of Nations auspices or independently of the League, was a demonstration of the Soviets' continued desire to form a common front against Nazi aggression.[62] Chamberlain, the obsessive anti-communist, would resist to the last any cooperation with the Soviets against Germany, retaining the view that cooperation with the latter against the former was preferable.

Chamberlain felt besieged from all sides but his overall assessments of various countries in the European chess game remained one that justified his plans for continued efforts to reach an understanding with Hitler. Three days after the Soviet offer he wrote:

> with Franco winning in Spain by the aid of German guns and Italian planes, with a French Government in which one cannot have the slightest confidence and which I suspect to be in closish touch with our opposition, with the Russians stealthy and cunningly pulling all the strings behind the scenes to get us

[60] *Ibid.*, p. 632.
[61] William Manchester, *The Last Lion: Winston Spencer Churchill, Alone (1932-1940)*, p. 295.
[62] Martin Gilbert, *Britain and Germany Between the Wars* (New York: Barnes and Noble, 1964), pp. 132-133.

125

involved in war with Germany (our Secret Service doesn't spend all its time looking out of the window), and finally with a Germany flushed with triumph, and all too conscious of her power, the prospect looked bleak indeed.[63]

Chamberlain's idiosyncratic reflections, which caused him to lash out at those calling for "a clear, decided, bold, and unmistakable lead," demonstrate the trap the British elite had set for itself and from which they appeared unable to walk away even after the invasion of Austria and the inevitability of aggression against Czechoslovakia. Chamberlain and those who thought like him wanted Franco to triumph over an elected Republican government which they believed was too left wing. They were unwilling to defend the republic even when it became clear that Franco was being backed by Germany and Italy who were using Spain as a proving ground for their weaponry. Yet Chamberlain now decried that Franco's expected victory was the result of aid by the fascist powers.

Germany was "flushed with triumph and all too conscious of her power." But that begged the question of what Britain had done and planned to do to keep Germany from becoming a threat to the rest of Europe. Chamberlain's hopes that Germany would gain its hegemony over central and Eastern Europe by 'beavering away' – that is through subtle aggression – had been dashed by Hitler's naked aggression against Austria.

France meanwhile was derided by Chamberlain because it continued to call for common action with Britain against German aggression. This meant that Chamberlain could not have "the slightest confidence" in its government. The common outlook of the Labour Party in Britain as well as the forces arrayed behind Eden and Churchill with the French government put all of these groups beyond the pale of the single-minded British prime minister.

As for the Soviet 'string-pullers', the reality was that the British Secret Service, and other Western secret services, had been unable to gather reliable information about Soviet internal operations. Only Chamberlain's passionate hatred of socialism and socialists of all stripes could make him believe that the Soviets and not Germany were the troublemakers in Austria,

---

[63] Keith Feiling, *The Life of Neville Chamberlain*, pp. 347-348.

Czechoslovakia, or Spain. The Czech Communists, for example, as the French ambassador in Moscow informed the British embassy (which passed the message on to Halifax), had behaved in an "exemplary" fashion.[64] In no way was the only group in Czechoslovakia whose string the Soviets could conceivably pull behaving provocatively towards Germany. But such facts would only have clouded Chamberlain's strategy as he faced bleak prospects largely of his own making.

Chamberlain was however hardly alone among members of the political elite of Britain and France who, without evidence, were convinced that the Soviets were master-minding events. Named ambassador to Moscow in 1936, Robert Coulondre was allowed to see the secret service's top-secret document on Soviet involvement in French affairs. The file contained "useless verbiage," Coulondre would recall as he wrote his memoirs of his years as an ambassador. Then he added: " This report, if it did not satisfy my curiosity, filled me with admiration for the Soviets. I had just observed, even before my departure, one of the strangest and most dread-inspiring aspects of the Kremlin's power: the secret character of its activity." Having learned that French spies found no traces of Soviet interference in French life, Coulondre could nonetheless complain of "continuous mixing-in of the Comintern in its [France's] affairs."[65]

Chamberlain seemed to be in an increasingly defensive mood about his actions and options because of the increasing intensity of the attack on his policies. So, for example, Winston Churchill, himself historically an obsessive anti-communist, was calling for a Grand Alliance against Nazi aggression that would include the Soviets. This, of course, dovetailed with Stalin's ideas. Chamberlain wrote incredibly that he had given serious consideration to such a proposal before Churchill made it but had rejected it after discussions with Halifax, the Chiefs of Staff, and Foreign Office "experts." From this he had determined that the idea lacked "practicability."[66] Again, there was a great deal of self-delusion here. Halifax was, like Chamberlain, too obsessed with communism to consider the obvious fact that it was Germany and not the Soviets who were proclaiming their

[64] *DBFP*, Series 3, Vol. 1, Doc. 333, p. 391, 28 May 1938.
[65] Robert Coulondre, *De Staline à Hitler: Souvenirs de Deux Ambassades 1936-1939* (Paris: Hachette, 1950), pp. 15-16. Translation from the French by the authors.
[66] *DBFP*, Series 3, Vol. 1, Doc. 333, 28 May 1938.

right to control central and eastern Europe. The senior people in the Foreign Office did not reject a Grand Alliance and the main person who did was Alexander Cadogan, who Chamberlain himself had given his exalted position. Cadogan, whose dismissive attitude to Austria we have already seen, believed "Czechoslovakia is not worth the bones of a single British Grenadier"[67]; for him the question of the worth of an alliance with the Soviets to defend Czechoslovakia could be of little interest. As for the Chiefs of Staff, the military scenarios that Chamberlain had asked them to consider all assumed Soviet neutrality rather than partnership with Britain and France.

The fact was that the Chiefs of Staff had indicated earlier to the government that the Soviets could prove a valuable ally in a war with Germany. In November 1937, the Chiefs of Staff sub-committee of the Committee of Imperial Defence had outlined the strategic pluses and minuses of having the Soviets as an ally in such a war. The minuses included the danger that Soviet involvement could draw Japan into the war. The pluses included the deterrent effect that Soviet air forces could have on German decisions to risk a war with a Grand Alliance of the Soviets, France and Britain. Germany still lacked land superiority over France and her superiority in the air was likely to be seen as insufficient compensation to risk war especially if she had to take into account Soviet air power.[68]

Chamberlain, having promoted inaction and indeed collaboration (for example in the Anglo-German Naval Agreement) in the face of German rearmament and German aggression, now used the consequences of these decisions to justify further inaction. Czechoslovakia, he argued, was indefensible because "the Austrian frontier is practically open." Germany could easily seize Czechoslovakia and the only way to get her out would be to declare war on Nazi Germany. But, because of Germany's military buildup (and of course Chamberlain's unwillingness to consider an alliance with the Soviets), there was no guarantee of the outcome of the war. "I have therefore abandoned any idea of giving guarantees to Czechoslovakia, or the French in connection with her obligation to that country."[69]

---

[67] *The Diaries of Sir Alexander Cadogan*, p. 63.
[68] *DBFP*, Series 2, Vol. 19, Doc. 316.
[69] Keith Feiling, *The life of Neville Chamberlain*, p. 348

On 24 March 1938 Halifax conveyed the British rejection of a Soviet proposal to the Soviet ambassador in London.[70] That same day Chamberlain, without mentioning Austria at all and feigning ignorance of German intentions with regards to Czechoslovakia, told Parliament that the Soviet proposal "would appear to involve less a consultation with a view to settlement than a concerting of action against an eventuality that has not yet arisen."[71] The conference, warned Chamberlain, could tend to "aggravate the tendency towards the establishment of exclusive groups of Nations," that is the creation of blocs, and this could prove "inimical to the prospects of European Peace." Given his efforts to establish a four-power European agreement that excluded the Soviets, this comment was, at the very least, disingenuous.

Chamberlain, in his speech to Parliament, suggested that his government was particularly concerned with addressing the issue of the treatment of the German minority in Czechoslovakia. This was pandering to Hitler's claims of German rights of interference on behalf of nationals in other countries of German descent. Since Czechoslovakia, unlike Germany, was a democracy and its German citizens enjoyed more civil rights than Germans in Germany, the suggestion that Hitler had a right to intervene in Czech politics on behalf of members of the "master race" was particularly obnoxious. But Chamberlain gave credence to the Nazi argument for interference on ethnic grounds.

The Opposition supported the Soviet call for a conference, causing Chamberlain to proclaim that his own position on the Czech issue had the support of all nations except the Soviet Union itself.[72] He was misleading the House, presumably to encourage the British public to believe that the Opposition was unrealistic. Czechoslovakia, obviously, was not supportive of a policy that rejected a concerted response to German aggression against her, but could not say anything for fear of German reprisal. France attempted publicly to minimize foreign policy differences between itself and Britain (indeed the main thing these two countries were able to agree upon throughout the early Nazi period was not to publicize their differences, though these

---

[70] *DBFP*, Series 3, Vol. 1, Doc. 116, p. 101.
[71] Neville Chamberlain, *In Search of Peace* (New York: Putnam's Sons, 1939), p. 85.
[72] Martin Gilbert, *Britain and Germany Between the Wars*, p. 133.

were usually obvious to an informed observer). But privately the French government made clear that it disagreed dramatically with the Chamberlain approach. Phipps, who had been transferred from Berlin to Paris as ambassador, wrote Halifax on 15 March 1938 that Paul-Boncour, the Minister of Foreign Affairs, "urged that His Majesty's Government should declare publicly that, if Germany attacked Czechoslovakia and France went to latter's assistance, Great Britain would stand by France."[73]

Even the United States government was beginning to express its doubts about appeasement of the dictators. Though neutrality acts had been passed by an isolationist congress from 1935 to 1937, Roosevelt, in a speech in October 1937, called for a "quarantine" against international lawbreakers. Though he was vague about what course of action he intended, he suggested the possibility of a naval blockade of aggressor nations. Roosevelt held discussions with the British ambassador regarding a joint blockade of Japan which had renewed its war of aggression on China. He sent a naval officer to London to hold talks with his British counterparts and his Under Secretary of State Sumner Welles called for a conference on international law where Roosevelt could pressure the British leaders to abandon their appeasement policies.[74] In early 1938 Chamberlain rejected such a meeting and dismissed the American President's "quarantine" talk as "utterings of a hare-brained statesman."[75] Eden indicates that Chamberlain's rejection of the American initiative, which provided a way out of the appeasement strategy to which his government seemed wedded, precipitated his withdrawal from Cabinet. Chamberlain had made his decision without even consulting his Foreign Secretary.[76] Without British support,

[73] *DBFP*, Series 3, Vol. 1, Doc. 81, p. 50.

[74] Thomas G. Paterson, J. Garry Clifford, and Kenneth J. Hagan, *American Foreign Relations: A History Since 1895*, Volume Two (Lexington, MA: D.C. Heath and Company, 1995), pp. 159, 179.

[75] *Ibid.*, p. 159.

[76] Eden's official reason for resigning was that Chamberlain had undermined his authority with the Italian ambassador by contradicting Britain's public position in favour of sanctions against Italy. But while this would have been sufficient reason for resigning, Eden wrote in his memoirs that the rejection of the European summit with American participation, long a goal of Eden's, was the more serious blow to efforts to rein in the dictators. Anthony Eden, *The Eden Memoirs: Facing the Dictators* (London: Cassell, 1962), pp. 562-563. This is also mentioned in Winston Churchill, *The Gathering Storm* (Kingsport, Tennessee: Houghton Mifflin, 1948), p. 254.

Roosevelt was in no position to confront the isolationists in Congress.

Chamberlain not only lacked the support of other nations that he claimed but even faced some resistance within his own Cabinet despite Eden's departure. Hore-Belisha asked Liddell Hart, an opponent of appeasement, to prepare notes that he could use to sway Cabinet opinion away from Chamberlain's course. Hart wrote that "we are blind if we cannot see that we are committed to the defence of Czechoslovakia." France had renewed her assurances to Czechoslovakia, aware that if the latter fell under the German dictator's heel that there would be no other front from which Germany might fear attack should Germany decide to make war on France. Hart, unlike Chamberlain, did not believe that Germany looked only eastwards. While it might choose initially to focus its military efforts in that direction, its appetite for territory and power went in both directions and so the futures of all non-fascist European countries were linked.[77]

The government had other concerns. Oliver Harvey, private secretary first to Eden and then to Halifax in their capacity as Secretary of State for Foreign Affairs, wrote in his diary on 19 March 1938 of the pusillanimity of the leading government figures. He noted Halifax's willingness to accept German economic hegemony in central Europe despite his objection to the "methods employed." Though Harvey was himself against new British commitments to countries threatened by dictatorships, he wrote: "Halifax is terribly weak where resistance is required and neither he nor the P.M. have such abhorrence of dictatorship as to overcome the innate mistrust of French democracy and its supposed inefficiency." Without Eden, felt Harvey, there was no one to spur the Cabinet to rearm more quickly. "My colleagues are dictator-minded, as A.E. used to say, and it is true," Harvey concluded sadly.[78]

But publicly they could not show their preference for dictators over a French democracy in which leftists and anti-fascist forces generally were, in their view, too strong for the protection of private property and the avoidance of war with Germany. One day before Harvey made his diary notes, Cabinet member Oliver

[77] Liddell Hart, *The Memoirs of Captain Liddell Hart*, Volume 2, (London: Cassell, 1965) pp. 41-143.
[78] John Harvey, ed., *The Diplomatic Diaries of Oliver Harvey* (London: Collins, 1970), pp. 121-122.

Stanley summed up Parliament's hypocritical stance, noting that "80% of the House of Commons are opposed to new commitments but 100% favour our giving the impression that we will stand resolutely to the Dictators." Chamberlain indicated his agreement with this estimate.[79] He gave a demonstration of Stanley's point by claiming in Parliament that his government was doing its utmost to rearm Britain and having his ministers proclaim that Britain enjoyed air superiority over any other country.[80]

In fact, Chamberlain and his Cabinet, as we have seen, had accepted the Chiefs' of Staff assessment that Germany was superior in the air. In response however to the persistent criticism of Britain's air force, Chamberlain sacked Lord Swinton, the Cabinet minister in charge of the Air Ministry. Sir Warren Fisher, the Permanent Under-Secretary in the Treasury, pointed to Swinton as the culprit for Britain's weak air force. But, Sir Kingsley Wood, Swinton's successor, produced a report that made clear that it was the Treasury, not the Air Ministry, that was responsible for Britain's lack of preparedness. In 1934 "the Treasury had opposed acceleration of aircraft production," wrote Wood. The Treasury at that time, of course, was headed by Chamberlain. In December 1937, Lord Swinton, on behalf of the Air Ministry, had submitted a rearmament plan to the Committee of Imperial Defence, only to be rebuffed on financial grounds. On 12 March 1938, Swinton received a letter suggesting a quota for his ministry that, in Wood's view, could have translated into air inferiority for Britain for a considerable period.[81]

The government, whatever its public face, seemed more concerned at this juncture with pressuring France to remove its guarantee from Czechoslovakia than with planning full-scale rearmament. To the delight of the anti-socialist Chamberlain, the French Cabinet headed by the Socialist Leon Blum was replaced in April 1938 by a more conservative government. Phipps, an anti-Nazi but a loyal servant of his government, followed instructions to work behind the scenes to insure that one of the ministers replaced in the change of government was the Foreign Minister Paul-Boncour.[82] Paul-Boncour was viewed by

[79] Ian Colvin, *The Chamberlain Cabinet*, p. 110.
[80] Britain, *Parliamentary Debates*, 5th Series, Vol. 32, Cols. 1558-1560, 230.
[81] Ian Colvin, *The Chamberlain Cabinet*, p. 120.
[82] Telford Taylor, *Munich: The Price of Peace*, pp. 580-581.

Chamberlain's government as too staunchly committed to the mutual assistance pacts France had signed in its efforts to have allies in case of German threats of aggression. They were pleased to see him replaced by Georges Bonnet who they expected would prove more amenable to their viewpoint.

Chamberlain and Halifax wasted little time in letting the new French Foreign Minister know that Britain was unwilling to be part of any attempts to defend Czechoslovakia against German aggression. They met with the new Prime Minister, the veteran centrist politician, Edouard Daladier, and Bonnet on 28 April. Responding to a request from Bonnet that the Chiefs of Staff of the two countries meet with regard to the military situation, Halifax insisted that any such contacts "not give rise to any obligation regarding the employment of defence forces."[83]

Bonnet may not have been particularly upset to hear such a reply. Unlike Paul-Boncour, he was an appeaser, who, like Halifax, was obsessively anti-communist before he was anything else. On 1 May 1938 the German Ambassador in France reported to the German Foreign Ministry:

> Bonnet...begged us most earnestly not to compel France...to take up arms by reason of an act of violence in favour of the Sudeten Germans. Both France and...Britain too...would exert their utmost influence to induce the Prague Government to adopt an accommodating attitude up to the extreme bounds of possibility; for he considered any arrangement better than world war, in the event of which all Europe would perish, and both victor and vanquished would fall victims to world communism.[84]

Such a message could only encourage Hitler towards an aggressive course in Czechoslovakia and other countries. Obviously if the leaders of the major democracies had convinced themselves that war with Germany, regardless of the cause, meant social revolution, they would be too paralyzed to respond to German aggression against smaller nations. While Hitler shared the elites' revulsion against the egalitarianism embedded in communist ideology, so at odds with his own emphasis on racial superiority and the martial spirit, his desire for German conquests overrode any fears of threats to wealth and property.

[83] *DBFP*, Series, 3, Vol. 1, Doc. 164, p. 199.
[84] *DGFP*, Series D, Vol. 2, Document 144, p. 254.

Indeed, as we saw in Chapter Three, the German dictator, himself not a product of the propertied classes, used anti-communism in a cynical fashion because of his awareness that the "rich idle classes" could be mesmerized by such rhetoric.

Prime Minister Daladier was less defeatist than his foreign minister. In their conversations with the British leader, Daladier affirmed that the French army was sufficiently prepared to "confront the German army victoriously."[85] This confirmed the views of the British Chiefs of Staff. Chamberlain, whose opposition to the war ministries' requests for a much greater injection of funds into rearmament was presumably unknown to the French, suggested that more time was needed to develop Britain's and France's defences. He suggested to the French that the defence of Czechoslovakia seemed an unrealistic objective, with the difficulty increasing "in proportion as Germany proceeded with the refortification of the Rhineland." This was an interesting point, remindful of the parricide who asks mercy of the court on the grounds that he has become an orphan.

Daladier and Chamberlain differed on most issues. Chamberlain wanted France and Britain to put pressure on Czechoslovakia to come to an understanding with the Sudeten Germans. Daladier responded correctly that democratic Czechoslovakia had the best record of European countries in dealing with minorities. It was Nazi Germany that had the worst record and upon whom pressure should be applied. Recounting France's inaction when the Rhineland was militarized and when Austria was invaded – and avoiding mentioning that Britain had put pressure on France to do nothing –, Daladier is reported to have said: "war could be avoided if Great Britain and France made their determination quite clear to maintain the peace of Europe by respecting the rights and liberties of independent peoples." Further, with regard to Czechoslovakia: "if, however, we were once again to capitulate when faced by another threat, we should then have prepared the way for the very war we wished to avoid."

But, while Daladier suggested that Hitler's ambitions for expansion far exceeded even Napoleon's, Chamberlain disagreed. He made plain that he was not willing to gamble the lives of "men, women and children of our own race" to oppose Hitler. The two leaders, he argued, should let President Edouard

[85] *DBFP*, Series 3, Vol. 1, Doc. 164.

Benes of Czechoslovakia know "the limits" within which he could count upon France and Britain. This was the diplomatic way of letting Daladier know that France could not count on Britain at all on this issue and ought to ignore its own treaty obligations with Czechoslovakia. When Bonnet questioned whether Britain would come to France's aid if Hitler refused to leave the Czechs alone after concessions were made to the Sudetens – concessions that France would demand from Czechoslovakia to satisfy Chamberlain – Halifax bluntly replied "no."

Daladier, who would later succumb to British government pressure to accept the route of working out deals with Germany, had views similar to Eden's and Churchill's about the folly of appeasement. While public reports of the meeting would fail to reveal the huge gap separating the views of the French and British prime ministers,[86] Daladier expressed starkly the bankruptcy of the approach that France and Britain had followed to that point: rather than avoiding war, they were following policies that encouraged Hitler to make war and allowed him to win the acquiescence of otherwise cautious elements within the German High Command. Daladier's plea, according to the records of the meeting, included the following observations:

> German policy...was one of bluff, or had certainly been so in the past. When Herr Hitler had ordered the reoccupation of the Rhineland, this policy had been opposed by the German Higher Command, who feared its consequences...but Hitler had bluffed and had reoccupied the Rhineland. He had used this method and had succeeded. Was there any reason why he should cease to use such methods if we left him an open road and so ensured his success?...We were at present still able to put obstacles in her path, but if we failed to do so now, we should then, in his view, make a European war inevitable in the near future, and he was afraid that we should certainly not win such war, for once Germany had at her disposal all the resources of Central and Eastern Europe, how could any effective military resistance be opposed to her?

---

[86] Chamberlain wrote on 1 May 1938: "fortunately the papers have had no hint of how near we came to a break over Czechoslovakia." Keith Feiling, *The Life of Neville Chamberlain*, p. 353.

With great foresight, Daladier predicted that smaller nations in central and eastern Europe, once they saw that France and Britain were unwilling to defend their independence, would submit to German hegemony. Then, with no fears of attacks from the east, Hitler would "turn west" as he had said he would in *Mein Kampf.*

A war of France and Britain with Germany therefore was inevitable and the sooner the better. Time was on Germany's side if it continued to swallow up countries and regions, "increasing her material strength and her political influence with every successful advance."

None of this had any impact on the British resolve to come to terms with Hitler. If anything, Daladier had been too delicate with his hosts. The fact was that Hitler was not engaged in blind bluffing when he marched troops into the Rhineland or Austria. The message that the Baldwin and Chamberlain governments conveyed to Germany by a variety of means, as we have seen, allowed the Nazi dictator to take aggressive actions with reasonable assurance that Britain and its French ally would take no counter-action.

Once the immovability of Chamberlain and Halifax became obvious, Daladier, unwilling to have France fight Germany alone or with only the Soviet Union as an ally, became defeatist. Interestingly, Chamberlain kept from his Cabinet the impassioned plea made by Daladier and also made no mention of information from Bonnet that the Czech crisis would soon come to a head.[87]

After the 28 April meeting Britain and France had effectively abandoned Czechoslovakia to Germany. But public opinion in neither country would have allowed them to admit their callous decision. Indeed, the need for more time to appease public opinion caused Chamberlain on one occasion to bluff Germany into forestalling a planned coup in Sudetenland. Chamberlain recognized that he could not convince the British people that Germany had a right to invade Czechoslovakia; instead he would work to insure that Germany got its way by means of "beavering away." On 21 May, the British government, having detected suspicious troop movements in the Sudeten region, publicly warned Germany that it could not guarantee that it would avoid

[87] Ian Colvin, *The Chamberlain Cabinet* , p. 123.

the use of force in responding to aggression against Czechoslovakia. Alexander Cadogan made clear in his diaries that the government continued to have no intention of using force against Hitler over Czechoslovakia but hoped that threats might forestall action by Hitler before the government could put pressure on the Czech government to accede to Hitler's demands. At the 22 May Cabinet meeting, reported Cadogan, the Cabinet was "quite sensible – and anti-Czech."[88] In the minds of the British leaders, the attempts by this small nation to preserve their national integrity were simply irritants in the way of great power diplomacy. Significantly, the Cabinet was, at this critical point, "anti-Czech" rather than "anti-Nazi;" its venom was reserved for the victim not the perpetrator of the crime. Nonetheless the bluff a day earlier had worked and any plans Hitler had for a coup in Sudetenland were postponed.

Also, on the 22nd, just one day after the tough British government note to Germany, Halifax sent a revealing telegram to Phipps in Paris. He instructed him to make sure the French government "should not be under any illusion" that the British government's position on the Czech crisis had changed. France, along with Britain, must put pressure on Czechoslovakia, not Germany, in order to resolve the crisis.[89] Aware of the misgivings France retained about the defeatist position that Britain had imposed upon them, Halifax was at pains to have Phipps understand that it would be "highly dangerous" for the French to have any hopes that Britain now intended to go as far as war to protect Czechoslovakia. Nine days later, to drive the point home even further, Halifax sent a telegram that emphasized that France must put pressure on President Benes himself. He wanted the French government to let Benes know that if a deal with the Sudetens was not reached because he failed to compromise enough, "the French Government would be driven to reconsider their own position vis-à-vis Czechoslovakia."[90]

Meanwhile, negotiations between the Sudeten nationalists, backed by Hitler, and the Czech authorities were not progressing. Britain, anxious to have Czechoslovakia make enough concessions to prevent a German invasion, applied pressure exclusively on the Czechs. Chamberlain's government

---

[88] *The Diaries of Sir Alexander Cadogan*, p. 79.
[89] *DBFP*, Series 3, Vol. 1, Doc. 271, pp. 346-347.
[90] *DBFP*, Series 3, Vol. 1, Doc. 355, p. 419.

proposed the appointment of a British investigator. Benes, anxious to maintain the independence of his nation, initially rejected the intervention of a foreign power in Czechoslovakia's internal affairs, for whatever the Germans or the British may think, Sudetenland was part of sovereign Czechoslovakia. Britain would not accept the rejection and the British ambassador in Prague informed President Benes that if he did not accept the British proposal, the government would make both the proposal and the rejection public. France joined Britain in pressuring Benes, who finally was forced to capitulate.

Worse, the British, still hiding from the public their true aims in Czechoslovakia, required the Czechs to ask publicly for the investigation that was being imposed upon them. In Halifax's distorted view, expressed in a letter to Nevile Henderson in Berlin on 25 June, it would be helpful for the Czech government (as opposed to his own) "if it can be represented that initiative in proposal had been theirs – and that His Majesty's Government had acceded to it."[91] Of course, that would mean that if Lord Runciman, the proposed British investigator, made a proposal that the Nazis rejected, Britain, not having initiated the Runciman mission, would not be bound by Runciman's recommendations. A letter from Henderson to Halifax a day later echoed the "anti-Czech" sentiments that Cadogan revealed as having dominated Cabinet discussions of apparent German plans for a coup in Sudentenland. "I do not envy Lord Runciman the difficult and thankless job which he is undertaking. The Czechs are a pig-headed race and Benes not the least pig-headed among them."[92] Henderson let the German government know of the ruse that made it appear that the Czechs were asking for a mediator whom Britain was in fact imposing upon them. He informed Halifax that he had done so.[93] Britain, anxious that Germany not use force to get its way with Czechoslovakia, wanted the Nazis to know that "diplomacy" was being used to cause the Czechs to be more submissive to Hitler's demands.

As the next chapter demonstrates, Chamberlain believed the aim of Runciman's investigation was to persuade the Czechs to give in to Hitler's exaggerated demands. This would pave the way for formal meetings with Hitler that would allow for the formal

---

[91] *DBFP*, Series 3, Vol. 2, Doc. 541, pp. 3-4.
[92] *DBFP*, Series 3, Vol. 2, Doc. 551, p. 11.
[93] *DBFP*, Series 3, Volume 2, Doc. 544, p. 6.

Anglo-German "understanding" that British leaders, led by Chamberlain, had been seeking since Hitler's arrival in power.

CHAPTER SIX

FORMAL COLLUSION: THE CHAMBERLAIN-HITLER MEETINGS

Neville Chamberlain's government had formally decided to abandon Czechoslovakia early in 1938. Yet Czechoslovakia's future became the pretext for having several meetings with Hitler in September 1938. The decision to cede Czechoslovakia's fate to German policy considerations was in line with the notion of giving Germany a "free hand" in the East in return for a 'hands off' policy in the West that had dominated Cabinet thinking in Britain from the time Hitler came to power. But until late in 1938 such a policy had been arrived at informally through diplomatic channels and state visits to Germany by Cabinet officials. There had been no meetings between Hitler and a British head of government and therefore no formal understanding at the highest instances of government.

From the time he came to power, and indeed in the years while he was prime minister in waiting, Neville Chamberlain believed that an overall understanding with Hitler and Mussolini was necessary if a war involving Britain was to be avoided. Firm in his view that Hitler wanted war only with the Soviet Union, and supportive of a war that might knock out an ideological adversary of the British ruling classes, Chamberlain did not consider Nazi Germany an inevitable enemy of Britain. But he worried that misunderstandings between Hitler and the West, particularly France, could lead Britain into a war against Hitler. He was determined to avoid this eventuality. The conundrum he faced was that popular opinion, supported by the Labour Party and the dissident Tories Eden and Churchill, was anti-Hitler. To meet openly with the German dictator with a view to determining jointly the fate of various European nations and the African and Asian colonies of Europe would have been scandalous. Chamberlain therefore seized upon the Czech crisis as a single issue requiring immediate resolution that could only be achieved through a dialogue directly with Hitler.

Public opinion supported the right of the Czechoslovak state to continue in existence with its territorial integrity intact. So Chamberlain's public statements that he sought a dialogue with Germany that would produce beneficial results for the Czechs met a positive response. Only members of the Cabinet and top-ranking foreign affairs civil servants would have known that Chamberlain's government had no interest in defending the Czechs. They alone knew that the government blamed the Czech defenders rather than the German aggressors for the failure of these two nations to resolve the Sudetenland "problem" invented by Hitler's government.

Chamberlain made plain to his sister in a letter on 11 September 1938, four days before his first of three meetings with Hitler, that his goal was to reach a more far-reaching arrangement with Nazi Germany than simply a settling of the Czech issue. "There is another consideration...and that is the plan...if it came off, it would go far beyond the present crisis, and might prove the opportunity for bringing about a complete change in the international situation."[1]

On 13 September 1938, just two days before the Berchtesgaden meeting with Hitler, Chamberlain admitted to the king that there was little to discuss regarding Czechoslovakia with Hitler. He was determined to take Sudetenland from Czechoslovakia and annex it to Germany. The only way Czechoslovakia could avoid an invasion was to capitulate. Wrote Chamberlain:

> ...reports are daily received... Many of these (and of such authority as to make it impossible to dismiss them as unworthy of attention) declare positively that Herr Hitler has made up his mind to attack Czecho-Slovakia and then to proceed further East. He is convinced that the operation can be effected so rapidly that it will be all over before France and Great Britain could move and that they will not then venture to try to upset a fait accompli.

> On the other hand, Your Majesty's representative in Berlin has steadily maintained that Herr Hitler has not yet made up   his mind to violence. He means to have a solution soon – this month – and if that solution, which must be satisfactory to himself, can be obtained peacefully, well and good. If not, he is ready to march if he should so decide.[2]

---

[1] Keith Feiling, *The Life of Neville Chamberlain* (London: Macmillan, 1946), p. 360.
[2] J. W. Wheeler Bennett, *King George VI* (Toronto: Macmillan Company of Canada, 1958), p. 346.

Chamberlain did not bother to mention to the king that Hitler was correct in his assessment that the British government did not intend to defend Czechoslovakia against military attack. Nor did he mention the role he, Chamberlain, had played in convincing the Daladier government in France to take the same capitulationist position on the Czech issue. But he was honest enough not to pretend to believe that Britain could, through diplomatic means, convince Hitler to withdraw his demand that Sudetenland be ceded to Germany. Instead, relying on information from Nevile Henderson, he made it clear that the only issue was whether Hitler would resort to violence to get the territory he wanted. The German ruler would only refrain from military action if Czechoslovakia ceded the Sudeten.

With Germany chafing at the bit to seize the disputed German-speaking territories under Czech control, Chamberlain informed the king:

> In these circumstances I have been considering the possibility of a sudden and dramatic step which might change the whole situation. The plan is that I should inform Herr Hitler that I propose at once to go over to Germany to see him...I should hope to persuade him that he had an unequalled opportunity of raising his own prestige and fulfilling what he has so often declared to be his aim, namely the establishment of an Anglo-German understanding preceded by a settlement of the Czecho-Slovakian question.[3]

While Chamberlain did not provide the king with details of what outcomes would constitute the "understanding" sought with Germany, he suggested the framework for this "understanding." If a peaceful solution to the crisis over Sudetenland could be found, the two powers could come to terms with "the prospect of Germany and England as the two pillars of European peace and buttresses against communism."[4]

The perspective of Chamberlain's letter is interesting. Hitler, he readily admits, has plans "to attack Czecho-Slovakia and then to proceed further East." How can this be squared with the "prospect" that this belligerent state can join England as a pillar of peace in Europe? The answer lies in the other role that Germany will play jointly with Britain: that of a buttress against

[3] *Ibid.*, p. 346.
[4] *Ibid.*

communism. A war in the East that will result in German military engagement with the Soviets is not, from this point of view, a war at all. It is an attempt to restore a conservative social order that Chamberlain equates with "peace."

Chamberlain recognized however that, even if his Cabinet had long since decided against any military involvement in the Sudeten crisis created by the Nazis, he could not win public acceptance for an "understanding" with Hitler if Hitler created a bloodbath in Czechoslovakia to get his own way. He confided to the king his notion of a "peaceful solution" to the crisis.

> Since I assume that he will have declared that he cannot wait and that the solution must come at once, my proposal would be that he should agree that, after both sides had laid their case before Lord Runciman and thus demonstrated the points of difference, Lord Runciman should act as a final arbitrator. Of course I should not be able to guarantee that Dr. Benes would accept this solution, but I would undertake to put all possible pressure on him to do so.[5]

The word "arbitrator" here is misleading. Chamberlain is quite clear in his letter that Hitler will only accept a solution that allows him to annex the Sudeten region. Only one outcome of the Runciman report is expected and that is capitulation to Nazi demands. As Chamberlain set off for Berchtesgaden, the site of the first of three Chamberlain-Hitler meetings, he had not diverged from his government's position that Britain would not and should not protect Czechoslovakia's territorial integrity. Instead he sought to find a peaceful solution to the Sudeten issue acceptable to Hitler but also saleable to the British public. This would be preliminary to the wide-ranging agreement between the two powers that would make them together the continent's protectors against communism. "All possible pressure" would be put on Czechoslovakia to yield to the Nazi dictator's imperial expansionism in order that an "Anglo-German understanding" could be reached that would unite these two pillars of anti-communist "peace."

At the Berchtesgaden meeting on 15 and 16 September 1938, Hitler talked tough. He demanded that Britain state firmly that under no circumstances would it go to war with Germany; otherwise he intended to abandon the Naval Treaty.

[5] *Ibid.*, p. 347.

Chamberlain, while revealing openly to Hitler that Britain would not object to a German attack against the Soviets, was evasive, expressing his desire for peaceful cooperation between Britain and Nazi Germany but unwilling to rule out the possibility of an eventual war between the two countries. Indeed, since Chamberlain required a guarantee that Germany would never attack other countries in western Europe or any British colonies, Hitler's insistence that no action by Germany could lead to a bellicose British response was absurd.

There are two documents that record the Berchtesgaden meeting, both of which are included in the Documents of British Foreign Policy.[6] One is Chamberlain's account of the meeting written from memory after the event. The other is the minutes of the meeting recorded by Dr. Paul Schmidt, the German translator for Hitler. Schmidt was an opponent of Nazism and his records of meetings have been universally accepted by historians as accurate and fair. In any case, the two versions are quite similar though Schmidt's version is more detailed and most of the references that follow, unless otherwise indicated, are excerpted from Schmidt's account.

Chamberlain opened the meeting by expressing his heartfelt support for Hitler's achievements. "He, Mr. Chamberlain, however, regarded the Führer as a man who, from a strong feeling for the sufferings of his nation, had carried through the renaissance of the German nation with extraordinary success. He had the greatest respect for this man." This was undoubtedly far more than flattery for the occasion. Though publicly Chamberlain had to appear to disapprove of Nazi dictatorship, privately he was quite taken with Hitler. Hitler was aware of this because of private reports he had received. For example, the Duke of Cobourg, a German descendant of Queen Victoria and an Eton schoolfellow of Chamberlain and Eden, had visited England in January 1936. His family ties and personal relations allowed him to have audiences with leading political figures in Britain. He reported his discussions to the German authorities. Chamberlain had invited the duke to dinner and the duke reported their conversation as follows: "Chaimberlain (sic) hates Russia. His son has studied in Germany and has heard Adolf Hitler speak in Munich. His accounts are so enthusiastic that Chaimberlain (sic) would very much like to see the Führer himself one day."[7]

[6] *DBFP*, 3rd Series, Vol. 2, Doc. 895, p. 338.

145

Chamberlain emphasized his desire for an overall understanding with Hitler, even suggesting that discussions regarding Czechoslovakia need not occur until their second day of meetings. Records Schmidt's text:

> He had come to Germany in order to seek by means of a frank exchange of views, the solution of the present difficulties. He hoped...that on the basis of this exchange of views...he could then, with double confidence work further for an Anglo-German rapprochement.

Hitler, as Chamberlain revealed to his Cabinet several months later, was blunt at Berchtesgaden about wanting "a free hand in Eastern Europe."[8] Indeed he wanted Britain and Germany to provide one another with absolute guarantees that they would never go to war one with the other. Hitler told Chamberlain belligerently:

> Germany had limited the strength of her fleet, of her own free will to a certain proportion of British naval power. The precondition for this agreement was, of course, the mutual determination never again to make war on the other contracting party. If, therefore, England were to continue to make it clear that in certain circumstances she would intervene against Germany, the precondition for the Naval Agreement would cease to hold, and it would be more honest for Germany to denounce the agreement.[9]

Chamberlain's first response to Hitler's threat was rather awkward, if not downright stupid. He asked "whether this denunciation would be contemplated by Germany before a conflict broke out or at the outbreak itself." It would be irrelevant whether or not one nation renounced a treaty with another nation once it had declared war on the other.

Hitler, conveniently ignoring that the Naval Treaty had been a virtual gift from Britain, a complete abandonment of its partners in the Versailles Treaty, "replied that, if England continued to recognize the possibility of intervention against Germany, while Germany had herself concluded the Naval agreement with the

---

[7] *DGFP*, Doc. 531, p. 1061, January 1936.
[8] *CAB* 23/99 0.122, 3 May 1938.
[9] *Ibid.*

intention of never again making war on England, a one-sided disadvantage for Germany must ensue; it would therefore be more sincere and more honest in such a case to terminate the treaty relationship."

Discussion soon turned to the Czechoslovak situation which Hitler did not wish to leave to the second day. But Chamberlain later returned to the subject of the Naval Agreement and allowed that "a very reasonable agreement had been made about naval strengths in the belief that there could be no question of war between the two countries." If war between the two countries had since become a possibility, the basis for the Naval Agreement, as Hitler suggested, disappeared. But Chamberlain wanted to disabuse Hitler of any notion that Britain contemplated war with Germany. True, Britain had issued warnings to Germany not to act hastily over Sudetenland. "But he must add that no proper distinction was made on the German side between a threat and a warning." He elaborated:

> When two people are on the point of going into conflict with one another they must be perfectly clear in advance of the consequences of such a conflict. Britain had acted in this sense, and had made no threats but had only uttered a warning. It was now the business of the Führer to make a decision on the basis of these facts which were known to him. No reproach could be made against England for giving this warning; on the contrary, she could have been criticized for failing to give it.

In other words, Chamberlain was giving Hitler the first of many hints to come that Britain's protestations over German sabre-rattling against Czechoslovakia constituted solely a "warning," a set of words with no likely follow-up action, rather than a "threat," an indication that if Germany did x, Britain would follow up with y action. This proved insufficient for Hitler. He made clear his demand for a free hand and indeed at this point seemed not even to limit that demand to central and eastern Europe.

> ...the Führer declared that he must adhere to the fundamental view whereby the basis of this treaty was to be seen simply and solely in a kind of obligation of both parties in no circumstances to make war on one another. If therefore England showed from time to time that she must, nevertheless, in certain

147

circumstances, reckon with a conflict against Germany, the logical basis of the Naval Agreement was done away with. While one party undertook a voluntary limitation of its naval strength, the other party left all possibilities open; and it was precisely at the moment when a warning was given that the disadvantage for the former party made itself felt.

According to Chamberlain's own notes:

> He then launched into a long speech...all he wanted was Sudeten Germans. As regards the 'spearhead in his side' he would not feel safe unless the Sudeten Germans were incorporated in the Reich; he would not feel he had got rid of the danger until the abolition of the treaty between Russia and Czechoslovakia.

> I said: 'Supposing it were modified, so that Czechoslovakia were no longer bound to go to the assistance of Russia if Russia was attacked, and on the other hand Czechoslovakia was debarred from giving asylum to Russian forces in her aerodromes or elsewhere; would that remove your difficulty?'

Chamberlain's response is interesting. Hitler referred to the Soviet-Czech treaty, a purely defensive treaty, and implied that he feared an attack by these two countries. Chamberlain recognized the absurdity of such a position and, aware from the CID report which his Cabinet had approved that Germany wanted to seize territories to its east, went straight to the heart of the matter. What should be done if Germany wished to attack "Russia"?

Chamberlain made clear that Britain would not oppose such an attack. Indeed it was prepared, if that would improve German-British relations, to put pressure on Czechoslovakia to change its treaty with the Soviets in such a way as to provide the Soviets with no assistance in case of a German attack.

As they completed their first meeting, Chamberlain and Hitler were agreed on two points that would provide a framework for a deal between them. The Anglo-German Naval Agreement, which both men recognized as giving Germany a free hand in eastern Europe, must be respected and the two countries must agree never to go to war again. There was however still no completed deal between Hitler and Chamberlain as they finished the meeting. But a common understanding was beginning to emerge. Hitler wanted a "free hand" to do as he chose. Chamberlain obviously could not grant a "free hand" across the board. If Hitler seized control over western Europe, Britain and its Empire would be in jeopardy. So he focused on eastern Europe and particularly the Soviet Union, going about as far as a leader of another country could in encouraging Hitler to believe that if he invaded the Soviet Union, Britain would place no obstacles in his way. Indeed Britain would attempt, through pressure on Czechoslovakia, to pave the way for German aggression on the Communist state.

Before the German and British leaders met again, Chamberlain, still seeking his overall agreement with Hitler, forced a Czech capitulation to German demands to allow Sudetenland to be annexed to Germany. Basil Newton, the British ambassador to Prague, revealed in a note to Halifax, the heavy-handed pressures that were required to win the Czech surrender.

> I have very good reason from an even better source to believe that...reply handed to me by Minister for Foreign Affairs should not be regarded as final. A solution must however be imposed upon Government as without such pressure many of its members are too committed to be able to accept what they realize to be necessary.
>
> If I can deliver a kind of ultimatum to President Benes, Wednesday, he and his Government will be able to bow to *force majeure*. It might be to the effect that in view of his Majesty's Government the Czechoslovak Government must accept the proposals without reserve and without further delay failing which His Majesty's Government will take no further interest in the fate of country.
>
> I understand that my French colleague is telegraphing to Paris in a similar sense.[10]

Next day at two in the morning President Benes was awoken to receive the Anglo-French ultimatum. Though he protested on behalf of his government, he had no recourse but to submit. Britain and France pledged to defend what would remain of Czechoslovakia from aggression. In his letter of acceptance,

[10] *DBFP*, Series 3, Vol. 2, Doc. 979, p. 425.

Benes underscored this pledge. In the aftermath of Munich, as we shall see in Chapter 7, the British assurance to Benes was rendered meaningless.

Chamberlain had sought a swift Czechoslovak capitulation to smooth the way for more talks with Hitler aimed at reaching an overall settlement between the "two pillars of European peace and buttresses against communism." One day after the Czech surrender of the Sudetenland to Germany Chamberlain began two days of meetings with Hitler at Godesberg (22 September and 23 September 1938, continuing into the early hours of the 24th). Here, building on their discussions at Berchtesgaden, the two leaders colluded to give Germany a "free hand" in central and eastern Europe with the understanding that Germany would attempt to destroy the Soviet Union.

Notes of the Godesberg meeting were made both by Dr. Paul Schmidt, the German translator, and Ivone Kirkpatrick, the British translator.[11] Chamberlain reported to Halifax by telephone that the first meeting on the 22nd was most unsatisfactory. Kirkpatrick's notes show that the next meeting on the 23rd was equally discouraging for Chamberlain. Hitler and Chamberlain argued about what a joint memorandum ought to state. They also argued about a matter of fact: which of Germany and Czechoslovakia had mobilized its army first. Chamberlain was frustrated by Hitler's intransigence on a matter about which the British prime minister was well informed. Nevertheless, after a private meeting on the 23rd with Hitler, Chamberlain emerged in a positive mood and gave an entirely favourable report on the meeting with Hitler first to a group of senior Cabinet ministers and then to a meeting of the entire Cabinet. What had happened to change his mind?

Chamberlain had arrived at Godesberg expecting Hitler to be pleased that Czechoslovakia had been forced to cede Sudetenland to Germany without a struggle. Instead Hitler protested that the procedure envisaged by the two leaders at Berchtesgaden for the cession of the German-speaking region was too slow. This involved a plebiscite among the Sudetens regarding their future, international supervision of the transfer of territory from Czechoslovakia to Germany, and the opportunity

[11] Kirkpatrick's report is found in *DBFP*, Series 3, Vol.2, Doc. 1033. The account of the meeting presented here is taken from that document except for the last part of the meeting which only Schmidt attended.

for anti-Nazi individuals in the region to leave before German occupation began. Now Hitler demanded that Germany be allowed to occupy Sudetenland immediately with the plebiscite and the departure of anti-Nazis to occur under Nazi military rule. Hitler also insisted that demands made by Poland and Hungary against Czechoslovakia ought to be satisfied at this point as well. In other words, he would not be content until this country, created by the Versailles Treaty, had been so dismembered and humiliated as to be impotent.

Chamberlain was frustrated that Hitler was making new demands without offering agreement on a general settlement of European issues. Though the two men agreed that their countries should come to an agreement that would reaffirm the Anglo-German Naval Agreement and guarantee no future wars between them, Hitler still seemed to Chamberlain unwilling to announce the limits of his ambitions. But in a private meeting he had with Hitler in the wee hours of the morning just before he took his leave from the Nazi dictator, Hitler provided the formulation which Chamberlain wished to hear. Dr. Paul Schmidt was the only witness and he describes the meeting as follows:[12]

> ...at 2:00 in the morning Chamberlain and Hitler took leave from one another in a completely friendly tone after having had, with my assistance, an eye to eye conversation. During the meeting, with words that came from his heart, Hitler thanked Chamberlain for his efforts for peace. He remarked that the solution of the Sudeten question is the last big problem which remains to be treated. Hitler also spoke about a German-Anglo rapprochement and cooperation. It was clearly noticeable that it was important for him to have a good relation with the Englishman. He went back to his old tune: 'Between us there should be no conflict,' he said to Chamberlain, '*we will not stand in the way of your pursuit of your non-European interests and you may without harm let us have a free hand on the European continent in Central and South-East Europe*. Sometime we will have to solve the colonial question; but this has time, and war is not to be considered in this case' (author's translation)[13]

[12] Dr. Paul Schmidt, *Statist auf Diplomatischer Buhne 1923-45* (Bonn: Athenaum-Verlag, 1949), pp. 406-7.
[13] Here is the original German text of the italicized sentence: " wir werden Ihnen bei der Verfolgung Ihrer auereuropaishen Interessen nicht im Wege stehen, und Sie konnen uns ohne Schaden auf dem europaischen Festlande in

It is clear in Schmidt's minutes that Chamberlain did not protest anything that Hitler said in the excerpt above. Indeed, as he notes, their meeting ended "in a completely friendly tone." The events of the next several days demonstrated that Chamberlain believed that he and Hitler had now reached the "Anglo-German understanding" that the two leaders craved. Hitler had limited his demand for a "free hand" in Europe to "Central and South-East Europe" and had given Britain free rein in its own non-European colonial pursuits. Despite a rising anti-Hitler crescendo of public opinion, Chamberlain convinced his Cabinet that Hitler was being cooperative regarding Czechoslovakia and that it remained prudent to allow that country to be dismembered rather than risk war with Germany. Not only did he not protest to Hitler the Nazi dictator's unvarnished insistence on a free hand in the East, he failed to report to either of the two Cabinet meetings what Hitler had said or his own response. Clearly, Chamberlain regarded Hitler's statement and his own warm response to it as a private deal between two leaders. He was unwilling to repeat it, much less defend it, to his colleagues or his country. But as he prepared for the next meeting with Hitler at Munich, he knew best how his meeting with Hitler had finished. At long last he had the "general agreement" that he had confided with the king to be his general goal. He had a deal with Hitler. The minutes of the Cabinet meeting are revealing:

> Did Hitler mean to go further? The Prime Minister was satisfied that Herr Hitler was speaking the truth when he said that he regarded this as a racial question. He thought he had established some degree of personal influence over Herr Hitler....Herr Hitler had said that if we got this question out of the way without conflict, it would be a turning point in Anglo-German relations. That to the Prime Minister, was the big thing of the present issue. He was also satisfied that Herr Hitler would not go back on his word once he had given it.[14]

So Chamberlain was enthusiastic that Godesberg had produced a "turning point in Anglo-German relations." He neglected however to let the Cabinet know that this "turning point" had been reached at a meeting where Hitler insisted upon Germany's

Mittel-und Sudosteuropa freie Hand lassen."
[14] Ian Colvin, *The Chamberlain Cabinet* (London: Victor Gollancz, 1971), p. 162.

right to a free hand in Central and South-East Europe as an integral part of a package that included Britain and Germany forswearing war the one upon the other and Germany abiding by the provisions of the Anglo-German Naval Agreement. In fairness, he did not tell the Cabinet that Hitler's territorial demands had now all been met. But by referring to the Nazis' demands in Czechoslovakia as "racial," he implied that non-German peoples of central and eastern Europe would not become victims of Nazi German expansionism.

Despite his personal enthusiasm after the late-night chat with Hitler at Godesberg and his deceitful presentation of the substance of Hitler's demands, Chamberlain did not have an easy time of convincing his electorate or even his own Cabinet to submit to Hitler's wishes. Hitler's unwillingness to abide by the agreement made at Berchtesgaden coupled with public opinion caused Lord Halifax, however temporarily, to tire of appeasing the Nazis. On 23 September, Chamberlain's second day of meetings with Hitler at Godesberg, he received a telegraph from Halifax saying:

> It may help you if we give you some indication of what seems a predominant public expression as expressed in press and elsewhere. While mistrustful of our plan but prepared perhaps to accept it with reluctance as alternative to war, great mass of public opinion seems to be hardening in sense of feeling that we have gone to limit of concession and that it is up to the Chancellor to make some contribution...it seems to your colleagues of vital importance that you should not leave without making it plain to Chancellor if possible by special interview that, after great concessions made by Czechoslovak Government, for him to reject opportunity of peaceful solution in favour of one that must involve war would be an unpardonable crime against humanity.[15]

Chamberlain did indeed have a "special interview" with Hitler. But at his early morning *tête-à-tête* with the Nazi dictator, the modalities of the German takeover of the Sudeten region figured rather small. The two men had worked out an arrangement that put flesh on the notion of "two pillars of European peace and buttresses against communism": Hitler would have a "free hand" in central and eastern Europe while Britain would pursue its

[15] *DBFP*, Series 3, Vol. 2, Doc. 1058, p. 490.

imperial interests untrammelled. The fate of a small nation such as Czechoslovakia was of little moment within the context of such overarching objectives.

Even the defeatist Cadogan, who had never supported intervention on Czechoslovakia's behalf under any circumstances, was appalled by the turn of events. Hitler had rejected compromise and sent a memorandum to the Czech government that included the new demands he had made at Godesberg. On 24 September, the day Chamberlain returned from Godesberg, Cadogan recorded his horror both at the depravity of Hitler's memorandum to Czechoslovakia and Chamberlain's support of "total surrender." In his diary, Cadogan said that appeasers like himself had "salved our conscience" about "ceding people to Nazi Germany" by insisting on an "orderly cession." He was aghast that all the "safeguards" that had been demanded were rejected by Hitler[16].

Chamberlain's position on this issue and his demeanour at the "Inner Cabinet" meeting that afternoon "completely horrified" Cadogan: "I was completely horrified – he was quite calmly for total surrender. More horrified still to find that Hitler has evidently hypnotized him to a point. Still more horrified to find P.M. has hypnotized H. [ed. note: Halifax] who capitulates."

David Dilks, editor of Cadogan's diaries, adds at this point:

> Chamberlain told the inner ring of ministers that he thought he has 'established some degree of personal influence over Herr Hitler' who would not, he felt satisfied, go back on his word. Later in the day the Prime Minister said in full Cabinet that he believed Hitler "extremely anxious to secure the friendship of Great Britain...It would be a great tragedy if we lost an opportunity of reaching an understanding with Germany." He thought he had now established an influence over Herr Hitler and that the latter trusted him and was willing to work with him.[17]

The records of the Godesberg meeting suggest that much of this was illusion. There was no indication that Chamberlain had any influence over Hitler. As for going back on his word, Hitler had

---

[16] David Dilks, *The Diaries of Sir Alexander Cadogan, O.M., 1938-1945*, (london: Cassell, 1971), pp. 103-04.
[17] *Ibid.*, p. 104.

demonstrated his total unreliability by breaking the agreement over the process for the Czechs' surrender of Sudetenland made just a week earlier.

Yet, if we keep in mind Chamberlain's perspectives on Hitler from 1933 onwards and on communism from well before that time, it is not surprising why he concluded that Hitler's candid comments at two in the morning amounted to an "Anglo-German understanding." Chamberlain and much of official Britain had long maintained that what Hitler wanted was a "free hand" in central and eastern Europe, a chance to attack the Soviet Communist state and grab much of its territory. With the exception of a few individuals such as Churchill, Eden and Vansittart, the ruling elite had viewed these German objectives blandly. The opponents had warned that Hitler would not limit himself to eastern Europe, that ultimately he would pose a threat to western Europe and to Britain's overseas colonies. So, for Chamberlain, to have Hitler limit his demand for a free hand to central and eastern Europe and to grant Britain *carte blanche* to pursue its "non-European interests" was tantamount to having his own position vindicated over those of Hitler's doubters in the British ruling elite.

Chamberlain chose however, as noted, not to repeat Hitler's early morning comments to his Cabinet colleagues. Rather than admit that he had thrown Czechoslovakia to the wolves to achieve larger – and completely immoral – objectives, he pretended that he had, in fact, defended Czech interests as well as could be done under the circumstances. In the light of public opinion at the time, he no doubt considered this more prudent than a candid defence of collusion to give Hitler a free hand in central and eastern Europe.

For a few days Chamberlain had to reckon with recalcitrance on the part of his Minister of State for External Affairs. While Halifax seemed prepared at the meetings on the 24th of September to accept Chamberlain's capitulation to Hitler on Czechoslovakia, by the next day, influenced by Cadogan, he changed his mind. At the Cabinet meeting, he informed Chamberlain that he could not support either the acceptance of Hitler's memo or further coercion of Czechoslovakia. During the meeting Chamberlain passed to Halifax a note indicating that the minister's change of mind was "a horrible blow to me." He also mentioned his concern that the French might now decide to stand by their treaty obligations to Czechoslovakia: "If they say they will go in, therefore dragging us in, I do not think I could accept responsibility for the decision."[18]

On September 26, the Foreign Office, on the authority of Halifax, issued a press statement: "...if, in spite of the efforts made by the British Prime Minister, a German attack is made upon Czechoslovakia, the immediate result must be that France will be bound to come to her assistance and Great Britain and Russia will certainly stand by France."[19]

Chamberlain, "to Halifax's surprise," was dismayed by the appearance of the communiqué.[20] Briefly, he seemed a defeated man. Halifax and other members of his Cabinet were abandoning his foreign policy. He had an agreement between himself and Hitler that he could not reveal, and the turn of events threatened to evolve into a war between the West and Germany. He contemplated resigning as prime minister.

Several days later the situation would be totally reversed. He would return triumphantly from Munich, supported by near-unanimity in Cabinet and by the enthusiastic majority of the British population. Chamberlain's political skills proved important in producing this turnaround. But his success also owed much to the strong support he had for a sellout to Hitler from key figures including Simon, Hoare and Inskip in his Cabinet, Sir Horace Wilson, and the ambassadors to Berlin and Paris, Henderson and Phipps respectively (Phipps's opposition to the Nazis seemed to crumble after he was transferred from Berlin to Paris).

Chamberlain had to take action on four fronts. First, he had to convince Hitler to act with restraint for a few days. Secondly, he had to prevent Czechoslovakia from taking actions or expressing opinions that Germany might construe as provocative. Thirdly, he had to convince France to cooperate with Britain in forcing Czech capitulation. Finally, he had to bring a hostile British public opinion around to the view that Czech capitulation would produce a lasting peace in Europe.

[18] *Ibid.*, p. 105.
[19] Winston Churchill, *The Gathering Storm* (Kingsport, Tennessee: Houghton Mifflin, 1948), p. 309.
[20] Telford Taylor, *Munich: The Price of Peace* (New York: Doubleday, 1979), p. 863 fn.

Chamberlain's strategies to achieve these four goals might be summarized as follows. He used secret messengers to let Hitler know that he should ignore tough official statements that might emerge in the next few days from Britain and France regarding Czechoslovakia. Meanwhile, as we shall see, he deceived France into believing that Britain would join France in taking a tough stand with Germany but that this required that France take no precipitous aggressive action without British consent. His government then let Czechoslovakia know that they could not depend on either France or Britain. Finally, he called for the digging of trenches in Britain and the issuing of gas masks so that he could broadcast to the population how important it was that he avoid war if at all possible.

The Foreign Office's response to a Czech proposal for mobilization demonstrated that Halifax had not truly left the camp of the appeasers. At first the Foreign Office demanded that Czechoslovakia not mobilize but, after a flurry of telegrams,[21] it agreed that such a mobilization could take place as long as it was not publicized. It was a ridiculous compromise because, of course, a mobilization is impossible without publicity. The Czechs broadcast the mobilization by radio and informed the Czech population that the mobilization was proceeding with the approval of the French and British governments. Halifax then sent instructions to Henderson to "at once assure Herr Hitler on behalf of Prime Minister and myself" that the broadcast was misleading. It wasn't but Halifax's need to let Hitler believe otherwise demonstrated his unwillingness to go very far in risking war with Nazi Germany in order to protect Czechoslovakia.[22]

The French leaders however appeared, at least at first, to be more difficult to dissuade than Halifax from a course of resisting Hitler's aggression. Prime Minister Daladier had caved in to Chamberlain's position on Czechoslovakia in April 1938. Persuaded himself that Hitler's appetite for territory was insatiable, he proved unwilling to stick with a principled anti-Nazi position in the face of Britain's penchant for collaboration with Hitler. Having been put in power by forces opposed to Leon Blum's Popular Front, Daladier faced a great

[21] *DBFP*, Series 3, Vol. 2, Docs. 1022, 1023, 1027, 1031, 1035, 1044, 1047, 1049, 1059, 1062.
[22] *DBFP*, Series 3, Vol. 2, Doc. 1090, p. 517.

deal of opposition at home to continuation of the Franco-Soviet mutual assistance pact and indeed to the policy of resisting Nazi aggression generally. With Britain also in the camp of the "appeasers," Daladier's ability to take a tough stance against the Nazis was considerably hampered.

Now however Daladier seemed to be at the end of his rope. The differences between Daladier's position and Chamberlain's as the leaders of the two countries met in London on 25 September were dramatic. Ashamed that France had consented to bullying Czechoslovakia to accept the Chamberlain-Hitler terms agreed upon at Berchtesgaden, he was enraged that now Hitler wanted even more. Even more forcefully than in April, he argued that it was time for France and Britain to resist Hitler's aggressions even if that meant war. What he found in London however was that Chamberlain's views had not shifted on essentials since April. While Chamberlain was prepared to regret that the Berchtesgaden conditions would not be met, he made light of this fact and defended Hitler's position. His ministers strongly implied that Britain would not come to France's defence if it went to war with Germany over Hitler's broken promise.[23]

When Daladier protested that Hitler had reneged on the agreement to allow international supervision of the surrender of territories, the minutes show that Chamberlain demurred.

> As regards the first point raised by Daladier, the proposal made in the German memorandum was not to take these areas by force, but only to take over areas handed over by agreement. The German troops will only be admitted for the purpose of preserving law and order which the German Government maintained could not be done effectively in any other way.

Daladier pointed out that occupation by German troops would leave democrats in the ceded territories "to the axe and the executioners of Herr Hitler." The Czech lands and Slovakia would be cut off from one another and dependent on German approval for their political and economic links to be maintained. "Herr Hitler's demand amounted to the dismemberment of Czechoslovakia and German domination of Europe."

[23] Minutes of the meeting are found in *DBFP*, Series 3, Volume 2, Doc. 1093, pp. 520-535.

Chamberlain's view was more cheery. The question of the fate of Hitler's opponents in Sudetenland could be settled after the German troops arrived. Similarly, the referendum called for at Berchtesgaden could be held under German occupation. The German troops, he stressed again, echoing Hitler's language, were needed "to preserve law and order," an interesting formulation since there was no evidence that law and order had broken down in the region when it was under Czech control. The planned German occupation was itself the main threat to order in the area.

Chamberlain kept pressing Daladier as to what France would do if Hitler refused to return to the conditions agreed upon at Berchtesgaden, as he surely would refuse, in Chamberlain's estimation. Daladier responded bluntly that: "in that case each of us would have to do his duty." He had called up one million Frenchmen "to go to the frontier" and their enthusiasm for the justice of the Czech cause convinced him that the French people rejected further surrenders to Hitler's immoderate demands.

But Chamberlain would not accept this answer as complete or final. Did the French General Staff have plans for an attack on Germany? France could not, after all, give direct assistance to Czechoslovakia. John Simon now joined the *de facto* cross-examination of Daladier with a fatuous question as to whether Daladier had mobilized troops "just to man the Maginot Line" or with the intention of possibly declaring war and taking "active measures with their [French] land forces." Daladier responded that France was not bluffing and would consider air attacks against Germany. Simon then pointed out that if the French government used their air force against Germany, this would "involve a declaration of war and active hostilities." While manning the Maginot line was purely defensive behaviour, an air attack would make France the aggressor. "He therefore wished to ask whether the French Government contemplated such a use of the air force against Germany."

Simon's intent was clear. Britain was obligated to protect France against German attack. Its obligations were less clear if France started a war with Germany. Chamberlain and Simon were unwilling to accept that France, to fulfil its treaty obligations with Czechoslovakia, had a duty under certain circumstances to launch an attack on Germany. Yet it was Chamberlain who pointed out the obvious: that France could not assist

159

Czechoslovakia directly. In short, the British message was that France should regard itself as capable of doing nothing for Czechoslovakia.

Daladier exploded, pointing out the absurdity of any suggestion that France had the right only to mobilize its land forces to do nothing and no right to do anything in the air at all. He also suggested that the German system of fortifications – the Siegfried line – was not especially strong as yet and France could break through it.

> M. Daladier wished, however, to make it clear that he wished to speak more of the moral obligations of France than of war and strategy...It should be remembered that only a week ago he had agreed...to dismember a friendly country bound to France not only by treaties but by ties centuries old...Like a barbarian, M. Daladier had been ready to cut up this country without even consulting her and handing over 3 1/2 millions of her population to Herr Hitler...It had been hard, perhaps a little dishonouring...This would not suffice for him [Hitler]. M. Daladier asked at what point we would be prepared to stop and how far we would go.

Daladier added that he was not prepared to accept Hitler's new demands because they meant "the destruction of a country and Herr Hitler's domination of the world and all that we valued most." Simon told Daladier the British agreed with him "in every way" and then disproved it by returning to his questions about whether France was prepared to fight Germany and if so, how. Daladier then suggested that France, Britain and Czechoslovakia should implement the Anglo-French proposal of July 1938. This would require Germany to accept the new boundary that an international commission would determine.

This was impractical, noted Chamberlain, because of Hitler's insistence on an immediate solution to the Czech issue. Chamberlain, contradicting Daladier, implied that the Germans were more ready for battle than the French. Britain, he pointed out, had received "disturbing accounts of the condition of the French air force." If Germany dropped a "rain of bombs" upon Paris, could France defend its capital? Would Russia help out? The British government, he said, had received "very disturbing news about the probable Russian attitude." Pointedly making no mention of any possible aid Britain might provide France in her hour of need, Chamberlain said: "It would be poor consolation if, in fulfilment of all her obligations, France attempted to come to the assistance of her friend but found herself unable to keep up her resistance and collapsed."

Daladier responded emotionally and asked directly: "Was the British Government ready to give in and to accept Herr Hitler's proposals?" He challenged Chamberlain's claims both about France's war readiness and about the Soviet attitude. France was "perfectly capable of mobilizing an air force and attacking Germany." The Soviet Union had 5000 aeroplanes, of which at least 800 had been sent to Spain. They had proved quite effective in putting Italian and German planes out of commission. And what of Britain, he asked? Britain's naval superiority would mean that Germany could be blockaded.

Samuel Hoare intervened to counter Daladier's optimism. The impact of the naval blockade would not be immediate. While he did not challenge the fact that the Soviets had a large air force, he was sceptical about their willingness to participate in a war to defend Czechoslovakia. As for the United Kingdom, it was only willing to act if its actions would prevent Germany overrunning Czechoslovakia.

Hoare was effectively declaring British neutrality. While Daladier's point was that Anglo-French cooperation could achieve victory, he could not guarantee that Germany would not overrun Czechoslovakia first. Indeed it was almost a certainty that Germany would overrun Czechoslovakia and would leave that country only after attacks against German territory forced Hitler to vacate Czech territory.

Chamberlain simply sidestepped direct questions that Daladier now asked. Daladier asked whether His Majesty's Government accepted Hitler's plan. Answer: it was Czechoslovakia, not Britain, that had to accept or reject Hitler's proposal. Did Britain intend to pressure Czechoslovakia to accept the German ultimatum? Answer: Britain had no means to compel Czechoslovakia. Finally, did Britain believe France should do nothing in the face of Hitler's belligerence? Answer: it was France's decision alone how to react to Hitler. What such evasion added up to however was the conviction on the part of the Chamberlain government that Hitler's proposal must be accepted.

Chamberlain now resorted to a clever, if immoral, gambit. To appease both France and British public opinion, he pretended to accept a tough Anglo-French communiqué warning Hitler of the consequences of invading Czechoslovakia. Meanwhile, through secret interlocutors, he let Hitler know that this was a facade and that the British government was working towards a solution based on Hitler's Godesberg ultimatum. While appearing to meet France halfway, the British government in fact used its influence to persuade France that the chief goal should be to prevent Germany from overrunning all of Czechoslovakia. This could best be achieved, argued Chamberlain and Halifax, if Czechoslovakia, under French pressure, acceded to Hitler's demands. Secure in the deal he had made with the German dictator at Godesberg, Chamberlain colluded with Hitler to insure that Germany got its way on Czechoslovakia without France declaring war on Germany.

Late in the evening on 25 September, Chamberlain sent a message to Henderson in Berlin. Henderson then communicated the message by phone to Ernst von Weizsacker, German State Secretary. The next day Weizsacker wrote a minute on the call as follows:

> The British Ambassador telephoned to me yesterday evening a request from the British Prime Minister that the Führer should take no notice of any reports on the course of his present negotiations with the French and the Czechs unless they came directly from himself. Any press or other messages which might appear previously should be disregarded as pure guesswork.[24]

Weizsacker continued by noting that, according to Henderson, Chamberlain's position was beset by "increasing difficulties" and that "false moves" by Germany could only complicate his problems. His "increasing difficulties," of course, meant the growing opposition at home to his policies in the wake of Hitler's bullying memorandum to Czechoslovakia. Chamberlain was conspiring with Hitler behind the backs of his Cabinet, the Foreign Office, the House of Commons, and the British public,

[24] *DGFP*, Series D, Vol. 2, Doc. 610, p. 936.

among all of whom there was growing disillusionment with the prime minister's approach to Hitler.

On 26 September, having warned Hitler in advance, Chamberlain tried to calm his French guests. Chamberlain summarized the situation in three sentences. The Czechoslovak government was determined to resist. The French government was prepared to fulfil its treaty obligations to Czechoslovakia. Britain stood by its long-standing position that it could not afford to see France overrun or defeated by Germany and would come to France's defence if France was in danger. The meeting communiqué announced a "full accord" between Britain and France "on all points" and added that General Gamelin, commander-in-chief of the French Chiefs of Staff, had met with the British Minister for the Co-ordination of Defence. The communiqué's tone suggested that Britain was prepared to stand by France in the defence of Czechoslovakia. Halifax issued a press release that made explicit the implicit threat to Germany in the communiqué. But Hitler, of course, had already been warned by Chamberlain to ignore statements that came from any source but himself.

The day of the communiqué Chamberlain again used a third party to convey the same message to Hitler. This time it was the German Chargé d'affaires, T. Kordt, who sent the following "very urgent" telegram to the German Foreign Ministry:

> Prime Minister asked me to transmit the following strictly confidential information:
>
> Reports to be expected in immediate future in British and foreign press on final Czech rejection of German memorandum are not last word. Chamberlain asks that statement on result of his action be awaited.[25]

Also, on 26 September, Chamberlain sent Sir Horace Wilson, his personal advisor, to convey two messages to Hitler. The first message was a written one. Its style friendly but firm, it entreated Hitler to renounce the use of force against Czechoslovakia since he could get all he wanted through negotiations in which Britain would take Germany's part. While the note did not directly threaten British military participation against Germany if it used force against Czechoslovakia to get

[25] *DGFP*, Series D, Volume 2,Doc. 605, p.933.

163

its way, that possibility was unmistakably present in the urgent tone of the entreaty.

The second message was oral and was delivered by Wilson in his conversation with Hitler before the letter was handed over to the dictator. It sugarcoated the letter. While the tough letter would soon become public, the Wilson-Hitler conversation would remain confidential for many years. Ivone Kirkpatrick, the translator, was present, and his notes[26] demonstrate that Wilson made clear that Chamberlain's tough note was a response to British outrage with Germany rather than a reflection of the prime minister's own convictions. Wilson informed Hitler (who was, in any case, already aware of it) that British public opinion had turned dramatically against Germany once Hitler's memorandum to Czechoslovakia had been published.

Wilson, accompanied by Nevile Henderson, emphasized the valiant efforts by Chamberlain to accommodate Hitler's wishes. Hitler, in turn, was impatient and downright rude despite the grovelling tone of his guests. The minutes note, for example:

> After the Prime Minister had returned from Berchtesgaden he had believed that Herr Hitler and himself could reach agreement on terms which would fully meet German wishes and have the effect of incorporating the Sudetenland in the Reich. He had succeeded in bringing his colleagues, the French government and the Czech government to his way of thinking, because he had convinced them that Herr Hitler and himself had agreed upon a solution within the framework of peace...

> Herr Hitler interrupted to vociferate in staccato accents that the problem must be solved forthwith without any further delay.

> Sir Horace Wilson continued that the Prime Minister fully appreciated, but the source of the difficulty lay in the manner in which it was proposed to proceed.

> Here Herr Hitler made gestures and exclamations of disgust and impatience.

[26] *DBFP*, Series 3, Vol. 2, Doc. 1118, pp. 554-557.

Nevile Henderson stated several times that Chamberlain "would see to it" that the Czechs capitulated to German demands. "Herr Hitler surely trusted Mr. Chamberlain," he noted. Significantly Hitler's answer was: "unfortunately Mr. Chamberlain might be out of office any day." Here was a fatal weakness in the Hitler-Chamberlain collusion that provided a free hand to Germany in the east in return for a hands-off policy in the west. Hitler placed little faith in agreements made between himself and the leaders of a democratic country since those leaders could easily fall in an election or party cabal and the agreement then be discarded.

Before meeting with Wilson again the next day (27 September 1938), Hitler had made a speech in which he hurled abuse at President Benes and the Czech people. Chamberlain had responded with a press communiqué that emphasized Britain's commitment to require Czechoslovakia to give up Sudetenland. This included the proviso however that Germany had to agree to settle the terms of the land surrender without resort to force.[27]

Despite Hitler's arrogant responses of the previous day, Wilson and Henderson persisted in presenting a message from Chamberlain that contradicted the Anglo-French communiqué and Halifax's press release.[28] Britain's goal, they insisted, was to see that Germany got its way but without a resort to force. Force, they warned, could lead to France declaring war on Germany; and if that led to a French attack on Germany, Britain would feel obliged to stand by France's side. Wilson was at pains however to make clear to Hitler that Britain was opposed to any French attack on Germany under any circumstances. "We did not know exactly in what form the French would decide to fulfil their obligations, but if in the fulfilment of these obligations France decided that her forces must become actively engaged, then for reasons and grounds which would be clear to Herr Hitler and to all students of the international situation, Great Britain must be obliged to support her."

The "ifs" and "musts" in Wilson's statement were meant to be weasel words and indeed he made his statement about Britain's

---

[27] *DBFP*, Series 3, Vol. 2, Doc. 1121, p. 559.

[28] The English version of the September 27 meeting, prepared by Ivone Kirkpatrick, is found in *DBFP*, Series 3, Vol. 2, Doc. 1129, p. 564. The German version of the meeting, prepared by Dr. Paul Schmidt, is found in *DGFP*, Series D, Vol. 2, Doc. 634, p. 963. Except where indicated references here are to the English-language version.

position several times to insure that Hitler would understand that Britain wished to restrain rather than encourage French hostilities against Germany. But Hitler remained defiant. As the German minutes of the meeting suggest, Wilson then went a step further to make Hitler aware of Britain's real intentions with regards to the Czech question.

> Sir Horace Wilson apparently wished to continue the conversation, but the British Ambassador advised him against doing so. On his departure, while alone with the Führer in the room, he said to him that a catastrophe must be avoided at all costs and he would still try to make the Czechs sensible ("I will try to make those Czechos sensible.")[29]

> The Führer replied that he would welcome that, and further repeated emphatically once more that England could wish for no better friend than the Führer...

During the meeting Wilson demonstrated the continued importance to the Chamberlain government of the argument that Germany was an ally against the Soviet menace, or the "disruption...from the East." Digressing completely from the Sudetenland issue at hand, he talked about the potential of an Anglo-German alliance. State the meeting minutes:

> There was however one more thing to say and he would try to say it in the tone which the Prime Minister would have used had he been himself present. Many Englishmen thought with him [Sir Horace Wilson] that there were many things which ought to be discussed between England and Germany to the great advantage of both countries...they included arrangements for improving the economic position all round. He himself and many other Englishmen would like to reach an agreement with Germany on these lines. He had been struck, as also had many others in England, by a speech in which Herr Hitler had said that he regarded England and Germany as bulwarks against disruption, particularly from the East. In the next few days the course of events might go one way or another and have a far-reaching effect on the future of Anglo-German relations generally.

[29] The bracketed sentence is in English in the original German document.

After meeting with Wilson for the second time, Hitler responded to Chamberlain's letter. He reiterated and defended the position he had taken in his letter to Prague at the time of Godesberg. He assured his British friend that, contrary to the Czech government's view, Germany's immediate occupation of Sudetenland would not result in the oppression of the conquered peoples. He concluded:

> In these circumstances I must assume that the Government in Prague is only using a proposal for the occupation by German troops in order, by distorting the meaning and object of my proposal, to mobilize those forces in other countries, in particular in England and France, from which they hope to receive unreserved support for their aim, and thus achieve the possibility of a general warlike conflagration. I must leave it to your judgment whether, in view of these facts, you consider that you should continue your effort, for which I would like to take this opportunity of once more sincerely thanking you, to spoil such manoeuvres and bring the Government in Prague to reason at the very last hour.[30]

This is proof that, contrary to myth, Hitler was not frustrated by Chamberlain's efforts. Indeed he encouraged the British prime minister to press on. Hitler recognized that Chamberlain, despite his public posture otherwise, was putting pressure on Prague rather than Berlin. The two, having come to terms at Godesberg on their general foreign policy goals, were colluding to insure that Czechoslovakia and France gave in to the terms of Hitler's memo. It was now up to Chamberlain to get France, which was completely unaware of the double game being played by Chamberlain, on side.

***

On 27 September 1938, Halifax sent Phipps, the British Ambassador in Paris, a telegram that demonstrated he was now on board again with Chamberlain's view of events.[31] The telegram recognized the likelihood that German troops would enter Czechoslovakia two days later. But its emphasis was on the uselessness of efforts at saving Czechoslovakia. It mentioned

---

[30] *DBFP*, Series 3, Vol. 2, Doc. 1144, p. 578.
[31] *DBFP*, Series 3. Vol. 2, Doc. 1143, pp.575-576.

several times that little could be done to save that country and that a world war over a German invasion would not change that fact. "The latest information requires us to face the actual facts," wrote Halifax.

> It is necessary that any action by France in discharge of her obligations and by ourselves in support of France should be closely concerted, especially as regards measures which would be likely immediately and automatically to start a world war without unhappily having any effect in saving Czechoslovakia.

Halifax indicated to Phipps that the British government's strategy was to restrain France from reacting to a German assault on Czechoslovakia. "We should be glad to know that French government agree that any action of an offensive character taken by either of us henceforward (including declaration of war, which is also important from view of United States), shall only be taken after previous consultation and agreement."

The likelihood that the United States would wish to involve itself in a war against Germany at this time was known to be remote. Waiting for an American response would stall any French and British response. No doubt by the time the Americans had responded officially, Germany would have completed its takeover of Czechoslovakia. Then the Chamberlain government would have been able to maintain, as it did after the invasion of Austria, that it was too late to help that benighted nation and therefore certainly not worth the bloodshed of a world war.

With Bonnet rather than Paul-Boncour in charge of the Foreign Office in France, Phipps had little difficulty in securing agreement to this new approach so at odds with the communiqué issued just one day earlier by France and England. Phipps telegrammed Halifax on 27 September 1938 from Paris:

> Minister for Foreign Affairs tells me that the French Government are in entire agreement not to take any offensive measures without previous consultation with and agreement by us.

His excellency feels more and more that it behoves us both to be extremely prudent and to count our probable and even possible enemies before embarking on any offensive act whatsoever.[32]

With France in line, Chamberlain's attention turned towards changing British public opinion which had become especially belligerent towards Germany after the announcement of Hitler's bullying demands that the Czechs simply accept an immediate German invasion of Sudetenland. Chamberlain had contempt for the opinions of the population as a whole whom he had once described as "an immense mass of very ignorant voters of both sexes whose intelligence is low and who have no power of weighing evidence."[33]

Chamberlain also had an acute sense of drama and the importance of timing. On 19 September 1938, after his return from Berchtesgaden and before his next meeting with Hitler at Godesberg, he wrote to his elder sister that "two things were essential." First, "the plan should be tried just when things looked blackest, and second, that it should be a complete surprise."[34] Now he had decided that what had to look blackest was not the treachery of Germany but the fate of the British people should war become necessary. So the government ordered the distribution of gas masks and the digging of trenches.

The decision to dig trenches and distribute gas masks was purely propagandistic. It made no sense from a military point of view. Lord Ismay, who was secretary to the Committee of Imperial Defence at the time of Munich, wrote in his memoirs of his puzzlement regarding the government's behaviour. Ismay had taken at face value the reactions of most government ministers as well as the British public to Hitler's bullying memorandum to the Czechs and expected that war could break out at any time. He indicated his concerns to Sir Thomas Inskip, Minister for the Co-ordination of Defence, that the territorial anti-aircraft units responsible for London's defence had not been called up. Neither had the fighter squadrons of the Auxiliary Air Force. Inskip replied that such actions were unnecessary. Within days

[32] *DBFP*, Series 3, Vol. 2, Doc. 1150. p. 582.
[33] Keith Middlemas and John Barnes, *Baldwin: A Biography* (London: Weidenfeld and Nicolson, 1969), p. 257.
[34] Keith Feiling, *The Life of Neville Chamberlain* (London: Macmillan, 1946), p. 363.

however came the announcement of gas masks and trenches. Ismay was flabbergasted that such irrelevant measures were being proceeded with while the real measures necessary for the defence of the capital, measures he had brought to the government's attention, were ignored.[35]

In reality, however, Inskip was right. No measures were needed for the defence of London at that time because the government had no intention of going to war with Germany over Czechoslovakia.

The measures taken by the government however allowed Chamberlain to make a radio broadcast to the British people on 27 September that suggested his intention to abandon the Czech people: "How horrible, fantastic, incredible it is that we should be digging trenches and trying on gas masks here because of a quarrel in a far-away country between people of whom we know nothing."[36] He did not mention that he had no support from the British military for his trenches-and-masks policy. Ignoring Hitler's treachery altogether, Chamberlain presented himself as the peacemaker. "I shall not give up the hope of a peaceful solution, or abandon my efforts for peace, as long as any chance for peace remains," intoned the prime minister. He added that he was prepared to meet Hitler for a third time in Germany if that might contribute to a peaceful solution.

Chamberlain was relatively forthright that a peaceful solution meant the surrender of the Czechs to the Germans. "However much we may sympathise with a small nation confronted by a big and powerful neighbour, we cannot in all circumstances undertake to involve the whole British Empire in war simply on her account. If we have to fight it must be on larger issues than that." Such a statement, of course, begged the question of where Britain drew the line: what issues were large enough to justify a war with Germany? Apart from the obvious point that Chamberlain was admitting that Britain was unprepared to halt aggressors in Europe if their target was small nations, his broadcast deliberately understated the importance of Czechoslovakia's fate. Unmentioned were the crucial strategic importance of Czechoslovakia and the strengthening of

---

[35] *The Memoirs of General The Lord Ismay* (London: Heineman, 1960), p. 91.
[36] Neville Chamberlain, *In Search of Peace* (New York: Putnam's Sons, 1939), pp. 174-5.

Germany's military might as a result of its domination over that country.

Chamberlain repeated his performance the next night in Parliament. By then, though no public announcement was made, Chamberlain had received an invitation from Hitler to go to Munich. William Manchester describes the parliamentary debate that evening as "a piece of stage management."[37]

Chamberlain's trenches-and-gas-masks gambit, coupled with his broadcast and parliamentary performance, helped to pave the way towards public support for the sellout of Czechoslovakia at Munich on 29 September. While the public generally may have been fooled, astute contemporary commentators saw through the prime minister's ploy.[38] Writing the preface to his autobiography on 2 October 1938, the historian R.G. Collingwood commented:

> To me, therefore, the betrayal of Czechoslovakia was only a third case of the same policy by which the 'National' government had betrayed Abyssinia and Spain; and I was less interested in the fact itself than in the methods by which it was accomplished; the carefully engineered war-scare in the country at large, officially launched by the simultaneous issue of gas-masks and the prime minister's emotional broadcast, two days before his flight to Munich, and the carefully staged hysterical scene in parliament on the following night. These things were in the established traditions of Fascist dictatorial methods; except that whereas the Italian and German dictators sway mobs by appeal to the thirst for glory and national aggrandizement, the English prime minister did it by playing on sheer stark terror.[39]

At Munich on 29 September 1938 four powers – Germany, Britain, France and Italy – determined the fate of Czechoslovakia without Czechoslovak participation. The British government took all steps necessary to insure that the Czechs were not allowed to think they would have any say in deciding their own fate. Newton, the British Ambassador in Prague, sent a

---

[37] William Manchester, *The Last Lion: Winston Spencer Churchill 1932-1940* (Boston: Little Brown and Company, 1988), p. 349.
[38] See, for example, Pierre Van Passen, *Days of our Years* (New York: Garden City Publishing, 1939), Chpr. 9, especially pp. 484-85.
[39] R.G. Collingwood, *An Autobiography* (Oxford: Oxford University Press, 1939), pp. 165-166.

telegram on 29 September, informing Halifax that he would omit a few words from Halifax's instructions when he spoke to the Czech Foreign Minister. Halifax had asked Newton to convey to the minister Britain's wish that he not express any disagreement with the timetable of events about to be agreed upon at Munich before the decisions had actually been made. Wrote Newton: "I will omit these words lest he should take them to imply that it would be open to Czechoslovak Government to formulate objections afterwards."[40]

Following the signing of the Munich agreement, Chamberlain and Hitler had a private meeting. The declaration that followed this meeting stated in part: "We regard the agreement signed last night and the Anglo-German Naval Agreement as symbolic of the desire of our two peoples never to go to war with one another again."[41] Just fifteen days earlier, Hitler had made plain the insoluble link in his mind between the free hand and the Anglo-German agreement added to a commitment never to go to war again with Britain. With Hitler's clarification at Godesberg that the free hand applied only to eastern Europe, Chamberlain was now prepared to sign a document that echoed Hitler's language at Berchtesgaden as he explained the rewards to Britain of giving Germany a free hand, that is everlasting peace and a strict adherence to the Naval Agreement.[42] In other words, he chose to echo the language Hitler used at Berchtesgaden to describe the policy of a free hand.

Hitler received what he wanted at Munich. Czechoslovakia was dismembered. The Sudetenland was ceded to Germany while other territories were ceded to Poland and Hungary. Czechoslovakia lost roughly a third of its population and its Czech and Slovak halves were no longer contiguous.

Czechoslovakia had now been abandoned by all of her allies except the Soviet Union. But the Soviet assistance pact with

[40] *DBFP*, Series 3, Vol. 2, Doc. 1217, September 29, 1938, p. 621
[41] *DBFP*, Series 3, Vol. 2, Annex to Doc. 1228, p. 640.
[42] Donald Cameron Watt suggests that Chamberlain "persuaded Hitler to sign a declaration of Anglo-German friendship." He portrays a sullen Hitler at Munich, resentful that Chamberlain had deprived him of war. But, whatever Hitler's mood at Munich, the declaration of friendship did no more than make public his private words to Chamberlain at Berchtesgaden that he was willing to maintain the Naval Agreement in return for British guarantees that the two countries would never go to war again. Donald Cameron Watt, *How War Came: The Immediate Origins of the Second World War, 1938-1939* (London: Heinemann, 1989), p. 29.

Czechoslovakia provided for Soviet involvement only after France discharged her obligations under the French-Czech agreement. Benes had asked to have such a clause in the treaty because ruling circles in Czechoslovakia found it unacceptable that the country should ever be dependent solely on the aid of a Communist country. Rudolph Beran, leader of the country's Agrarian Party, the largest single party in the nation, did not hide from Germany that he would welcome her help in the struggle against communism.[43]

Britain failed to consult the Soviet Union as it made its plans regarding Czechoslovakia and provided the Communist nation little information. Chamberlain's bitter anti-communism makes this unsurprising. Yet Chamberlain faced criticism at home from Opposition politicians and Winston Churchill who believed that the Soviets had a role to play in the unfolding crisis. He responded by alleging that the Soviets were militarily too weak to be a factor.

As we have seen, the French questioned this point of view. Yet the French military rejected an offer of fighter aeroplanes from the Soviets. They even refused the plans of the design of a Soviet fighter model considered by the French experts to be superior to any model the French air force had. The reason was that to accept Soviet help would have been humiliating to France.[44] Similarly, the British military refused a Soviet offer to deliver to them the plans for the construction of a tank which, according to British experts, was superior to any model Britain had produced or designed.[45]

The British were aware that the Soviets intended to provide whatever assistance to Czechoslovakia they might be allowed to provide. Halifax had decided to confirm Soviet willingness to implement their obligations under their treaty with Czechoslovakia while the Godesberg meeting was under way. Halifax had asked Rab Butler, Parliamentary Under-Secretary of State in the Foreign Office, to approach Maxim Litvinov, the Soviet Foreign Minister, in Geneva regarding Soviet intentions in the case of a German attack on the Czechs.[46] Next day Butler

---

[43] *DGFP*, Series D, Vol. 2, Doc. 62, p. 141 (27 February 1938) and Doc. 105, p. 195 (27 March 1938).
[44] Robert Coulondre, *De Staline à Hitler*, (Paris: Hachette, 1950), pp. 126-7.
[45] Liddell Hart, *The Memoirs of Captain Liddell Hart*, Vol. 1 (London: Cassell, 1965), p. 390.
[46] *DBFP*, Series 3, Vol. 2, Doc. 1043, p. 480, 23 September 1938.

responded at length, indicating the Soviet readiness to stand by their obligations.[47] The Soviets did not share a border with Czechoslovakia and so, without the permission of either Roumania or Poland, they could only help out Czechoslovakia in the air. This alone could prove valuable.

But it was possible, by having recourse to the League of Nations, to win the Soviets the right to have their armies cross through other countries to get to Czechoslovakia. The Soviets were prepared to join other nations in asking the League to give the Soviet Union permission to let its armies march into Czechoslovakia. Litvinov felt however that a preferable course was to have Britain, France, the Soviet Union and Roumania meet to discuss the practical military assistance that could be given to Czechoslovakia. Butler rejected the suggestion.

The Czechs recognized that the major European powers regarded the Soviet Union, not Nazi Germany, as a pariah. On the evening of 30 September 1938, M. Vavrecka, the Czechoslovak minister of propaganda, gave a broadcast in which he mentioned the reasons why his country had not called upon the Soviet Union for help.

> We had to consider that it would take the Russian Army weeks to come to our aid – perhaps too late, for by that time millions of our men, women and children would have been slaughtered. It was even more important to consider that our war by the side of Soviet Russia would have been not only a fight against Germany but it would have been interpreted as a fight on the side of Bolshevism. And then perhaps all of Europe would have been drawn into the war against us and Russia.[48]

Harold Ickes reports in his diary on 2 July 1939 on conversations he had with Benes while the Czech president was lecturing at the University of Chicago. "He was particularly explicit in saying that, at all times during the Czechoslovakian crisis, Russia was not only willing to carry out every obligation that it had entered into, it was willing to go further."[49] "To go further" could only mean that the Soviet Union was prepared to

[47] *DBFP*, Series 3, Vol. 2, Doc. 1071, pp. 487-498.
[48] F.S. Northedge, *The Troubled Giant* (New York: F.A. Praeger,1966), p. 535.
[49] *The Secret Diary of Harold Ickes*, Volume 2 (New York: Simon and Shuster, 1954), p. 675.

assist Czechoslovakia even if France abstained from helping, as the Vavrecka broadcast after Munich implicitly recognizes.

But Vavrecka was no doubt right about the probable response of the democracies if Czechoslovakia accepted Soviet aid in resisting naked Nazi aggression. Neville Chamberlain regarded Germany and Britain as the "two pillars of European peace and buttresses against communism," as he had confided to King George VI. He had colluded with Hitler at Berchtesgaden and Godesberg to provide Hitler with a free hand in eastern and central Europe in return for guarantees of peace in the West and non-intervention by Germany in Britain's colonial ventures. England and Germany were to be, as Sir Horace Wilson put it, "bulwarks against disruption, particularly from the East." The fate of Czechoslovakia was small potatoes in the context of an "Anglo-German understanding" that would give Germany the responsibility of maintaining "order" to its east. "Order" meant an eventual war against the Soviet Union which had created disorder by nationalizing property and providing an inspiration to the 'disorderly' of other countries.

It was this notion of order that was behind Neville Chamberlain's claim that the four-power meeting at Munich on 29 September 1938 represented "peace in our time." For Chamberlain, the three meetings he had held with Hitler had produced not simply or mainly a solution to the Czech crisis. Rather an overall plan for European global and social stability, in which Britain and Germany were the guarantors of "peace," had been concluded. As we have seen, Chamberlain understood that this "peace" excluded warfare only in western Europe while allowing Germany to make war eastwards and eventually to challenge the right of the Soviet Union to exist. The next chapter examines the consequences of this "peace agreement."

CHAPTER SEVEN

FROM MUNICH TO THE FALL OF PRAGUE: TRYING TO MAINTAIN "THE DEAL"

Chamberlain was flush with victory upon his return from Munich. He had achieved the "Anglo-German cooperation" that he had sought and was hailed by the British public for having kept the country out of war. But Chamberlain soon learned that Hitler, fearing that the next government of Britain might be led by an anti-Nazi, placed less store by the agreement than he, Chamberlain, did. Over the next eleven months, before circumstances forced him to declare war on Hitler, Chamberlain tried in a variety of ways to convince Hitler that Britain was a reliable partner and that the "free hand" in central and eastern Europe would be maintained.

But that required that Hitler keep to his promise of limiting his aggressions to the nations to his east. Military intelligence soon revealed to Chamberlain that Hitler was, in fact, planning to attack western nations as well. This led Chamberlain to follow a dangerous and ultimately unsuccessful double game: on the one hand, he tried to demonstrate to Hitler that Britain would not tolerate a violation of the "understanding" the two men had reached at Godesberg and Munich. The British guarantee to Poland was key to this strategy. It meant that Germany would face a two-front war if it attacked in the West – and if as expected Poland would reciprocate the guarantee given to her. On the other hand, he made it clear to Hitler via secret emissaries that if Hitler stuck by his part of the unwritten agreement at Godesberg, so would Britain. He could have his free hand in the east if he acted in ways that convinced Britain he had no designs on western Europe. Ultimately however, Hitler was too suspicious of the impermanence of democratic governments to be willing to regard an agreement with Chamberlain as unshakeable. His non-aggression pact with Stalin and the agreement of the two dictators to hand over the non-Ukrainian areas of Poland to Nazi Germany demonstrated his lack of faith in Chamberlain's ability to make good on "Anglo-German cooperation." Britain was forced by the logic of its guarantee to Poland to declare war on Germany.

This chapter traces developments from Munich to the events preceding the British decision to provide the unilateral guarantee to Poland. It demonstrates that while evidence mounted that Hitler was planning an attack on the nations west of Germany, Chamberlain refused to give up his notion that Germany and Britain together were the "two pillars of European peace and buttresses against communism." He worked to restore the agreement that he believed Hitler and he had hammered out together. We argue here as well the untenability of the well-established view that Britain and France turned against Hitler because he invaded the remnants of Czechoslovakia. The leaders of both countries were reconciled to the disappearance of Czechoslovakia in the weeks following Munich and indeed accepted that all the countries of central and eastern Europe would become vassal states to Nazi Germany. But though the dismemberment of Czechoslovakia as such caused Chamberlain little grief, German actions in connection with the dismemberment confirmed for him earlier reports that Hitler was indeed planning an assault on the West. When Germany handed Ruthenia to Hungary, the accepted view of appeasers in Britain and France that Hitler was planning to attack the Ukraine and not the West was dashed to pieces. This forced the British and French governments to take action. Because of public disgust with Hitler's brutal overthrow of the Czechs, these governments fostered the view that they were indeed reacting to Hitler's aggression against the remnants of Czechoslovakia.

***

French Prime Minister Daladier was ashamed of his role in abandoning Czechoslovakia at Munich. So were many of the Foreign Office officials in Britain, including Sir Alexander Cadogan and Lord Strang. Strang, who accompanied Chamberlain to Munich, recalled that Chamberlain felt otherwise:

> ...the Munich Conference was a distressing event...What was disturbing was that, at an international conference, four Powers should have discussed and taken decisions upon the cession to one of them of vital territory belonging to a fifth state, without giving a hearing to the Government of that State. The decision, after it had been reached, was merely communicated at the dead of night to representatives of the government concerned by two

> of the participants in the conference, for immediate acceptance under brutal duress...Mr. Chamberlain though his original proposal had been for a conference of the four powers and Czechoslovakia, did not seem afterwards to have been much disturbed by this.
>
> On his return to the hotel, as he sat down to lunch, the Prime Minister complacently patted his breast-pocket and said: "I've got it."[1]

"It," in Chamberlain's mind, was an enduring "peace" agreement, not an opportunity to buy time for military preparations against the aggressive Nazi state. On 3 October 1938, Lord Swinton, a trusted Conservative, told Chamberlain that he would support him if the prime minister was simply buying time for rearmament. Swinton reported to Ian Colvin the reply from Chamberlain: "But don't you understand? I have brought back peace."[2] Though Hitler had revealed at Berchtesgaden and Godesberg that he expected a free hand in central and eastern Europe, Chamberlain, as we have already seen, did not see this as in contradiction with the seeking of peace. Peace, in his lexicon, meant simply peace in western Europe.

Within days however Hitler had made a speech that revealed the fragility of the "deal" Chamberlain had made with the Führer during their three meetings of September 1938. At Saarbrucken on 9 October, Hitler noted: "It only needs that in England instead of Chamberlain, Mr. Duff Cooper or Mr. Eden or Mr. Churchill should come to power, and then we know quite well that it would be the aim of these men immediately to begin a new World War." With this in mind, said Hitler, he had decided "to continue the construction of our fortifications in the West with increased energy."[3]

Neville Chamberlain decided that he must demonstrate to Hitler that he alone made foreign policy for Britain. Hitler need not fear that Chamberlain would be unduly influenced by an ever-changing public opinion or by the opinions of other leading

[1] Lord Strang, *Home and Abroad* (London: Andre Deutsch, 1956), pp. 146, 148.
[2] Ian Colvin, *Vansittart in Office* (London: Victor Gollancz, 1965), p. 270.
[3] Winston Churchill, *The Gathering Storm* (Kingsport, Tennessee: Houghton Mifflin, 1948), pp. 328-329.

politicians less steadfast in their support of the new "Anglo-German understanding." Once again, secret interlocutors were crucial to the process of conveying a message to Germany that could not be conveyed openly. George F. Steward, a member of the Prime Minister's office at 10 Downing Street from 1929 to 1940, was Chamberlain's intermediary. Steward took Chamberlain's message to Dr. Fritz Hesse, a representative in London both of a German news agency and of German Foreign Affairs Minister von Ribbentrop. In turn, Hesse passed on the information to Herbert von Dirksen, German ambassador in London, who reported it to Ernst von Weizsacker, German State Secretary, a pipeline to Hitler.

Hesse provided Dirksen with a detailed account of his conversation with Steward, whom he described as "a confidential agent of Neville Chamberlain." The thrust of Steward's information to the Germans was that Chamberlain was devoted absolutely to the cause of Anglo-German cooperation and that the German government would aid its own cause best by acting in ways that bolstered Chamberlain's popularity at home. In the days leading to Munich, revealed Steward, Chamberlain had acted without consulting his Cabinet or the Foreign Office and had demonstrated his ability to turn public opinion around. But the anti-Nazi forces in Britain remained strong and Chamberlain's continued ability to contain those forces depended upon his winning the next election. German praise of Chamberlain's peace efforts, an end to German attacks on British Opposition politicians, and care not to appear to be bullying Czechoslovakia or boasting about its new territorial acquisitions would be Germany's contribution to Chamberlain's re-election.[4]

As we have seen, while much of Chamberlain's Cabinet had little stomach for the complete sell-out of Czechoslovakia that Hitler demanded at Godesberg, he retained the complete support of such ministers as Simon, Hoare and Inskip. Halifax, though he had great personal reservations about the prime minister's position and almost broke from the prime minister entirely, re-entered the fold quickly and did Chamberlain's bidding. Wishing to convey to Hitler however that he had almost the degree of power in Britain that the Führer exercised over Germany, Chamberlain exaggerated the extent to which he had single-handedly delivered the Munich agreement to Hitler. This

[4] *DGFP*, Series D, Vol. 4, Doc. 251 [enclosure 2], pp. 305-08.

made sense because the essence of the Anglo-German agreement was the private conclusions of two individuals at Berchtesgaden, Godesberg and Munich. Only if Hitler believed that Chamberlain could keep his side of the bargain could a deal be maintained between the two men.

And so Steward, speaking for Chamberlain, informed Hesse that before Munich Chamberlain "made decisions entirely alone with his two intimate advisers and in the last decisions had no longer asked the opinion of any member of the Cabinet, not even of Lord Halifax, the Foreign Secretary." Nor had he "received assistance or support of any kind from the Foreign Office." In short, Chamberlain had "ignored the provisions of the British Constitution and customary Cabinet usage."

Next, Steward informed Hesse that the Foreign Office was hostile to Germany because of the events leading to Munich. It was important therefore that "all major questions should be dealt with direct, thus bypassing the Foreign Office and also Sir Nevile Henderson." The latter, though pro-German, cooperated with the Foreign Office and "was not completely reliable when forwarding communications."

British public opinion on Munich remained fragile, warned Chamberlain's representative. German actions that made it appear that the Nazis were intervening in British public life could only inflame the situation in Britain. Hitler's speech in Saarbrucken was no doubt what Steward had in mind but he was too diplomatic to give examples. Instead he cautioned the Germans that if they wished to help Chamberlain, they should not attack his opponents and thereby give the latter the chance to curry public favour by attacking German interference in British domestic politics.

> On the other hand, if we wished to do something positive, it was especially important for us to emphasize again and again that we trusted Chamberlain because he wanted peace and for us to stress our wish to live in lasting friendship with the British people. As a matter of fact it was desirable for propaganda to be put out which would manifest the desire on the part of Germany for friendship between the British and the German peoples.

Meanwhile, Germany would improve its public image in Britain if it avoided "boasting and bullying" with regard to the Czech question. It should not "threaten too much with our military strength," as Hesse put it. In any case, Chamberlain's attitude had not been determined by Germany's military capacities relative to Britain's. He "had never been dictated by a consciousness of military weakness but exclusively by the religious idea that Germany must have justice and that the injustice of Versailles must be made good."

"In order to strengthen Chamberlain's position," Hesse related, Steward, on behalf of the prime minister, was suggesting that Germany must come to an agreement with Britain on the "disarmament question." If Germany did, Chamberlain would go to the country in a general election on a platform that stressed Anglo-German cooperation. Germany therefore had it within her means to "stabilize pro-German tendencies in Britain."

It was, of course, highly irregular for British foreign policy to be conducted in this manner. As he boasted he had done with Munich, Chamberlain was by-passing his Cabinet and the Foreign Office to reaffirm his collusion with Hitler. Interestingly, the Foreign Office learned of his treachery but chose to respond gingerly. Sir Alexander Cadogan's diaries indicate that on 28 November 1938 an Intelligence Service officer brought him evidence of contact between 10 Downing Street and Fritz Hesse. Cadogan reported this information to Halifax, who spoke to Chamberlain about it the next day. Chamberlain appeared to be aghast and Halifax believed that he was genuine. Cadogan was quite sceptical. Nonetheless, Sir Horace Wilson advised Steward against indiscreet conversations and Cadogan believed that "this will put a brake on them all."[5] As we shall see, secret contacts between the prime minister and Hitler via intermediaries without the participation of the Foreign Office or the full Cabinet would continue despite the uncovering of the Steward-Hesse meeting.

The message from Chamberlain focused on image more than substance, placing few limits on German ambitions but counselling Germany to use moderate rhetoric as it proceeded. Hitler remained intractable, both in his impatience for territorial expansion and in his mistreatment of the Jews of Germany. The

[5] David Dilks, *The Diaries of Sir Alexander Cadogan, O.M., 1938-1945.*(London: Cassell, 1971), p. 126

latter caused only minor consternation on Chamberlain's part. On 10 November, the Nazi authorities decided to punish collectively the German Jews for the assassination of a secretary in the German embassy in France by a Polish Jew. They unleashed a reign of terror against Jewish homes and businesses. "Kristallnacht," the night when the windows of Jewish homes were smashed and their occupants savagely beaten or murdered, was reported in the British press. The British people learned of the murders of many of the Jewish victims of Nazi hatred. They learned also that many Jews had been arrested and sent to concentration camps. Chamberlain's reaction, as reported by Sir Kingsley Wood, Air Minister, was:

> "Oh, what tedious people these Germans can be!"
> said Neville Chamberlain when he read the reports of
> the anti-Jewish riots and the measures which
> followed. "Just when we were beginning to make a
> little progress!"[6]

The British government and elites had refrained from saying or doing anything as Hitler, after taking power, progressively stripped the German Jews of their citizenship rights. Anti-Semitism was rampant among the elite but, no doubt, even more important was that they did not wish to undermine the 'pillar of peace' and 'buttress against communism' just because he had plans to deport or fry an unpopular minority. Chamberlain's flippant comment demonstrated little concern for Hitler's victims. His only concern was how his deal with Hitler would continue to play in the court of public opinion once Hitler's newest outrages were generally known to the British public.

After his three deal-making meetings with Hitler in September, Chamberlain was anxious to forge an even closer alliance, including a military alliance of the Munich powers against the Soviet Union. To cement his agreement with Hitler on Czechoslovakia, Chamberlain allowed Germany even more of Czechoslovak territory than the Munich agreement made necessary. Nevile Henderson, British representative on the International Commission that drew the new boundary between Germany and Czechoslovakia, made the peculiar argument that he had determined "to pin the Germans down to a line of their

---

[6] Leonard Mosley, *On Borrowed Time* (New York: Random House, 1969),p. 125.

own choosing" so that they could not later come back and demand even more territory.[7]

Though the Munich Agreement provided for Czechoslovak involvement in the boundary decision-making, the British and French caved in to German demands afterwards to exclude the Czechs.[8] Later indeed, they did not protest the *Vienna award* which disposed of Czechoslovak territory without consultation with either of them. This "award" had been made in November 2, 1938 by Germany and Italy without reference to the remaining two Munich partners.

The Germans understood why the Chamberlain government was being so accommodating. Dirksen, then German Ambassador in London, recorded the extent to which the prime minister and his closest associates were prepared to go to reach a formal agreement with Germany on a range of issues:

> Nevertheless, leading British Cabinet Ministers were loath to let the links with Germany break during these weeks. In various speeches Chamberlain, Lord Simon, and Lord Templewood, amongst others, directly or indirectly requested Germany to produce a programme of her wishes for negotiations; colonies, raw materials, disarmament, and limitations of sphere of interest were mentioned. In a long interview during a week-end visit, Sir Samuel Hoare approached me with these ideas.[9]

In a report written on 31 October 1938, Dirksen informed the German government of what he had learned from conversations with Hoare, who was Home Minister, as well as Transport Minister Leslie Burgin and a number of other individuals in political life within Chamberlain's circle.[10] "Chamberlain has complete confidence in the Führer," he reported. The British prime minister was planning to make proposals for "a continuation of the policy initiated at Munich." This was because he regarded a "lasting rapprochement" between

---

[7] Nevile Henderson, *Failure of a Mission* (New York: G. P. Putnam's Sons, 1940), p. 175.
[8] R. W. Seton-Watson, *From Munich to Danzig* (London: Methuen, 1939), p. 119.
[9] Herbert Von Dirksen, *Moscow, Tokyo, London: Twenty Years of German Foreign Policy* (Norman: University of Oklahoma Press, 1952), p. 212.
[10] *DGFP*, Series D, Vol. 4, Doc. 260, pp. 319-323.

Germany and Britain "as one of the chief aims of British foreign policy."

While Chamberlain was keen to have disarmament on the agenda for discussions to widen the British rapprochement with Germany, Dirksen wrote that Chamberlain understood German trepidation about limiting its air capabilities. He sympathized with German fears of the powerful Soviet air force. Sir Samuel Hoare "let slip the observation that, after a further *rapprochement* between the four European great powers, the acceptance of certain defence obligations, or even a guarantee by them against Soviet Russia, was conceivable in the event of an attack by Soviet Russia."

In practice, such a guarantee would provide British muscle against attempts by smaller nations, aided by the Soviet Union, to resist German aggression. If the Soviet Union intervened militarily to defend a victim of German aggression, the four European powers would no doubt be asked to consider this an act of aggression against Germany. As we saw in Chapter 6, Vavrecka, the Czech minister for propaganda, had feared that Czech resistance aided only by the Soviet Union might call forward such an all-European attack on Czechoslovakia.

Dirksen was "certain" that Chamberlain wanted progress on disarmament because he wished to "save face at home" in the wake of the humiliation many felt over Munich. The armaments question was the "starting point for the negotiations vis-à-vis the public."

But the British leaders were not fooled into thinking that Hitler was finished gobbling up territory. A reduction in armaments was not meant to place limits on Hitler's acquisitions in central and eastern Europe. On October 12, Joseph Kennedy, U.S. Ambassador to Britain and advocate of Western cooperation with Hitler, reported to Secretary of State Cordell Hull the substance of an extended conversation with Halifax.[11] For an hour and a half the two men drank tea and chatted in front of Halifax's fireplace "while he outlined to me what I think may be the future policy of His Majesty's Government."

Halifax confided in Kennedy that he did not believe Hitler wanted war with Britain. As for Britain, it was only willing to go

[11] *Foreign Relations of the United States*, 1938, Vol. 1, pp. 85-86.

to war with Hitler if there was "direct interference with England's Dominions." Britain and France, believed Halifax, should strengthen their air defences dramatically. "Then after that to let Hitler go ahead and do what he likes in Central Europe." "In other words," added Kennedy, "there is no question in Halifax's mind that reasonably soon Hitler will make a start for Danzig, with Polish concurrence, and then for Memel, with Lithuanian acquiescence, and even if he decides to go in Rumania it is Halifax's idea that England should mind her own business."

Halifax's approach, if Kennedy's impressions can be relied upon, was callous. England's future lay in "maintaining her relations in the Mediterranean, keeping friendly relations with Portugal, he hopes Spain, Greece, Turkey, Egypt, Palestine...plus England's connection in the Red Sea, fostering the Dominion connections, and staying very friendly with the United States, and then, as far as everything else is concerned, Hitler can do the best he can for himself." In brief, Halifax was candidly admitting that Britain had now allowed Germany a free hand in central and eastern Europe. Whatever reservations Halifax held after Godesberg, he was back on board with Chamberlain now.

Chamberlain, like Halifax, was not much interested in rearmament meant to increase Britain's capacity for a war on the European continent. On 31 October, 1938, the very day Hoare offered Germany a British alliance against the Soviet Union, Chamberlain told his Cabinet:

> Our policy is one of appeasement. We must aim at establishing relations with the Dictator Powers which will lead to a settlement in Europe and a sense of stability. A good deal of false emphasis has been placed...in the country and in the Press...on rearmament, as though one result of the Munich agreement has been that it will be necessary to add to our rearmament programmes.[12]

Trusting that Germany, if properly reassured, would move exclusively to the east, Chamberlain was responding to Hitler's fears that Western rearmament was aimed at making war on Nazi Germany. At the Cabinet meeting on 7 November 1938,

[12] Ian Colvin, *The Chamberlain Cabinet* (London: Victor Gollancz, 1971), p. 173.

Chamberlain, joined by Inskip, Kingsley Wood, and John Simon, resisted suggestions for increased rearmament.[13] Despite his past support for a strong bomber force as a deterrent to those who might attack Britain, Chamberlain now resisted expansion of Britain's bomber force. It would be hard to represent this expansion to Germany as purely defensive, he worried.

Chamberlain risked Britain's defence by bending over backwards not to stir Hitler's paranoia about Western intentions. On 24 November 1938 Harold Nicolson noted in his diary the revelations of Austin Hopkinson at a meeting of a group of MPs who met to discuss foreign-policy issues. The Tory MP, who had been parliamentary secretary to Thomas Inskip, was outraged that his former minister was being scapegoated by Chamberlain for Britain's failure to rearm properly. He had turned down an offer to be the Conservative Party's whip in the House so that he could be in a position to defend Inskip and question government policy on rearmament.

> The Government are really not telling the country the truth. He [Hopkinson] had seen Kingsley Wood, and the latter had admitted quite frankly that we can do little without a Minister of Supply, but to appoint such a Minister would arouse the anger of Germany.

> That is a dreadful confession.[14]

Halifax was more concerned about the nation's defences than the prime minister but, as his conversation with Kennedy revealed, he shared the prime minister's perspective on the free hand for Germany in central and eastern Europe. He further outlined this perspective in a letter to British Ambassador to France, Sir Eric Phipps, on 1 November 1938.[15] "Genuine agreement" was needed between Britain, Germany and France, he argued. Such agreement had to start from the premise of "German predominance in Central Europe." The French, he thought, had resisted this notion for many years but at Munich had gone a long way to its acceptance. Effectively abandoning central and eastern Europe to the Nazis, Halifax had a clear vision of the foreign and defence policies that should guide Britain and France:

[13] *Ibid.*, pp. 173-175.
[14] Harold Nicolson, *Diaries and Letters 1930-1939* (New York: Athenaeum, 1968), pp. 380-1.
[15] *DBFP*, Series 3, Vol. 3, Doc. 285, pp. 251-253.

> In these conditions it seems to me that Great Britain and France have to uphold their predominant position in Western Europe by the maintenance of such armed strength as would render any attack upon them hazardous. They should also firmly maintain their hold on the Mediterranean and the Near East. They should also keep a tight hold on their Colonial Empires and maintain the closest ties with the United States of America.

Halifax distorted the events that led to France's having to retreat from her important role in central Europe. He wrote that "the rising strength of Germany" and "France's neglect of her own defence" had led to the need for the Munich agreement. This conveniently ignored that Germany's rising strength resulted from her numerous treaty violations and that Britain had pressured France not to take appropriate countermeasures to force respect of these treaties. It also ignored the fact that British policy since the coming to power of the Nazis had accepted and indeed welcomed increasing German power in central and eastern Europe.

Elsewhere in his note to Phipps Halifax alludes to the British attitude regarding the rise of Nazi Germany's power in central Europe. "The greatest lesson of the crisis has been the unwisdom of basing a foreign policy on insufficient strength...It is one thing to allow German expansion in Central Europe, which in my mind is a normal and natural thing, but we must be able to resist German expansion in Western Europe." Again, however, Halifax is distorting the recent past and contradicting himself to boot. On the one hand, he suggests that Britain's foreign policy regarding central Europe has been unsuccessful because Britain and its allies were unwisely militarily weak. On the other, he states that Germany's preeminence in central Europe is "normal and natural." Why then would Britain have opposed it? The simple truth, as we have seen, is that Britain did not oppose it.

Nor did the British Cabinet oppose further expansion of Germany in central Europe, for example into Poland. Halifax's note suggests that Germany, in the immediate future, will "consolidate herself in Central Europe." Poland's right-wing dictatorship, reasoned Halifax, could not ally with the Soviet Union. So if France, "having once burnt her fingers with

Czechoslovakia," breaks her alliance with Poland, that country "can presumably only fall more and more into the German orbit."

Germany's next step in its expansionist campaign after exercising control over Poland, guessed Halifax, might be "expansion into the Ukraine." Halifax indicated to Phipps that he hoped France "would protect herself – and us – from being entangled by Russia in war with Germany." Yet, hypocritically, he hesitated to advise France to break its treaty with the Soviets. The Soviets, from this perspective, should be expected to help protect France from a German invasion but should not expect the same favour if Germany seized Soviet territories. An important subtext to Halifax's position is that he understood that his government was gambling with the security of the West by maintaining the Chamberlain-Hitler deal. Otherwise, why would France need to maintain a treaty with the Soviets to deal with a possible invasion of France by Germany?

Less sanguine than Halifax but equally defeatist was Alexander Cadogan, Chamberlain's appointee to replace the fierce Nazi critic Robert Vansittart as Permanent Undersecretary for Foreign Affairs. "We are back in the old lawless Europe and have got to look out for ourselves," he wrote in his diary on 7 November 1938.[16] Unlike Halifax, he recognized that British policies had helped contribute to the recreation of "the old lawless Europe." If Britain had wanted to maintain the Versailles agreement, he argued, it should have reacted when Hitler marched into the Rhineland at a time when British and French forces could easily have dealt a body blow to the Führer.

Chamberlain, having consented to the free hand for Germany in central and eastern Europe, continued to be dismissive about the prospects of war. He told a City luncheon party in the House of Commons in mid-December that Germany would pause to look at Britain's military and financial might before daring to risk war with Britain.[17] Still naively believing Hitler's word that Germany's expansionist interests were limited to territories to Germany's east, Chamberlain saw no point in massive rearmament to fight battles in western Europe. Though he could not publicly admit the free hand, he, like Halifax, was

---

[16] David Dilks, *The Diaries of Sir Alexander Cadogan*, p. 123.
[17] Iain Macleod, *Neville Chamberlain* (London: Muller, 1961), p. 272.

committed to keeping Britain out of any war that might be provoked by German actions in central and eastern Europe.

Germany was confident enough of its relationship with the British government in the post-Munich period to carry out a secret discussion with the British leaders on 7 December regarding German plans for future territorial conquests. Vansittart, present at the meeting, wrote scathingly in his diary of the German proposal.

> Not content with having dismembered Czechoslovakia, the Germans now wish to do the same to Poland and wish us to connive officially at their ambition by double-crossing the Poles. Such an attitude is impossible for any honourable nation to adopt, and the sooner it is dismissed the better. The answer that may be made to this is that Germany will soon take the corridor anyhow. That is pure defeatism in the first place, and in the second place such a consummation is unnecessary if Poland will readjust her relations sensibly with Russia...the Ribbentrop school is already bent on detaching the Ukraine from Russia and breaking up the present Russian regime from within. The Germans think they can overturn the Stalin State...We should then have in Germany a regime that had installed in Russia a regime favourable to itself, and had completely paralyzed Poland by annexing the corridor. If that is not a total domination of Europe, I don't know what is. And we are apparently expected to be foolish enough not only to connive, but to consent to it in advance. In addition we are expected to make substantial colonial concessions. Besides colonies we are also to give them a large loan...[18]

Three days later William Bullitt, the American Ambassador in Paris, discussed Anglo-French foreign policy with U.S. Interior Secretary Harold Ickes. Bullitt was party to much confidential information from the French leadership because France had made it a priority to improve its friendship with the Americans. Though Bullitt was an ardent supporter of the Munich Agreement, he reported darkly on the turn of thinking among the leaders of the two largest European democracies. Ickes wrote in his diary on 10 December that Bullitt "thinks that it is now the policy of England and France to permit other nations to have

---

[18] Ian Colvin, *Vansittart in Office* (London: Victor Gollancz, 1965), p. 284.

their will of Russia." Germany, predicted Bullitt, would attempt to seize the Ukraine while Japan would try to conquer Siberia. Both, he thought, would break from the strain of attempting to accomplish such vast expansions. "But, by leaving Russia to her fate, England and France will be diverting the threat of Germany from their own lands."[19]

***

Chamberlain and Hitler signed a Friendship Declaration at Munich. France made plans for a similar declaration with Hitler. The assassination of the secretary in the German embassy in Paris caused a slight delay. On 6 December 1938, the agreement was signed.

On 24 November 1938, before signing the agreement with Germany, France invited the British leaders for talks on the pending agreement.[20] Daladier indicated the assassination of the German secretary had set the talks back. Interestingly, he made no mention of the Kristallnacht pogrom as a setback. The French government appeared no more upset at the increase in state-sanctioned violence against German Jews than did Chamberlain.[21]

Though Chamberlain remained convinced at this time that Hitler had no aggressive intentions regarding western Europe, both he and Daladier raised issues about the other's readiness to provide aid should Germany strike against one of their countries. Chamberlain asked for and received reconfirmation of French assurance that if Germany attacked Britain, France would come immediately to its assistance. France complained that the two British divisions that Britain promised to send to France in case of a German attack were insufficient in light of the diminished importance of Czechoslovak land forces after Munich. Chamberlain did not give in. He tried to justify Britain's concentration on other defence problems.

---

[19] *The Secret Diary of Harold Ickes, Volume 2* (New York: Simon and Shuster, 1954), p. 519.
[20] The talks are minuted in *DBFP*, Series 3, Vol. 3, Doc. 325, pp. 285-311.
[21] Daladier was also silent before manifestations of anti-Semitism in his party, the Radical Socialist Party. Richard Millman, *La question Juive entre les deux guerres: Ligues de droite et antisemitisme en France* (Paris: Armand Collin, 1992), p. 281.

Chamberlain, as suggested above, remained unafraid that Britain would be vulnerable to German air power. The gas masks and trenches pre-Munich publicity stunt notwithstanding, Chamberlain did not take seriously the threat of a German knockout blow against Britain. This had been merely an excuse to gain the British public's support for the Munich Agreement with Hitler. He told Daladier that "you could terrify people by indiscriminate bombing, but you could not win a war." The combination of Britain's military preparedness and poor visibility from the skies over the country would "make it very difficult for enemy bombers to work effectively."

At this meeting Britain made plain its complete abandonment of what remained of Czechoslovakia and requested that France formally follow suit. Halifax proposed that the guarantee of Czechoslovakia's new boundaries be a joint guarantee of the four signatories to Munich. That guarantee "would only come into force as a result of a decision by three of the four powers." In other words, Fascist Italy, Germany's closest ally, would have to agree to join with France and Britain to repel a German invasion of Czechoslovakia. There was, of course, no chance that this would occur.

Daladier, who had given in to the British leaders on several occasions before, was not willing to go as far as them on this occasion. It would be immoral, he insisted, for France, after having failed to live up to its obligations to Czechoslovakia in the past, now to allow that country to simply be annihilated. He pointed out to Chamberlain and Halifax that Czechoslovakia's situation was deplorable. It had been forced to give up more territories even than the Munich agreement required.

Halifax's response reflected his unconcern with Daladier's moral objections to abandoning Czechoslovakia. "The Czechoslovak army had diminished in importance and there was to be an important German road across Czechoslovak territory," he pointed out. France and Britain could therefore do little to implement any guarantee that they made to that unfortunate country. It seemed of little importance to Halifax that Anglo-French policy had helped to weaken Czech defences against Germany; rather, now that Czechoslovakia was so weak, it was said to be futile to claim to be able to defend it.

Revealingly, the minutes indicate Halifax's concern that Czechoslovakia might ask for British and French assistance for support of a policy "not entirely in conformity with German wishes." That would constitute a "provocation" to Germany. From the point of view of the British Foreign Secretary, then, Czechoslovakia was to be a vassal to Germany. It had no right to consider pursuing policies "not entirely" consistent with Germany's desires.

Chamberlain did not pretend that Britain expected or indeed wanted Germany to end its territorial expansion with a gradual gobbling up of Czechoslovakia. He raised the question of Germany's likely moves on both Polish and Soviet territory, specifically the Ukraine. Though he claimed that Germany would be "subtle" rather than resort to crass military action, it is unlikely that he believed his own words. The prediction that he and Halifax had made a year earlier that Hitler would "beaver away" to erode Austria's independence had been proven wrong. Hitler was an impatient bully rather quick to resort to military force.

In any case, Chamberlain himself was not especially subtle in his meeting with the French in pointing out his hopes that Germany would now begin to deliver on the promise that the Nazi regime had embodied for the British elite from day one: the destruction of the Soviet Union. "There had been indications that there might be in the minds of the German Government an idea that they could begin the disruption of Russia by the encouragement of agitation for an independent Ukraine." He pressed straight to the heart of the matter with France: if Germany were involved in efforts to create an independent Ukraine, "it would be unfortunate" if France became "entangled" in the matter on the Soviet side. French Foreign Minister Bonnet confided that France was also aware of German intentions to help create an independent Ukraine. Chamberlain then asked what the French attitude would be to Soviet calls for aid on the grounds that the independence movement was in fact a German-created undermining of Soviet territorial integrity. Bonnet was blunt: France only considered itself under obligation to the Soviet Union if Germany launched a direct attack against Soviet territory. Chamberlain indicated satisfaction with this response.

Obviously the two powers considered it acceptable for the Nazis to finance and arm forces that would detach portions of the Soviet state from the Communist rulers. Their anti-communist obsession blinded them to the obvious fact that the Soviet Union was a major potential ally in resisting an expansionist and militarily powerful Germany. The military implications of a Nazi puppet state in the Ukraine were given little consideration. It was, after all, as Halifax wrote Phipps, "normal and natural" for Germany to expand eastward. That such expansion should involve a rolling-back and perhaps ultimate destruction of Communist power had long been a goal of the elites of Europe. They were no more willing in 1938 than in 1933 to recognize the danger of allowing Nazi Germany to expand its sphere of control and influence.

In the treaty signed by France and Germany on 6 December 1938, Germany renounced her claims on the French provinces of Alsace and Lorraine that had been under German control from 1870 to 1918. Talks followed the signing. Robert Coulondre, the French ambassador in Germany, whose attitude was coloured by his anti-communism, wrote to Bonnet his impressions on 15 December 1938.[22] He said Germany's determination to expand in the East was "undeniable." But it had no intention for the moment of making conquests in the West. "The one is the corollary of the other," he said of Germany's very different attitudes to East and West. Now that Germany had annexed nations and territories where German speakers predominated, its goal was to achieve *lebensraum*. That meant a focus on central and eastern Europe that gave the Nazis no time to pursue quarrels with the West. Coulondre was as clear and as callous as Halifax in summing up Germany's intentions.

> To secure mastery over Central Europe by reducing Czechoslovakia and Hungary to a state of vassalage and then to create a Greater Ukraine under German control – this is what essentially appears to be the leading idea now accepted by the Nazi leaders, and doubtless by Herr Hitler himself.

> ...Among those who approach him [Hitler], a political operation is thought of which would repeat, on a larger scale, that of the Sudetens: propaganda in Poland, in Roumania and in Soviet Russia in favour

[22] Frederick L. Schuman, *Night Over Europe* (New York: Alfred A. Knopf, 1941), p. 69.

of Ukrainian independence; support eventually given by diplomatic pressure and by the action of armed bands; Ruthenia would be the focus of the movement. Thus by a curious turn of Fate, Czechoslovakia, which had been established as a bulwark to stem the German drive, now serves the Reich as a battering-ram to demolish the gates of the East...

Coulondre's warlike picture of the immediate future demonstrates that France, like Britain, was committed to peace in the West, not peace in all of Europe. His notion that Ruthenia would be the focal point for the German drive to create a German-dependent "independent" Ukraine was shared by the leaders of France and Britain. Germany had refused Hungary's request after Munich to have Ruthenia incorporated into its territory. Coulondre was repeating the popular view that this was because Ruthenia, a predominantly Ukrainian-speaking area, gave Germany a border with Roumania's and Poland's Ukrainian regions and would therefore be pivotal to German plans to detach Ukrainian territories from the three countries that included large Ukrainian-speaking populations. It would be the spearhead for an attack on the Soviet Union. Therefore it remained, for the moment, part of the Czechoslovak state while Germany considered its future. As we see later in this chapter, events regarding Ruthenia would contribute to a change in Anglo-French attitudes to Germany in March 1939.

Bonnet was as convinced as Coulondre that Germany was uninterested in peace but intended to expand only eastwards. On 6 December, 1938, the very day of the signing of the treaty with Germany, he let France's ambassadors know his perspective. The Minister of Finance in Daladier's Cabinet writes as follows of the actions that day of his fellow minister:

> Bonnet, himself, in an official note to all Ambassadors, declared that the impression he had derived from those conversations [ed. with German political leaders] was that the German policy was henceforward oriented towards the struggle against Bolshevism. The Reich was revealing its will of expansion towards the East.[23]

---

[23] Paul Reynaud, *La France A Sauvé l'Europe* (Paris: Flammarion, 1947), p. 575. Translated from the French by Clement Leibovitz.

One day earlier Bonnet had informed Phipps of his intention to "loosen the ties that bind France to Russia and Poland."[24] Eight days later Charles Corbin, the French ambassador to Britain, reported to Halifax the substance of conversations between Bonnet and von Ribbentrop. The German Foreign Minister told his French counterpart that there were no obstacles to good relations between the two countries provided that France did not interfere with German plans. These, wrote Halifax to Phipps, "appeared to M. Bonnet to be mainly concerned with possibilities in the East."[25] Revealingly, the French Ambassador told Halifax that the conversation of the two foreign ministers "did not appear to amount to much." France at the time seemed to consider it normal to be put on notice by Germany to mind its own business and not to sniff into Germany's affairs, particularly in Eastern Europe.

Dr. Paul Schmidt, who was the German interpreter at the Bonnet-Ribbentrop meeting, confirms in his memoirs that Bonnet had expressed to Ribbentrop France's disinterest in Eastern Europe.[26] Indeed it would appear that Bonnet was mainly interested in getting the Germans to persuade Italy to be more reasonable in the discussions that France and Italy were having over control over Tunisia. While he would later deny having told Ribbentrop that France was unconcerned with the fate of Poland or Czechoslovakia, he gave no indication that France was concerned with their fate. He also was quite explicit that France would not object to Germany's provision of military assistance to Ukrainian nationalists who would then attack the Soviet Union.[27]

Bonnet was concerned not to let the Germans be angered by statements that he made for domestic consumption suggesting that France had not given Germany a free hand in the East. For example, on 26 January, he made a public statement indicating that France continued to abide by the terms of its agreements with the Soviet Union and Poland. Two days earlier however he had called in the German ambassador in Paris, Count Johannes von Welczeck, and given him advance notice of this address,

---

[24] *DBFP*, Series 3, Vol. 3, Doc. 407, p. 397, note 1.
[25] *DBFP*, Series 3, Vol. 3, Doc. 427, p. 427.
[26] Dr. Paul Schmidt, *Statist auf Diplomatischer Buhne, 1923-45* (Athenaum-Verlag, Bonn, 1949), p. 424.
[27] A. Scherer, "Les 'Mains Libres' à l'Est," *Revue d'histoire de la Deuxième Guerre Mondiale*, No. 32 (October 1958), pp. 16-18.

reading him several passages that he noted were meant only "for domestic purposes."[28]

Bonnet saw the German-French accord as an important device not only in French foreign policy but also in its domestic policy. Count von Welczeck reported that Bonnet had said "an agreement with Germany in whatever form would equally consolidate the position of Daladier and Bonnet and would strengthen their policy of ganging up on and excluding the Communists."[29]

The continuing willingness on the part of the British (and now French) government to explain away Germany's impressive rearmament programme with reference to Germany's Eastern ambitions is evident in this excerpt from Halifax's letter to Phipps:

> M. Corbin went on to say that the French Government had information that some reinforcement of the German army was in progress in the direction of creating eight new divisions, strengthening the reserves and some reorganization of the Higher Command. The French Government took the view that these measures were designed to have certain offensive advantage but that they were again inspired rather by the possible requirements of the situation in the East than elsewhere.[30]

Halifax failed to question what Germany's military requirements in the East would be relative to the extensive armament that was occurring. The belief that Hitler's sights were targeted exclusively on the East was too strong; the dream that Hitler could "begin the disruption of Russia" was too entrenched.

***

We have seen that Chamberlain's response to Kristallnacht was flippant. Yet informed British sources recognized that this was a prelude to "elimination" of the Jews. The malevolent behaviour of the Nazis demonstrated that they regarded the Jews as sub-human. After having rained death and destruction on the Jews on 10 November, the government imposed further

[28] *Ibid.*, p. 20.
[29] *Ibid.*, p. 10.
[30] *DBFP*, Series 3, Vol. 3, Doc. 427, p. 427.

penalties on the Jews that assumed their collective guilt for the murder of Herr Von Rath, the murdered employee of the German embassy in Paris. The government imposed a collective fine of a billion marks (about 420 million dollars) on a community whose property it had been progressively expropriating since 1933. It also passed a number of new laws that discriminated against the Jews. Among these was a law that required the Jews to forfeit to the state monies they received from insurance claims relating to Kristallnacht damages. The state, having unleashed destruction on Jewish property, now wished to reap a reward for such damage. On 16 November 1938, Sir G. Ogilvie-Forbes, the British representative in Berlin (Nevile Henderson was convalescing in Britain), wrote in his report to Halifax:

> I think that the murder of Herr Von Rath by a German born Polish Jew has only accelerated the process of elimination of the Jews which has for long been planned. This project, had it proceeded according to schedule, was cruel enough, but the opportunity offered by Grynszpan's criminal act has let loose forces of medieval barbarism...In spite of statements to the contrary, there can be no doubt that the deplorable excesses perpetrated on the 10th November were instigated and organized by the Government...I did not meet a single German of whatever class who in varying measure does not, to say the least, disapprove of what has occurred. But I fear it does not follow that even the outspoken condemnation of professed National Socialists or of senior officers in the army, will have any influence over the insensate gang in present control of Nazi Germany.[31]

Sir Ogilvie-Forbes was a supporter of Chamberlain's foreign policies. As British ambassador to Spain, his reports were sympathetic to Franco. Yet he recognized the suffering of the Spanish people. Similarly, while he wanted a British settlement with the Nazis, he was shocked by the brutality of the "insensate gang" who ran Germany. It was becoming fairly obvious as well that as Germany conquered much of central and eastern Europe, ever-larger populations of Jews and gypsies, among other minority groups loathed by the Nazis, faced extermination.

---

[31] *DBFP*, Series 3, Vol. 3, Doc. 313, p. 277.

Chamberlain was not shocked by the "tedious" Germans. On 11 November, a day after the well-reported pogrom in Germany, he wrote a letter to his sister Hilda in which he omitted any comment on Kristallnacht. Instead he lamented the German press's continued hostility to Britain and the failure of the German government "to make the slightest gesture of friendship." While the whole world raged at Hitler's barbarism, Chamberlain was absorbed with the German government's unfriendliness to himself.[32]

Nonetheless, Chamberlain was aware that public opinion in Britain was turning against appeasement of a regime with murderous intentions towards many of its own citizens. He took advantage of a meeting between Colonel Pirow, South Africa's Minister of Defence, and Hitler, to offer Hitler Britain's view on a "final solution" for the "Jewish problem" in Germany, while at the same time affirming his support for a free hand for Germany in eastern Europe. Pirow, a South African of German descent, was an admirer of Hitler and an anti-Semite. Yet Chamberlain viewed him as an acceptable conduit to Hitler for the British prime minister's views on the question of the Jews. Meeting with Pirow before the latter set out in late November, 1938, to meet with Hitler, Chamberlain indicated that he wanted to see "a solution satisfactory to all the interested parties" on the issue of the future of German Jewry. Pirow was instructed to let Hitler know that if he proved flexible on this issue, Chamberlain would not oppose new initiatives by Hitler in central and eastern Europe, particularly concerning the "Polish corridor." Pirow presented to Chamberlain a plan that had the support of a section of the British elite who viewed Hitler's extreme anti-Semitism as a sticking point in British-German relations. With funding from rich Jews around the world, German Jews would be evacuated to a faraway land, such as Madagascar or somewhere in west Africa. Hitler would achieve his goal of a "Judenrein" Germany while the Jews, who would be allowed to take half their property with them, would be allowed to live. Pirow would later report that his proposal was sympathetically received by Goering but not by Ribbentrop or Hitler. Hitler rejected any outside intervention in what he regarded as a German domestic issue and proposed that Germany and Britain come to an agreement on global spheres of influence with Germany to be master of the European continent and Britain to have control of most of the rest of the world.[33]

[32] D.C. Watt, *How War Came* (London: Heinemann, 1989), p. 91.

***

Much of the British establishment remained out of step with the growing outrage against the Nazis, fuelled by the dismemberment of Czechoslovakia, the pogrom against German Jews, and Hitler's speech against the British opposition. Oliver Harvey, secretary to Halifax and past secretary to Eden, and Lord Strang at the Foreign Office were among the minority of conservatives who concluded that their government and the Conservative Party were going too far to appease Hitler. Though they reluctantly supported Munich because they were unsure that Britain and France could win a war with Germany, they deplored the country's continued lack of military preparedness. Their informed joint assessment of the problem, as expressed by Harvey in his diary, may sound surprising coming from such conservative sources:

> Strang and I agree that the real opposition to re-arming comes from the rich classes in the Party who fear taxation and believe Nazis on the whole are more conservative than the Communists and Socialists: any war, whether we win or not, would destroy the rich idle classes and so they are for peace at any price. P.M. is a man of iron will, obstinate, unimaginative, with intense narrow vision, a man of prewar outlook who sees no reason for drastic social changes. Yet we are on the verge of a social revolution.[34]

Chamberlain indeed had no desire to support drastic social changes that would reduce the supposed threat of Communism and clung to the secret agreement with Hitler that his three meetings in September had produced. Communism for him was the product of Soviet agitation and not social inequalities in various countries. Hitler, with his requirement for *lebensraum* and his hatred of Communists, would take care of the social revolutionaries of the East. Chamberlain was unflinching in his support for the free hand for the Nazis in central and eastern

---

[33] Charles Bloch, "Les relations anglo-allemandes (30 septembre 1938-28 avril 1939) 1," *Revue d'histoire de la Deuxième Guerre Mondiale*, No. 18 (April 1955), p. 45.

[34] *The Diplomatic Diaries of Oliver Harvey* (London: Collins, 1958), p. 222. The diary entry was for 18 November 1938.

Europe at least for as long as he believed that Hitler was true to his side of the bargain: hands off of the West.

But reports soon abounded suggesting that Hitler was not maintaining his side of the collusion with Chamberlain. The first such report appears to have come from Sir Ogilvie-Forbes in Berlin on 6 December 1938, the very day that the Franco-German agreement was signed. Wrote the British Chargé d'Affaires in Berlin:

> There is a school of thought here which believes that Herr Hitler will not risk a Russian adventure until he has made quite certain that his Western flank will not be attacked while he is operating in the east, and that consequently his first task will be to liquidate France and England before British rearmament is ready.[35]

This report did not cause much alarm. But over the next several months such reports became frequent. On 15 December, for example, Cadogan wrote in his diary that Ivone Kirkpatrick, First Secretary at the British Embassy in Berlin, had word from a German friend that Hitler would bomb London in March.[36] Kirkpatrick, writing after the war, denied having indicated a fixed date but confirmed that his sources suggested Hitler wanted the capacity to make a surprise air attack against London.[37] The report was taken seriously enough for Chamberlain to call a Cabinet meeting. But the British prime minister had invested too much of his political capital in his trust of the Nazi dictator and concluded that Germany would only attack Britain if it appeared to threaten "Hitler's eastern ambitions." This it would take pains not to do.[38]

Ogilvie-Forbes had come to similar conclusions. He wrote to Halifax at the beginning of 1939 that Germany lacked agricultural and mineral resources that it could acquire most easily via conquest in the East, particularly in the Ukraine. It would only attack the West if the West seemed to stand in the way of such conquest. Using language that demonstrated the peculiar notions of war and of Europe on the part of the

---

[35] *DBFP*, Series 3, Vol. 3, Doc. 403, pp. 386-88.
[36] *The Diaries of Sir Alexander Cadogan*, p. 130.
[37] Ivone Kirkpatrick, *The Inner Circle* (New York: Macmillan, 1959), pp. 136-138.
[38] Telford Taylor, *Munich: The Price of Peace* (New York: Doubleday and Company, 1979), p. 943.

Chamberlainites, Ogilvie-Forbes then looked at ways to "avoid an European war." In other words, Hitler's conquest of eastern Europe did not constitute a war in Europe. Europe to Ogilvie-Forbes was only its western half. Apart from counselling Western defeatism with regards to eastern Europe, the Chargé d'Affaires advised that Britain make every effort to encourage close relations with "moderate Nazis" such as Field-Marshall Goering so that they could restrain "extremists" like Ribbentrop, Goebbels and Himmler.[39] Both "moderates" and "extremists" were warmongers but the "moderates" believed the French and British would not interfere with Germany's planned conquests in the East; so, unlike the "extremists," they wanted to head eastwards immediately rather than knock out the Western powers first.

Chamberlain was already pursuing a policy of personal contacts with "moderate" German Nazi leaders. Oliver Harvey's diary entry of 2 January 1939 was filled with outrage that "mountebank Montagu Norman," the governor of the Bank of England, was about to pursue talks with Reichsbank leaders without reference to the Foreign Office. Halifax was not consulted about the planned visit. Harvey, reflecting the Foreign Office view that Chamberlain and his closest supporters exposed Britain's weaknesses to Germany by their grovelling attitude, commented:

> Such a visit can only do harm – by encouraging the pro-German proclivities of the City, by making American and foreign opinion think we are doing another deal with Germany behind their backs – another example of the P.M.'s pro-nazi tendencies – and finally in Germany itself where it will be regarded as proof of our anxiety to run after Hitler.[40]

Cadogan wrote to Norman, asking that he be non-committal in his discussions with the German bankers. Norman responded violently, revealing in the process that he had discussed his plans closely with Chamberlain and Sir Horace Wilson. "We thus see a further use of P.M.'s policy of working behind his Foreign Secretary's back and keeping a side-line out to the dictators."[41] But the precise nature of the talks among Chamberlain, Wilson and Norman are unknown.

[39] *DBFP*, Series 3, Vol. 3, Doc. 515, pp. 561-564, 3 January 1939.
[40] *The Diplomatic Diaries of Oliver Harvey*, pp. 234-235.
[41] *Ibid.*, 4 January 1939, p, 235.

Herbert von Dirksen, the German ambassador in London, was satisfied that elite opinion in Britain, as reflected particularly in press coverage, supported Chamberlain's agreement to give Germany a free hand in central and eastern Europe. Dirksen reported to his Ministry on 4 January 1939 about British newspaper opinion regarding Germany's likely efforts to detach the Ukrainian-speaking territories from Soviet and Polish control.[42] Dirksen wrote that the British press took as a given that Germany remained expansion-minded and that it sought the formation of a "Greater Ukrainian State." Such reports predicted that the time would soon arrive when Germany demanded Danzig and the Polish-controlled Ukrainian territories. "In doing so, she will use the demand for 'the right of self-determination' with the same success as against Czechoslovakia." Reports on German intrigues in "Carpatho Ukraine" (also known as Ruthenia), and its support of Ukrainian nationalist groups in Poland and Soviet Ukraine also appeared.

Dirksen was encouraged by the tone of these reports. Before the Munich agreement itself was signed, he noted, the British press had taken a hostile stance towards Germany. "Whereas in the latter question the British press from the start took the view that Britain could not disinterest herself in the fate of Czechoslovakia, such statements with respect to Poland and the Soviet Union are now entirely lacking."[43]

While cautious in his predictions about British reactions to German moves on Polish or Soviet territory, Dirksen believed that "authoritative circles," following Chamberlain, would "accept a German expansionist policy in eastern Europe." Like Chamberlain, Dirksen believed that Western European public opinion generally was most likely to accept this policy if Germany was not too precipitous and bullying.

[42] *DGFP*, Series D, Vol. 4, Doc. 287, pp. 364-367.
[43] Though Dirksen did not comment upon it, the changed attitude of the press had much to do with the change in France's attitude to its various alliances. Before Munich France had made it appear that it would defend Czechoslovakia from German aggression because it had a mutual defence pact with that country. If the French went to war with Germany, it was feared that Britain would join the war on France's side in conformity with the Anglo-French treaty for mutual defence. Having abandoned Czechoslovakia, France was now distancing itself from its remaining defence pacts. So there was little fear that French moral scruples would force Britain into a war with Germany over Poland or the Ukraine.

> If, on the other hand, a Ukrainian state were to come
> into being with German help, even if this were of a
> military nature, under the psychologically skilful
> slogan freely circulated by Germany:
> "Self-determination for the Ukrainians, liberation of
> the Ukraine from the domination of Bolshevist
> Jewry," this would be accepted by authoritative
> circles here and by British public opinion, especially
> if consideration for British economic interests in the
> development of the new state were an added
> inducement for the British.

The view that a German move against Ukraine was imminent
became general among the appeasers in early January 1939.
They saw signs of it in unrelated events. So, for example, French
Chargé d'Affaires, M. de Montbas, wrote improbably to Bonnet
on 5 January that Germany's plans to force Czechoslovakia into
a monetary and customs union were a first stage of a takeover of
Ukrainian territories.[44] Chamberlain, holding conversations with
French leaders on 10 January before going to Italy, wondered
whether sudden Italian intransigence in dealings with France
was related to the impending attack on Ukraine. Bonnet
responded that the Italian attitude may have been a ruse by
Germany's closest ally to keep France busy in the Mediterranean
and unable to intervene in Ukraine if she had any inclination to
do so – as we have seen, she had no such inclination.[45]

Not everyone was sanguine about the impact of a German
takeover of Ukraine. The British Air Attaché, Wing Commander
Douglas Colyer, reported to Halifax on 12 January the opinion
of the French Head of the Second Bureau of the Air Army,
Lieutenant Colonel de Vitrolles. The Second Bureau was the
French military intelligence service. De Vitrolles believed that
France and Britain should take a strong position against German
acquisition of the various Ukrainian territories. As Colyer
summed up de Vitrolle's attitude: "If we let Germany get away
with the Ukraine it would be too late for us to do anything, but
wait our turn for execution."[46]

Such a report had little impact on Halifax whose view that only
a German attack on the West need be taken seriously by Britain

---

[44] Frederick L. Schuman, *Night Over Europe*, pp. 55-77.
[45] David Dilks, *The Diaries of Sir Alexander Cadogan, O.M.,
1938-1945*.(London: Cassell, 1971), p. 135
[46] *DBFP*, Series 3, Vol. 3, Doc. 536 and enclosure, pp. 583-5.

was fixed. But the number of reports warning of a German assault on the West now reaching Halifax was alarming. On 17 January, Strang wrote a report from reliable sources concerning conversations between Hitler and the Polish leader, Colonel Beck, at Berchtesgaden.[47] After saying that it is likely that Beck had made some agreements with Hitler, Strang wrote:

> This story would also fit in with reports we have had of Hitler's intention to attack in the West this spring, and the signs that Germany intends to pick a quarrel with Holland point in the same direction. Germany cannot conduct a war on two fronts in present circumstances, and material conditions will make it easier for her to operate in the West than in the East. Furthermore, it is easier for Germany to secure her rear in the East during an operation in the West than to secure her rear in the West during an operation in the East. The attraction of Hungary and perhaps other States into the anti-Comintern pact, and the attraction of Poland into the German orbit by promises in the colonial sphere, would give Germany an assurance of at least benevolent neutrality along her Eastern frontier.

Ironically, given Chamberlain's sycophantic attitude to Hitler and Nazism, Strang suggested that Britain had to confront the possibility that Hitler had added an anti-British obsession to his obsession with Jews and Communists. Munich, where Britain demonstrated that it would not interfere with Hitler's plans, could have the "ironic" result of making Hitler see Britain as his worst enemy and promote "the determination to finish with her."

It was not Munich as such that promoted such anti-British feelings in Berlin. Rather it was the sense that Chamberlain and the British elite generally were unreliable allies because in a democracy they could be overthrown and replaced with politicians sympathetic to the victims of Nazism. Hitler's fears expressed in November 1938 were not vanquished by Chamberlain's rather silly efforts to present himself as an equivalent to a British Führer. German newspapers, which, under Hitler, were *de facto* organs of the state, often voiced the same suspicions as Hitler. In late October 1938, the *Frankfurter Zeitung*, for example, gave dictatorship's objection to an agreement with a democracy. It railed against the British

[47] *DBFP*, Series 3, Vol. 3, Doc. 541, p. 590.

government because it could not stop Winston Churchill or Lloyd George (the latter a late convert to opposition to Nazism) from making "provocative" radio speeches. Nor could it prevent a Churchill replacing a Chamberlain in office in Britain or a Mandel replacing Daladier in France.[48]

The German Embassy in London sent conflicting reports home about Chamberlain's ability to keep public opinion with him. Dirksen, as noted, had warned that Germany had to act slowly and subtly so as not to arouse anti-Nazi feelings in Britain that had been especially evident in the weeks before Munich. Hitler's impatience to expand his Reich however rendered such advice futile.

Halifax regarded the situation as critical enough to inform the Americans on 24 January of Britain's concerns. His message to Mallet in Washington for the American President reflected British hypocrisy on the issue of German aggression – that it was all right if limited to the East and criminal if it was directed to the West.[49] There had been indications, he wrote, in November, that Hitler was planning further campaigns in the East. But, of course, Halifax had not thought it necessary to inform the Americans of his knowledge of such plans at the time. By December the prospect of "establishing an independent Ukraine under German vassalage was freely spoken of in Germany." Again however Halifax had chosen not to inform the Americans. Now however there were reports that Hitler, encouraged by the "extremists" who rejected the view of "moderates" that only the East was a target, was planning to attack the West. Some of this information came from Germans "anxious to prevent this crime;" some from foreigners with access to the top German leadership. Beck, noted Halifax, had received recent assurances from Hitler that Germany would not attack Poland.

Halifax explained to President Roosevelt that the period of danger would start at the end of February. Informing the president that Chamberlain might issue a warning to Germany in his speech on 28 January, he suggested that a prior public declaration by the president would be helpful. President Roosevelt obliged.

[48] Telford Taylor, *Europe on the Eve*, (Garden City, New York: Doubleday, 1979), p. 470.
[49] *DBFP*, Series 3, Vol. 4, Doc. 5, pp. 4-6.

At the Cabinet meeting on 25 January 1939, Halifax updated the members on this distressing news. Chamberlain was only partly convinced though he conceded that "we might be dealing with a man whose actions were not rational."[50] He agreed that Britain would have to intervene if Germany attacked Holland. But he hesitated before the suggestion that he make an immediate declaration to that effect because that would make the commitment binding! Later he qualified Britain's commitment with the caveat that Britain would intervene only if Holland resisted a German assault. It did not appear to occur to him that Britain's willingness to intervene or lack thereof might determine the Dutch attitude to the usefulness of resistance.

Chamberlain even seemed uncharitable in discussing a possible attack on France. While Britain only faced the possibility of attack by Germany, France could be attacked from several quarters, he complained. But Chamberlain was unclear whether this meant that he only believed Britain had a duty to come to France's assistance if it was attacked by Germany.

Chamberlain recognized that Britain would have to increase its defence expenditures to meet the new situation. But he continued to disbelieve that Hitler could have turned against him and therefore resisted the large-scale increases in expenditures that some of his ministers deemed necessary. So, for example, at the Cabinet meeting of 2 February, the Cabinet considered the defence of Belgium. Sir Leslie Hore-Belisha, Minister of War, reminded the Cabinet that it had not previously been his role to equip the army for a continental role. Now however he "proposed to equip four divisions of the Regular army and two mobile divisions on the Continental scale and similarly to equip the Territorial divisions."[51] Chamberlain balked at the bill for this proposal: 81 million pounds. He also continued to oppose a declaration that Britain would come to the aid of the Low Countries if they were attacked. His focus was exclusively on the defence of Britain because he still believed that his deal with Hitler could be glued back together.

Chamberlain's warning speech to Germany re-emphasized the spirit of Munich.[52] Rejecting the view of opponents who

[50] Ian Colvin, *The Chamberlain Cabinet* (London: Victor Gollancz, 1971), pp. 179-182.
[51] Ian Colvin, *The Chamberlain Cabinet*, p. 183.

denounced Munich as a sellout that had led to increased German irresponsibility, Chamberlain hid behind the aura attached to his office. He claimed that his critics did not know the full circumstances that he alone knew when Munich was signed. In retrospect we know that this argument was hollow. His speech avoided dealing with such delicate issues as whether the military balance between the democracies and Hitler had changed since Munich and if so, in whose favour. He also avoided the issue of why he continued to oppose an alliance with the Soviet Union against Hitler when this country alone among the eastern powers had the ability to make it difficult for Hitler to carry on successfully a war on both eastern and western fronts.

Chamberlain's warning to Hitler was that Britain's military power was impressive and growing more so all the time. He stressed naval construction, aircraft production, anti-aircraft defences, and the construction of shelters. He also mentioned plans for evacuation of the population, beginning with children. Chamberlain did not say a single word on bombers. The defensive capabilities of Britain were singled out to the exclusion of offensive capabilities even though bombers, for example, could have been considered a strong deterrent. Echoing Franklin Roosevelt, the British prime minister claimed that he would not stand idly by as demands were made "to dominate the world by force." But he added: "I cannot believe that any such challenge is intended." Then he noted that "differences" among nations could be settled peacefully as they were at Munich.

The wording of the Chamberlain speech was carefully crafted to send Germany a particular message. That message could easily be decoded as follows: 'There are rumours that you intend to move to the West. This would be a direct challenge to our sphere of influence and I will not stand for it. Personally, I do not believe the rumours are true. I am therefore prepared to offer you the same services that proved of such use to you at Munich. You can feel safe concerning your Western boundaries. As proof of our peaceful intentions, we do not put any stress on bombers, we do not intend to create a Ministry of Supplies, and we do not intend to bring Churchill into the Cabinet.'

[52] Neville Chamberlain, *In Search of Peace* (New York: Putnam's Sons, 1939), pp. 249-57.

Hitler, in turn, tried to put Chamberlain's mind at ease regarding German intentions. On 30 January he made a speech that underlined Germany's desire for peaceful relations with Britain. He reiterated his position that Germany had no designs on any part of the British Empire and that it wanted only cooperation and peace with Britain and France.[53] He then gave one of his bully warnings to the West: "In the future, we shall not tolerate the Western Powers attempting to interfere in certain matters which concern nobody except ourselves in order to hinder natural and reasonable solutions by their intervention."

Chamberlain responded positively to the speech, believing it showed Hitler was trying to avoid "another crisis."[54] What he could not say publicly was that having conceded central and eastern Europe to Germany, he did not feel threatened by oblique threats to the West not to intervene when Germany made moves in central and eastern Europe. Next day, Dirksen could report to Germany that "the Fuhrer's speech had laid the foundation for the contemplated exchange of visits between the two Ministers of Economics and for a further active development of economic questions between Germany and Great Britain."[55]

The British government's continued willingness to grant Hitler a free hand in central and eastern Europe was demonstrated by events in February. On 7 February Halifax informed the American government that the British government would consider a German attack against either Holland or Switzerland as an attempt to dominate the world.[56] Interestingly, at that date, neither an attack against Czechoslovakia or Poland was to be seen in that light. Such attacks presumably were to be judged "normal and natural," to use Halifax's previously-quoted words.

On 18 February Nevile Henderson wrote Chamberlain about a meeting he had had with Field-Marshal Goering that morning. "What guarantee had Germany that Mr. Chamberlain would remain in office and that he would not be succeeded by 'a Mr. Churchill or a Mr. Eden' government?" he had asked Henderson.[57] This repeated Hitler's concern the previous autumn that democracies were unreliable partners for the Reich.

---

[53] *DGFP*, Series D, Vol. 4, Doc. 305, Note 1, p. 397.
[54] *Ibid.*, p. 430.
[55] *DGFP*, Series D, Vol. 4, Doc. 305, p. 397.
[56] *DBFP*, Series 3, Vol. 4, Doc. 87, p. 83.

Yet Chamberlain now believed that he had received the gesture of friendship from Hitler which he had claimed he lacked the previous November. Or so he wrote Henderson on 19 February. He seemed to be clutching at straws. The Duke of Cobourg, a minor German subaltern, had spoken to a society for Anglo-German Friendship and had used a sentence from a Hitler speech that emphasized the need for close relations between the two countries.[58] It was enough however to convince Chamberlain that the deal he had struck with Hitler at Godesberg and reconfirmed at Munich was still in effect. Despite the continuing warnings about German preparations for an attack on the West, he wrote Henderson:

> Things look as though Spain might clear up fairly soon. After that the next thing will be to get the bridge between Paris and Rome in working order. After that we might begin to talk about disarmament...If all went well we should have so improved the atmosphere that we might begin to think of colonial discussions. But people get so frightened and 'het up' about them that we should have to approach the subject with the greatest care.

The triumph of fascism in Spain unsurprisingly did not trouble Chamberlain, who, like most of the British elite, supported Franco over Spain's democratic forces. Chamberlain seemed to have moved little on issues involving Germany, including the idea of finding colonial possessions for ultra-racist Germany.

Chamberlain's optimism paralleled Henderson's. Henderson had returned to Berlin on 13 February after a four-month absence and was soon convinced that Germany wanted "peace," which in the Chamberlain-Henderson lexicon translated into: 'Hitler wants war only in the East.' There was greater scepticism in the Foreign Office but Cadogan believed the doomsayers were even less realistic than Henderson. Henderson, he believed, was "bewitched" by the Nazis. Vansittart, by contrast, "out-Cassandras Cassandra in a kind of spirit of pantomime." Of the two however, he thought Vansittart likely the "sillier" party.[59]

---

[57] *DBFP*, Series 3, Vol. 4, Doc. 118, p. 121.
[58] *DBFP*, Series 3, Vol. 4, p. 591.
[59] *The Diaries of Sir Alexander Cadogan*, p. 151.

By the end of February the Foreign Office was receiving disturbing reports pointing to German military preparations for the occupation of the rump Czechoslovak state.[60] Halifax was alarmed and communicated these reports to Washington. Chamberlain was not alarmed. He believed that Germany was demonstrating again that its expansionist interests lay solely in the East, as agreed upon at Godesberg. Sir Henry (Chips) Channon reported in his diary on 7 March the upbeat mood of the prime minister as they dined at an exclusive club. "He thinks the Russian danger receding, and the danger of a German War less everyday, as our rearmament expands."[61] There was no Russian military danger to Britain. What Chamberlain meant was that he thought Germany was on schedule for its assault on Ukraine, less likely than ever to be impeded by the Soviet government. As Britain improved its defences, it became an improbable target for German attack, making it likely that the policy debate among the Nazis would be won by the "moderates" who wanted to attack eastwards rather than to the west.

On 9 March Henderson wrote to Halifax recommending that Germany be given not only a free hand in the East but economic aid.[62] The *quid pro quo* would be German concessions in disarmament. Disarmament however would not mean abandoning its expansionist aims in eastern Europe. Instead, getting German cooperation for disarmament meant "acquiescing to a certain extent in Germany's aims in Central and South-Eastern Europe." Disarmament and peace, for Henderson, as for the British elite generally, continued to mean only peaceful relations in western Europe. It did not strike this admirer of Hitler[63] as unethical to provide economic assistance to a nation he believed was preparing for military assaults against other countries. His letter made clear that a German war with the Soviets was inevitable and that war with Poland, while hopefully avoidable, might also occur. It was "inevitable" that Germany would regain Memel and Danzig "on the basis of self-determination to the Reich," though "the most that we can hope for" is that it will occur peacefully. There was little chance, by contrast, that Germany could avoid a war with the

---

[60] *The Diaries of Sir Alexander Cadogan*, p. 153.
[61] Robert Rhodes James, ed., *Chips: The Diaries of Sir Henry Channon* (London: Weidenfeld and Nicolson, 1967), p. 185.
[62] *DBFP*, Series 3, Vol. 4, Doc. 195, pp. 210-216.
[63] In the letter, Henderson wrote: "I have little faith in the gratitude of nations, though I believe that Hitler is not lacking in that rare quality."

Soviets. Sounding like an agent for the German government rather than his own, Henderson argued:

> Hitler made it very clear in *Mein Kampf* that *Lebensraum* for Germany could be found in expansion eastward, and expansion eastward renders a clash between Germany and Russia some day or other highly probable. With a benevolent Britain on her flank, Germany can envisage such an eventuality with comparative equanimity. But she lives in dread of the reverse and of the war on two fronts.
>
> The best approach to good relations with Germany is therefore of avoidance of constant and vexatious interference in matters in which British interests are not directly or vitally involved and the prospect of British neutrality in the event of Germany being engaged in the east.
>
> ...The *Drang nach Osten* is a reality, and the *Drang nach Westen* will only become so if Germany finds all the venues to the east blocked or if western opposition is such as to convince Hitler that he cannot go eastward without first having rendered it innocuous.

While such a slavish acquiescence to German demands may sound extreme, it was simply a more candid admission of the British government's approach than contained in some of the documents we have discussed above. In plain English it argues for the deal that Chamberlain arranged in his September 1938 meetings with Hitler. Hitler could have a free hand in central and eastern Europe and feel free to try to 'disrupt' the Soviet menace. Henderson's main concern was that Hitler not feel that the West would take advantage of his Eastern adventures to lead an assault on Germany. So his advice was that Britain should do nothing that might cause German leaders to believe that the free hand offered before and during Munich was now being withdrawn.

That same day William Bullitt, the American Ambassador to Paris, reported to the Secretary of State on his luncheon conversation with Premier Daladier and the Polish Ambassador in Paris. The Polish Ambassador made an accusation against France and Britain for which Henderson's memo, if known to him, would have been one more piece of evidence.[64] Since

Munich, he noted, neither Britain nor France had resisted the German advance in central and eastern Europe. Indeed they were "anxious to have Germany turn her hostile intentions towards Russia." Instead, it was Poland, Hungary and Roumania, who feared the impact of German domination, who were left to fend alone against the Nazis. Daladier did not dispute the accusation. He knew it was utterly correct.

***

The traditional historical view is that Britain and France regarded the invasion of the rump Czechoslovak state on 15 March 1939 as a new departure because unlike the takeover of Austria and the Sudeten, the area in question was not German-speaking. No longer could the argument that Hitler was mysteriously supporting self-determination for Germans and nothing more be defended. As we have seen however, the British and French leaders looked with equanimity on Hitler's creation of a Ukrainian puppet state. They also had accepted in the weeks and months following Munich and indeed, in the case of the Chamberlainites, long before, that central and eastern Europe would fall vassal to Nazi Germany. It therefore seems implausible that the takeover of the remnants of Czechoslovakia could in itself have caused a dramatic change in Anglo-French relations with Germany.

Indeed in the weeks preceding the takeover of Czechoslovakia the British and French leaders were aware that it was impending and felt no need for a change in Britain's or France's foreign policy.[65] As noted earlier, Halifax had received word of Germany's intentions at the end of February. But no blunt British warnings were delivered to Germany to suggest that an invasion of Czechoslovakia would be unacceptable to Britain. Chamberlain was in an ebullient mood about Anglo-German relations on 7 March, according to "Chips" Channon. On 8 March the United States government obtained the minutes of a German government meeting held that day during which Hitler announced the expected occupation of Czechoslovakia on 15 March.[66] There are indications that Britain received the same

---

[64] *FRUS*, Foreign Relations, 1939, Vol. 1, pp. 29-31.
[65] Sydney Aster, *The Making of the Second World War* (New York: Simon and Shuster, 1973), p.21; Donald Cameron Watt, *How War Came* (London: Heinemann,1989), p. 164.
[66] *FRUS*, Diplomatic Papers, 1939, Vol. 1, pp. 672-673, as reproduced in part

information. During discussions about the invasion in the British House of Commons on 20 March, the opposition presented evidence that knowledge of the impending invasion was widespread in government circles in both Britain and France in the weeks leading to the aggression. Rab Butler, the government's spokesman against the charges, avoided the specific evidence as he attempted unconvincingly to protest his government's innocence.[67]

Yet, on March 9, Chamberlain, having read Henderson's communication with Halifax, gave an optimistic report at a press conference. He predicted that French-Italian relations would soon improve and indicated his high expectations of a forthcoming visit to Germany by Oliver Stanley, President of the Board of Trade. Next day, on Chamberlain's advice, Samuel Hoare gave an address in which he cheerfully anticipated an era of cooperation in Europe.[68]

On 11 March Cadogan noted in his diary that Major General Sir Vernon Kell, head of M.I. 5, "came to raise my hair with tales of Germany going into Czechoslovakia in next 48 hours." In turn, Cadogan told Halifax and Chamberlain of this warning.[69] The message to Cadogan from M.I. 5 was clear and unequivocal. "The German Army will invade Bohemia and Moravia at six a.m. on March 15." Yet, Chamberlain, after speaking to Cadogan, neither called a Cabinet meeting nor a meeting with his service chiefs.[70]

Despite his knowledge of the impending invasion, Chamberlain was evasive when Clement Attlee, the Labour party leader, questioned him in the House about the government's willingness to stand by its guarantee to Czechoslovakia. "I might add that the proposed guarantee is one against unprovoked aggressions on Czechoslovakia," said the prime minister, downgrading any presumption of an existing guarantee to a proposal.[71] "No such

in *Soviet Peace Efforts on the Eve of World War* 11, (Moscow: Progress Publishers, 1976), Doc. 97, pp. 183-184.
[67] *Parliamentary Debates, House of Commons*, 28 March 1939.
[68] Telford Taylor, *Munich: The Price of Peace*, p. 256.
[69] *The Diaries of Sir Alexander Cadogan*, p. 155.
[70] Leonard Mosley, *On Borrowed Time*, (New York: Random House, 1969), p. 151.
[71] As we have seen, the only guarantee Britain was willing to give to Czechoslovakia was one in which Germany and Italy, but not the Soviet Union, participated alongside Britain and France. Since three parties of the four would have to agree to punish a violator of Czech independence, the guarantee would

aggression has yet taken place," he swiftly added. The government, following Henderson's advice, did not wish to talk tough and appear to be thwarting Hitler; rather it stuck its head in the sand, ignoring its own certain knowledge that the assault on the remnants of Czechoslovakia would occur the next day.

On 14 March, Halifax did send Henderson a mildly-worded message to be conveyed to the German government.[72] "His Majesty's Government have no desire to interfere unnecessarily in matters with which other Governments may be more directly concerned than this country," wrote Halifax. Yet the British government hoped that Germany would not take actions that would impair the efforts the two countries were taking to improve their economic relations. Halifax would not defend Czechoslovakia's right to exist but instead preferred to caution that Germany behave prudently in its handling of the Czech situation so that the general atmosphere of confidence existing between Britain and Germany would not be impaired.

Henderson went perhaps even lower than Halifax in a discussion that day with the German State Secretary. He attempted to impress upon him "the extreme importance of the form in which Germany handled the situation" and hoped nothing would be done that might prevent Oliver Stanley's visit to Germany.[73] While the fate of a nation weighed in the balance, Henderson could think only of "form" and of economic talks between Britain and Germany.

The U.S. Chargé d'Affaires in Germany wrote Cordell Hull that same day of British indifference to the fate of Czechoslovakia:

> The British Counsellor, who returned from London today, states that the British Foreign Office, is inclined to regard any move by the Germans in Czechoslovakia with calmness and will advise the British Government against assuming a threatening attitude when in fact it contemplates doing nothing. He stated in short that "the British Government were reconciled to a possible extreme German action in Czechoslovakia."[74]

be useless. At the time of the invasion, the guarantee had not been issued, though Czechoslovakia had a right to believe, on the basis of promises from Britain and France before and after Munich, that these two countries would protect the independence of her post-Munich territories.

[72] *DBFP*, Series 3, Vol. 4, Doc. 247, p. 250.
[73] *DBFP*, Series 3, Vol. 4, Doc. 248, p. 250.

One day before the invasion of Czechoslovakia, then, the British were unwilling to react to an invasion. Indeed that day Halifax discussed with his entourage what Britain was prepared to fight for and what it was not willing to fight for. Oliver Harvey wrote in his diary:

> ...Slovakia declared herself independent with German support...reports that Germany is appointing two *Staathalters* for Prague and Bratislava, and troops move in tonight.

> We had a meeting in H's room to discuss the position. It was agreed that we must make no empty threats since we were not going to fight for Czechoslovakia any more than for Danzig, although we would fight for Switzerland, Belgium, Holland, or Tunis.

Revealingly, two weeks before the British unilateral guarantee, there was no intention to defend Poland against Germany. Britain would risk war over France's overseas colonies such as Tunisia but not over eastern Europe.

Chips Channon's reaction first to the impending invasion and then the invasion itself demonstrates the thinking of the Chamberlainites as Hitler proceeded to act in bad "form," that is using an invasion rather than threats to take control of Czechoslovakia. In his diary on 14 March, Channon wrote much what he had written after Kristallnacht: "It looks as if he [Hitler] is going to break the Munich agreement, and throw Chamberlain over...Hitler is never helpful."[75] Next day, with the invasion having taken place, he wrote that Hitler's "callous desertion of the PM is stupefying." From this Cabinet minister's point of view, Hitler and Chamberlain were part of the same brotherhood and Hitler had betrayed a brother.

The prime minister, in any case, responded blandly to the actual invasion. Cabinet met on 15 March after the invasion had been announced and Chamberlain defended the German government and stressed that the British guarantee could not apply under the circumstances. "Our guarantee was not a guarantee against moral pressure," he said irrelevantly with reference to the

[74] *FRUS*, Foreign Relations, 1939, Vol. 1, p. 38.
[75] *Chips*, p. 185.

unprovoked German attack, according to Cabinet minutes. "German actions had all been taken under the guise of agreement with the Czechoslovak Government. The Germans were therefore in a position to give plausible answers."[76] A "guise" that everyone knew was fraudulent would be the thin reed the British government would hang on to in order not to live up to its responsibilities towards the Czechs.

Chamberlain's address to the House of Commons that day repeated the German version of events leading to the invasion. He also made use of a laughable technicality to claim that the British guarantee to Czechoslovakia was null and void. With German encouragement, the Slovak Diet had declared the independence of Slovakia. That meant that the nation whose borders Britain had sworn to defend from foreign aggression no longer existed thanks to "internal disruption."[77] This left unclear why Britain accepted a declaration of independence occurring under circumstances of external intervention. But, more to the point, it took the immoral view that foreign aggressors did have the right to seize the Czech lands if Slovakia separated from the Czechoslovak state. Though he had precise knowledge of events leading to Germany's invasion of Czechoslovakia, Chamberlain claimed that there were so many charges of breach of faith on both sides of the German-Czech divide that he did not wish to take sides. He noted, without comment, that the Czechoslovak president had signed a document calling for German "protection" for the country. While in Cabinet he had admitted that German-Czech agreement was only a "guise," in the House he pretended that Germany's naked aggression was little more than an overly-enthusiastic implementation of an amicable agreement between two countries.

Overall, Chamberlain's message was that British foreign policy regarding Germany would not change. Oliver Stanley's visit to Berlin would be postponed but otherwise nothing essential was to change. The spirit of Munich had been offended[78] but must be

---

[76] Ian Colvin, *The Chamberlain Cabinet*, p. 186.

[77] Great Britain, House of Commons, *Parliamentary Debates*, Vol. 45, cols. 435-440.

[78] Halifax suggested to Chamberlain that he mention that the invasion was not in the spirit of Munich. Chamberlain agreed to do so but minimized the German aggression by saying that he "thought that the military occupation was symbolic, more than perhaps appeared on the surface." Sydney Aster, *The Making of the Second World War*, pp. 29-30.

recreated. Using his language of appeasement, he lectured the House:

> It is natural, therefore that I should bitterly regret what has now occurred. But do not let us on that account be deflected from our course. Let us remember that the desire of all the peoples of the world still remain concentrated on the hopes of peace and a return to the atmosphere of understanding and good will which has so often been disturbed. The aim of this Government is now, as it has always been, to promote that desire and to substitute the method of discussion for the method of force in the settlement of differences. Though we may have to suffer checks and disappointments, from time to time, the object that we have in mind is of too great significance to the happiness of mankind for us lightly to give it up or set it to one side.

Taken at face value, this speech shows Chamberlain to be a foggy-brained pacifist unaware of the significance of Germany's final destruction of the Czechoslovak state. The speech however is insincere. As we have seen, "our course" was not one of "peace" for "all the peoples of the world" but simply for the people of western Europe. Chamberlain had given Hitler a free hand in the territories east of Germany and looked anxiously forward to a war between Hitler and the Soviets over Ukraine. "The object that we have in mind" was not peace but the destruction of the Communist state and consequent social stability in Europe where radical movements were perceived by conservatives as emanating from Soviet agitation rather than local conditions.

If Czechoslovakia had to disappear for this goal to be obtained, that was a tragedy that could not be avoided. John Simon, defending Nevile Henderson against charges that he had not warned the government about Hitler's planned aggression, demonstrated the moral bankruptcy of British policy. Quoting the German propaganda chief, Joseph Goebbels, he noted that the central tragedy was: "The State of Czechoslovakia has ceased to exist." Nothing could be done to alter this and therefore the guarantee ceased to exist.[79] The guarantee, in other words, was only valid if an assault on Czechoslovakia was unsuccessful.

[79] *Ibid.*

Privately, Halifax went further. Still on 15 March, he wrote to Phipps to brief him on a conversation he had with the French Ambassador. He wrote:

> The ambassador then proceeded to make some obvious comments upon the recent action of the German Government, with which I concurred, adding that the one compensating advantage that I saw was that it had brought to a natural end the somewhat embarrassing commitment of a guarantee in which we and the French had both been involved.[80]

The callousness of Chamberlain and Halifax in the face of Hitler's destruction of Czechoslovakia was fairly typical of the reaction of members of their social class. Charles Ritchie, one of Canada's most distinguished diplomats, was part of the diplomatic corps in the Office of the High Commissioner for Canada in London at this time. He travelled in elite circles and his diary entry for March 15, 1939 spoke volumes about the willingness of the British elite to maintain the Chamberlain agreement with Hitler with its implicit granting of a free hand to Hitler.

> Posters in the streets announce German troops enter Prague. My neighbour said at lunch, 'It may seem cynical but I really cannot get excited over this. I do dislike all this sentimentality about the Czechs – as long as the Germans are going towards the east...' This seems to be the general view among the 'people one meets at dinner.'[81]

Next day Liberal leader Archibald Sinclair asked Chamberlain in the House whether his government would lodge a protest against the invasion. Chamberlain replied that he could not answer the question without notice. Asked by another member whether his government would warn the German government not to harm the Czech leaders, Chamberlain responded: "I think it wrong to assume that the German Government have any such intention."[82] It was a strange answer given the Nazis' record of

---

[80] *DBFP*, Series 3, Vol. 4, Doc. 280, p. 273.
[81] Charles Ritchie, *The Siren Years: A Canadian Diplomat Abroad, 1937-1945* (Toronto: Macmillan, 1977), p. 31.
[82] Great Britain, House of Commons, *Parliamentary Debates*, Vol. 345, Col. 613.

ruthless repression of their opponents. Yet, one day later, Chamberlain's attitude had hardened considerably. Why?

***

On 17 March 1939 the government became aware that Hitler had decided to give Ruthenia to Hungary. This was a shock to the government. As we have seen, for some time, government leaders had assumed that Hitler's next move was into Soviet Ukraine. The Czech-controlled Ruthenia, a province largely consisting of Ukrainians, was seen as strategically necessary for Germany's plans in this regard. After Hitler had denied Hungary's request for control of Ruthenia in the wake of Munich and left it as part of Czechoslovakia, it was assumed that Hitler wanted Ruthenia for his Eastern campaign. For that reason Poland, fearful of Hitler's intentions regarding Galicia, the dominantly Ukrainian-speaking territory under its control, had supported Hungary's request to Germany for Ruthenia.

Now however Hitler was abandoning Ruthenia. For the British and French governments, that was alarming. Did it mean that the Nazis were temporarily abandoning their expansion eastwards to turn against the West? Indeed the significance of a German disinterest in Ruthenia was universally understood. In a memo written on 27 July 1939, Schnurre of the German Foreign Office in Berlin recorded a conversation he had with the Soviet Chargé d'Affaires, Astrakhov. Trying to calm Soviet fears of hostile German objectives, Schnurre pointed out that "the solution of the Carpatho-Ukrainian[83] question had shown that here we did not aim at anything there that would endanger Soviet interests."[84]

Chamberlain did not know what German intentions were regarding Ruthenia until 17 March. Ruthenia had declared its independence on 14 March and established a provisional government. On 16 March he answered a question from Attlee in the House on the fate of Ruthenia by indicating that Hungary had demanded that the new Ruthenian government surrender control of the province to Hungarian forces.[85] The Foreign Office learned that day that Hungarian forces were occupying

---

[83] Carpatho-Ukraine is another name for Ruthenia.
[84] *DGFP*, Series D, Vol. 6, Doc. 729, p. 1008.
[85] Great Britain, House of Commons, *Parliamentary Debates*, Vol. 345, col. 613.

Ruthenia.[86] But the British government remained unaware of the German government's attitude to these events.

On March 17 at 19:30, Halifax received a telegram from the British ambassador to Budapest who informed him that the German ambassador had confirmed that Germany was uninterested in Ruthenia and prepared to let Hungary occupy the area.[87] Eighty minutes after receiving the news, Halifax sent Henderson a telegram with a message to be conveyed to the German government. The message was that the British government not only regarded the invasion of Czechoslovakia as a violation of the spirit of Munich but also that they considered the changes effected in Czechoslovakia "devoid of any basis of legality."[88]

Ironically, earlier that day, Henderson had approached Weizsacker, the German Secretary of State, for arguments that Chamberlain could use to quell British public opinion regarding German military action in Czechoslovakia.[89]

On the night of 17 March, Chamberlain, having learned just hours before about the Germans' changed position on Ruthenia, made a tough speech in Birmingham denouncing the German invasion of Czechoslovakia.[90] The tone was completely at odds with his statements in Parliament the two previous days.

Chamberlain's turnaround has been attributed to his need to make a dramatic gesture to public opinion in order to avoid being forced to resign. Harold Nicolson noted in his diary on 17 March that if Chamberlain did not reverse his policy, he would probably be forced out by government MPs and replaced by Halifax with Eden becoming Leader of the House.[91] Leonard Mosley writes that Chamberlain tore up the original speech he had prepared for Birmingham with Sir Horace Wilson after Wilson spoke to him shortly before he gave the speech. Mosley suggests that Wilson, with his spies in Parliament, informed the prime minister that a servile speech on the lines of his address to

[86] *DBFP*, Series 3, Vol.4, Doc. 286, p. 277.
[87] *DBFP*, Series 3, Vol. 4, Doc. 305, p. 290.
[88] *DBFP*, Series 3, Vol. 4, Doc. 308, p. 291.
[89] *DGFP*, Series D, Vol.6, Doc. 16, pp. 16-17.
[90] Keith Feiling, *The Life of Neville Chamberlain* (London: Macmillan 1946), p. 400.
[91] Harold Nicolson, *Diaries and Letters* 1930-1939 (New York: Athenaeum, 1968), p. 393.

Parliament two days earlier would cost him his job as prime minister.[92] But Chamberlain had faced such a challenge before Munich and had skilfully used scare tactics to bring the population and the politicians back on his side. He was committed almost fanatically to his deal with Hitler and the view that it could not be preserved if Britain appeared willing to frustrate Germany's efforts in the East.

It seems more probable that what Wilson told Chamberlain was that Germany had awarded Ruthenia to Hungary. The "Russian danger" – the danger that Germany would decide to do something other than attack the Soviet Union – had not receded, as Chamberlain had so confidently claimed ten days earlier. Hitler was not so clearly committed to moving eastwards first.

Halifax, who believed German control of eastern Europe was "normal and natural" and none of Britain's business, clearly believed that something had changed on 17 March 1939, the night Britain learned of Germany's grant of Ruthenia to Hungary. He summed up his views in a candid letter that day to Sir Ronald Lindsay, the British Ambassador to the United States. The letter described two views of how Britain ought to approach foreign policy. On the one hand was the approach of collective security which took the position that all peaceful nations should intervene to prevent violations of treaties. The other was the approach of avoiding commitments unless Britain was itself threatened with attack. In Halifax's summation, the proponents of both sides were motivated purely by their notions of British self-interest rather than any larger commitment to a common good. Those who resisted collective security generally believed Britain faced no direct threat from Germany; their opponents believed that it did. "I had little doubt that recent events would have the result of leading many people to examine afresh the latter method of seeking to gain security," wrote Halifax with reference to collective security.[93]

In other words, Halifax, until recently an opponent of collective security, believed that Britain was now under threat of German attack. He did not say why he had come to this conclusion. But the coincidence of the Ruthenia decision provides a strong hint about the reasons for his shifting views.

---

[92] Leonard Mosley, *On Borrowed Time*, pp. 180-1.
[93] *DBFP*, Series 3, Vol. 4, Doc. 394, pp. 364-366.

Of course, one cannot dismiss the importance of Chamberlain's need to calm outrage at his initial craven response to Nazi immorality in Czechoslovakia. Events over the next two weeks however indicated that Chamberlain had an agenda that went beyond calming parliamentarians and citizens enraged with the latest Nazi outrage. He was clearly worried about Hitler's intentions towards the West, though, at the same time, he wished, if possible, to resurrect his secret deal with Hitler. Chapter 8 examines the double game played by Chamberlain as he attempted vainly to recapture the "Munich spirit" with Hitler: Hitler could have what he wanted in the East and could "disrupt" the Soviets with the blessing of Britain and France. He must however leave the West alone. This time however Chamberlain recognized that Britain had to demonstrate to Hitler that it could react if he broke his part of the deal. As we shall see, to the bitter end, even after World War Two had erupted, Chamberlain sought the chimera of Berchtesgaden, Godesberg and Munich, never completely giving up the idea of a British alliance with the Nazi dictator to create an anti-Communist "peace" in Europe.

CHAPTER EIGHT
TRYING TO SAVE THE DEAL:
FROM THE GUARANTEE OF POLAND TO 1940

It is a fact that Britain and France declared war on Nazi Germany two days after the Germans invaded Poland on 1 September 1939. But this chapter argues that it is misleading to claim, as many historians do, that Britain and France went to war with Germany "over Poland." The truth is far more complicated. A year earlier the leaders of both Britain and France were prepared to allow Germany to do as it wished in central and eastern Europe. This would be a *quid pro quo* for leaving the West alone. In fact, even in September 1939 these countries were prepared to restore to Germany the "free hand" in these regions that they had offered at Munich. What then had changed?

The argument of this chapter is that Poland was used by Britain and France for their own ends. After Germany granted Ruthenia to Hungary, the Western leaders were persuaded by military intelligence reports suggesting that Hitler would attack the West before moving into eastern Europe. Neville Chamberlain, still desperately clinging to his secret deal with Hitler that gave the latter a "free hand" in the lands east of Germany, now accepted a double-barrelled strategy. On the one hand, appeasement would continue. But, on the other, it was necessary to improve the defences of Britain and France in case Hitler was prepared to attack their territory. This required time and an alliance with Poland that would make that country Hitler's likely first target would buy several months, it was believed. An alliance of Britain with Poland would warn Hitler that a single-front war with the West was impossible; he would have to be prepared to fight on two fronts at once should he attack the West and this Britain knew, from its security sources, Germany was largely unprepared to do. It therefore became important to Chamberlain to secure an alliance with Poland that would provide reciprocal guarantees against German attack. So Britain and France, which had not wanted to get entangled with Poland at all, found themselves providing that country with a unilateral guarantee against German aggression that included recognition of Poland's dubious claim to Danzig, a guarantee given in the expectation that Poland would make it reciprocal.

225

Danzig had been part of Prussia and then Germany from 1793 to 1919. Danzig was populated mainly by Germans but Poland's insistence on a seaport during the Versailles negotiations had resulted in Poland being given important authority over Danzig. Danzig became nominally a free city but Poles had equal weight with Danzigers in managing its waterways and harbour and Poland controlled its foreign policy. The League of Nations was mandated to protect the city's independence but its members showed little willingness for the task. Danzig's strategic importance as well as the chauvinism of the Polish leaders militated against their cession of the port city and the Corridor to Germany despite the close ties that the Polish leaders cultivated with Hitler from 1934 to early 1939.

The unilateral guarantee was the first stage towards winning what Britain and France really wanted: a reciprocal guarantee from Poland. Meantime, Chamberlain implemented secret discussions with the Germans meant to restore the "Anglo-German understanding" of Godesberg and Munich. The Germans were assured that if they returned to their original plans of subordinating eastern Europe and leaving the West alone, the Western powers would do nothing to save Poland or any other country within the recognized German sphere of influence. Ultimately, however, Hitler feared that the leaders of the democracies were too easily replaceable by firm anti-Nazis who he feared would take advantage of his eastern campaigns to attack Germany's western flank.

When Hitler attacked Poland on 1 September, no deal had been reached with the western countries. Britain and France declared war but then did nothing to help Poland. A "phoney war" between the Germans and the British-French alliance occurred for over seven months until the Nazis began a relentless assault on Western countries, leading to French capitulation in June 1940. This chapter argues that throughout the "phoney war" Chamberlain and his supporters continued through secret diplomacy to try to revive the Chamberlain-Hitler collusion of 1938, though increasingly they believed that Hitler was unstable and needed to be replaced. His alliance with the Soviet Union, made just before the invasion of Poland, was seen as apostasy, though some elements of the ruling elite continued to hold out hope that he could be made to see the light. He could have eastern Europe and attack the Soviets with Western blessings if he renounced his claims on Western territory. If however Hitler could not be persuaded to live up to his deal with the British, Chamberlain's government was prepared to negotiate with Nazis who would. Meetings were held with Nazis and military representatives willing to overthrow the unpredictable Hitler and replace him with Nazis and other authoritarian nationalists willing to accept a division of Europe in which Germany looked only eastwards for conquest.

***

Throughout the period from Hitler's accession to power through to the invasion of Czechoslovakia in March 1939, Neville Chamberlain had been committed to the view that the Nazis could be given a free hand in Eastern Europe but must not lay a hand on Western Europe. Yet at a Cabinet meeting on 8 February 1939 Chamberlain, not for the first time, resisted an open declaration that Britain would defend Holland if it was attacked by Germany. On 31 March 1939, by contrast, the Chamberlain government gave a unilateral guarantee to Poland to protect that country, including the disputed port of Danzig, against foreign aggression. Holland had not moved to Eastern Europe and Poland had never left the region. So what had changed?

Before 17 March 1939, as we have seen, Chamberlain remained committed to the Chamberlain-Hitler deal. He feared that an open declaration regarding Holland might be taken as an unfriendly gesture by Germany. By the end of March however he had reason to believe, particularly in the wake of the award of Ruthenia to Hungary, that Hitler was stabbing him in the back. He wanted to restore his deal with Hitler but once he gave his guarantee to Poland, he crossed the Rubicon. No longer could Hitler see the British leader as a collaborator. From the Nazi point of view, even without the government in Britain having changed, the policy that the Chamberlain-Hitler deal embodied had been abandoned by the British government. Chamberlain's various efforts to convince Hitler otherwise would not bear fruit.

The decision to provide a guarantee to Poland came gradually in the wake of the Ruthenia decision and of public disgust with Hitler's barbaric treatment of the Czechs. At a Cabinet meeting on 18 March, the Chamberlain-Hitler deal already seemed in tatters. The Cabinet, convinced of the danger of Hitler attacking the West before beginning further Eastern campaigns, decided that it was important strategically to force Hitler to fight on two fronts. This required one or more Eastern allies. So, while a few days earlier Chamberlain and his close associates regarded Central and Eastern Europe as Hitler's sphere of influence, military strategy now required that they make alliances with countries they had formerly decided it was "natural and normal" for Hitler to control.[1]

At the 18 March Cabinet meeting several ministers openly called for an alliance with the Soviets. Leslie Hore-Belisha, never one of the appeasers, wanted "frank and open alliances" with Poland and Russia as well as major steps to increase Britain's military strength. Walter Eliot argued it was "most important to get in touch with Russia." Chamberlain, by contrast, according to Cabinet minutes, "thought that Poland was very likely to be the key of the situation." But Chamberlain was unprepared just yet to discuss how an alliance with Poland would be effected. The two-fronts policy was crucial "if" Germany was intent on "world domination," that is, if Germany was not content with simply the free hand in Central and Eastern Europe.

A great deal of effort was expended in the weeks and months that followed in finding out whether "world domination" really was Germany's goal or whether Hitler was prepared to return to his more limited goal of a German sphere of influence enunciated in the wee hours at Godesberg and implicit in the Munich Agreement. The doubts were present not only in Chamberlain's comments in Cabinet on 18 March but also in a letter from Halifax to Phipps two days later. Mentioning doubts about reports of a German ultimatum to Roumania, Halifax indicated that the conquest of Czechoslovakia showed that German expansionism went beyond a desire to consolidate ethnic Germans within the German state. This meant that no country was safe "if this should prove to be part of a definite policy of domination."[2] In other words, Halifax, who had long conceded German domination of territories to its East, feared – but was not absolutely convinced – that Germany had designs on the West.

---

[1] Ian Colvin, *The Chamberlain Cabinet* (London: Victor Gollancz, 1971), p. 189.
[2] *DBFP*, Series 3, Vol. 4, Doc. 446, p. 400.

Halifax believed however that prudence called now for a measure of collective security. Halifax had assumed his portfolio after his predecessor's resignation in disgust that the prime minister rejected even tentative efforts in the direction of collective security. Now however Halifax argued:

> In the circumstances thus created it seems to His Majesty's Government in the United Kingdom to be desirable to proceed without delay to the organization of mutual support on the part of all those who realize the necessity of protecting international society from further violation of fundamental laws on which it rests.[3]

What "circumstances" had been created? As we noted in chapter 7, Halifax explained to Sir Ronald Lindsay that he was reluctantly embracing the doctrine of collective security because Britain could no longer simply assume that the country and its Empire were not objects of Nazi designs.[4]

***

The guarantee to Poland coming so soon after the fall of Czechoslovakia would come as a surprise to many observers for two reasons. First, as Simon Newman observes, it was feared that the appeasers would attempt to gloss over Hitler's brutal invasion and insist that Germany remained a reliable ally.[5] Secondly, in the months preceding the guarantee, Britain had given Poland every reason to believe that it would do nothing to prevent the free port of Danzig from falling under Germany's control.[6] In December, as relations between the German and Polish-speaking communities in Danzig broke down, the Poles were informed that Halifax intended to ask the League of Nations to end its protection of the city as of 16 January 1939. The Polish leader, Colonel Beck, was able to convince the

---

[3] *DBFP*, Series 3, Vol. 4, Doc. 446, p. 400.
[4] *DBFP*, Series 3, Vol. 4, Doc. 394, pp. 364-366.
[5] Simon Newman, *March 1939: The British Guarantee to Poland* (Oxford: Clarendon Press, 1976), p. 106. Newman quotes the views of Ivone Kirkpatrick at the British Embassy in Berlin. Kirkpatrick expected the "optimists" in Cabinet to use the lull after the invasion of Czechoslovakia to "tell us that Hitler has renounced his evil ways and that in consequence we have nothing to fear."
[6] As we saw in Chapter 7, the Poles were quite right. In fact, Chamberlain, Halifax and other leading Cabinet ministers were clearly prepared to let Hitler do as he wished in central and eastern Europe generally.

League to postpone such a decision. But, as Anita Prazmowska writes, Polish politicians feared that Britain was prepared to sacrifice Danzig to achieve an overall Anglo-German settlement.[7]

Yet, by 21 March, the main lines of Britain's new foreign policy with respect to Poland were spelled out by Lord Halifax as he and Lord Strang met with Bonnet, the French Minister for Foreign Affairs, and his private secretary. Halifax informed the French representatives that he had instructed his ambassador to Poland to stress to the Poles the importance Britain placed on the preservation of Polish independence. While Britain would prefer that Germany and Poland resolve peacefully the issue of Danzig, it would not allow Germany to use the Danzig issue as a pretext to challenge Polish independence. The British government, the ambassador was told to say, was now committed to resisting German aggression no matter where in Europe it might occur.[8] The countries enumerated by Halifax included France, Great Britain, Holland, Switzerland, Roumania, Poland, and Yugoslavia. Interestingly, the one nation threatened with German aggression that he did not mention was the Soviet Union. "Or whoever it might be" might cover that nation; and then again it might not.

Bonnet indicated that France shared Britain's view that "it was absolutely essential to get Poland in." This would be the way for bringing in the Soviets who had a border with Poland and could then cross Polish territory to fight Germany. Halifax sidestepped the question of Soviet participation altogether. He indicated to Bonnet that France and Britain must argue to the Poles that the weakening of these two Western nations would leave Poland defenceless against German aggression. In short, the West now feared attack in their corner of Europe and therefore was willing to form an alliance with Eastern European countries to make it unlikely that Germany could count on a fight on only one front at a time.

Western self-interest argued for an alliance with Roumania as well as Poland. On 22 March 1939, Alexis Leger of the French Foreign Office briefed Campbell in the British Embassy in Paris on the French position regarding the German occupation of

---

[7] Anita Prazmowska, *Britain, Poland and the Eastern Front 1939* (London: Cambridge University Press, 1987), p. 35.
[8] *DBFP*, Series 3, Vol. 4, Doc. 458, pp. 422-427.

Memel one day earlier. Leger said that the French did not believe that Memel in German hands gave the Germans greater capacity for making war against Britain and France. On the other hand, as Campbell put it: "it was because Roumania could supply Germany with the means of carrying on such a war (means which she at present lacked), that it was necessary to protect that country."[9]

On 28 March, Halifax sent to Sir Ronald Lindsay, the British Ambassador in the United States, a message to be delivered to the United States President. It included the following:

> It is important to Germany to avoid a war on two fronts, and her recent behaviour has stiffened the attitude at any rate of Poland and created strong apprehension in other countries in Central and Eastern Europe. It is Germany's purpose gradually to neutralize these countries, to deprive them of their power to resist, and to incorporate them in the German economic system. When this has been done, the way will have been prepared for an attack on the Western European powers.[10]

In October 1938, Halifax had told Joseph Kennedy, American Ambassador in London, that Britain should mind her own business even if Germany moved into Roumania. In November 1938 he wrote to Phipps that Central and Eastern Europe should be Germany's domain while the West should hold on to the Mediterranean and the Middle East. But by March 28, 1939, with Germany having put her move against Ukraine in cold storage, Halifax feared an attack on the West. He now therefore embraced the notion of European-wide collective security against Germany.

At the Cabinet Committee on Foreign Policy meeting on 27 March 1939, Chamberlain, referring to Roumania and Poland, articulated the new strategic concerns of the government. Roumania was needed in an alliance with the West because a naval blockade of Germany, a key component in British strategy for a potential war with that country, would be weakened if Germany had access to Roumanian oil. Poland was vital "because the weak point of Germany was her present inability to

---

[9] *DBFP*, Series 3, Vol. 4, Doc. 493, p. 468.
[10] *DBFP*, Series 3, Vol. 4, Doc. 549, pp. 526-528.

conduct war on two fronts, and unless Poland was with us, Germany would be able to avoid this contingency."[11]

There was disagreement about whether to include the Soviet Union. Chamberlain underlined the opposition to Soviet participation on the part of both Roumania and Poland and suggested that Italy, Spain and Portugal would also turn against Britain if it made common cause with the Communists. But the decision not to pursue an alliance with the Soviets was hardly a broadly-based agreement. As Ian Colvin notes: "Once more the decision had been taken by very few minds, had been presented to the Foreign Policy Committee as an adopted plan, and would be told to the Cabinet when finalized."[12] Yet the Chiefs of Staff had informed the government on 18 March that a warning to the Germans to leave Roumania alone would only have a chance of acting as a deterrent if both the Soviet Union and Poland were part of an Eastern front against Germany. The Chiefs indicated that if a decision had to be made on military grounds to choose either the Soviets or Poland as an ally, the Soviet Union was the better prospect.[13] Chamberlain however, proved unbending in his unwillingness to have the Communist country, which he had hoped Germany would crush, as an ally.

At the 27 March meeting Chamberlain expressed his readiness to give Poland a unilateral guarantee of military assistance in case of attack. While he would prefer that Poland give reciprocal guarantees to Britain and France, he was prepared if necessary to provide the unilateral guarantee.[14] Halifax commented that "there was probably no way in which France and ourselves could prevent Poland and Roumania from being overrun." Still it was necessary to be prepared to go to war rather than "doing nothing."

The Chiefs of Staff reported the following day that a key military consideration was that a guarantee to Poland and Roumania could encourage intransigence from those two countries in their dealings with Hitler. That could "precipitate a European war before our forces are in any way prepared for it, and such a war might be started by aggression against Danzig alone."[15] Yet reports the next day suggested that Colonel Beck,

[11] Ian Colvin, *The Chamberlain Cabinet*, pp. 192-193.
[12] *Ibid.*, p. 193.
[13] Simon Newman, *March 1939*, pp. 119-120.
[14] *Ibid.*, pp. 151-154.

the Polish leader, was undecided whether to seek an alliance with the British/French combination or with the Germans.[16] The one concession the British could make to Poland that Germany would never make was the recognition of Danzig as part of Polish territory. So, despite a recommendation by the Chiefs of Staff against inclusion of Danzig in any guarantee, Cabinet decided on 30 March to offer a unilateral guarantee to Poland, including Danzig. As Simon Newman comments on a guarantee that encouraged Poland to be belligerent with the Germans:

> It is significant that their chosen method was designed to result in somebody else's war first. For the British were still conscious of their weakness. As Halifax told his Private Secretary a few days later, he 'wanted to gain time because every month gave us 600 more airplanes.' What better way to gain time, given that war was considered inevitable, than to direct the German military machine against the Poles.[17]

Chamberlain rejected the suggestion that the guarantee be simply against 'unprovoked aggression.' He wanted a guarantee that the most sceptical Pole could accept. As Czechoslovakia demonstrated, Germany would always claim technically to have been provoked. In the Polish case, the Polish demand that Danzig be considered part of Poland might be termed a provocation.

Many factors militated against granting a guarantee to Poland. Danzig was overwhelmingly a German city and Hitler's claims with respect to the city and the Polish Corridor were among the most justifiable he had. Before providing the guarantee, Britain had never supported Poland's claim to the port city. Poland was a dictatorship that suppressed its minorities. It had also behaved shamelessly in 1938 when Germany was bullying Czechoslovakia to make its own expansionist demands against the beleaguered nation. It had sent an ultimatum to Czechoslovakia in September 1938 claiming the region of Teschen at a time when Czechoslovakia was in no position to reject it. The only serious reason given in Cabinet for guaranteeing Poland was the military assessment that Germany could not manage a war on two fronts.

[15] *Ibid.*, p. 155.
[16] *Ibid.*, pp. 171-173.
[17] *Ibid.*, pp. 196-197.

Yet, as noted, Halifax, without contradiction from any member of Cabinet, made plain the fact that Britain and France could not defend Poland. Indeed in the early days of the war it became clear that, despite their belief that Hitler could not fight on two fronts, they would not open a second front to draw fire away from Poland.

There are two possible explanations of why Britain and France drew Poland into an alliance that sealed the latter's fate and insufficient documentation to choose between them. One explanation is that it would provide the Allies with additional time to rearm and later to make peace with Germany from a position of military strength. Germany would be restrained from an attack on the West by the knowledge that such an attack would also mean war with Poland. If it chose however to attack Poland, Britain need not respond since Germany would conquer Poland in a few months. Poland could then be abandoned with the rationalization developed for Austria and Czechoslovakia: since the country no longer existed, nothing could be done to save it. Another possible explanation is that Britain hoped that its original goal of luring Germany towards an exclusive focus on Eastern expansion could be restored. If Hitler attacked Poland, he would be brought face to face with the Soviets and the temptation to move into Soviet Ukraine would be great.

The first explanation is consistent with the pessimistic scenario that Chamberlain provided his sister Hilda in a letter on 2 April. He believed Hitler planned to attack Poland, annexing part of it to Germany and making the rest a protectorate. Next Hitler would absorb Lithuania and the other Balkan states, following which he might make an alliance with the Soviets[18] and then attempt to conquer the British Empire.[19] Here was a scenario for Germany much at odds with what the prime minister had believed scant weeks ago when he thought his deal with Hitler remained in force. He now informed his sister that the guarantee to Poland was necessary to prevent a German-Polish alliance. Stated otherwise, Britain did not believe Poland was in imminent military danger from Germany. Rather it believed Britain was in danger of facing a German-Polish settlement if it did not act quickly to prevent it.

[18] Chamberlain would soon revert to the position that a German-Soviet alliance was impossible for ideological reasons.
[19] Roy Douglas, *1939: A Retrospect Forty Years After* (London: Macmillan, 1983), p. 93.

On 4 April, Colonel Beck, in London for talks, provided Halifax with a reciprocal guarantee to Britain, though he refused to commit his country to the defence of Roumania.[20] Two days later Halifax noted that Poland, according to Count Raczynski, Polish Ambassador to Britain, did not want "immediate negotiations" with Germany. Writing to Sir Howard Kennard, the British Ambassador to Poland, Halifax observed that Britain had no intention "to force, or even to urge" Poland to enter such negotiations.[21] A year earlier democratic Czechoslovakia was denounced by Britain for unwillingness to make concessions to Nazi Germany. Now however dictatorial Poland was not even to be urged to make concessions, though the issue, the fate of a German-speaking population, was the same. It seemed of little concern to the British government that Poland might provoke the German dictator into an invasion.

Britain's support for Poland once the guarantee was provided was hardly generous. Hitler certainly was not convinced that the British guarantee of Poland meant a great deal. On 22 August 1939, he told his generals that Britain had refused Poland a loan for rearmament, granting only credits so that Poland was forced to buy its arms in England "although England cannot make deliveries." "This suggests that England does not really want to support Poland."[22] Indeed Britain had stalled when Poland requested economic help and military equipment to prepare to deal with a German invasion. Focusing on coal exports and Britain's perceived need for a devaluation in Poland's currency, Britain did not give the impression of being a forceful ally of a country under the gun of Hitler.

On 22 August 1939, Hitler would outline for his commanders in chief his decision to attack Poland before attacking the West. Hitler often changed the facts to suit his purposes. But on this occasion he confirmed Chamberlain's fears as expressed in the letter to his sister and demonstrated that the West had successfully induced the Nazi dictator to attack Poland before attacking the West.

> It was clear to me that a conflict with Poland had to come sooner or later. I had already made this decision

[20] *DBFP*, Series 3, Vol. 5, Doc. 1, p. 3.
[21] *DBFP*, 3rd Series, Vol. 5, Doc. 18, p. 52
[22] *DGFP*, Series D, Vol. 7, Doc. 192, p. 203.

in the spring, but I thought that I would first turn against the West in a few years, and only after that against the East. But the sequence of these things cannot be fixed. Nor should one close one's eyes to threatening situations. I wanted first of all to establish a tolerable relationship with Poland in order to fight first against the West. But this plan, which appeared to me, could not be executed, as fundamental points had changed. It became clear to me that, in the event of a conflict with the West, Poland would attack us.[23]

The cynicism of the British government in setting Poland up for a German assault is nicely summed up by Liddell Hart.

Since World War II, when the practical absurdity of the Polish guarantee has come to be better appreciated than it was at the time, it is commonly excused, or justified, by the argument that it marked the point at which the British Government declared: 'We were blind, but now we see.' I have too many recollections, and records, of discussions during this period to be able to accept the view that this sudden change of policy was due to a sudden awakening to the danger or to the moral issues. In Government circles I had long listened to calculated arguments for allowing Germany to expand eastward, for evading our obligations under the League covenant and for having other countries to bear the brunt of an early stand against aggression.[24]

***

Chamberlain remained no more committed to the defence of small nations against aggression than he had been at Munich. He was dismissive of Mussolini's invasion of Albania on Good Friday, 1939. That day Rab Butler, Parliamentary Under-Secretary of State in the Foreign Office, went to Chamberlain for instructions and was told: 'I feel sure Mussolini has not decided to go against us.' Butler expressed fears for the Balkans generally and Chamberlain told him: 'Don't be silly. Go home to bed.'[25] Chamberlain was even more cynical when he wrote his sister. He indicated his disappointment that Mussolini

[23] Hitler's explanation of his reasons for deciding to attack Poland is found in *DGFP*, Series D, Vol. 7, Doc. 192, pp. 200-04.
[24] *The Memoirs of Captain Liddell Hart*, Volume 2 (London: Cassell, 1965), p. 221.
[25] Lord Butler, *The Art of the Possible* (London: Hamish Hamilton, 1971), p. 79.

had not made the coup look like an agreed-upon arrangement between the two countries, "thus raising as little as possible questions of European significance."[26] Once again, Chamberlain was more concerned with form than substance. He wanted Mussolini to behave as Hitler had behaved when he seized the remnants of Czechoslovakia. Plainly, aggression as such was no issue for this proponent of appeasement. The issue was whether an aggressor was "against us" or had raised "questions of European significance," by which he meant "Western European significance" since Albania, of course, WAS a European nation.

Nor had Chamberlain given up on trying to convince Hitler not to raise "questions of European significance." On 31 March 1939, T. Kordt at the German Embassy in London wrote the German Foreign Ministry that the Chamberlain government insisted the unilateral guarantee to Poland was not a step towards encirclement of Germany.[27] From 23 to 26 April a Roumanian delegation, consisting of Grigore Gafencu, Minister for Foreign Affairs, and Viorel Tilea, the Roumanian minister in London, had conversations in London with Halifax and three Foreign Office officials: Cadogan, Ingram and Strang. When Gafencu reported that Hitler believed Britain was standing in the way of German development, Halifax asked him to find out from Hitler what the British government "were doing that was wrong."[28] The answer, according to Gafencu, was that Germany wanted Britain to leave Europe to Germany and the rest of the world to itself. Next day Chamberlain joined the talks. Gafencu noted that Hitler had not opposed an Anglo-French guarantee for Roumania but insisted that the Soviets must be left out. Hitler, he said, believed that Germany, Britain and France had a common interest in saving Europe from the Soviet danger. "The Prime Minister said he gathered therefore that Herr Hitler's dislike and fear of Russia had not diminished."[29] He was obviously relieved that his fears of a German-Soviet agreement, expressed earlier in the month in his letter to his sister, might be unwarranted.

On 27 April 1939, Norton of the British Embassy in Warsaw complained that the officials of the Berlin Embassy, even with

---

[26] William Manchester, *The Last Lion: Winston Spencer Churchill 1932-1940* (Boston: Little Brown and Company, 1988), p. 421.
[27] *DGFP*, Series D, Vol.6, Doc. 137, pp. 172-173.
[28] *DBFP*, Series 3, Vol. 5, Doc. 278, p. 303.
[29] *DBFP*, Series 3, Vol. 5, Doc. 279, pp. 309-315.

Henderson absent from Berlin, were "falling for the Nazi propaganda stuff that Poland is the menace to peace."[30] On 15 May, Henderson, back in Berlin, met Weizsacker, the German Secretary of State, and assured him, as the Secretary wrote, that a war over Poland "would be conducted defensively by the Western powers."[31] This was hardly the only instance where Britain tipped off Germany that it did not intend to defend Poland and was looking for a general settlement with Germany that could either precede or postdate a German assault on Poland.

We noted in Chapter 7 that Chamberlain, through a confidential agent, had established contacts with Ribbentrop, bypassing the Foreign Office and the British Ambassador. Cadogan had received information on these contacts through British Intelligence. Contacts through special channels did not stop. On 3 May 1939 Cadogan entered in his diary:

> Went to see H.J.W. [Wilson] about a telephone intercept, which looks as if No. 10 were talking 'appeasement' again. He put up all sorts of denials, to which I don't pay attention. But it is a good thing to show we have our eye on them.[32]

Adam Von Trott, a former Rhodes Scholar, was sent by Germany to England on a fact-finding mission in early June of 1939. During his eight-day stay, he was invited for a weekend to Cliveden with Halifax, Inskip, Lothian and other political leaders. He reported that Halifax told him that Britain was prepared to fight Germany if necessary but wished to avoid war.[33] Halifax spoke of the division of the world into spheres of influence that he had envisaged after Munich. It was a faithful recreation of the vision he had expressed at the time in his letter to Phipps in Paris.

> After the Munich Conference, he had seen the way open for a new consolidation of Powers, in which Germany would have the preponderance in Central and South East Europe, a 'not too unfriendly Spain and Italy,' would leave unthreatened British positions

---

[30] *DBFP*, Series 3, Vol. 5, Doc. 301, p.. 352-353.
[31] *DGFP*, Series D, Vol. 6, Doc. 385, p. 503.
[32] David Dilks, *The Diaries of Sir Alexander Cadogan, O.M., 1939-1945* (London: Cassell, 1971), p. 178.
[33] Von Trott's report is found in *DGFP*, Series D, Vol. 6, Doc. 497, pp. 674-685.

in the Mediterranean and the Middle East, and with pacification in the Far East also becoming possible.

Lord Astor said that "unfortunately" people in Britain regarded the invasion of Czechoslovakia as an indication that further, similar conquests were imminent. Lord Lothian went much further. He told Von Trott that he recognized that at times Germany was required to use force to achieve "her vital rights." He regarded the "military occupation and disarming of Czecho-Slovakia as being an unavoidable necessity for Germany in the long run." Lothian had been appointed British Ambassador to Washington though he had yet to assume the post. Henderson had identified him to the Germans as someone who spoke with authority for the Chamberlain government. Lothian suggested to Von Trott that Germany consider giving Czechoslovakia national independence on the condition that she disarm and cooperate with Germany. He added that he did not wish to be identified as the source of the idea because he "wants to avoid the suspicion that he has not yet been converted from his ideas of reconciliation with Germany." But because Lothian was influential with Chamberlain and Astor and their circles, Von Trott thought it important to mention his name.

Lothian thought that the move he was suggesting would have a beneficial impact on British public opinion. It would lead to the gradual "elimination of all material and moral differences" between Germany and Britain. "Economically the German living space would naturally have to extend far beyond the present limits," Lothian had told Von Trott. But that should not lead to the elimination of the nations which Germany would then dominate economically. Again, for the Chamberlainites, form was the issue. Germany could use coercion to get its way in Central and Eastern Europe but it should provide a *pro forma* independence to these nations so that it could not be accused of aggression. Such attention to form would help British supporters of Germany in responding to public disgust with German expansionism.

Von Trott also met with Chamberlain. "The Astors have access to him at any time," wrote the German visitor, "so that the meeting came about quite naturally." Chamberlain told Von Trott that he had not given his guarantee to Poland "gladly." Rather he felt forced to do it because Hitler's actions had caused the British public to oppose any further concessions to Germany.

He was however still desirous of pursuing a policy of appeasement or a "German-British settlement," as he called it.

> Basically he still desired a peaceful settlement with Germany. From the day he had taken up office he had stood for the view that the European problem could only be solved on the line Berlin-London...at Prague Germany had gone over to the 'destruction' of other nations and that thereby all Germany's neighbours were forced into a kind of self-defence psychosis. If Germany would restore confidence in this respect he would again be able to advocate a policy of coming to meet us half-way.

Indeed, once public distrust of Germany had been surmounted, wrote Von Trott, Chamberlain "would again be able to advocate concessions." Chamberlain assured Von Trott that Germany could ignore anti-appeasement Tories such as Churchill, Eden and Duff Cooper as well as the Labour party. "Because of his large majority he need not pay any great attention to the opposition."

Von Trott discussed the positive views of German-British cooperation that Halifax and Chamberlain had expressed with Lord Dunglass, a private secretary to Chamberlain. Dunglass agreed to try to influence Oliver Stanley, president of the Board of Trade, to make a parliamentary statement accommodating to Germany. Stanley indeed made such a speech.

On 3 June Dunglass's brother handed Von Trott a memorandum that the latter found very encouraging. "It is at any rate interesting that such positive views are to be found in the immediate entourage of the Prime Minister," wrote Von Trott. The memorandum, which demonstrates how slavishly some appeasers still held to their views, is here quoted in full:

> The democracies say: We will not make any concessions until you put away your pistols!
>
> The dictators reply: We will not put away our pistols until you make concessions!
>
> The democracies, remembering Czecho-Slovakia and Albania, say: How can we know whether you will put away your pistols after we have made concessions?

The dictators, remembering the Versailles Treaty and France's broken promise, reply: How can we know whether you will make concessions after we have put away our pistols?

The result is an *impasse*. Consequently, the democracies and dictators are sitting back and waiting for a sign. The dictators dissatisfied and therefore impatient, are waiting for concessions to be granted. The democracies, satiated and therefore content, are waiting for the pistols to be put away.

Here is the vital point:

The democracies are making the pistols an issue. That is wrong. The pistols are of secondary importance. The dictators, however, are making the concessions an issue. That is right. The concessions or their nonexistence, are the reasons for the pistols. – There can be no agreement on the question of the pistols. Pistols speak only to pistols and their language is war. Therefore drop the pistols.

But there is already agreement that concessions will

be made one day-

Let today be that day!

On 13 June 1939 Henderson, meeting with Weizsacker, "spoke of London's willingness to negotiate with Berlin." Weizsacker's notes observed that Henderson was "acting on instructions." Speaking personally, Henderson went further than his government was prepared to go. He would concede the continent of Europe to Germany if Britain's control of the sea was conceded.[34] On 27 June, Weizsacker reported another conversation with Henderson in which the British ambassador complained that Chamberlain was being forced to implement Labour's foreign policy although he remained committed to "the path of peace."

Reports coming to Germany from Britain suggested that there was little likelihood of a return to the British position before March 17. One report on 29 June, for example, confirmed that Chamberlain and the inner Cabinet opposed war and supported a

[34] *DGFP*, Series D, Vol. 6. Doc. 521, pp. 718-719.

compromise over Danzig and the Corridor. But any tentative moves they made in the direction of compromise were met by cries of "No more appeasement" from the British population. The report concluded that Britain would not agree to peaceful relations on German terms.[35]

On 10 July Herbert Von Dirksen, the German Ambassador to Britain, also complained that the British public "have taken the initiative from the Government and drive the Cabinet on." Dirksen however expressed some hope that a "small but influential group" in Cabinet who opposed war might yet bring an end to what he called the "negative policy of encirclement" of Germany.[36]

Chamberlain was still hoping in July to becalm public opinion. He insisted on the traditional summer recess though Opposition members suggested it was irresponsible to recess Parliament while a crisis situation continued. To insure that his own party supported the recess, he made the vote on it a confidence issue. But ending the parliamentary criticisms of Hitler was only part of his strategy. A press truce between Germany and Britain was another. Henderson, on Chamberlain's behalf, proposed such a press truce to Weizsacker.[37]

From 18 to 20 July conversations were held between Dr. Helmut Wohlthat, an important German official[38] attending a whaling convention in London, and Horace Wilson, Joseph Ball[39] and Robert Hudson, officials close to Chamberlain. Wilson was, of course, the prime minister's major confidante while Hudson was the junior minister of Overseas Trade. Relying on Wilson's and Hudson's version of the meetings, Sydney Aster titled a chapter dealing with the matter, "Appeasement Cremated."[40] German records of the meetings however suggest a more appropriate title would have been: "Appeasement Alive and Running Amok."

As Aster notes, the Foreign Office had been excluded from these talks. Hudson and Wilson sent their notes to the Foreign Office

---

[35] *DGFP*, Series D, Vol. 6, Doc. 630, pp. 875-878.

[36] *DGFP*, Series D, Vol. 6, Doc. 645, pp. 891-893.

[37] *DGFP*, Series D, Vol. 6, Doc. 671, p. 922.

[38] Dr. Wohlthat was in charge of the German Four Year Economic Plan. He was a close collaborator of Goering.

[39] Ball was a senior officer in British Counter-Intelligence.

[40] Sydney Aster, *The Making of the Second World War* (New York: Simon and Shuster, 1973), Chapter 13, pp. 243-259.

after Halifax complained to Chamberlain about his ministry's exclusion.[41] But their conspiratorial behaviour should raise doubts about the accuracy of their reports. It was not in their interest or Chamberlain's to admit to the Foreign Office that they had shamelessly attempted to steer British policy back on the road to appeasement.

In his record of his conversation with Dr. Wohlthat, Hudson began by claiming that the German Embassy had asked him if he would meet with the visiting official. The German version suggests that the British leaders approached Dr. Wohlthat through the intermediary of a Norwegian member at the whaling convention. But, as Dirksen wrote to the German Foreign Ministry on 24 July, public opinion in Britain was so inflamed against appeasement that negotiations with Germany must be undertaken in strictest secrecy.[42] It would have been politically dangerous for Hudson to admit that Chamberlain's office had initiated a meeting with the Germans.

Hudson's report of the meeting indicated that he offered Germany a loan to help reconvert German military industries into peacetime industries. While admitting that he conceded to Wohlthat that south-eastern Europe fell "in the natural economic sphere of Germany," his report implied that no territorial concessions were discussed.[43] The Foreign Office was unhappy with Hudson's proposal, which apparently involved a loan to the Nazis of at least a billion pounds.[44] Lord Gladwyn of the Foreign Office reported to Cadogan that "the immediate effect of this piece of super-appeasement...has been to arouse all the suspicions of the Bolsheviks, dishearten the Poles...and encourage the Germans into thinking we are prepared to buy peace."[45]

The "Bolsheviks" and Poles would have been far more suspicious if they read the German records of the meetings between Wohlthat and Chamberlain's representatives and subsequent meetings of Horace Wilson with Dirksen. According to Dirksen, what Wilson had proposed to Wohlthat was: a) a pact of non-aggression to be understood as renunciation of

---

[41] *Ibid.*, pp. 149-150.
[42] *DGFP*, Series D, Vol. 6, Doc. 710, p. 970.
[43] *DBFP*, Series 3, Vol. 6, Doc. 370, p. 407.
[44] According to Lord Gladwyn (Gladwyn Jebb) of the Foreign Office. *DBFP*, Series 3, Vol. 6, Doc. 370, p. 93.
[45] *Ibid.*

aggression in principle; b) a pact of non-intervention which would delineate the respective spheres of interest.[46] In his report on 21 July 1939 to the German Foreign Ministry, Dirksen emphasized that Wilson had made it "perfectly clear" to Wohlthat "that Chamberlain approved this programme." Also:

> Sir Horace Wilson definitely told Herr Wohlthat that the conclusion of a non-aggression pact would enable Britain to rid herself of her commitments vis-à-vis Poland. As a result the Polish problem would lose much of its acuteness.

Wilson informed Wohlthat that the government expected to call an election in the autumn. It believed that it could win either on a platform of the need to prepare for war or of a lasting Anglo-German agreement. But it preferred to run on the latter platform.

Wohlthat's own report of his meeting with Wilson, written on 24 July, paralleled Dirksen's.[47] He added that Wilson had insisted that Britain's recent feverish pace of rearmament was forced by Opposition pressures. Britain wanted negotiations with Germany but would be negotiating from a position of military strength.

Wilson had produced a memorandum approved by Chamberlain that included the points on which agreement would have to be reached between Britain and Germany to prevent war.[48] Wilson said that the negotiations between the two countries would have to involve "the highest ranking personages" and yet be secret. Initially they would exclude Italy and France until "a joint German-British policy" had been reached and could be refined in agreements among the four countries.

> ...If the Greater German policy in respect of territorial claims was approaching the end of its demands, the

---

[46] *Documents and Materials Relating to the Eve of the Second World War, Volume 2* (Salisbury, North Carolina: Documentary Publications, 1978), pp. 67-72.

[47] *DGFP*, Series D, Vol. 6, Doc. 716, pp. 977-983.

[48] Sydney Aster, *The Making of the Second World War*, claims that Wohlthat invented a story because he was not being taken seriously by his superiors. But he provides no shred of evidence for this claim. Wohlthat's evidence parallels Dirksen's and there is no reason to discredit it. Lord Gladwyn, who should know better than Aster, asserts the credibility of Wohlthat's report. See *The Memoirs of Lord Gladwyn* (London: Weidenfeld and Nicolson 1972), p. 93

Führer could take this opportunity of finding, in conjunction with Britain, a form which would enable him to go down in history as one of the greatest statesmen and which would lead to a revolution in world opinion.

Wilson emphasized that Germany was not being asked to restore territory nor indeed to give up its objective of domination of eastern Europe. What Wilson proposed, said Wohlthat, was:

Mutual declarations of non-interference by Germany in respect of the British Commonwealth of Nations and by Great Britain with respect to Germany. I drew attention to the fact that it was not only a question of the frontiers of States and possessions, but also of territories of special interest and of economic influence. For Germany this would apply especially to East and South East Europe. Sir Horace replied that this point needed especially careful political wording and that the political definition would probably best result from an examination of Germany's economic interests.

On military questions, Wilson proposed a joint Anglo-German declaration on arms limitations. But "the Air Agreement and the Army Agreement should take into account the special strategic and military conditions of the British Empire and of the German Reich in Central Europe." Just what the German Reich in Central Europe might require was not elaborated but it was clear that the Chamberlain policy of conceding Central and Eastern Europe to Germany remained alive.

On 1 August 1939, Dirksen reported to the German Foreign Office that Wilson had confirmed to him personally the offer made to Germany via Wohlthat. "It appeared that the basis of the Wohlthat-Wilson conversation remained in force," wrote the German Ambassador. Wilson was quite conciliatory, even observing that armaments control rather than disarmament was the military goal of the British proposal. But Wilson stressed on several occasions during his conversation with Dirksen that "the greatest secrecy was necessary at the present stage." If talks were to be held between Germany and Britain, the Chamberlain government would be forced to resign if their existence became known before agreement had been reached. Public opinion simply remained too anti-German at the time. "The thing above all was to convince the British public that confidence was warranted," as Dirksen interpreted Wilson's message.[49]

In his memoirs in 1952, Dirksen recalled the various secretive efforts made by the Chamberlain government to produce a last-minute Anglo-German agreement that would stave off war. Recalling his meeting with Wilson, he wrote:

> A general election was due in the autumn. By then Chamberlain would have to stand before the electors with the clear alternative: either "the compromise with Germany has been successful," or "we must prepare for war with Germany." I was plainly told by both Lord Halifax and Sir Horace Wilson that Parliament and public would accept either of these solutions unanimously. Hitler, too, heard it from the press magnate Lord Kemsley in a long conversation with him...

> Thus the British Cabinet had the unusually difficult task of carrying through a dual foreign policy. On the one hand there were the negotiations with Moscow, which had to be kept alive; on the other hand, a compromise on a broad front had to be achieved with Germany. If the compromise failed, the formation of an Eastern front would have to be achieved. If it succeeded, the Moscow negotiations would lose their importance. In view of the excited feelings in Britain, contacts with Germany had to be made in the utmost secrecy.[50]

A variety of such contacts occurred. On 29 July, for example, Kordt of the German Embassy had a visit from Charles Roden Buxton, a Labour politician. Dirksen, writing to Weizsacker three days later, suggested that Buxton, whose proposals were widely at odds with those of his party, was acting on Chamberlain's behalf. Buxton had not claimed to be speaking for Chamberlain but on 31 July, Chamberlain made a speech in the House that referred to the Anglo-French Agreement of 1904 and the Anglo-Russian Treaty of 1907. Buxton had earlier referred to these agreements. Dirksen was also struck by the fact that Buxton, like Wilson in his conversation with Wohlthat, had used the phrase "spheres of interest" rather than the more usual

[49] *Documents and Materials, Volume 2*, pp. 116-123.
[50] Herbert Von Dirksen, *Moscow, Tokyo, London* (Norman: University of Oklahoma Press, 1952), pp. 226-227.

diplomatic phrase, "spheres of influence." Buxton's proposal called for Germany to promise to leave the British Empire alone, to give "some kind of autonomy" to Bohemia and Moravia, and to agree to a "general reduction of armaments." In return:

> Great Britain promises fully to respect the German spheres of interest in Eastern and South-Eastern Europe. A consequence of this would be that Great Britain would renounce the guarantee she gave to certain states in the German sphere of interest. Great Britain further promises to influence France to break her alliance with the Soviet Union and to give up her ties in Southeastern Europe...

> Great Britain promises to give up the present negotiations for a pact with the Soviet Union.[51]

On 2 August, Lord Kemsley, just back from Germany where he had met with Hitler, spoke to Dirksen to whom he confirmed Wilson's statement that Chamberlain could win House support for either war preparations or a far-reaching agreement with Germany. Lord Kemsley, wrote Kordt, "spoke with pleasure of his conversation with Reichsleiter Rosenberg (charming personality) to whom he had said that Chamberlain was in his way the Führer of England, similar to Hitler and Mussolini."[52]

Yet the government, while desperate to reach an agreement with Hitler, remained unwilling to openly re-embrace appeasement for fear of public reaction. Halifax, for example, expressed an interest in an incognito visit to Britain by Goering to Swedish businessman Birger Dahlerus. Dahlerus was to act as an intermediary to arrange the meeting (which, in the end, did not occur). But, as Halifax explained in his minute of the meeting:

> It was, however, essential that I should know nothing about it officially and I should not even wish to have any communication sent to me directly by those taking part in the meeting [with Goering]. He could, if he so desired, always communicate with me through Sir H. Wernher, but if any official connection were ever to be established, it would only do mischief and create quite unnecessary and undesirable misunderstandings.[53]

[51] *Documents and Materials*, pp. 105-112.
[52] *Documents and Materials*, pp. 113-114.
[53] *DBFP*, Series 3, Vol. 6, p. 484.

While some historians, particularly Donald Cameron Watt, have suggested that the British placed little store upon their last-minute negotiations with Germany,[54] this is clearly untrue. As Nicholas Bethell observes, pressure from the British and French prevented Poland from fully mobilizing its considerable land army until 30 August. The result was that "a quarter of the Polish Army never reached its units,"[55] thereby seriously reducing the length of time that the Polish army could withstand the German attack.

***

Chamberlain and his circle publicly talked tough to Germany in the months leading to World War Two and privately tried to resurrect the Chamberlain-Hitler deal. Their treatment of the Soviet Union was rather different. Chamberlain wanted no part of a mutual assistance pact with the hated Bolsheviks. But he was forced into negotiations because of the combined pressures of public opinion, the Opposition, and a section of the Conservative Party.[56] The anti-communism of Chamberlain and the British elite generally made reaching such an understanding impossible. Having argued for so long that Germany could help eliminate the Soviet Union and that a war with Germany could only help the communist cause throughout Europe, Chamberlain remained hostile to the Communist state.

In the negotiations with the Soviets, the British made little effort to achieve success. So, for example, early in the talks Halifax met with Soviet Ambassador in London Ivan Maisky. Maisky suggested that Britain and France ought to make assistance to Poland and Roumania contingent on these countries' adoption of a reasonable attitude to assistance from the Soviets. Halifax was non-committal, indicating that this could not be forced upon these countries but that "we should not certainly exclude such a possibility from our mind."[57] The same day, however, Halifax wrote Kennard, the British Ambassador to Poland, that he had

[54] Donald Cameron Watt, *How War Came:The Immediate Origins of the Second World War, 1938-1939* (New York: Pantheon, 1989), p. 502.
[55] Nicholas Bethell, *The War Hitler Won September 1939* (London: Allen Lane, 1972), p. 28.
[56] *DBFP*, Series 3, Vol. 5, Doc. 1, p. 8; *The Diaries of Sir Henry Channon*, entries of 15 and 17 May 1939, p. 199.
[57] Halifax to Seeds, British Ambassador to Moscow, 12 April 1939, *DBFP*, Series 3, Vol. 5, Doc. 42, pp. 82-84.

told Count Raczynski of Maisky's demand and indicated that "I had told him that I could not feel this to be a very helpful contribution."[58] This was clearly not what he had said to Maisky. But why, in any case, attempt to further Polish-Soviet enmity by repeating to Raczynski a tough proposal from Maisky? Certainly neither the British nor the French made a habit of letting the Poles know everything about negotiations that might affect their future. It should be added that the British General Staff had often underlined the importance of having Soviet troops enter Poland or Roumania for these countries to defend themselves against German aggression. Sir William Seeds, the British Ambassador to Moscow, stressed the same point with Halifax.[59] French Foreign Minister Bonnet and Lloyd George had also made this clear.

The Soviets made a formal proposal to Britain and France for an alliance against aggression on 18 April 1939. Among other provisions, the three countries would agree to provide all necessary aid to one another in case of aggression against any one of them. All three would guarantee the "Eastern European States situated between Baltic and Black Seas and bordering on U.S.S.R." against aggression.[60]

The British reaction was hostile. Cadogan suggested rejection.

> If we are attacked by Germany, Poland under our mutual guarantee will come to our assistance, i.e. make war on Germany. If the Soviet are bound to do the same, how can they fulfil their obligation without sending troops through or aircraft over Polish territory? That is exactly what frightens the Poles.[61]

But what if Poland were to be attacked by Germany? Britain was in no position to make her guarantee good whereas the Soviets would be able to help fend off an aggression. The British were vague with the Poles as to how the island nation would go about aiding a country bordering on Nazi Germany. They did not put the obvious case to the Poles that Soviet involvement in an anti-Nazi alliance was crucial to dealing with a German invasion of Poland, whatever Poland's fears of Communist subversion.

---

[58] *DBFP*, Series 3, Vol. 5, Doc. 50, p. 98.
[59] *DBFP*, Series 3, Vol. 5, Doc. 50, p. 98.
[60] Seeds to Halifax, 18 April 1939, *DBFP*, Series 3, Vol. 5, Doc. 201, pp. 228-229.
[61] *The Diaries of Sir Alexander Cadogan*, p. 175.

They did not do so because, like the Polish dictators, they feared Communist ideology more than Nazi guns.

Halifax recognized that the Soviet proposals would be judged modest and appropriate in the court of public opinion. He therefore informed Ambassador Phipps in Paris that it was important that the proposals not be made public nor the negative reaction of the British and French governments.[62] There were initially important differences in the responses of the two governments. France was prepared to accept the Soviet proposal for a triple pact in which Britain, France, and the Soviet Union were required to respond to German aggression against any of the three. Daladier pointed out to Lord Halifax that Germany would have to cross Polish and/or Roumanian territory to get to the Soviet Union and so, by definition, any German attempt to attack the Soviets would result in Britain and France being required to declare war on Germany. Lord Halifax significantly saw things otherwise. With the free hand still in mind as a goal, he pointed out to Daladier that it was possible that Germany might attack the Soviets "with Polish or Roumanian connivance or acquiescence." In such a case, the guarantees to Poland and Roumania provided by Britain and France would not come into play. He made clear that in such circumstances Britain and France should provide no guarantees to the Soviet Union. "We should in fact be undertaking a heavier obligation since unless Poland and Roumania resisted, our guarantee to them would not come into force."[63] Given Poland's friendly relations with Nazi Germany before March 1939, Halifax was not referring to a dim possibility.

Britain also wanted the Soviets to give unilateral guarantees to Poland and Roumania with no reciprocal guarantee from France and Britain to defend the Soviets from German reprisals for enforcing the guarantee.[64] France proposed that the Soviets guarantee assistance to France and Britain if either of these countries were attacked by Germany after fulfilling obligations they had undertaken to protect certain nations from German aggression. Once the Soviets joined the war effort, France and Britain would be obliged to defend Soviet territory from German attack. But this sidestepped what was to happen in the most likely scenario: the Soviets would be obliged to defend Poland

---

[62] *DBFP*, Series 3, Vol. 5, Doc. 232, p. 254, 20 April 1939.
[63] *DBFP*, Series 3, Vol. 5, Doc. 576, 21 May 1939.
[64] *DBFP*, Series 3, Vol. 5, Doc. 277, p. 295, Phipps to Halifax, 24 April 1939.

or Roumania from a German attack.[65] Proposals of this kind could only convince the Soviets that France and Britain had every intention of allowing Germany to destroy the Soviet Union if it so wished. With Germany wooing the Soviets to accept a treaty of non-aggression, the West's failure to negotiate seriously with the Soviets was bound to have dire consequences. But, as we have seen, Chamberlain deluded himself that a German-Soviet agreement would never be concluded.

Halifax's summary of British goals in the negotiations with the Soviets, set forth in a note to Kennard in Warsaw on 28 April, demonstrates why a treaty with the Soviets would ultimately be unreachable. Britain was interested in using the Soviets for whatever it could get and insistent on offering nothing in return. The British goals, according to Halifax, were:

> (a) not to forego the chance of our receiving help from the Soviet Government in case of war;

> (b) not to jeopardize the common front by disregarding the susceptibilities of Poland and Roumania;

> (c) not to forfeit the sympathy of the world at large by giving a handle to Germany's anti-Comintern propaganda;

> (d) not to jeopardize the cause of peace by provoking violent action by Germany.[66]

The British and the French disagreed about the likely German reaction to a British-French-Soviet alliance. Halifax held talks with the French in Geneva and wrote Cadogan on 21 May about the exchange of views. Halifax repeated his view that the tripartite alliance might provoke a violent response from Hitler. Daladier's view, as expressed by Halifax, was the opposite:

> Unless we concluded such an agreement quickly we should increase rather than diminish the risk of an act of force by Germany. Such an act could only be averted if Germany could be convinced that if she embarked upon this course she would meet with effective resistance. Without collaboration of Russia assistance could not be effective.[67]

[65] *Ibid.*
[66] *DBFP*, Series 3, Vol. 5, Doc. 408, p. 461.

Halifax then made clear what the Soviets suspected all along: if Germany's intentions were to attack the Soviet Union, with Polish or Roumanian compliance, Britain had no intention of trying to stop her. Halifax's words here bear repeating:

> M. Daladier added that an attack by Germany on Russia which did not bring our Polish and Roumanian guarantees into play was most unlikely to occur. We should in fact not be increasing our obligations much by accepting triple pact. I replied that if as he himself had pointed out what Russians feared was attack by Germany with Polish or Roumanian connivance or acquiescence we should in fact be undertaking a heavier obligation since unless Poland and Roumania resisted, our guarantee to them would not come into force.

Halifax, like Chamberlain, would clearly have liked to have been able to return to the early post-Munich period when he thought that Nazi ambitions could be contained within eastern Europe, including the Soviet Union. From his perspective, as we have seen, once it became clear that Germany had turned its aggressive intentions westwards, it became necessary to have an alliance with eastern countries so as to limit the possibility that Germany could fight a war on the western front alone. Such an alliance however remained unnecessary if Britain's new eastern allies chose to let Germany use their territory to attack the Soviet Union. A German attack on the Soviet Union would signal that Hitler did not mean to attack the west after all. It was therefore critical for Halifax that Britain and France not place themselves in the position where they would have to defend the Soviet Union against Germany. After all, it was Communist Russia, not Nazi Germany, that the British elite found most ideologically offensive. Why defend the Communist state if doing so became unnecessary for the defence of Britain and its Empire? Why not instead continue to seek an "Anglo-German agreement"?

***

On 1 September 1939, Germany invaded Poland. From the very start, Germany bombed the civilian population indiscriminately.

---

[67] *DBFP*, Series 3, Vol. 5, Doc. 576, pp. 623-625.

Britain was pledged to assist Poland to the best of her ability. This implied retaliatory air raids against at least German military targets, if not against civilian ones as well.

But Chamberlain and his circle, while disappointed that Germany had carried out the invasion, still sought peace with Germany. The declaration of war was put off for two days. Mussolini was asked to use his good offices to intercede for peace. Both Halifax and Bonnet reacted enthusiastically to Mussolini's proposal for a new Munich-style conference to determine Poland's fate. But the majority of the members of the British House of Commons, against the advice of Chamberlain and Halifax, insisted on a declaration of war, and France too was forced to follow suit.[68] When war was declared, the Cabinet, hoping to turn Germany around through negotiations, feared that the waging of a serious war would ruin this possibility. Kingsley Wood, Air Minister, argued against a proposal to bomb the Black Forest where the German army held large depots of munitions on the grounds that this would be a blow against private property. The same held for Essen's armaments factories. Instead the air force would restrict itself to dropping propaganda leaflets over Germany. Major-General Sir Edward Spears would later comment: "It was ignominious to stage a confetti war against an utterly ruthless enemy who was meanwhile destroying a whole nation, and to pretend that we were thereby fulfilling our obligations."[69]

Chamberlain wrote his sister on 10 September, explaining why the declaration of war had been delayed and why a rather limited war was being waged. Regarding the former, he mentioned three reasons: Mussolini's proposal of a conference (which Hitler ignored); France's desire to evacuate women and children from cities and mobilize its army before declaring war; and finally "the secret communications that were going on with Goering and Hitler." These communications had appeared "promising," making it appear that "it was possible to persuade Hitler to accept a peaceful and reasonable solution of the Polish question in order to get to an Anglo-German agreement, which he [Hitler] continually declared to be his greatest ambition."[70]

[68] A.J.P. Taylor, *The Second World War: An illustrated History* (London: Penguin, 1976), p. 36.
[69] Major-General Sir Edward Spears, *Assignment to Catastrophe* (London: William Heinemann, 1954), p. 31.
[70] Keith Feiling, *The Life of Neville Chamberlain* (London: Macmillan, 1946) pp. 416-417.

At the time of Munich, Chamberlain was already clear that Hitler's notion of reasonable solutions meant having his way. In terms of Poland, that would have to mean at a minimum, that Germany would take control over Danzig and the Polish corridor. So it would appear that even as Germany was ruthlessly invading Poland, Chamberlain was attempting to arrange a solution that would give Germany more territory. As we shall see, he was prepared to go much further and abandon Poland to Germany altogether.

Chamberlain was unwilling to use all of Britain's military might against Germany to try to limit the latter's ability to concentrate her full attention on seizing Poland. He confided to his sister that he did not think a military victory over Germany was possible. Instead he sought to "convince the Germans that they cannot win." He did not want to "bomb their munitions centres and objectives in towns, unless they begin it." Despite Britain's pledges to Poland, its prime minister was unwilling to launch retaliatory air raids against her German invader. Only German air attacks on Britain itself would merit retaliation in his view. Germany remained free to bomb the Polish people without having to protect its own cities against the British air force.

It is interesting to compare such concern for delicacy in dealing with the Germans and a degree of indifference to the Poles with Britain's reaction to the Soviet invasion of Finland. Britain offered unconditional military help to Finland and drew up plans for war with the Soviet Union.[71] Plans for an attack on the Soviets even continued after Finland made peace with the Soviets. As we shall see in Chapter 9, the Finnish affair demonstrated that both France and Britain wanted to turn the war against the Nazis into a war with the Soviet Union, a turn of events that required an alliance with the Nazis with or without Hitler.

The British ruling class, as we have seen, hated communism to a man. Fascism, by contrast, was admired by most of its members, and many admired its most extreme example: Hitler's Nazism. The outbreak of war with Germany would not sweep away such admiration. Nicholas Bethell has documented the case of the Duke of Westminster, a known anti-Semite and admirer of

[71] Winston S. Churchill, *The Gathering Storm* (Boston: Houghton Mifflin Company, 1948). pp. 560-561

Germany, who, on 12 September 1939, assembled a group of opponents of the war, including Lord Arnold, Lord Rushcliffe, and the Duke of Buccleuch.[72] At the meeting Westminster, the wealthiest man in the British Empire, read a document opposing the shedding of blood by "the two races which are the most akin and most disciplined in the world." The document advocated giving Danzig to Germany and removing all obstacles to German economic expansion in southeastern Europe. The group was later joined by Lord Ponsonby, a former Cabinet minister. Bethel writes:

> Men such as these were the gilded tip of the iceberg. Lurking below there were many thousands of right-wingers in England, as in other countries, who had been captivated by Hitler and his New Order. Even now, after the outbreak of the war, they were ready to give him their support.[73]

A copy of the document reached Chamberlain who handed it to a senior British counter-intelligence officer, Joseph Ball, one of his intermediaries less than two months earlier in dealing with Wohlthat. Ball had also served as Chamberlain's confidential agent for the purpose of providing a link between the prime minister and the Italian Ambassador to London. Reporting his discussion of the document with Chamberlain to Sir Horace Wilson, Ball revealed the prime minister's sympathy for the views of Westminster and his supporters. But he reported that they were foolish to express such views "at the present juncture." He believed that Churchill was aware of the existence of the Westminster group and will "press hard for their immediate and categorical rejection." "It is difficult to see how the P.M. can avoid giving him some assurance," Ball added revealingly. As Nicholas Bethell, who treats Chamberlain with great respect, comments: "The Prime Minister did not contemplate doing a deal with Hitler, but he wished to have his hands free to allow German expansion towards the East. That seems to be the alarming implication behind Ball's note."[74] The implication however is hardly surprising in light of our knowledge of Chamberlain's long-standing efforts, capped by the Munich agreement, to provide Germany a free hand in the East in return for peace in the West.

[72] Nicholas Bethell, *The War Hitler Won* (London: Penguin, 1972), pp. 175-180.
[73] *Ibid.*, p. 176.
[74] *Ibid.*, pp. 177-178.

***

Efforts to find a suitable "present juncture" for an overall agreement with Nazi Germany however were not given up by Chamberlain and his closest associates. The events of World War Two are largely beyond the scope of this book but some references to other works on this subject establish the continuity between attempts to come to terms with Hitler in the 1930s and their persistence even as Britain and France finally went to war with Nazi Germany. A good starting place is *The British Case* by the Right Honourable Lord Lloyd of Dolobran, of which some mention was made in the first chapter. It is a document that other histories of this period have completely ignored. Written at the end of 1939 and published early in 1940, *The British Case* has a preface by Lord Halifax written in November 1939 that makes clear the government's endorsement of its contents. Lloyd was an important member of the British Conservative party and would serve as a Cabinet minister in Churchill's wartime government.

Halifax notes that *The British Blue Book,* published by the government at the start of the war, gave the diplomatic history of the origins of the war. "Lord Lloyd has penetrated deeper," he claims, looking at the underlying causes of a war which is a conflict "between forces that support our civilization and forces that are in revolt against it."[75] Halifax emphasizes in his preface that nation-states in Europe give expression to "Christian conceptions of freedom." Lloyd also focuses on the need to defend the concept of the nation-state as the cause for which Britain is fighting. Nationalities, he argues, must have the right to a state which defends their culture. Using this argument, he defends Britain's willingness to allow Hitler to absorb Austria and the Sudetenland. Hitler's aggressions in these cases can be justified in terms of self-determination for people of German heritage (the assumption being that language alone creates a "national" grouping). On the other hand, the German seizure of non-German areas of Czechoslovakia and its division of Poland between itself and the Soviets violate the principle that nationalities have the right to a national state.

---

[75] The Right Honourable Lord Lloyd of Dolobran, *The British Case* (Toronto: William Collins Sons, 1940), p. 9.

But Lloyd is clear that Britain is not fighting for democracy. There is no question of trying to force Germany to abandon fascism. Indeed he speaks eloquently in favour of the fascist regimes. They are presented as "nationalist reactions to the menace of anarchy" and Spain's fascists, for example, rather than the overthrowers of an elected government, are presented as the protagonists of "the national uprising in Spain in 1936." Penetrating deeper into British official thinking, to paraphrase Halifax, Lloyd observes:

> Our most ancient and very faithful ally, Portugal, enjoys today greater prosperity than ever before in the modern world under the wise but authoritarian government of Senhor Salazar. The government of Poland itself was definitely authoritarian. Above all, the Italian genius has developed, in the characteristic Fascist institutions, a highly authoritarian regime which, however, threatens neither religious nor economic freedom, or the security of other European nations.[76]

The dividing line in Europe, writes Lloyd, "is not, as has been sometimes absurdly suggested, between democratic and non-democratic states." Instead it is between states that recognize "independent nationalities" and those who do not. Of course, it depends on one's definition of "nations" and "European nations." Italy had invaded Ethiopia in 1935 but, of course, Ethiopia was not a European nation and therefore, presumably, in Lloyd's view, had no right to preserve its independent nationality. Just months before he wrote his book, Italy had also seized control of Albania, geographically a European nation though presumably in Lord Lloyd's eyes, not very European after all. Here was a continuation of the double-speak which we have seen the Baldwin and Chamberlain governments utilized extensively, reducing nations to European nations and Europe to its western half.

The heart of "the British case" against Hitler, in Lloyd's view, appears to be its opportunist alliance with the Soviets in August 1939. The Soviets, in his view, were not to be seen as Europeans anymore than the Albanians despite the fact that their European land mass was greater than that of any other European nation. Instead they were 'Orientals' and enemies of Christianity. Poland, writes Lloyd, is "the natural bastion of the European

[76] *Ibid., p. 37.*

defence against Oriental incursions." It was Poland that repelled the Bolshevik armies in 1920 so that "once again, Germany and Europe was saved by Poland."[77] Hitler had not only betrayed Poland but had joined with the very Bolsheviks Poland had repelled. Lloyd makes clear that the Nazi alliance with the Soviets was the final straw for Britain. He writes:

> This was Herr Hitler's final apostasy. It was the betrayal of Europe. It meant the sacrifice on the altar of Communist ambition not only of Eastern Poland but of other independent states. It had one purpose only: to supply not the German people with food but the German army with munitions for a war against England and France designed (and since October 6th, admittedly so) to enforce the reorganization of the whole of Europe east of the Rhine along lines planned by Germany in the interests of Germany.[78]

Lloyd is, of course, correct in stating that Britain and France went to war with Germany because Germany was planning to attack them. He is also correct in stating that Germany intended this invasion as a prelude to seizure of all the European territories east of the Rhine. This begs the question however of whether Britain would have been willing to go to war with Germany if it had simply planned to seize the parts of eastern Europe not yet under its control rather than to launch pre-emptive assaults on western Europe to ensure no interference with its eastern European aims. As we have seen, the Chamberlain-Hitler collusion of September 1938 formalized Britain's informal policy of letting Hitler have a free hand in eastern Europe in return for assurances that he would leave the West alone. But Lloyd, defending Britain's appeasement of Germany before March 1939, is very clear that it was not the invasion of Prague, the taking of Memel, or threats to Poland that prevented the conclusion of "an honourable peace" with the Nazi regime. Rather it was "the conclusion of the German-Soviet pact." Since Lloyd's book had the endorsement of Britain's Minister for External Affairs, his statements about how official Britain had regarded Hitler and why they were now sufficiently disappointed in him to go to war with Germany deserve statement in full:

---

[77] *Ibid.*, p. 48.
[78] *Ibid*, pp. 53-54.

For all the other acts of brutality at home and aggression without, Herr Hitler had indeed been able to offer an excuse, inadequate indeed, but not fantastic. The need for order and discipline in Europe, for strength at the centre to withstand the incessant infiltration of false and revolutionary ideas – this is certainly no more than the conventional excuse offered by every military dictator who has ever suppressed the liberties of his own people or advanced to the conquest of his neighbours. Nevertheless, so long as it could be believed that the excuse was offered with sincerity, and in Herr Hitler's case the appearances of sincerity were not lacking over a period of years, the world's judgment of the man remained more favourable than its judgment of his actions. The faint possibility of an ultimate settlement with Herr Hitler still, in these circumstances, remained. However abominable his methods, however intolerant he might show himself of the rights of other European peoples, he still claimed to stand ultimately for something which was a common European interest, and which therefore could conceivably provide some day a basis for understanding with other nations equally determined not to sacrifice their traditional institutions and habits on the bloodstained altars of the World Revolution.

The conclusion of the German-Soviet pact removed even this faint possibility of an honourable peace.[79]

From the point of view of the British elite, in short, Hitler's persecution of Jews, Communists, Socialists, trade unionists, civil libertarians, and the mentally and physically handicapped, while lamentable, had been justified by "the need for order and discipline in Europe." The need to protect "traditional institutions and habits" against the World Revolution justified fascism from the British elite's point of view, as Lloyd explicitly noted earlier. It also justified Nazism presuming that Hitler kept it within bounds. Presumably parliaments, political parties, trade unions, and an independent judiciary, were not the crucial parts of the "traditional institutions" that Lloyd wished to protect. Hitler's "order and discipline" had protected owners of property against advocates of socialism and communism. That was enough. But then Hitler, overly ambitious for territorial aggrandizement, had made common cause with the Soviet Union, the epicentre for World Revolution. Interestingly, Lloyd

[79] *Ibid.*, pp. 54-5.

goes on to denounce the Stalin-Hitler deal, which he calls "apostasy" a second time, not because it destroyed Poland's national existence but because it gave the Soviets eastern Poland and the Baltic states, thus extending the region under Communist control. This, notes Lloyd, demonstrates the insincerity of Hitler's claims to have "concerns for the future of European civilization."[80]

It is important to note that Lloyd, speaking for British officialdom, after having defended fascism and made clear that democracy or its lack is not the dividing-line among European nations, suggests that the issue of the war is "the issue of European freedom." "European freedom" and "European civilization," in Lloyd's lexicon, clearly have little to do with civil rights and democracy. When he uses these words, he clearly uses the diplomatic code language that we discussed in Chapter One, in which everyone in the know understands what is really meant. Fortunately he provides enough context in his book to make it clear what "freedom" and "civilization" do not mean for him. He is less explicit about what they do mean but it is not difficult, reading between the lines, and putting his book in the context of elite opinion generally, to see that he means the preservation of the existing socioeconomic system with property in the hands of its "traditional" owners and relations between the social classes unchanged. He does also claim to defend national rights but, as we have seen, he defines them from the point of view typical in the official code language: they do not include the right to an independent national existence for Ethiopia, Albania, or Austria or Czechoslovakia's right to the territories granted it under the Versailles agreement.

***

It may seem extraordinary on first blush that Halifax would give the wartime government's blessing to a tract that extolled fascism and suggested that some of Germany's territorial ambitions could be excused on the grounds that they did not violate the "national principle." Why would Halifax risk the government's credibility to endorse without caveat a book that found little fault in Nazism as such and even implied that Hitler's behaviour before the conclusion of the German-Soviet pact, while egregious, did not justify war? The answer lies in the

[80] *Ibid*, p. 56.

secret British-German diplomacy that involved the highest circles of government in the early months of the war.

Until the war began, Chamberlain had rejected overtures from opposition forces in Germany, unwilling to jeopardize relations with the Hitler government. Historian Patricia Meehan has traced the fruitless efforts of opposition forces, led by former Leipzig mayor Carl Goerdeler, to convince Britain throughout 1938 and early 1939 that a tough Franco-British line with Hitler would lead to his overthrow by the German military.[81] With the war having erupted, however, Chamberlain, still anxious for a British-German peace, supported efforts to reach an agreement with the chiefs of the German General Staff to overthrow Hitler, though not necessarily the Nazis, and turn the war onto the Soviets. His thinking was described by one of his private secretaries, John Colville, in his diary. Six weeks after the outbreak of war, Colville, having conversed with Sir Arthur Rucker, Chamberlain's principal private secretary, wrote:

> Arthur Rucker says he thinks Communism is now the great danger, greater even than Nazi Germany. All the independent states of Europe are anti-Russian, but Communism is a plague that does not stop at national boundaries, and with the advance of the Soviet into Poland the states of eastern Europe will find their powers of resistance to Communism very much weakened. It is thus vital that we should play our hand very carefully with Russia, and not destroy the possibility of uniting, if necessary, with a new German Government against the common danger. What is needed is a moderate conservative reaction in Germany: the overthrow of the present regime by the army chiefs.[82]

The British Secret Service began negotiations on Chamberlain's behalf with individuals connected to the highest instances of the military. They were not trying to drive a hard bargain with Germany. Alexander Cadogan noted on 4 October the rather large plate the British were prepared to present to the Germans. In late September Hitler had proposed to Britain via Dahlerus, the still-active intermediary, talks based on a set of proposals which Cadogan summarized as follows:

[81] Patricia Meehan, *The Unnecessary War: Whitehall and the German resistance to Hitler* (London: Sinclair-Stevenson, 1992).
[82] Anthony Cave Brown, *The Secret Servant: The Life of Sir Stewart Menzies, Churchill's Spymaster* (London: Michael Joseph, 1988), p. 213.

> ...an independent Poland in economic vassalage to
> Germany and subject to military restrictions to
> prevent her being a threat to Germany. Germany
> would occupy the old Reich frontier in Poland.
> Germany would say nothing about Poland on the
> other side of the demarcation line – she was not
> interested in that. Frontier rectification in Slovakia –
> particularly in that region where Poland encroached
> last March. Disarmament. A colonial settlement,
> either by restoration of former German colonies or by
> 'compensation.' No war aims against France or
> England. No territorial claims in Europe and
> particularly not in the Balkans. This to be subject to
> 'suitable guarantees.' Ready to guarantee French and
> British empires. Settlement of Jewish question by
> using Poland 'as a sink in which to empty the Jews.'[83]

Cadogan's response to this set of proposals was: "All of this, or some of it, may be very nice, but we cannot trust the word or the assurance or the signature of the present rulers of Germany." Nicholas Bethell finds Cadogan's attitude, particularly his notion that what Hitler was offering was "very nice," to be "a strange one." It is not strange in light of what we know of the long-standing British acceptance of the need to give Germany a free hand in eastern Europe. Cadogan again reveals the tendency of official Britain to conflate Europe with western Europe. After indicating Hitler's demands for territory in eastern Europe, he claims that Hitler will make "no territorial claims in Europe."

Cadogan was sufficiently conciliatory in his meeting with Dahlerus to leave the latter to believe that British mistrust of Hitler, rather than Hitler's specific demands, was the major stumbling-block to peace.[84] Whatever Cadogan's intentions, he gave Dahlerus sufficient encouragement that the latter returned to Berlin to report to Hitler that negotiations with Britain for an early end to the war on the basis of Hitler's proposals were still possible.

It is unclear how seriously the British or the French were willing to entertain the idea of a new pact with a Hitler-led Germany in October 1939. It seems that by that time the British leadership did not trust his assurances that Germany would confine its aggressive behaviour to east and central Europe. Hence the

[83] Bethell, *The War Hitler Won, p. 370.*
[84] *Ibid., pp. 370-2.*

secret negotiations meant to overthrow Hitler while maintaining a fascist government in Germany. As Lord Lloyd had revealed forcefully, democracy was not an issue for the British leadership and neither was fascism.

On 1 November, Chamberlain, for the first time, informed his Cabinet of these negotiations. The purpose of the negotiations, as Anthony Cave Brown sums them up, was "to make an alliance with a German military regime from which Hitler and the Nazis had been extruded, one directed against Russia"[85] His own evidence suggests that both sides in the negotiations were, in fact, willing to have "moderate" Nazis, that is Nazis with designs only on eastern but not western Europe, included.

Churchill, whom Chamberlain had made first lord of the Admiralty when he established a wartime Cabinet, and other Cabinet members were "astounded" that "British agents had been negotiating with the enemy in time of war."[86] But the negotiations persisted. Unfortunately for the German conspirators, they had a Nazi secret service mole in their midst who reported their plot to the German authorities.[87] The result was that by the end of 1939 Chamberlain's efforts to establish peace with Germany had failed. Yet the character of the "peace" that was sought was consistent with what Chamberlain had sought before, during and after Munich with Hitler: there would not be peace at all but war with the Soviet Union, the power with whom any deal must be seen as "apostasy."

The Chamberlain government had chosen to seek an alliance with Germany, a country with which it was nominally at war, rather than to bomb Germany and make it difficult for that country to enjoy its easy victory over Poland. Unwilling to offend the German military leaders with whom they hoped to conclude an anti-Soviet accord, the British had declared war on Germany after that country's assault on Poland but had done nothing to aid the violated nation.

***

[85] Brown, *The Secret Servant*, p. 271
[86] *Ibid.*, p. 217.
[87] *Ibid.*, p. 213.

Through the early months of 1940, Chamberlain continued the "phoney war" with Germany, still unwilling to accept the notion of an all-out war with Hitler. Chamberlain was forced to give up his prime ministership after the German offensive in the West in the spring of 1940. Winston Churchill succeeded him on 10 May as head of a coalition government that included the Labour Party as well as the governing Conservatives. Though Churchill's own war aims were muddled, he was, as we have suggested, aware that Hitler and the Nazis represented a threat to Britain and its Empire and therefore little interested in notions of giving Germany a "free hand" in eastern Europe. Churchill did however give Cabinet and other governmental positions to most of Chamberlain's entourage and the "appeasers" of the 1930s kept up secret negotiations with the Germans until 1942.

Lord Halifax remained Minister of Foreign Affairs until late December 1940. His under-secretary, Rab Butler, sanctioned talks between Germans and non-Germans in contact with Goering, the supposed moderate of the Hitler government, and British representatives abroad. For example, in July 1940, Max zu Hohenlohe-Langenburg, a German national representing Goering, met in Berne with Britain's plenipotentiary in Switzerland, Sir David Kelly. Sir Samuel Hoare, whose long-time support for a "free hand" for Germany in the east we have seen, had become Britain's ambassador to Spain and used that posting to carry on contacts with Goering's representatives. Nothing came of such contacts because Churchill was determined to crush the Nazis rather than seek peace while they remained in power. Churchill confidentially informed Roosevelt however, as he asked for military assistance, that it was not beyond the realm of possibility that his government might be overthrown by forces favourable to a compromise agreement with Hitler Germany.[88]

When the Americans formally became part of the war effort, they protested to Churchill about meetings involving Foreign Affairs officials and representatives of the enemy Nazi government. Churchill put an end to these talks. But other talks that included American businessmen, American and British officials, and the Vatican continued throughout the war. The details of these talks are beyond the scope of this book.[89]

[88] Charles Bloch, *Le III e Reich et le Monde* (Paris: Imprimerie Nationale, 1986), 369-70.
[89] The negotiations are discussed in John Loftus and Mark Aarons, *The Secret*

The view that Hitler's great "apostasy," to use Lord Lloyd's term, was his failure to maintain a Western European alliance against the Soviets would not die even as the war came to a close and the news of Hitler's slaughter of Jews and gypsies was revealed. Leading American establishment figures often expressed views on this subject as retrograde as those expressed by the British elite. An example is provided in the diaries of the American Secretary of Defence James W. Forrestal who reports sympathetically the views of the United States ambassador to the Soviet Union, W. Averell Harriman, views that echo Lord Lloyd's racism against Asians and the peculiar nonsense that the Bolsheviks of Russia were not Europeans.

> Averell was very gloomy about the influx of Russia into Europe. He said Russia was a vacuum into which all movable goods would be sucked. He said the greatest crime of Hitler was that his actions had resulted in opening the gates of Eastern Europe to Asia.[90]

* * *

Chamberlain's secret negotiations with Nazi dissidents and generals, while fruitless, had a serious impact upon the government's handling of the war effort until the fall of the Chamberlain administration in May 1940. Not only did the government do nothing to help Poland, it did little either to punish Germany for its destruction of the Polish nation or to properly mobilize the British economy for a real war effort. Financial journalist Paul Einzig played a large role in exposing to the British public Chamberlain's failure either to put the economy on a war footing or to administer seriously the announced economic blockade of Germany. Writing in 1960 before the secret Chamberlain-Nazi negotiations had been exposed, Einzig was prepared to be charitable towards the prime minister his revelations in the *Financial News* probably helped to bring down. "I was and still am utterly convinced that Chamberlain had meant well," he emphasizes. But he adds: "There can be an excuse for Munich, but there can be no excuse or extenuation for the Government's reluctance to ensure that

War Against the Jews: How Western Espionage Betrayed the Jewish People (New York: St. Martin's Press, 1994), p. 90.
[90] Walter Millis, ed., *The Forrestal Diaries* (New York: Viking, 1951), entry for 29 July 1945, p. 79.

the utmost economic effort was made after the outbreak of the War and before the shooting war started."[91] A continuation of the half-hearted economic effort for another month or two, concludes Einzig, could have cost the country the Battle of Britain. Britain might have been short the requisite number of fighter planes needed to assert British supremacy in the air over its own territory during the Nazi blitzkrieg. Einzig details the extent of the government's economic sabotage of its own supposed war effort, indicating that ministers who disagreed with the course being followed by Chamberlain provided him with much of his information at the time:

> The exchange restrictions were leaking like a sieve, and so was the so-called blockade of Germany. Economic warfare in the form of preemptive purchases of essential materials in countries which were in a position to sell to Germany, was far from adequate. The conversion of industry for war requirements was proceeding at a very slow pace. The Treasury maintained its normal scrutiny of public expenditure. While in times of peace such scrutiny is an essential brake to extravagance, in time of war it necessarily entailed delays which Britain, unprepared as she was, could ill afford. On the eve of the Nazi invasion of the Low Countries the Government was still engaged in lengthy negotiations with some aircraft producers about the terms of compensation payable to them if they were to convert their works for war requirements and if orders placed with them were canceled subsequently as a result of an early termination of the War.[92]

Einzig correctly presumed that the reason for such laxity was that the government expected to come to terms with Germany at an early date. "Early in 1940 a leading Cabinet minister actually told a leading Financial Editor quite candidly that his newspaper was rendering a disservice by agitating for intensified economic war effort, because if we were to convert our economy to war requirements it would be very costly to reconvert it again to peace requirements."[93]

---

[91] Paul Einzig, *In the Centre of Things: Paul Einzig's Autobiography* (London: Hutchinson, 1960), p. 207.
[92] *Ibid.*, pp. 201-202.
[93] *Ibid.*, p. 201.

The government's complacency seemed irresponsible to Einzig. What he was unaware of was that its policies during the phoney war represented a continuation of its peacetime "appeasement" policies. The Chamberlain government, like its Baldwin and Macdonald predecessors, wanted an understanding with Nazi Germany that if Germany was prepared to leave the West alone, it could have a free hand in eastern Europe and make war on the Soviet Union without fear of British or French retaliation. The attempt, while officially at war with Germany, to form an alliance with the Nazi dictatorship to make war against the Soviets, seems little surprising in light of the diplomacy of the pre-war years. All that had changed was perceptions of Hitler as an individual. While the pre-war diplomacy assumed the need to negotiate with Hitler, anger that he had apparently reneged on his promise to Chamberlain at Berchtesgaden, Godesberg, and Munich to leave the West alone, sowed mistrust among Britain's leaders in the Nazi dictator.

Still, in the early months of the war Britain and France were busy trying to pull back from a major military confrontation with Germany. By contrast, they demonstrated keenness to attack the Soviet Union. The Finnish affair, dealt with in our last chapter, is best explained in light of the desire on the part of the Chamberlain and Daladier governments to fight Communism and the Soviet Union rather than Nazi Germany. As we shall see, a peculiarity of the early months of the war was the extent of French and British belligerency towards the Soviets. They were at war with Germany and not the Soviet Union but clearly wished to have things reversed.

CHAPTER 9
A CONFUSION OF ENEMIES

As we observed in Chapter 8, both Britain and France proved unwilling from September 1939 to the fall of France in June 1940 to follow up their declarations of war with military attacks of any consequence on Nazi Germany. Yet the two countries had bellicose plans at the ready: but they involved a plan of assault not on Germany, their declared enemy, but on the Soviet Union, a neutral power though it had benefited from its non-aggression pact with the Nazis to acquire important new territories in eastern Poland just as Poland, a year earlier, had acquired Czech territories thanks to friendship with Germany. This chapter outlines the continuation of the Soviet obsession on the part of the leaders of Britain and France. It demonstrates the continued irresponsibility of these leaders even after they had largely given up on their plans to make Hitler the chief vehicle for removing the Communist menace from Europe. While pretending to recognize Nazism as the great evil menacing European civilization, the governments of Chamberlain and Daladier continued to focus their main hostility against the socialist threat.

Though the French and British maintained that they could not overthrow Hitler and must eventually come to a compromise solution with Germany, they believed that they could overthrow the government of the Soviet Union and had elaborate plans ready to achieve this end. Their obsession with the Soviets was so great that even when the negotiations with the Nazis for a British-French-German alliance against the Communist powerhouse appeared to collapse, they could not stop planning the destruction of the Soviet Union. At one and the same time, they moaned that they lacked the men and the equipment to forestall a Nazi takeover of most of Europe, east and west, while they planned a reckless invasion of a country more than twice as populous as Germany, an invasion for which they were prepared to transfer their scarce resources of men and materiel.

Much of our information comes from *Les Documents Secrets de l'État-Major General Français*, documents in the possession of the French General Staff that were seized by the Nazis and then published. Historians have generally accepted the authenticity of these documents and William L. Shirer's excellent, if brief, account of France's attitude to Finland and the Soviets in early

269

1940 is based heavily on this set of "top secret" communications among the leading politicians and military leaders of wartime France.[1] The Nazis, as their preface suggested, wanted to demonstrate that the Allies, who appeared to be doing nothing, were trying to strangle the German economy. They had little obvious interest in trying to demonstrate that the Allies would rather be fighting the Soviet Union than Nazi Germany. The thrust of the "documents secrets" is borne out by other sources, including official British and Swedish foreign policy documents, and French archival materials as well as first-person accounts by participants in the key events such as Paul Stehlin, a young Air Force captain assigned to duties in the Finnish theatre. In post-war France, Stehlin would become Air Force Chief of Staff.

The argument made in favour of hostile action against the Soviet Union was that it was not a true neutral. While it was not fighting alongside Nazi Germany, it had secretly agreed with the Nazis to divide up Poland and had taken control of the Ukrainian portion of that hapless inter-war nation. More importantly, it was allegedly supplying the Nazis with an important percentage of Germany's petroleum needs. The Allied strategy during the "phoney war" was to use Britain's control of the seas to deprive Germany of trade. A defeat inflicted upon the Soviet Union, went this argument, was therefore a defeat inflicted upon the Nazis, and likely to force Germany to the bargaining table sooner rather than later as the resources to fuel its war machine diminished. Once the Soviet Union began to menace neutral Finland, the British and French could argue that Soviet behaviour towards small helpless nations was reminiscent of Nazi Germany's actions.

On the surface, then, anticommunism was not the motivating force in Anglo-French schemes to turn the war against the Soviets. But that surface is thin. In the first instance, as we have seen, Britain was actively involved in efforts during the early months of the war to produce an anti-Soviet alliance that would include Nazi Germany. Secondly, the argument that Soviet oil supplies were keeping the Nazi war machine in motion was patently false. The Soviets supplied about three percent of the Germans' oil needs while Roumania supplied four times more. A report in *Paris-Soir* on 5 April 1940 revealed the paucity of

---

[1]   William L. Shirer , *The Collapse of the Third Republic: An Inquiry into the Fall of France in 1940* (New York: Simon and Schuster, 1969), pp. 536-41.

oil shipments from the Caucasus to Germany: barely 750 tons of crude oil a day.[2]

Neither Britain nor France took lightly the prospect of invading neutral countries other than the Soviet Union. As the war began, France, for example, pledged to Belgium and Holland that it would not use their soil to launch attacks against Germany without receiving their explicit sanction. Such a pledge limited severely the possibilities for Britain and France to invade Germany.[3] France had fewer scruples with regards to Roumania, a far more important supplier of petroleum to Germany than the Soviet Union. It did not however consider an actual invasion of that country. France was prepared to block navigation on the Danube provided that the British were prepared to join in such a blockade. Its request for British cooperation was made however in late October 1939 while Britain was still carrying on its secret negotiations with the "German opposition" and the blockade did not occur.[4] Afterwards no serious attempt was made to revive the idea of a blockade on the Danube.

France and especially Britain were also keen not to intrude too obviously upon the neutrality of Norway and Sweden. The two powers recognized that Swedish ores were at least as important to the German war effort as Soviet oil.[5] Britain looked forward to intervention in Finland against the Soviets because it would provide a pretext to occupy the Swedish mines. When that pretext was gone, Britain lost interest in grabbing the mines. Even as Norway was about to fall to a German invasion, Britain could not bring itself to deprive Germany of the possibility of availing itself of Sweden's mineral riches. France proposed that the two countries blow up Sweden's mines and compensate Sweden financially for the loss. Sweden would be asked to consent to the explosion of this resource, but the destruction would occur with or without such consent. Britain however

[2] Charles O. Richardson, "French Plans for Allied Attacks on the Caucasus Oil Fields, January-April, 1940," *French Historical Studies*, Vol. 8, No. 1 (Spring 1973), pp. 134-35.
[3] General Gamelin, Armed Forces Chief of Staff, to Daladier, 1 September 1939, *Les Documents Secrets de l'État-Major General Francais*, Document 3 (Berlin 1941).
[4] Minister of Foreign Affairs to M. Corbin, French Ambassador to London, 24 October 1939, *Les Documents Secrets de l'État-Major General Francais*, Document 11.
[5] Paul Reynaud, the French prime minister, made the blunt comment that oil was not more important than iron ore at the ninth meeting of the Supreme Council in London, 27 April, 1940, *Les Documents Secrets*, Document 44.

regarded such action without Swedish consent, which it assumed would never be offered, as unconscionable.[6] It would ruin the Allies' reputations with other neutral powers.

Such delicacy however was never evident in British or French thinking regarding the Soviet Union. Even if they admitted that Soviet supplies to Germany were no more important than those of Roumania or Sweden, they were happy to argue that in the latter two cases, the neutrality of the country in question had to be considered while in the Soviet case it did not. Blockades could be considered to deal with supplies from Roumania or Sweden, but for the Soviet Union, an actual invasion, an effort to tear apart the country could be planned.

***

The Soviet Union had been as alarmed as France and Britain by the speed of the German takeover of Poland. Wishing to strengthen the Soviet frontier, which then lay only twenty miles from Leningrad, Stalin proposed a territorial exchange with Finland. The Finns, encouraged by the West, rejected the Soviet proposal.

The Soviets then invaded Finland on 30 November 1939 and though the Finns mounted a spirited resistance, the Finnish-Soviet pact of 12 March 1940, which ended hostilities between the two countries, largely granted Stalin's initial demands. In the interim, however, both France and Britain made a *cause célèbre* of the Finnish resistance. Having done nothing for Poland whose independence they had guaranteed, they were suspiciously anxious to help out a nation whom they were not bound to help. They provided material aid to Finland in December and thought to do much more. In January, General Gamelin, France's Armed Forces Chief of Staff, planned a naval expedition to the Russian-occupied port of Petsamo as well as a takeover of the ports and airports of the west coast of Norway as part of a plan to aid Finland in its battle with the Soviets. Sweden's mines would also be seized. As Gamelin later admitted, this effectively meant a declaration of war upon the Soviets.[7]

---

[6] *Ibid.*
[7] "Note du General Gamelin," March 10, 1940, *Documents Secrets*, No. 23.

272

The British government, while anxious to seize the mines in northern Sweden, was reticent about an early attack on Petsamo, which necessarily meant overt conflict with the Soviets.[8] The Supreme Council, the coordinating body for France and England during the war, agreed to put off the Petsamo operation indefinitely, though Britain agreed "that if we couldn't gain the acquiescence of the Norwegians and Swedes we must try the Petsamo project."[9] Even without Petsamo, France and Britain together envisioned sending 150,000 troops into the Scandinavian fray.[10]

The hysteria that the governments of France and Britain whipped up over Finland proved quite contagious, gripping even the Socialist Party of France[11] and the Labour Party in Britain. Labour chairman Hugh Dalton, reflecting on the mood of the time, would later recall:

> I was...shocked by the proposal, not only to supply Finland with arms, including aircraft, which were badly needed by France and ourselves, but to send an Anglo-French expeditionary force to fight in Finland against Russia. This seemed to me sheer political lunacy. It would, I thought, throw the Russians, with their vast manpower and material resources, into alliance with the Germans against us and the French. It would immediately and recklessly create just that tremendously powerful hostile combination which Western foreign policy should have been striving by all means to prevent. It might even make quite certain that we lost the war.[12]

Despite the fact that the Germans were massing troops on the Western Front, on 2 March, Daladier authorized sending 50,000 "volunteers" (they were troops but France and Britain used the fiction of volunteers to disguise the fact that they were making war on the Soviet Union) and a hundred bombers to Finland.

---

[8] David Dilks, *The Diaries of Sir Alexander Cadogan* (London: Cassell, 1971), 5 February 1940, p. 253.
[9] Roderick Macleod, *The Ironside Diaries 1937-1940* (London: Constable, 1942), p. 215.
[10] "Note du General Gamelin—Note relative à la participation de forces franco-britanniques aux opérations en Finlande," 10 March 1940, *Documents Secrets*, No. 23.
[11] Hugh Dalton, *The Fateful Years: Memoirs 1931-1945* (London: Frederick Muller, 1957), pp. 292-3.
[12] *Ibid.*, p. 293.

Britain, now leery of any diversion from the Western front, nevertheless agreed to send 50 bombers.[13]

Britain had been counting on Swedish and Norwegian participation in the defence of Finland. But both of these countries were anxious to avoid hostilities with the Soviets. The French did not help their cause when they told the Swedes they and the British were planning a full-scale war against the Soviets. On 2 March, the Swedish consul general in Paris communicated to King Gustave V a personal message from Daladier. France was about to send 50,000 men to Finland via the Norwegian port of Narvik. "The expedition fell within a general plan of attack against the U.S.S.R. Action was supposed to start against Baku on the 15th of March and against Finland the same day." The Swedish Foreign Minister, Gunther, was present at the meeting and took notes. Stockholm immediately refused to take part in such plans or to offer its ports as launching bases for an offensive against the Soviet Union.[14]

Military aid for Finland had become a pretext for a wider strategy of attack on the Soviet Union. On 19 January 1940, Prime Minister Daladier asked General Gamelin and the naval commander, Admiral Darlan, to prepare a study of Allied options for an "eventual destruction of Russian oil." The three hypotheses that the armed forces chiefs were to examine were: interception of ships carrying oil to Germany via the Black Sea; direct intervention in the Caucasus; and the facilitation of Muslim "movements of emancipation" in the Caucasus.

On 22 February General Gamelin provided his report to Daladier. Intervention in the Black Sea would have a minimal effect on Soviet oil shipments to Germany, he believed, and so his study focused on an Allied effort to attack Baku, the major centre for oil wells in Russia, as well as the secondary centre, Batum. Gamelin began by noting that an Allied intervention against the Russian oilfields could have one of two objectives and he gave no preference to one or the other. The purpose could be to deprive Germany of the oil it was receiving from the Caucasus or it could be "to deprive Russia of a primary resource

[13] *Ibid.*, p. 295.
[14] "La Suède Pendant la Guerre: Les Livres Blancs Suédois," in *Revue d'histoire de la Deuxième Guerre Mondiale*, Vol. 4, No. 13 (January 1954), p. 20. Les Livres Blancs were the official foreign policy documents of Sweden for the wartime period and were published by the Swedish Ministry of Foreign Affairs.

that is indispensable to its economy and thus to break down Soviet power," at the same time reducing supplies to Germany. The latter objective seemed pleasing to Gamelin who observed that an assault on Baku would not only have an impact on Germany "but it would deprive the U.S.S.R. of an important portion of Caucasian oil and Moscow, having need of almost its entire oil production for its motorized formations and its agricultural operations, the Soviets would quickly be placed in a critical situation." Later, returning to this theme, he suggested: "After a couple of months, Soviet difficulties could become so great that this country would run the risk of a total collapse."

Gamelin rejected any thought of a land invasion of Baku as logistically impossible. Instead, he recommended an air assault based either in Turkey, Iran, Syria, or Iraq. In either case, an agreement with either Turkey or Iran would be necessary whether for the creation of bases or the overflight of aviation on their territory. Six to eight groups of modern bombers would be required and, owing to France's lack of such bombers, most of the aircraft used would have to be British.[15]

After the war, Gamelin, confronted with the recklessness of planning to add to the Allies' enemies a well-armed country of 185 million when France felt unable to respond militarily to a nation of 85 million with which it was already at war, blamed the politicians. He had only answered the questions put to him by Daladier, he argued, doing his soldier's duty without indicating his political assessment of the government's proposal. But this is easily refuted. Gamelin had had no difficulty in chiding the government in September for accepting that Belgium would not be used as a staging-ground for attacks on Germany without its government's permission. Nor did he give his soldierly assessment of how best to attack the Soviet Union and then leave matters to the government. He sent several notes to Daladier in which he encouraged the prime minister to follow the recommendations of his study on how to destroy the Soviet oil fields. On 12 March 1940, he wrote:

> My personal assessment is that it is in our interest to pursue rapidly these studies of an attack upon Baku and Batum (especially by aviation). The operations to be conducted in this scheme of things would be a

[15] "Note du General Gamelin, Commandant en Chef des Forces Terrestres," —"Extrait"— *Les Documents Secrets*, No. 22.

> happy complement to those conducted in Scandinavia. But if the latter become impeded, that would be all the more reason to act in the Caucasus.[16]

Some historians, while noting the seriousness of the French regarding the attack on the Soviets, suggest that Britain was not truly committed to this course of action.[17] The French certainly had reason to believe otherwise. General Weygand, the French commander-in-chief in the Middle East, wrote Gamelin on 7 March regarding the joint planning he was undertaking with British officers to insure that Middle Eastern countries cooperated with the Allied efforts to bomb Baku and Batum. Air Marshall Mitchell, the British Air Force commander for the region, met with Weygand in Ankara and told him that he had received instructions from London "concerning the preparation of eventual bombing operations against Baku and Batum." Mitchell told Weygand that he intended to ask Marshal Cakmalk for authorization to use Turkish bases as intermediary bases for aeroplanes whose principal base would be Djezireh in Iraq. In turn, he asked Weygand to receive Iraqi permission to make use of Djezireh for the anti-Soviet assault.[18]

Three days later Weygand wrote Gamelin that General Wavell, British Commander in Chief in the Near East, had received a letter from the War Office asking him to analyze the operations required for an eventual attack on the Caucasus to be treated within the context of war against Russia. The War Office indicated that this eventual action would be under the control of the Army.[19]

On 14 March France's ambassador to Turkey received what he believed was a sympathetic response from Turkey's Foreign Minister to the French-English plans to storm the Caucasus.[20]

[16] *Les Documents Secrets*, General Gamelin to Daladier, 12 March 1940, No. 25.

[17] Charles Richardson, "French Plans," p. 136. It does seem indeed that British military and political leaders recognized that French plans regarding attacks on the Soviet Union were unrealistic, even insane. Nonetheless, the fact remains that, on the whole, with whatever degree of enthusiasm, British officialdom was prepared to participate in such schemes. Richardson indeed confirms this, noting that Britain "not only failed to veto French proposals for military action against Russia but at times took the initiative in preparing for such attacks." Richardson, p. 146.

[18] General Weygand to General Gamelin, 7 March 1940, *Les Documents Secrets*, No. 25.

[19] General Weygand to General Gamelin, 10 March 1940, *Ibid*.

[20] Monsieur Massigli, French ambassador to Turkey, to the Minister of War,

This was encouraging to Gamelin, who believed that Turkey should lead the land attack onto Soviet territory. Gamelin did not feel that the anti-Soviet plans of France and Britain need be re-examined in light of the armistice between the Soviets and Finland on 12 March. Despite France's weak air defences against Germany, Gamelin was now prepared to deploy four French *groupes d'aviation* in the war against the Soviets, leaving the Royal Air Force to provide five.[21] Since Britain continued to plot with France for an attack on the Soviet Union, it is clear that the resolution of the Finnish issue made little difference in that country's attitude to the Soviets. Finland had simply been a pretext for targeting the Soviet Union; even with that pretext gone, the leaders of the British and French political and military establishments were anxious to plan an attack on the Soviet Union.

Daladier was forced to resign as French premier a week after the Soviet-Finnish agreement because of perceptions that he had acted too slowly to make use of the Finnish events to launch an attack on the Soviets. Paul Reynaud, who succeeded Daladier as premier and formed a new Cabinet, wrote to the British government that it was unfortunate that the Finnish situation had been resolved. Had the Allies intervened to save Finland and thereby created a complete break with the Soviet Union, this break would "free us from the legal impediments which Soviet non-belligerence imposes on the extension of intervention in other theatres of operation."[22]

Turkey, it soon appeared, was, contrary to what was earlier believed, reticent about joining an Allied attack against the Soviets. While the government remained sympathetic to the Allies, it could not ignore that much of public opinion in Turkey held that eventually the Allies would come to terms with Germany and there was little point in taking sides. Massigli, the French ambassador in Ankara, wrote the Minister of Foreign Affairs on 28 March urging that the operation against Baku proceed as quickly as possible. It seemed to him that it would lead to paralysis of the Soviet Union and encourage Turkey to believe that it was safe to join with the Allies in blockading the Black Sea against German shipping.[23] The same day the

Paris, 14 March 1940, *Documents Secrets*, No. 26.
[21] Note of General Gamelin on the conduct of the war, 16 March 1940, *Documents Secrets*, No. 27.
[22] Charles Richardson, "French Plans," pp. 146-47.

Supreme Council approved plans for an immediate study by French and British experts of the proposal for bombing Soviet oilfields. The study was to focus on the likelihood of this yielding effective results, the repercussions of this operation for the USSR and the probable attitude of Turkey.[24]

As Massigli learned a few days later, Turkey would not participate in an offensive action taken against the Soviet Union. Massigli advised his minister that he did not feel that this should impede French action. Massigli saw no reason why France should require Turkish consent for an operation that would involve "the overflight of a small proportion of its territory."[25]

French and British planning of the bombing of Baku continued apace. On 2 April General Lelong, military attaché to the French embassy in London, wrote Gamelin of the detailed operations which were being worked out with the British. Subsequent messages over the next three days filled out these plans. Incredibly, as Norway approached its final days of freedom, Britain was offering to commit six squadrons to the destruction of Soviet refineries. Britain and France together would use 90 to 100 aeroplanes in the attack.[26]

On 17 April General Weygand informed Gamelin and Air Force Chief of Staff General Vuillemin that the attack on the Soviets should be delayed until the end of June or the beginning of July. This would allow enough time for the technical arrangements for the bombing attack to be perfected and give Turkey a chance to ready itself for a Soviet response to its collaboration, however unwilling, with the Allies in this attack. Giving little thought to what Soviet retaliation the Allies might face, Weygand wrote that "such an operation ought not to last longer than a few days and should consist of massive bombardments of places where destruction or fire is recognized to be most effective."[27]

---

[23] Massigli to Minister of Foreign Affairs, 28 March 1940, *Documents Secrets*, No. 28.
[24] "Projet de résolutions de la sixième séance du Conseil Suprême," 28 March 1940, *Les Documents Secrets*, No. 30.
[25] Massigli to Minister of Foreign Affairs, 1 April 1940, *Documents Secrets*, No. 32.
[26] Lelong to Gamelin, 2 April 1940, *Documents Secrets*, No. 33; "Notes sur les liaisons effectuées les 4 et 5 avril 1940 au G.Q.G. Aerien," and "Liaison effectuée au G.Q.C. Aerien le 5 avril 1940," *Documents Secrets*, No. 34.
[27] Weygand to Gamelin, 17 April 1940, *Documents Secrets*, No. 38.

Only ten days later however, as the French War Committee, which included all the ministers with responsibilities related to the war, discussed possible aid to Norway, it became clear that France's ability to defend itself against Germany, much less engage another large, militarized European power, was questionable. General Gamelin and his second in command, General Georges, told the ministers that France could not afford the luxury of sending more troops to Norway to join the 40,000 it had already dispatched. Rather France had to focus on defence of its own borders. Nonetheless, the meeting discussed the "question of eventual operations in the region of the Caucasus and in the Balkans."[28]

No such operations would occur though General Weygand continued his preparations in Syria for an assault on the Caucasus until he left for France on 17 May.[29] In April, Germany seized Denmark and Norway, in May Holland and Belgium. Finally, on 17 June, after six weeks of fighting that ended the phoney war, France capitulated to Germany. But the degree of planning that went into the aborted Allied effort to make war on the Soviet Union cries out for analysis. Why were two countries at war with Germany largely unwilling to attack that country and quite prepared to make war on the Soviet Union, first using the pretext of aiding the Finns and when that pretext was gone, with the flimsy pretence that the Soviet-German non-aggression pact was a full-scale alliance between the two countries?

Paul Stehlin, as a young captain about to be assigned to Finland, received this explanation from General Bergeret, associate to Air Force Chief of Staff General Vuillemin.

> Russia is henceforth associated with Germany. They are making war together so as to divide up Europe and looking to extend beyond that. Thus by striking the Soviet Union we will deprive Hitler Germany of resources that she needs, and at the same time we will move the war from our borders. General Weygand commands in Syria and in Lebanon the armed forces which will head in the general direction of Baku to stop the production of petroleum; from there they will

[28] Minutes of the meeting of the French War Committee, 26 April 1940, *Documents Secrets*, No. 41.
[29] Charles Richardson, "French Plans," p. 153.

go northwards to meet the armed parties of
Scandinavia and Finland on the way to Moscow.[30]

Stehlin, though far junior to Bergeret, could not contain himself
from expressing his view that this was a dangerous course of
action. Over the next few days, he learned that the other junior
officers who had been posted to this operation shared his view
that the operation was mad. Like him, they viewed the French
commanders as incompetents. The air force had no offensive
capacity, much of the armed forces' equipment was in disrepair,
and the operational plans were outdated.[31] It seemed incredible
that France and England believed they could launch a full-scale
war against the Soviet Union, which had the world's largest
army,
and still continue to be at war with Germany.

If the junior officers could see the obvious – that a war in the
Soviet Union left France and Britain in a weak position to
defend the continent, much less to carry out assaults on
Germany – , why were the senior officers so blind? Why were
their political commanders generally also fixated on the attack
on the Soviet Union? Why did they irresponsibly exaggerate
even among themselves the economic role of the Soviet Union –
which was, in fact, negligible – in fuelling the Nazi war
machine? Why pretend that a blow against the Soviets was, in
any meaningful sense, a blow against Hitler? Historian Charles
Richardson suggests some answers with regards to the French
supporters of a war against the Soviet Union. While some of
those who supported collective action to help the Finns were
long-time supporters of collective action against Nazi and
Fascist aggression, "for the first time they were joined by the
former appeasers of Hitler who were now eager for bold action
against Communist Russia."[32] The very men and women who
had insured that France gave no support to Austria,
Czechoslovakia, Ethiopia, Spain, and Albania, not to mention
Poland for whom the country had nominally gone to war, now
cried out for vengeance against the Soviet invaders of Finland.

Finland appealed to the Right for many reasons. Though it was
nominally a democracy, it was led by the generals who had

---

[30] Paul Stehlin, *Témoignage pour l'histoire* (Paris: Robert Laffont, 1964), p.
215.
[31] *Ibid.*, p. 217.
[32] Charles Richardson, "Allied Attacks," p. 131.

defeated the Communists' attempts to make a revolution in Finland during 1918 and 1919. Fascist movements had attempted coups in the country in 1930 and 1932 and exerted sufficient influence to have the Communist movement banned in Finland.

But the main attraction of Finland was that it was, however briefly, at war with the Soviet Union. It provided a pretext for an attack on the country that the Right detested and wanted destroyed. France and Britain brought the matter before the League of Nations to have the Soviet Union condemned even though they had made no effort to have the League condemn the Nazi invasion of Poland. The views of the Right were expressed succinctly by Professor Rougier of the Faculty of Arts at Besançon. Writing to former Prime Minister Camille Chautemps, who shared Rougier's thoughts with Prime Minister Daladier, Rougier observed:

> A unique opportunity arises for the Allies to liquidate the war in a few months, to unanimously rally American opinion and the opinion of neutral countries, to force Italy to make up with us, to provoke perhaps the fall of the Bolshevik regime, and to finally liquidate our domestic Communist Party. This unique opportunity is the U.S.S.R. aggression against Finland and the decisions of the League of Nations.[33]

Chautemps would become a supporter of General Pétain's accession to power in France in June, 1940, and capitulation to the Nazis. He served in various posts in the Vichy government and was found guilty after the war of collaborating with the enemy, though his sentence of five years in prison was later quashed.[34] Rougier also played an important role in the Vichy government.[35]

The view that Finland represented an "opportunity" to make war against both the Soviets and French Communists was widespread in France. Bourgeois newspapers made the small nation their central focus and were far more vicious in their attacks on the Soviet Union than in their attacks on Nazi

---

[33] Henri Amouroux, *Le peuple du désastre, 1939-1940: La grande histoire des Français sous l'occupation* (Paris: Robert Laffont, 1976), p. 221.
[34] William L. Shirer, *The Collapse of the Third Republic*, pp. 845, 856, 958.
[35] Henri Amouroux, *Le peuple du désastre*, p. 221.

Germany. As Charles Richardson observes, the strongest pressures on the French government for reprisals against the Soviets for the invasion of Finland came from those who had supported Munich and would soon support Vichy. Admirers of Mussolini and opponents of sanctions against Italy for having invaded Ethiopia, in short the Fascist-inclined, joined Professor Rougier in regarding Soviet actions in Finland as an "opportunity."

The government, which was a coalition of centrist and right-wing forces, was, from the start of the war, harsher in its dealings with the supporters of the Soviet Union in France than the supporters of Germany, though it was the latter against whom France had declared war. The government banned the Communist press because it had reported favourably the Nazi-Soviet nonaggression pact of 22 August 1939. Party leader Maurice Thorez told the Chamber of Deputies three days later, that the Nazi-Soviet pact notwithstanding, French Communists supported all military efforts to defend France against a German attack and were prepared to support the French government if it came to the defence of other countries, such as Poland, that the Nazis might attack. Such a concession was not welcomed by the government, which proceeded to ban the Communist Party outright and to forbid any of its elected members to remain in Parliament unless they renounced the Nazi-Soviet pact. This led to the expulsion of 53 of the 65 Communist members of the Chamber of Deputies.

Communists suffered harassment, censorship and arrest. Notes Richardson: "When contrasting this treatment to the leniency extended to the Republic's enemies on the right, one must conclude that the French government considered the Communists the chief threat to their internal security."[36]

The far Right was at least honest enough to admit that they regarded the Soviet Union and Communism as the enemies of the kind of Europe they wanted to see. They supported German Nazism and Italian Fascism and wanted France to adopt policies similar to those put in place by the dictators. The traditional Right as well as the Socialists had a harder time explaining why they wanted to focus their fight on the Soviet Union, making an assault against Germany unlikely and increasing the risk of a Nazi assault on France. So, for example, the conservative

[36] Charles Richardson, " French Plans," p. 132.

Senator Émile Mireaux, echoing Professor Regier, called the Soviet attack on Finland "a capital event." It would force Germany and the Soviets closer together and Soviet weakness would drag Germany down with its Communist ally. As historian Jean-Baptise Duroselle observes, not only was this reasoning absurd but it was also, with minor nuances, the view of the principal decision-makers in France, including Daladier, Gamelin, and Darlan. It is, in fact, difficult not to conclude that the leaders of France and Britain were lying even to themselves about what they were doing because what they were doing was so shameful. They were abandoning a war against Germany that they had not really begun to fight for a war against the Soviet Union.[37]

Daladier was clearly warned about the right-wing strategy, a strategy that was aided by right-wing dominance within the press. One of his diplomatic counsellors explained: "certain milieux want to make the U.S.S.R. appear to be enemy number one and use this to make arguments in favour of a shaky peace with Germany."[38] Many of these individuals had been opposed to war with Germany all along and now had a pretext to end that war and make war on the country they loathed most.[39] While Daladier may not have sympathized with this strategy and would prove an opponent of Vichy unlike many of the loudest defenders of a war for Finland, he played into the hands of the Right with many of his public statements. On 3 March he told a journalist that "I cannot see any difference between Bolshevism and Nazism if it is not the difference between plague and cholera." Further," Russia wants to spread the war as widely as possible in the hope that Bolshevism will thereby find a favourable terrain."[40]

****

In light of what we have discovered about British and French foreign policy throughout the Hitler period, none of the above should seem too surprising. The Chamberlainites and conservative French administrations had supported the concept of giving Hitler a free hand in central and eastern Europe

[37] Jean-Baptiste Duroselle, *L'Âbime 1939-1945* (Paris: Imprimerie Nationale, 1983), p. 90.
[38] Jean-Louis Crémieux-Brilhac, *Les Français de l'An 40: Tome 1: La Guerre Oui Ou Non?* (Paris: Gallimard, 1990), p. 226.
[39] *Ibid.*, p. 235.
[40] *Ibid.*, p. 229.

provided that he agreed to leave western Europe alone. Their hope was that Hitler, who they believed had rescued Germany from Communist revolution, would destroy the Soviet Union, the fount of social unrest in conservative demonology. They did not want to fight a war against Hitler because, apart from the fact that they had only minor disagreements with his policies, they believed that the social disruption caused by another war would cause proletarian revolts across the continent. Only Hitler's plans to attack Western countries and his "apostasy" in signing a pact with the Soviets that divided Poland between the Soviet Union and Germany caused France and Britain to declare war on Hitler. But they were reluctant to wage war on Nazi Germany and risk both social revolution and an end to their plans for destroying the Soviet Union. Britain negotiated with the Hitler government until Germany invaded Poland, offering as many assurances as possible of its commitment to let Germany have a "free hand" in central and eastern Europe. Afterwards, it negotiated with important Nazi and military figures who it believed were more conciliatory than Hitler, though the basis of the discussions remained the same: Germany could control central and eastern Europe and it would be encouraged to attack the Soviet Union. This time Britain and France would join in the attack.

As it became less and less likely that a compromise with Nazi Germany could be worked out, the Allies found their foreign policy objectives and methods of the 1930s in ruins. The Finnish crisis was an effort to pick up the pieces. Once again, Britain and France could turn attention away from Nazi Germany and make the Soviet Union out to be the principal threat to European countries. Communism, not Nazism, could be treated as the principal threat to Western civilization. The Allies had tumbled back through time to the period of the Bolshevik Revolution when they had found pretexts to try to overthrow a Communist state without admitting that their real aim was to negate the possibility of having a state whose underlying economic principle was neither capitalist nor feudal.

CONCLUSION

The argument that this book has made, simply put, is that Chamberlain made what he considered to be a formal deal with Hitler in September 1938 that gave the Nazi dictator control over central and eastern Europe in return for a solemn assurance that Nazi guns would never be aimed in the direction of western Europe or any corner of the British Empire. This collusion was the logical result of official British reaction to the Nazi government from the time Hitler came to power in 1933. From the beginning, the governments of Ramsay MacDonald, Stanley Baldwin and Neville Chamberlain, took the view that whatever Hitler's faults, he was the best if not only alternative to the Communists of Germany. Though they recognized that Hitler's intentions to rearm Germany in violation of the Versailles Treaty could ultimately represent a military threat to their own country, they were convinced that Hitler's focus was on expansion eastwards to grab the *lebensraum* that he claimed the German population required. The goals of Nazi expansionism would, they believed, inevitably produce a military clash between Hitler and Stalin that they hoped might result in a dismemberment of the Communist state. This would rid the elites of Europe of the Communist threat which had menaced them since 1917 and which they had been unable to extirpate in the aftermath of the establishment of the Bolshevik regime because of troop mutinies and demonstrations at home opposed to intervention in the affairs of the former Russian Empire. They were so obsessed with the perceived Communist danger that they were prepared to gamble on the security of their own country, wistfully hoping that Hitler would prove the instrument of their fondest goal. Though the French elite, more concerned than the British about the possibility of a German invasion of their country, were divided on this approach, the French right received a big boost in pursuing a pro-Hitler foreign policy from the British opposition to making anti-Nazism rather than anti-Sovietism the fundamental objective of Franco-British foreign policy.

The Anglo-German Naval Pact in 1935 and the British and French refusal to react to Germany's remilitarization of the Rhineland in 1936 grew out of this perspective of how the democracies should deal with Hitler on the one hand and Stalin on the other. Britain reconciled itself to the rearming of Germany and the march into the Rhineland before they had occurred. We argued that it did so because it was willing to countenance a free hand for Germany in the east and, in any case, was unwilling to see Hitler overthrown for fear that the next German government might be controlled by Communists. Prime Minister Baldwin was explicit in Cabinet that France, which considered repelling the Germans from the Rhineland, had to be made to see that Hitler was the best alternative available as leader of Germany if the communist danger in Europe was to be averted. With the free hand to Hitler conceded early on, it is fair to say that Britain accepted in advance both the takeovers of Austria and the Sudetenland. Indeed, as we have seen, Britain was prepared almost a year before Munich to let Hitler do as he wished in Czechoslovakia. Public revulsion however forced Chamberlain to attempt to get Hitler to modify his appetite at the same time using the Czech crisis as a pretext to meet three times with Hitler in an effort to get, as he admitted to the king, a "general agreement" with Germany that would unite the two nations against the Soviet Communists. The three Chamberlain-Hitler meetings in September 1938 formalized what had been an informal understanding between Britain and Germany to that point, with France, with varying degrees of enthusiasm and reluctance, concurring: Germany could do as it wished in central and eastern Europe and the democracies were not to intervene, particularly should Germany carry its warfare to the Soviet Union. Racism against Slavic peoples made this betrayal of the interests of much of Europe on the altar of antibolshevism appear more palatable.

The "deal" between Hitler, on the one hand, and Chamberlain and Daladier, on the other, at Munich, which in turn simply confirmed the deal worked out by Chamberlain and Hitler at Berchtesgaden and Godesberg, fell apart because when push came to shove, Hitler had more faith in British and French democracy than the rulers of Britain and France themselves. While he trusted Chamberlain and Halifax, he was convinced that the pro-Nazi foreign policy that Britain and France were following would not outlive the prime ministerships of Chamberlain and Daladier. Aware that public opinion in both countries was against the Fascist dictators and their intimidation of both their own peoples and aggression against their neighbours, Hitler believed that he had to face the possibility of a return of the Popular Front in France or of a government in Britain led by a firm anti-Nazi such as Churchill, Eden, or Cooper. Such governments, he reasoned, would disavow the free hand in the east that he had received from the leaders of Britain and France and take advantage of a German assault on eastern and central Europe to attack Germany from the west. Unwilling to risk having to fight on two fronts at once, he began plans to attack the West so as to neutralize the Western countries before he invaded more countries of central and eastern Europe to pursue his *lebensraum*.

Chamberlain received reports of Hitler's change of plans from late 1938 onwards but tended to discount them until March 17, 1939 when he learned that Ruthenia, Czech territory which was seen as crucial to Hitler's supposed plans to create a puppet Ukrainian state that would justify Germany invading the Soviet Union, had been handed by Hitler to Hungary. To stall for time and to cause Hitler to rethink his strategy, Chamberlain, who had long written off Poland and especially Danzig and the Polish Corridor as within the German sphere of influence, gave Poland assurances of British support against any attack by Germany. France followed with a similar guarantee. In practice, the two countries had no intention of going to war with Germany on Poland's behalf but wanted to confront Hitler with the unpalatable possibility of a two-front war. This was meant to get Hitler to behave more moderately and feverish negotiations began to restore the Chamberlain-Hitler understanding and avert war. These came to nought because Hitler proved to be more influenced by the "extremists" than the "moderates." So war was declared but, rather than fight, Britain and France negotiated with the so-called moderates in an ultimately failed bid to remove Hitler from the equation but to restore the free hand in central and eastern Europe to Germany and unite Germany with France and Britain to make the Soviet Union the enemy. In violation of their guarantee to Poland, France and Britain did nothing to punish Germany for its murderous assault on its eastern neighbour, preferring to continue their efforts to get Germany to divide up Europe with them and stick to whatever agreement was reached. Only the fall of the Chamberlain government removed the official efforts to reach a peace agreement with a Nazi-led Germany.

It is important not only that the truth of what transpired in Britain and France as Germany rearmed comes out but also that the underlying causes be exposed. There is an assumption in much writing on this period and on other periods that the leaders of the democracies, however conservative their economic and social policies, are democrats. While they may be interested in the protection of the property and privileges of elites, they are considered to be willing to fight for and perhaps lose their battles within a framework of mass democracy and elected governing bodies. Unfortunately such an assumption is often untrue. It is quite clear from the evidence of the 1920s and 1930s that the elites in Britain and France, as well as other countries, were contemptuous of the parliamentary regimes they were forced to work under, hostile to labour parties and trade unions, and terrified of Communists and large-scale strikes. Largely unwilling to allow sufficient redistribution of wealth and power to weaken the ideological threat posed by socialism and communism, many members of the elites welcomed the fall of democracy in such countries as Italy, Spain, Portugal and Germany. The enthusiasm of the big businessmen and landlords of the fascist countries for the new regimes, regimes whose establishment owed much to the bankrolling of the dictators by vested interests, confirmed the increasingly anti-democratic views of the British and French establishment. While they happily moaned the lack of democracy in the Soviet Union, they made excuses for the right-wing dictators, suggesting that the countries they led were somehow unsuited to democracy. Unfortunately, it would seem that when wealth is too greatly concentrated, the powerful social class controlling that wealth will stoop to any level to maintain their privileges. The general incompatibility of democracy with plutocracy seems to be confirmed by the behaviour of the British and French elites of the 1930s.

We conclude however by pointing out once again that even if most of the leaders of the democracies were not truly democrats, the citizens of these countries generally were. And it was the decency of the people as a whole that ultimately led to the breakdown of the Chamberlain-Hitler collusion. Hitler's faith that British democracy would not accept a "free hand" for Germany in central and eastern Europe led to his resolve to crush that country before he proceeded with his eastern agenda. The strength of popular feeling against Hitler's foreign and domestic policies, which almost prevented Munich, narrowed the Chamberlain government's manoeuvrability considerably as the war began. Negotiations with the German government that had continued in the period after the guarantee to Poland had to be kept secret and the negotiations with the German military after the war started were kept under even closer wraps. About a month after the war began, Joseph Kennedy, the American Ambassador to Britain and a critic of Britain's decision to declare war on Germany, asked John Simon, then the Chancellor of the Exchequer, why Britain did not pull out of the war. Simon, himself pessimistic about the war with Germany, responded that if the government "were to advocate any type of peace, they would be yelled down by their own people, who are determined to go on."[41] In the end, whatever either Hitler or Chamberlain thought of British democracy was irrelevant. It continued to exist and to assert itself, getting in the way of deal-making by the elite with the dictators of Europe. The fact that the leaders of both Britain and France felt compelled in the end to make war on Germany is a testimony to the strength of democracy in both these countries in this period despite the efforts of their leaders to keep the people out of decision-making. Unfortunately, though historians have tried ever since to tell us that the leaders and the people were at one in standing up to the dictators, our evidence argues that the opposite is true. It was the voice of the people, not of the elites that was raised up against Hitler and that forced the British government to launch a war that would ultimately destroy the fascist regimes of Germany and Italy.

[41] Nicholas Bethell, *The War Hitler Won* (London: The Penguin Press, 1972), pp. 283-284.

APPENDIX

THE HISTORIANS AND THE CHAMBERLAIN-HITLER COLLUSION

Most of the evidence in this book has been readily available to historians of the period leading to the Second World War. Yet most historians of the period deny that Britain gave Nazi Germany a "free hand" in central and eastern Europe before 1939 or ignore the issue altogether. They deny that Chamberlain's "appeasement" of Hitler implied sympathies for fascist ideology or Hitler's aims of German conquest. While they generally admit the fierce anti-Sovietism of the British rulers, they insist that there was no collusion between the leaders of Britain and France, on the one hand, and Germany on the other, to have the Nazis invade and dismember the Soviet Union. This chapter outlines their conclusions and evidence and suggests that, whatever the intent of these historians, there is a great deal of self-delusion to their arguments. We also point out however that some historians do present evidence that buttresses the argument that the British and French rulers were prepared to grant Hitler a free hand in eastern Europe and were anxious to provoke a war between Germany and the Soviet Union. They document the pro-fascist sentiments of political and military leaders or they demonstrate the cynicism of the British or French governments with regards to Hitler's conquests. But few of these historians examine closely the Chamberlain-Hitler meetings of September 1938 and so none demonstrates, as this book does, that there was formal collusion between Hitler and Chamberlain to give Hitler undivided control over the fate of central and eastern Europe. Indeed, with only a few exceptions, as noted in the chapter, even most of the critical historians draw back from their evidence and there is a strong tendency to exonerate Chamberlain from accusations that he truly condoned Hitler even among authors who freely admit the widespread anti-democratic sentiments within the ruling elites of Britain and France. He is presented as a kindly, if quite naive, pacifist, who was fooled by Hitler's assurances because he was so desirous of preventing another war. This is a view totally opposed in the current book which presents the evidence that Chamberlain was, in fact, promoting war between Nazi Germany and the Soviet Union and that the defence of the property rights of the rich was, in practice, the value that Chamberlain cherished most. On the whole the argument of this chapter is that historians, reluctant to believe that a long-standing parliamentary democracy could be lead by a man who believed an alliance with Nazism was the best way to preserve "Western civilization," that is capitalist and even feudal rights, have ignored or fudged crucial evidence.

A.J.P. Taylor's important work, *The Origins of the Second World War*, serves as a useful point of departure. First released in 1961, its suppositions and conclusions have framed much of the subsequent debate about both underlying and immediate causes of the war. Taylor was anxious to produce an objective history of the years leading to the war and to question earlier claims that Hitler followed a predetermined plan of conquests which Western leaders ought to have deciphered if they had the moral courage to face facts. His underlying argument is that the leaders of Britain and France pursued traditional diplomatic courses of action and that war resulted when it finally became clear to them that Hitler, despite earlier pretences, had an insatiable appetite for conquests and could not be dealt with through diplomatic means. Even then they would have preferred to continue to make compromises with Nazi Germany and some Nazi officials were also prepared to compromise. But events finally made it impossible for either side to turn back. Taylor suggests that it is wrong to use hindsight to condemn political leaders and foreign affairs officials for being unable to transcend their conventional assumptions regarding diplomacy among nations or to disregard the mixed signals the Nazi regime gave the Western nations. On the whole, while he dislikes the word appeasement, Taylor argues that Chamberlain and his associates were indeed interested in peace and pursued rational policies meant to avoid war. They ought not to be condemned for that in his view by historians who know things about the Nazis that had not yet been revealed to Chamberlain's generation in office.

Taylor's influential book has been rightfully criticized for its relative inattention to ideology. In Taylor's particular interpretation of the diplomatic record, little thought is given to the underlying ideas that politicians, civil servants or military officials brought to their consideration of options in dealing with fascist regimes. Taylor does observe that there were many English and French citizens who believed that fascism was superior to communism and indeed suggests that many French right-wingers believed Hitler was preferable to Leon Blum. But he only rarely indicates that the admirers of fascism included the government leaders — he does mention Halifax's toadying statement to Hitler in November 1937 that Nazi Germany was "the bulwark of Europe against Bolshevism"[1] – and never explores ideological as opposed to merely strategic aspects of foreign policy. As Alan Cassels puts it, Taylor "deals with foreign policy *in vacuo.*" Neither political movements nor ideologies play a real role in his account of events.[2]

The result is that Taylor takes Chamberlain's commitment to peace at face value, and does not question the subtext of statements by Chamberlain, Halifax and other ministers that equate abandonment of various countries to Hitler with peace. Indeed he makes Churchill and Vansittart, men who correctly predicted the threat which Hitler posed to the Empire, seeming villains while presenting Chamberlain in a positive light.

> Churchill had recently fought a long campaign against concessions to India; his opposition to concessions in regard to Germany was the logical sequel to this. Vansittart and some other senior members of the foreign service took much the same view. It was a view which shocked most Englishmen and which, by its apparent cynicism, deprived its holders of influence on policy. Power, it was held, had been tried during the first World war and afterwards. It had failed; morality should take its place.[3]

The view that Chamberlain and company represented morality in foreign policy determination while Churchill and Vansittart represented only power politics demonstrates clearly Taylor's bias. He adds that "non-interference in other countries was a long-standing tradition of British foreign policy, advocated by John Bright and by Chamberlain's father in his Radical days" and "Chamberlain was adopting towards Nazi Germany precisely the attitude which the Labour movement had always demanded should be adopted towards Soviet Russia."[4] He does pose the central question of this book though only to dismiss it.

---

[1] A.J.P. Taylor, *The Origins of the Second World War* (Harmondsworth, Middlesex: Penguin, 1979), p. 175.
[2] Alan Cassels,"Switching Partners: Italy in A.J. P. Taylor's *Origins of the Second World War*", In Gordon Martel, ed., *The Origins of the Second World War Reconsidered: The A.J.P. Taylor Debate after Twenty-five Years* (Boston: Allen and Unwin, 1986), p. 88.
[3] Taylor, *Origins*, p. 173.
[4] *Ibid.*, p. 173.

The British and French governments acknowledged Soviet Russia only to emphasize her military weakness; and this view, though it rested no doubt on their information, represented also their desire. They wanted Soviet Russia to be excluded from Europe; and therefore readily assumed that she was so by circumstances. Did their wishes go further? Did they plan to settle Europe not only without Soviet Russia, but also against her? Was it their intention that Nazi Germany should destroy the 'Bolshevik menace'? This was the Soviet suspicion, both at the time and later. There is little evidence of it in the official record, or even outside it. British and French statesmen were far too distracted by the German problem to consider what would happen when Germany had become the dominant power in Eastern Europe. Of course, they preferred that Germany should march east, not west, if she marched at all. But their object was to prevent war, not to prepare one; and they sincerely believed – or, at any rate Chamberlain believed – that Hitler would be content and pacific if his claims were met.[5]

Taylor does not so much interpret differently the evidence presented in this book as he ignores it. He seems, in particular, to have avoided the German documents in foreign policy, including Dr. Paul Schmidt's accounts of the Chamberlain-Hitler meetings. The result is that he claims that the Godesberg meeting "ended in failure" and that Chamberlain, faced with a choice between war and Britain's "abdication as a Great Power," leaned to the latter.[6] He apparently sees no necessity to support the absurd claim that Chamberlain, a zealous imperialist, was so much the pacifist that he sought to abandon Britain's role as a leading nation in world affairs. Yet Taylor's own evidence often seems to contradict his claims that Chamberlain was simply taking Hitler at his word and could not be expected to judge him at various junctures through the lenses that he could wear as the war finally approached. He makes clear that Chamberlain's government was desperate, after Munich, to escape their guarantee to the Czechoslovak government to respond to any aggression upon the territories that remained within the rump Czechoslovak state. Indeed they were "concerned to get out of such commitments in central Europe as they already had."[7] In short, Taylor, while suggesting

[5] *Ibid.*, p. 204.
[6] *Ibid., p. 223.*
[7] *Ibid.*, p. 245.

that Chamberlain was concerned with moral persuasion of Germany to limit her aims and respect nationalities such as the Czechs, equally suggests that his government did not fool itself into believing that they had won Hitler over to their view at Munich. Rather they wished to distance themselves from the necessity of having to intervene when Hitler committed his various depredations within central and eastern Europe.

Interestingly, while rejecting after slight discussion the notion that anti-communism and anti-Sovietism played a far-reaching role in the formulation of British foreign policy, Taylor, at least some of the time, endorses the view that Britain was prepared to grant a free hand to Germany in the east. This is true, for example, in his explanation of why British appeasers began gradually to move towards a policy of opposing Hitler rather than making concessions to him. He suggests there was a backlash in Tory ranks against the fierce German criticisms of Churchill and Duff Cooper, the strongest advocates of massive rearmament.

> They believed in mutual non-interference. Hitler could do what he liked in Eastern Europe; he could demolish Czechoslovakia or invade the Ukraine. But he must leave British politicians alone.[8]

Taylor makes no more effort to square his claims that Chamberlain was motivated by moral principles with his claims that his government was prepared to throw all of eastern Europe to the wolves than he attempts to square Chamberlain's supposed willingness to believe Hitler with his anxiety not to have to enforce a guarantee of Hitler's good behaviour in Czechoslovakia. Within his framework such claims ultimately do not have to be reconciled because his emphasis is on the chance character of events.

Taylor's underplaying of the importance of ideology in the formation of foreign policy is particularly evident in his handling of the issue of Chamberlain's hostility towards any alliance of the democracies with the Soviet Union against Nazi aggression. Writes Teddy Uldricks:

> He seriously underestimates the strength of anti-communism as a motive force in British foreign policy, not only toward Soviet Russia, but in regard

[8]   *Ibid.*, p. 245.

to Germany as well. Thus, Taylor notes, the Great Purges (especially the destruction of the Soviet officer corps) reinforced the prime minister's belief that the USSR was scarcely worth having as an ally, but he misses the more important point that Chamberlain was doctrinally opposed to any real alliance with the communist state – even if Stalin had been a benevolent ruler instead of a bloody tyrant.[9]

Taylor, along with many other historians, points out that the British government in the 1930s did not want to make the economic sacrifices necessary to put the country on a war footing. Britain's economic position had been weakening since before World War One and continued to deteriorate after the war. Faced with the Great Depression of the 1930s, it had little desire to match the fanatical Nazis in devoting a large portion of national resources to mobilization for war. It preferred to focus on peaceful negotiations of contentious issues with Germany and other states. But this begs the question of why Britain did not confront Germany early on in the Nazi period when the arms advantage of Britain and France was overwhelming and they could force Hitler either to respect Versailles limitations on German arms or leave office.

While the tone of Taylor's *Origins* is apologetic for the Chamberlain government, his acceptance that the government cared little about the fate of eastern Europe and his claim that Britain and France were launched by events into war and were not fighting over any great principles could hardly be of comfort to those who wished to argue that World War Two was a struggle of freedom and democracy against Nazi tyranny and oppression of Jews and other nationalities. Indeed in 1975 in a summary of events leading to the war that opened his book on World War Two, Taylor portrayed both Chamberlain and Halifax in a more sinister light than in *Origins*. He interpreted Halifax's visit to Hitler in November 1937 as a green light to Germany in Danzig, Austria, and Czechoslovakia provided that Hitler handled his takeovers judiciously. As for Chamberlain: "In his view, Germany even under Hitler was a lesser evil than Soviet Russia, and German predominance in eastern Europe, however unwelcome, would be a barrier against Communism."[10]

[9] Teddy J. Uldricks, " A.J.P. Taylor and the Russians," In Gordon Martel, ed., *The Origins of the Second World* War *Reconsidered* , p. 172.
[10] A.J.P. Taylor, *The Second World War: An Illustrated History* (London: Penguin, 1976), p. 30. The book was originally published one year earlier by

Simon Newman, writing in 1976, attempted to refute much of the Taylor thesis and to paint the Chamberlain government as firm anti-Nazis whose war with Hitler in September 1939 did indeed result at least in part from their defence of principles of individual and national rights. Newman countered Taylor's claims that Britain had little interest in central and eastern Europe with evidence that Britain was intensifying its economic involvement in the region even as it was appeasing Hitler. "The Foreign Office strategy, executed with Chamberlain's express consent, had been to resist German expansion in central and southeastern Europe by economic means."[11] Apart from moral objections to a German takeover of various nations, the British government, argues Newman, were sensitive to the fact that a German-dominated central and eastern Europe would threaten Britain's control of the waterways that linked the various components of the British Empire.

Newman does establish that Britain tried to improve its relatively weak investment and trade links with eastern Europe during the 1930s. But he fails to establish that this was part of a grand strategy to prevent a German military takeover of the region and indeed there is no logical reason why increased British trade in eastern Europe would have caused Germany to pause before invading the various states of the region. The focus on economic policy however allows Newman to avoid a serious examination of what had changed in British-German relations between Munich and the unilateral guarantee to Poland. He states: "But the political commitment that was then made to Poland is at least more understandable if we accept that British policy in 1938 was not based on willingness to grant Germany a free hand in central and south-eastern Europe."[12]

For Newman, demonstration of a supposed British economic stake in keeping the Nazis from seizing eastern Europe results in a conclusion that there is little need to examine what had changed from Munich to the guarantee of Poland. British policy had been consistently to defend the integrity of eastern European countries. As we have seen throughout this book, an

Hamish Hamilton.

[11] Simon Newman, *March 1939: The British Guarantee to Poland: A Study in the Continuity of British Foreign Policy* (London: Oxford University Press, 1976), p. 150.

[12] *Ibid.*, p. 53.

examination of the actions and attitudes of Chamberlain, Halifax, Henderson, Simon and other policy-makers simply does not bear this out. It is also clear that, while British leaders should have been concerned about the threat that Hitler's control over eastern Europe would pose to the British Empire, voices such as Churchill's and Vansittart's that emphasized this threat were drowned out by the voices of those obsessed with the vision of Hitler's destroying the Soviet Union.

Newman unfortunately pulls optimistic conclusions from thin evidence. We have seen that the British and French were little concerned about Hitler's treatment of his own people, including the Jews of Germany. Kristallnacht was viewed as a nuisance because it hurt Hitler's image with the public in Britain but no more. Newman however writes:

> Although there is little reference to these excesses in the British Cabinet minutes, they were widely reported in Britain and affected public opinion deeply. According to Cadogan, writing much later, 'Hitler's open atrocities against the Jews in the autumn of 1938 certainly deeply impressed Chamberlain....And of course Halifax was no less shocked.'[13]

It seems remarkable that a remark by Cadogan well after the events of November 1938 would be more suggestive to Newman than his own evidence that the Cabinet did not agonize over the issue of its dealings with a regime that persecuted a religious minority among other groups. As we have seen, Chamberlain, at the time, worried not about the victims of Nazi persecution but of the impact of this persecution on his government's ability to convince the British people that the Nazis were partners with Britain in defending western Christian civilization against Oriental Communist barbarism.

The Soviet Union figures weakly in Newman's account. He admits that the Chiefs of Staff insisted that Soviet help was necessary if Polish resistance to a Nazi invasion were ever to be successful. He then adds: "The decision to guarantee Poland, however, was not taken on the basis of strategic considerations alone. For instance neither the professional diplomats nor the politicians shared the assumption that Russia would in fact help

---

[13] *Ibid.*, p. 71.

when the time came. Intentions had to be judged as well as capabilities, and the ideal strategic configuration was not always politically feasible."[14] Newman, like Taylor, fails to deal with the impact of ideological hatred of the Soviet Union on the conduct of British foreign policy. The Soviets, after all, had been attempting since 1934 to form a united front against fascism between themselves and the parliamentary democracies. They had provided the arms that allowed democratic Spain to hold out for three years against the Nazi and Fascist-supplied Franco forces. They had made plain to the democracies in 1938 their willingness to join in any plans to defend Czechoslovakia against German aggression. On what basis then were the Soviets, with their anti-fascist record, to be regarded as poorly-intentioned, while Poland, which had collaborated with Hitler until March 1939 – even picking up a piece of Czechoslovakia after Munich – was to be regarded as well-intentioned? Like Taylor, it would appear, that Newman wishes to avoid a thorough investigation of the underlying thinking of policy makers.

By the late 1980s it was common for historians to go much further than Taylor or even Newman in proclaiming the essential decency and high moral principles of the appeasers. Newman's questionable refutation of Taylor's claims that the British government cared little about the fate of eastern and central Europe was largely unchallenged. The view that the governments of Britain and France eventually went to war with Germany over matters of principle rather than because of a particular, unfortunate set of events, as Taylor would have it, became further entrenched. In 1986, P. M. H. Bell's contribution to the "Origins of Modern War" series, entitled *The Origins of the Second World War in Europe* to distinguish it from Taylor's work, provided the state-of-the-art overview of then-current conclusions about the period leading up to World War 2. Bell suggested that anti-communism played more of a role in determining British policy than Taylor believed but rejected the view that it is central to understanding British policy overall. He admits that conservatives liked Germany's anti-Sovietism but then adds:

> The effect of these ideological issues on the course of British policy was limited. In the general matter of relations with Germany, the policy which became

[14] *Ibid.*, p. 120.

> known as 'appeasement' arose from hard considerations of strategic and economic interests, as well as from the soothing climate of opinion represented by the League, pacifism, and disarmament, or from anti-Bolshevik zeal.[15]

"Anti-Bolshevik zeal" from Bell's point of view played a role in preventing an alliance with the Soviets, an admission that makes more sense than Newman's suggestion that there was scepticism about whether the Soviets would fight if there was a German attack on one of its allies.

Bell writes admiringly of Chamberlain, explaining Chamberlain's change of heart about Hitler in March 1939 as a response to the invasion of Prague.

> Chamberlain too saw the issue in moral as well as power-political terms. He was a loyal and upright man, and in March 1939 he felt that he had been double-crossed. Even more, the growth of nazi power now palpably threatened the whole system in which he had spent his life and to which he was devoted – Parliament, the rule of law, the workings of business, the rules of decent behaviour.[16]

This is, of course, a view of Chamberlain which this book demonstrates to be untrue. Neither he nor his government placed a primary value on parliament or the rule of law. Halifax's endorsement of Lord Lloyd's book defending fascists even as the British and French were nominally at war with Germany (though not yet with Japan and Italy) demonstrates the limited importance that the British elite gave to parliament. Chamberlain's flattering comments to Hitler, his cynicism regarding the granting of a free hand to both Germany and Japan to attack Soviet-held territories, and his willingness to negotiate with Nazis even after the war started reveal that he was not especially "loyal and upright." His good mood after Hitler made plain at Godesberg that Germany would leave the West alone if it had a free hand in the East questions the extent to which he believed "moral" arguments should carry the day.

---

[15] P.M.H. Bell, *The Origins of the Second World War in Europe* (London: Longman, 1986), p. 107.
[16] *Ibid.*, p. 108.

Bell presents Britain's timidity before Hitler in contradictory terms. He excuses the apparent British indifference regarding Hitler's rearmament program and his illegal militarization of the Rhineland by noting that Britain had "discounted" these events before they occurred and therefore reacted with alarm to neither.[17] Yet Britain's subsequent desire to "appease" Hitler is explained in terms of Britain's military unpreparedness and unwillingess to risk the enmity of more than one of Germany and Japan. He sees no need to explain either why Britain "discounted" Hitler's rearmament rather than stopping it or why it failed to fully rearm afterwards to deal with the German threat.

Bell, following in the tradition of Taylor, Newman, and many other historians, excuses Britain's acquiescence in Germany's takeover of Austria and Sudetenland. He mentions the huge crowds that met Hitler in his hometown in Austria without noting that most Austrians opposed the *Anschluss* and that Hitler sent in troops before they could vote on the issue of becoming part of Nazi Germany. He justifies Munich by noting that Prague, unlike Warsaw, was unharmed by World War 2.[18] He claims that the Soviets were won over to the pact with Hitler because he offered them territory and Britain did not, largely ignoring the fruitless attempts of the Soviets to make an alliance with the Western democracies. Britain's negotiations with the Soviets in 1939 are said to have stalled because "when the British committed themselves to Poland, they to all intents and purposes ruled out an alliance with the USSR unless they threw the Poles overboard first."[19] This ignores, as we suggested in Chapter 7, that Britain was aware that Poland could not be defended without Soviet help. Unsurprisingly Bell presents the view that Britain gave its guarantee to Poland to warn Hitler against future aggressions no matter where rather than to present Hitler with the uncomfortable prospect of a two-front war.

Apologia for the appeasers reached a new plateau with the publication in 1989 of the massive work by Donald Cameron Watt, *How War Came: The Immediate Origins of the Second World War 1938-1939*. Watt not only confirms much of Newman's version of events but goes farther in asserting the uprightness and morality of Chamberlain and his ministers and in denouncing their contemporaries who suspected they were in

[17] *Ibid.*, pp. 205, 209-210.
[18] *Ibid.*, pp. 228-229, 242.
[19] *Ibid.*, p.261.

bed politically with the German Nazis. In Watt's account, the Cabinet in the months leading to Munich was moved by a desire to prevent a war such as World War One which they believed could only result in millions of deaths and in national bankruptcy. Aware of Britain's limited resources for making war, they felt that disaster would result if they were forced at once to confront German assertiveness in eastern Europe, Italian threats in the Mediterranean, and Japanese aggressiveness in the Far East. Watt recounts the standard line that Chamberlain and his ministers believed that nations would, except in rare instances, behave morally towards one another and expected that Britain's charitable treatment of Germany at Munich was more likely to lead to peace than war.

Watt's assumptions about the good intentions of the British government as it pursued appeasement policies cause him to read the documents of this period in a most peculiar light. So, for example, he reports that Chamberlain was sceptical in November 1938 when given reports that Hitler might strike in the Balkans, Asia Minor, or India. He expected instead that Hitler's next moves would be in eastern Europe. This we have seen in Chapter 7 was undoubtedly true. But Watt's view of Chamberlain's reaction to these possibilities is: "He [ed. Chamberlain] was one of those who feared that Hitler was planning to strike eastwards in conjunction with Poland against the Ukraine."[20] As we saw in Chapter 7, Chamberlain, Halifax, Daladier, and Bonnet, among other leading officials in Britain and France, relished the prospect of a Nazi attack on the Soviet Ukraine. Their words make it clear that it is delusion to say that any of them, especially Chamberlain, "feared" an attack on Ukraine.

Watt observes that the British Cabinet wished to strengthen "moderate" forces in Germany. "The full Cabinet, meeting on November 30, agreed that Britain should do what it could to strengthen the moderates."[21] But Watt provides no discussion of what the moderates stood for against what the extremists stood for. As we have seen, the "moderate" Nazis, like Goering, were individuals who believed that the Chamberlain-Hitler deal would be respected by Britain and France and that Germany could set out to conquer all the territories it wished to its east without

---

[20] Donald Cameron Watt, *How War Came: The Immediate Origins of the Second World War, 1938-1939* (London, Heinemann, 1989), p. 91.
[21] *Ibid.*, p. 91.

worry of an unprovoked attack by the West. The extremists, rejecting the moderates' claims that a war with the West would be ruinous, argued that the West, despite the Hitler-Chamberlain understanding, would take advantage of German war-making in the east to attack Germany from the west with possibly ruinous consequences.

Watt traces the mood of Chamberlain as events unfolded after Munich. Chamberlain remained euphoric in mid-February 1939 when he met American Ambassador Joseph Kennedy in London. He excuses Chamberlain's initial unwillingness to denounce the German takeover of the remains of Czechoslovakia by suggesting that he was in shock and reacted "like some amputee needing time to recognize the full extent of his loss."[22] As we have mentioned above, Chamberlain's government had attempted ever since Munich to withdraw from its guarantee of what remained of that country; a German takeover of the Czechoslovak rump state was, in short, expected. Chamberlain's reaction was not spur of the moment and not a result of denial that Czechoslovakia had indeed been obliterated. Whether his change of heart two days later was a caving in to public opinion, genuine shock that Ruthenia had been given to Hungary, or some combination of the two, it was not the result of a sudden recognition that Hitler had betrayed Britain. This betrayal was expected but what was unexpected by Chamberlain was his personal conversion to the view that Hitler might, despite their deal, be intending to attack in the West.

Unlike Taylor who believes the appeasers tried to avoid war right to the bitter end, Watt trivializes the feverish and ultimately failed negotiations that preceded the war.

> To understand the negotiations that were to follow it is essential to realize that these were entered into on the British side with very little expectation of success but with the conviction that negotiation should be tried. No Cabinet member was prepared to accept the responsibility of not seeming to be willing to negotiate, to try any opening in the hope that somehow Hitler might be out-manoeuvred. They were certainly not prepared to allow Hitler to say that a refusal to negotiate left him no option for war.[23]

[22] *Ibid.*, p. 167.
[23] *Ibid.*, p. 502.

Clearly, if the negotiations were viewed as no more than *pro forma* by the British government, they would have ceased the moment war was declared. But as we saw in Chapter 8, they continued secretly but officially as the war raged until Chamberlain's departure from office.

Watt is not content to provide his own perspective on Chamberlain's motives; he believes it necessary to impugn Chamberlain's contemporaries who had a different view. He is particularly negative in his discussion of the two world leaders who saw through Hitler early on: Stalin and Roosevelt. The former, of course, was a brutal dictator and his reign of terror at home may excuse Watt's willingness to fail to credit his prescience with regard to Hitler's intentions. More surprising is his vitriol directed against the American president. He comments, in part:

> What is more surprising is to discover how the President's secretiveness, his distrust of his supporters, and his total confidence in his own judgment and vision were to encourage him to entertain a series of beliefs and convictions about those with whom he was dealing that left him very nearly as ill informed and as myopic in his judgment of European, indeed of world, politics as Stalin was. Like Stalin, he suspected a constant conspiracy on the part of British financial interests to accept Germany's terms for a division of Europe. Like Stalin he consistently misinterpreted Neville Chamberlain's horror and fear of European war as cloaking a psychological affinity for the totalitarian powers. Like Stalin with his fears of a Baltic invasion, Roosevelt imagined strategic threats to the United States where none existed. By contrast with Stalin, however, his intelligence sources were all second-hand and, in the main, grossly unreliable. Indeed some were certainly subject to Soviet influence.[24]

As an indication of how gullible President Roosevelt could be, Watt observes that he was "convinced by Claud Cockburn [ed. a Communist journalist], who had invented it, of the existence of the 'Cliveden Set,' allegedly a clique of British politicians and financiers who met at Cliveden, the country seat of Lord and Lady Astor in Buckinghamshire, a 'pro-German group with heavy backing' from the City and financial interests, and an ally

[24] *Ibid.*, p. 125.

304

of those Wall Street interests with whom the New Deal
ideologists from the President downwards felt themselves to be
at war."[25]

It is difficult to know where to begin in responding to such
statements. In the first place, it ought to be clear from the
evidence in this book that Roosevelt was right in all the
particulars mentioned by Watt. British financial interests and the
Conservative government that sought to represent them WERE
interested in an "understanding" with Germany that would mean
effectively a division of Europe in which central and eastern
Europe were conceded as a German sphere of influence.
Chamberlain DID admire the dictators and so did his
government as a whole. Roosevelt was a moderate reformer
whose minor movements in the redistribution of wealth in his
country were sufficient to cause reactionaries in the United
States, many of whom would have been quite happy with a
fascist regime in their country, to denounce him bitterly. He was
a wealthy capitalist with no affinity whatever for Communism or
class struggle. The suggestion that he got his ideas from known
Communists and leftists is absurd, a ruse to disguise the fact that
the essential information he was receiving was correct. Watt
forgets that the United States, like other countries, had diplomats
abroad who reported to the American leaders. The dispatches
from Joseph Kennedy, American Ambassador in London, while
they reveal his own sympathies for the Nazis, also indicate quite
clearly the extent to which he found that the British leadership
was at one with his views. As for the 'Cliveden set,' it is clear
from Adam Von Trott's correspondence, mentioned in Chapter
8, that it existed and that its members, who included the prime
minister, were broadly sympathetic to fascism.

Not all historians of Britain – nor of France – in this period are
as anxious as Donald Cameron Watt to disregard evidence
suggesting base motives for the conduct of foreign policy. As
early as 1942, historian Frederick Schuman concluded that the
leaders of Britain and France must have granted Hitler a free
hand in the East. The public statements of members of the
British elite not bound by government responsibilities suggested
the popularity of the free hand strategy among the class from
which the Cabinet was drawn. The government's persistent
belief that it could come to a deal with Hitler only made sense,
Schuman argued, if it had offered him a free hand in the East.[26]

[25] *Ibid.*, p. 127.

The famous Italian historian-politician Gaetano Salvemini came to the same conclusions[27] though both historians, writing at a time before many documents relevant to foreign policy-making in the thirties had been released by Western governments, had to rely on circumstantial evidence that allowed their detractors to claim that they were only speculating and had no hard evidence with which to brand the rulers of Britain in the 1930s as having collaborated with the Nazis. Unsurprisingly then, the toughest critique of British foreign policy-making to appear in the three decades following Schuman's scathing account does not emphasize the question of the free hand. Margaret George, an American specialist on British foreign policy, provides solid evidence of the primary role that anti-communism played in arguing for a policy of appeasement. She also makes note of the fact that when Labour MP Hugh Dalton challenged Stanley Baldwin to deny that the government was prepared to grant Hitler a free hand in the East, Baldwin's denial was in a form that suggested the MP was correct but that the government did not wish to have the odious label "free hand" attached to its dealings with Nazi Germany.[28]

Recently several historians have added to the story told by Schuman, Salvemini, and George. Robert Rothschild, for example, casts grave doubt on the approach of historians such as Watt and Newman. Rothschild, a political scientist, served in the Foreign Ministry of Belgium from 1937 to 1939 and later as an ambassador for many years at various postings. Apart from traditional sources, his account rests on his own personal experiences. Unlike Taylor, Newman, Watt, and others who suggest that a high moral sense motivated the appeasers, Rothschild suggests that fear of communism produced "anaemia of their moral force." He writes:

> In reality, in spite of the infatuation of naive intellectuals fooled by Kremlin propaganda, the communists in the countries that remained faithful to democracy would remain without great influence on the masses. Nevertheless, the ruling circles would continue to be haunted by a threat which – at that time – existed only in their imagination. Hanging on

[26] Frederick Schuman, *Europe on the Eve* (New York: A.A. Knopf, 1942).
[27] Gaetano Salvemini, *Prelude to World War 11* (London: Victor Gollancz, 1953).
[28] Margaret George, *The Warped Vision: British Foreign Policy, 1933-1939* (Pittsburgh: University of Pittsburgh Press, 1965), p.92.

> desperately to values of the past broken to pieces by the irresistible pressure of new times rather than by an inefficient Marxist conspiracy, they allowed themselves to be carried away by a deep wave of fear and repulsion which hid from them true perils. It was a myth, there is no doubt, that was a principal cause of the anaemia of their moral force.[29]

Rothschild, no left-winger, observes that the response in Britain and France to Hitler was that he was a welcome alternative to the Communists. He notes that Chamberlain, who interfered with Eden's handling of foreign policy concerning Italy, accused the Foreign Secretary of "antifascism," and named his sister-in-law official agent in Rome where she competed with the embassy for the attention of the Italian and British governments. Her corsage carried a golden insignia of the Fascist Party.[30] This evidence of Chamberlain's "profascism" clearly sits poorly with Watt's and Newman's portrait of an anti-fascist who only dealt with the dictators at all because he felt a compulsion above all to prevent another war in Europe. Rothschild discounts the much-restated argument of Chamberlain that Britain lacked the armed strength to combat Germany. It is a "specious" argument, he suggests, because it avoids the question: who was responsible for this lack of preparedness?[31]

Rothschild has little better to say about Eden, Halifax or Daladier. While Eden may have been "antifascist" from Chamberlain's point of view, he was, before 1938, an appeaser and he had, while still Secretary of State for Foreign Affairs, encouraged Ribbentrop to believe that Britain would not react if Germany annexed Austria. Halifax meanwhile had been won over by Hitler's anti-communism to take weak stands against Nazi aggression. As for Daladier, Rothschild points out that even after war against Hitler had been declared, he remained obsessed with combating Communism and was not convinced that the Third Reich as opposed to the Soviet Union was the main enemy.[32]

---

[29] Robert Rothschild, *Les Chemins de Munich: Une Nuit de Sept Ans 1932-1939* (Paris: Perrin, 1988), p. 87, trans. from French by the authors.

[30] *Ibid.*, p. 270.

[31] *Ibid.*, p. 374..

[32] *Ibid.*, pp. 280-3, 309.

Rothschild does not deal with the issue of the free hand in central and eastern Europe or the question of whether Western thinking about Hitler changed because of new information in early 1939 that the Nazis were thinking of attacking the West before they assaulted more of eastern Europe. He focuses upon public opinion as the precipitating factor in forcing the governments of France and Britain to finally stand up to Hitler. The new public opinion polls in Britain showed that by early 1938 most of the population favoured the country taking a tougher stance against the dictators. When public opinion polls were taken for the first time in France in late 1938, they showed a similar result. He believes that popular disgust with Hitler after the occupation of Prague finally forced the leaders of the two countries to face up to Hitler.[33]

Historian Michael Carley reinforces Rothschild's general observations about the role of anti-communism in determining foreign policy in France and Britain in a detailed study of Franco-Soviet trade negotiations in the period before World War 2. After demonstrating the Soviet willingness to make whatever concessions were necessary for a trade deal, he points out that the right-wing in France made it impossible for a deal to be reached. He notes:

> The Great Depression provided an opening. French heavy industry was in trouble; it broke with the ideological anti-Communism of the right, as it had begun to do in the 1920s, and sought business in the USSR. It found the Soviet side willing; French industrialists were the key to better political relations. But the Banque de France and Finance bureaucracies resisted, dragged their feet, made excuses for not financing Soviet exports. The "wall of money" hampered better relations with the USSR. The right-wing press still sent up its hue and cry. Behind it were powerful, rich men who frightened the ministers of the unstable French governments after Poincaré.[34]

Further:

> Franco-Soviet trade negotiations had thus failed as political negotiations failed. When the Soviets offered

---

[33] *Ibid.*, pp. 294, 295, 392.
[34] Michael Jabara Carley, "Five Kopecks for Five Kopecks: Franco-Soviet Trade Negotiations 1928-1939," *Cahiers du Monde Russe et Soviétique*, 33:1 (janvier-mars 1992), p. 50.

> "five kopecks for five kopecks," the French dallied over the bid and would not ante-up. How could they, when Communism and civil war threatened France; why should they, as long as a Soviet-German *rapprochement* seemed unlikely? When this latter assumption proved a fateful miscalculation, and the Soviet government concluded a non-aggression pact with the Nazis in August 1939, the French and British accused Stalin of perfidy and double-dealing. But when the Soviets' five kopecks were down on the table, it was the French who would not take the risk, and it was the British who did not want them to. The failure of Franco-Soviet trade negotiations is a little-known episode in the history of the Western powers' lamentable inability to provide for their own defence during the 1930s.[35]

Carley, in brief, establishes that the ideological anti-communism of the French forestalled a trade agreement with the Soviets, a measure that could have led as well to closer political links between the two countries. As we have seen, a section of the traditional political elite did accept the need for a defence pact with the Soviets but once the pact was concluded, it was largely sabotaged by the large right-wing within the elite who, even in the face of the Nazi threat, were unwilling to forge links with the Communist power. This is an example of the moral anaemia that Rothschild decries. But, of course, in and of itself, it does not establish that the British and French governments wanted to give a free hand to Hitler in central and eastern Europe, much less that Chamberlain formally negotiated such a deal with the Nazi dictator. The work of historian Wesley R. Wark, by contrast, provides much evidence of the "free hand," though it is beyond the scope of his inquiry to determine whether formal collusion with the Nazis occurred. In a masterful study of the intelligence operations in Britain from 1933 to 1939 and their impact on the government's response to Hitler's activities, Wark casts much doubt on the accounts of such conventional historians as Taylor, Newman, and Watt. Indeed, in Wark's work, the extreme anti-communism and racism of members of the elite, vastly understated in the traditional accounts, play a central role in the gathering of intelligence and the giving of advice to the government. Both the War Office and the Admiralty are open supporters of the free hand to Germany in central and eastern

[35] *Ibid.*, p. 51.

Europe in Wark's work while Halifax and Cadogan are presented as at least sometime supporters of this policy.

Wark makes plain that early appeasement of Nazi Germany cannot be explained in terms of the British government's fear of a war with that country. Until September 1936, that is after the Anglo-German Naval Agreement and the German occupation of the Rhineland, the British government was receiving underestimates of German rearmament. He notes that the government's signing of the Naval Agreement is sometimes attributed to Hitler's having told Simon and Eden in March 1935 that Germany had reached air parity with Britain. But, "the British were not, in fact, deceived."[36]

What then were British military planners telling the government? Major Whitefoord, head of MI3(b), the War Office intelligence unit, in a paper in June 1935 entitled "Germany and British Security in the Future," argued for a free hand for Germany in the east. This should not, he felt, be seen as a problem for Britain because "the annexation of purely Slav districts would weaken the racial cohesion of the Reich." Whitefoord expected and indeed hoped for a clash between Nazi Germany and the Soviet Union. "From a conflict between Germany and Russia, which would probably ruin our two potential enemies in Europe, we have little to lose, and might even gain considerably." Even if Germany were to become dominant in eastern Europe and threaten British interests, Whitefoord felt that Britain would not be best served by an alliance with "Russia and the weaker states in Europe." Instead it should concentrate on securing "firm defensive alliances in Western Europe coupled with an alliance with America to oppose any German attempt at world domination."[37] Whitefoord's views, Wark cautions, "may have been more extreme than those of his War Office colleagues," but their underlying military judgments were those that prevailed in the War Office until the government gave its guarantee to Poland in March 1939.[38] As Wark notes, the British had traditionally feared Russia as a threat to its position in the Middle East and India. Such concerns, "along with prevalent anti-Bolshevist attitudes" resulted in the War Office having "thrown away its

[36] Wesley R. Wark, *The Ultimate Enemy: British Intelligence and Nazi Germany, 1933-1939* (Ithaca:Cornell University Press, 1985), p. 44.
[37] *Ibid.*, p. 88.
[38] *Ibid.*

chances for objectivity." The War Office was not defeatist as the Foreign Office charged. Rather it regarded German rearmament as normal and expected the Nazis' goals "would be moderate and reasonable," that is restricted to conquests in eastern Europe.[39]

In September 1936, as it became clear that the regular German army would expand beyond 36 divisions, the War Office began to fear that Hitler's army "might one day threaten the West." For the next two years and more, both Army Intelligence and Air Intelligence exaggerated the extent of German rearmament. It was not however a simple case of military defeatism that caused the War Office to oppose any British involvement in defending Czechoslovakia against German aggression. "The War Office's latent antagonism to any Central European entanglement was rekindled and fed by a long-standing pessimism about the Czech powers of resistance."[40]

The Admiralty was as indifferent to the fate of eastern Europe as the War Office. Admiral Chatfield, first sea lord and chairman of the chiefs of staff from 1933 to 1938, focused on the Far East and "could see no vital interest in Europe that need involve Britain in war." In January 1937, responding to a Vansittart essay warning of German intentions in the east, Chatfield commented: "If Germany...tries to expand to the Southeast, we must, in my opinion, accept it. Europe must work out its own salvation in that quarter."[41] Though he focuses mainly on the intelligence units and war departments rather than on politicians and the Foreign Office, Wark notes:

> Chatfield was not alone in this kind of thinking. Others – such as Sir Alexander Cadogan and Lord Halifax at the Foreign Office, members of the War Office staff, and Chatfield's close friend and supporter the Cabinet secretary Sir Maurice Hankey – at times shared an uncertainty about whether Germany could or should be allowed to conduct her *Drang nach Osten.*[42]

Indeed, "even when German actions in Europe became threatening, the Admiralty sought to uphold the Anglo-German

---

[39] *Ibid.*, p. 89.
[40] *Ibid.*, pp. 90, 102.
[41] *Ibid.*, pp. 128, 144.
[42] *Ibid.*, p. 144.

Naval Agreement as the foreign policy key." Chatfield wrote the report of the chiefs of staff in March 1938 on the likely impact of Britain responding aggressively to a German assault on Czechoslovakia and it reflected his conviction that the east was not worth fighting for.

Though he is cautious in his assessment of the evidence, Wark concludes: "Both the Admiralty and the War Office developed visions of a limited liability policy that would rule out an Anglo-German clash so long as Hitler did not directly threaten Britain or the status quo in the West. "[43]

As mentioned earlier, Wark's research focuses mainly on the armed forces and only secondarily on the politicians. He accepts the traditional view of events after the invasion of Prague. He also tends to accept the view that Chamberlain's appeasement policies followed from his assessment that Britain was no longer a military match for Germany. But he makes clear that the information provided Chamberlain after September 1936 was overly-pessimistic. He does not however lay the blame for the use of this information solely on the military providers. The politicians, he notes, like the intelligence authorities, believed the totalitarian states could "combine efficiency with the ruthless exercise of power toward well-defined goals." This "suggests a weakening faith in the democratic system."[44] Here indeed is an interpretation of British elite behaviour in the 1930s well at odds with the traditional interpretations of which Watt's 1989 account, as noted, is the most apologetic for the leaders of Britain.

**

Even many contemporaries of Chamberlain, who opposed appeasement, could not believe that the British prime minister acted in full knowledge of the consequences of his actions or the full authority to act otherwise. For example, Dorothy Thompson, a liberal journalist, writing in 1939 before the outbreak of war, recognized that Munich plainly involved the granting of a free hand in the east to Hitler, and that it would have required incredible naiveté to believe that it did not. Yet she exonerated Chamberlain in the following words:

[43] *Ibid.*, p. 230.
[44] *Ibid.*, p. 238.

> It is very difficult to believe that when Chamberlain
> went to Munich he did not know that he was giving
> Hitler a free hand in the east and that he did not know
> exactly what giving that free hand would mean. But
> since Mr. Chamberlain is English it is possible that he
> really thought that Hitler would behave like an
> Englishman and take what he wanted in such a way as
> not to shock and horrify the world and stop at the
> right moment....

> If Chamberlain had ever read 'Mein Kampf' – which
> I am reasonably sure he has not done – he might have
> been aware a long time ago. But, being English, even
> that is doubtful. For the English mind believes only
> what it sees. It believes in the event, not in the plan.[45]

In fact, Chamberlain had read *Mein Kampf* and had received
many briefs about the implications of its contents. Vansittart,
Churchill, Phipps, Rumbold, Temperley, Liddell Hart, and
others who warned Chamberlain about the devastating
consequences that collaboration with Hitler could produce, were
as English as Chamberlain. Thompson's patronizing racialism
makes little sense.

Hamilton Fish Armstrong, editor of the prestigious American
journal, *Foreign Affairs*, also an opponent of appeasement, was
as willing as Thompson to rationalize the behaviour of the
appeasers even though he completely disagreed with them.
Writing just after Munich, he argued that Chamberlain's ability
to stand up to Hitler was limited by the extent to which
pro-Fascists were prominent in his Cabinet. He writes:

> It is fair to Prime Minister Chamberlain to note that
> many of his Conservative supporters, including,
> probably, members of his own Cabinet, felt more
> community of interest with Fascism than Communism
> and also instinctively preferred Germany to France.
> Among British reactionaries, liking for Germany and
> fear of Germany blended curiously. They pictured
> Hitler as a guardian of capitalism, intensely disliked
> the idea of lining up on the same side as Soviet
> Russia, even inside the League of Nations, and
> glossed over the fact that whatever one thought of the
> Communist theories to which the Soviet rulers still

[45] Dorothy Thompson, *Let the Record Speak* (Cambridge, Massachussetts:
Riverside, 1939), p. 325.

> paid lip service, and however repugnant the Stalin
> tyranny, Soviet Russia was for the time being a factor
> on the side of international peace.[46]

Armstrong is correct in pointing out that Conservatives often identified with the fascists but on what basis does he determine that Chamberlain was not amongst them? Chamberlain chose, after all, to exclude men like Churchill, Eden, and Vansittart who opposed appeasement from authority and to further the careers of men like Halifax, Cadogan, Nevile Henderson, Horace Wilson and John Simon who fit the description that Armstrong provides regarding Conservatives. Indeed after his meetings with Hitler he chose to hide information from his Cabinet that would demonstrate that he had formally agreed to give Hitler a free hand. Rather than a victim of conservative forces in Britain that supported an alliance with Hitler, Chamberlain was the leader of such forces.

***

The mythology of Chamberlain's essential decency is so strong that even the historians who have revealed his attempts to win a deal with the German military and Nazis *after* the war started have been unwilling to assail the prevailing view of the man. Nicholas Bethell, for example, as we noted in Chapter 8, reveals the deal which the Chamberlain government was willing to accept as a peace agreement with an essentially unreformed German government from which however Hitler would be removed. It included a *de facto* free hand for Germany in the east and a military combination of Britain and Germany against the Soviet Union. In other words, it not only restored to Germany the free hand promised in the meetings with Hitler in September 1938 but in return for a solemn promise by the German military that it would leave territories to Germany's west alone, it involved Britain in warfare with the Soviets. This ought to demonstrate that avoidance of war altogether was not Chamberlain's goal; his goal was to avoid war with Germany, which under fascist rule, remained in his view, within the ambit of "civilization." But Bethell, while indicating that it is upsetting that Chamberlain was party to such immoral negotiations, nonetheless exonerates him.

---

[46] Hamilton Fish Armstrong, *When There Is No Peace* (New York: Macmillan, 1939), p. 21.

> The victim of the tragedy of 1939 is of course Neville Chamberlain, the honest man so blind in his kindly tolerance that he gave Hitler the benefit of the doubt, a man of peace so un-violent that he was almost physically incapable of making decisions necessary to conduct and win a war. He believed in the goodness of human nature so deeply that he could not understand the mesmeric hold which Hitler had over the German people. In spite of all the facts and all the advice he was given, he persisted in his faith that his radio speeches and propaganda leaflets would detach the German people from Hitler and induce them to overthrow him.[47]

Reading between the lines, we can see that Bethell is saying that the British prime minister was a well-meaning idiot. His success in projecting himself publicly as a pacifist once again causes a historian, even one who recognizes his involvement in a rather seamy business, to excuse his behaviour on the grounds that the strength of his pacifist moral convictions made him "blind" to Hitler despite all the signs pointing to Hitler's intentions. This rather begs the question of why this prime minister, whom Bethell correctly describes as uncharismatic, was placed in office and then retained there by his Conservative colleagues. Were they also "kindly" dolts? Bethell's evidence suggests otherwise. Indeed he suggests that extreme anti-communism led to the attempt to negotiate an alliance with a right-wing German military-Nazi regime (minus the unpredictable Hitler) to fight the Soviet Communists. Limiting his analysis however to 1939, Bethell appears unaware that the "free hand" offered to Germany in central and eastern Europe – or relatively free, since Poland, for example, was to have nominal independence but to be, as Cadogan noted, a "vassal" of Germany – was not invented only after the war began. Yet his comments on the Western elites' attitudes to Germany and the Soviet Union in 1939 echo the evidence that this book provides of their attitudes throughout the period from 1933 to 1940, though with differences that we mention below. He writes in part:

> The Allied leaders likewise dismissed Russia as a military power and made only feeble attempts to recruit her to the anti-Nazi cause. Some of them, even after the outbreak, persisted in the belief that Russian communism was a greater danger than Hitlerism. In

[47] Nicholas Bethell, *The War Hitler Won: September 1939* (London: Allen Lane, 1972), pp. 415-416.

315

the last months of 1939 their theory of the Red Army's uselessness seemed confirmed by its poor performance against Finland, but they had totally miscalculated its ability to withstand defeats and learn from them, to build itself up into an efficient force on the bodies of dead comrades.

Likewise they were wrong about which ideology was more dangerous to western Europe. It was not a question of which was morally the worse, Hitlerism or Stalinism. The point was that while Stalin was for the moment in a defensive mood, content to consolidate his power in his own country, albeit by viciously repressive measures, Hitler was in a thoroughly aggressive mood, resolved to march deep into eastern Europe to obtain the living-space he believed his country was entitled to seize. Whether Hitler then planned to march against France and Britain is a moot point, but what is certain is that had such a Greater Germany ever been allowed to appear, it would have dominated the European continent and become an intolerable threat to British and French independence. Churchill foresaw this danger when it was still on the horizon. He even foresaw the day when he would make an alliance with Russia to meet this danger. But his was not in 1939 the view which dominated British and French thinking.[48]

The main problem with Bethell's formulation is that it is Britain which is made to appear the anti-Nazi nation and the Soviet Union the nation that needs to be recruited to the anti-Nazi cause. In fact, the Soviets followed a consistently anti-Nazi foreign policy from 1934 onwards, pressing on every occasion for a united front of the democracies and the Soviets against the fascist powers. The Comintern made popular fronts against fascism the mainstay of Communist Party work in every country. As most objective observers recognized, it was in the Soviets' national interests to have the expansion-minded Nazi regime in Germany defeated. But the leaders of Britain and France, more ambivalently in the latter case, were too occupied in the anti-Soviet cause to be much interested in the anti-Nazi cause. After all, it was the Nazis who were viewed as crucial to the success of campaigns to eradicate Communism from the face of Europe. By the time the British and French, concerned that Germany intended indeed to attack westwards before embarking on its seizure of lands in eastern Europe, finally stood up,

[48] *Ibid.*, p. 415.

however ambiguously, to Germany, the Soviets had given up hope that the western powers were serious in their opposition to Hitler or sincere in their efforts to gain an alliance with the Soviets. Their complete unwillingness to provide any guarantee to the Soviets along the lines of the British and French guarantees to Poland and Roumania led Stalin to make his devil's pact with Hitler. Bethell is, however, hardly unaware of these facts. Despite his efforts to defend Chamberlain personally, he writes revealingly of the thinking of the elites of Europe and America in a discussion of American debates in 1940 about whether to join the war on Britain's side. "The illusion created and fostered by so many prominent men in Western Europe and America, that Hitler was a necessary bulwark against communism, or 'Bolshevism' as it was then commonly termed, had only recently died in Britain and France, while in America it was still very much alive."

Anthony Cave Brown, another author who exposes the wartime attempts of the Chamberlain government to make an anti-Soviet alliance with a military successor government to the government of the Nazis, also defends the personality of Chamberlain and, in a general way, his policy of appeasement. Of Chamberlain he writes: " Chamberlain was a man of property, a son of a famous political family, and, so it seemed, he was as solid as his silver. " And of his foreign policy he says:

> Part of his foreign policy came to be called "appeasement," to be used by the extreme right and left, wrongly, as a euphemism for profascism, antibolshevism, and British moral weakness. In reality Chamberlain followed the same strategy as did Stalin and Roosevelt when they found themselves menaced by the great dictators: he played for time in which to rearm with the only weapon at hand, concessions to Hitler.[49]

Brown however then immediately contradicts himself by noting that Chamberlain did not intend to fight Hitler. It would appear then that he was in fact not simply playing for time to rearm against Hitler. Brown also admits that anti-Sovietism was the pivotal point of Chamberlain's foreign policy. But he tries to argue that these facts do not justify the notion that Chamberlain was profascist and/or antibolshevist because the source of

[49] Anthony Cave Brown, *The Secret Servant: The Life of Sir Stewart Menzies, Churchill's Spymaster* (London: Michael Joseph, 1988), p. 187.

Chamberlain's disgust with the Soviets was not their bolshevism as such but their efforts to force an Anglo-German war. But he offers no evidence of such Soviet scheming other than to state that Chamberlain believed it existed. As we have suggested earlier in this book, Chamberlain had no evidence for such a belief but was so viscerally anti-communist that he was happy to believe the rumours of such Soviet planning. Brown however, apparently unwilling to question someone who "was as solid as his silver," appears unwilling to accept the deep tarnish on that silver.[50]

***

One wonders how Brown and other of the Chamberlain defenders mentioned above would react to Chamberlain's claims to the king that imperial Britain and Nazi Germany were together the "two pillars of European peace and buttresses against communism "or to his sycophantic praise for Hitler's achievements at Berchtesgaden. Could they reconcile Chamberlain's supposed espousal of peace with his invitation to Hitler at Berchtesgaden to attack Russia without having to worry about Czech assistance to the Soviets? How would they explain Chamberlain's upbeat mood after his meeting with Hitler at Godesberg where the German dictator made clear that Germany would agree to keep its hands off the British Empire in return for "a free hand on the European continent in Central and South-East Europe?" How would they square Chamberlain's vaunted honesty with his cynical proposal to give Japan a free hand in Soviet Asia? Or his private statements that Mussolini would make life easier for him by making the seizure of Albania appear legal? Or his pro-Hitler statements to the Duke of Cobourg? More generally, one wonders at the exclusion from most of the works cited above − Rothschild and Carley are significant exceptions with Bethell and Taylor partial exceptions

---

[50] *Ibid.* Brown says in part:
   The principal ingredient of Chamberlain's two policies was that under no circumstances was there to be any agreement, written or spoken, with the Soviet Union. She remained *the* enemy. A second but no less important aspect of the policy was that under no circumstances should England fight Germany again. ..As Chamberlain suspected, Russia was seeking to precipitate a war between England and Germany that would leave Russia the most powerful nation in Eurasia, and as he declared in a letter to his sister on March 20, 1938, just before the world crisis began: 'With the Russians stealthily and cunningly pulling the strings behind the scenes to get us involved in war with Germany our Secret Service doesn't spend all its time looking out of the window.'

– of discussion of the positive views of fascism and Nazism within the British ruling classes generally. Why do they ignore Lord Lloyd of Dolobran's pro-fascist *The British Case* which Lord Halifax gave the government's seal of approval? Or the racist and pro-Nazi rantings of Nevile Henderson whose views were so important to the prime minister? No doubt it seems too painful for these writers to admit that the leaders of Britain in the 1930s were so consumed with fear and hatred of communism that most admired the fascist dictators who had used force to obliterate the socialist threat and to protect the property of the wealthy classes. The clear evidence of their own words that many members of the elites wished that Britain and France too could dispose of their mass-based democracies receives little mention. But the facts will not go away. While it would be wonderful to believe that the democracies in the 1930s were led by people who truly believed in democracy and civil liberties, all the evidence suggests indeed that they were led by members of elites who were, at best, ambivalent about the political systems within which they laboured. While perhaps few condoned in principle the thuggery used by fascists to rid their countries of social unrest, in practice their fear of losing their social privileges made them accept such behaviour as necessary under the circumstances. Their paranoid fear of Communism lead them to believe that Adolf Hitler's goals of expansion could be harnessed to the elites' goals of destroying the Soviet Union and ridding all of Europe of the Communist threat. In the process, as our evidence proves, they set aside all notions of decency and honesty and focused on their primary objective.

In fairness to the historians who steadfastly maintain the line that Chamberlain and company were decent, if deluded, individuals who followed the only course of action that was open to them if they wished to avoid a new European conflagration, a superficial reading of the foreign policy documents does support their conclusions. This is particularly so if one refuses to give any consideration to the German foreign policy documents, if one ignores most of Henderson's correspondence and some of Halifax's, and if one takes statements made by the government leaders in the House of Commons at face value. Even with all these caveats it is impossible to escape the many references to a free hand for the Germans in eastern Europe in the statements of the armed forces leaders and of the Committee of Imperial Defence which linked the government and military leaders. Even these rarely reach the history books though Wesley Wark's book is a significant exception here. There is however no justification for the exclusions mentioned above or for a failure to attempt to put into context the public statements of officialdom. Indeed, as we have argued throughout this book, British foreign policy in this period can only be understood if the indisputable references to the free hand are supplemented by a critical reading of the available documents more generally. "Europe" often is code for western Europe and "peace" often refers to peace purely in western Europe particularly when it is mentioned in the same sentence or paragraph that speaks of Nazi warfare or "conflict" in eastern Europe or against the Soviets. "Civilization" is equated with capitalism and its enemies are seen to include the Soviet Union but not the Nazis or other fascists. "Moderate" Nazis are not pacifists; instead they are Nazis who favoured maintaining good relations with the western democracies with the understanding that the latter would not intervene as Germany absorbed eastern Europe and made war on the Soviet Union. "Extremists," by contrast, did not trust British and French claims that they recognized a free hand for Germany in the east and argued that only a knock-out blow against the western powers could prevent them from meddling as Germany prepared an all-out assault eastwards.

INDEX

INDEX

Index

Index

Index

come to power, 68
and Jews, 182-3
and Lloyd George, 41
Newman, Simon, 2, 229, 229fn., 297-300, 306
Newton, Sir Basil, 149, 171, 172
Nicolson, Harold, 44, 49, 83, 88-90, 187, 221
Norman, Montagu, 202

Ogilvie-Forbes, Sir G., 198, 201-2
Orde, C.W., 56, 57fn.
Ormsby-Gore, W.G.A., 50

Paris-Soir, 264
Paul-Boncour, Joseph, 71, 130, 132, 133
Pétain, General, 275
Phipps, Sir Eric, 9, 73-74, 103, 130, 132, 137, 156, 167-8, 187-90, 219, 226, 250
Phipps, William, 30
Phoney war, 226, 264
Pirow, Colonel, 199
Poland, 2, 19, 188, 199, 203, 209, 212, 225-36, 243
and Danzig, 225-6, 229, 233, 242, 254, 255
Ponsonby, Lord, 255
Popular Front (France), 13fn., 44, 48, 49, 61
Prazmowska, Anita, 230

Raczynski, Count, 235, 249
Rhineland, remilitarization, 11, 43, 78, 86-88, 111-12, 301
Richardson, Charles, 280, 282
Ritchie, Charles, 219
Robins, Raymond, 28, 29
Roosevelt, Franklin D., 264
"quarantine" speech, 130
and Spain, 51
view of British foreign policy, 1, 8, 38, 304, 305
Rothschild, Robert, 306-10
Rougier, Professor, 281
Roumania, 230, 231, 248
Rucker, Sir Arthur, 261
Rumbold, Sir H., 69-70
Runciman, Lord, 138, 144
Rushcliffe, Lord, 255
Russell, Stuart, 90
Ruthenia, 18, 178, 195, 203, 225-7, 303

Salazar, Antonio de Oliveira, 6, 40, 257

Salvemini, Gaetano, 4, 306
Sargent, Orme, 48-49, 84-85, 122
Schmidt, Dr. Paul, 14fn., 16, 114, 145, 146, 150-2, 196, 294
Schuman, Frederick L., 4, 305-6
Schussnigg, Chancellor (Austria), 118, 119, 121
Seeds, Sir William, 249
Shirer, William L., 269-70
Simon, John, 41, 52, 53, 55-57, 63, 68, 71, 74-78, 154, 159-60, 184, 187, 218, 288
and Stresa, 79-80
visits Hitler, 79
Sinclair, Archibald, 219
Soviet Union
and Czechoslovakia, 148, 172-5
calls for alliance with Britain and France, 123, 248-50, 299, 316
early history, 25-40
and France, 12, 308-9
object of French and British wartime hatred, 263-78
and pact with Germany, 5, 177, 245, 258-60, 269, 301
and Simon Newman, 298-9
view of British foreign policy, 1, 3, 5, 8, 12, 15, 20
Spanish Civil War, 45-51
Spears, Major-General Sir Edward, 247
Stanley, Oliver, 131, 217, 240
Stalin, Josef, 2, 33, 129, 285, 304
Stehlin, Paul, 270, 279-80
Steward, George F., 19, 180-2
Strabolgi, Lord, 95
Strang, Lord, 45, 178, , 200, 205, 230, 237
Stresa, 10, 79-80, 86
Swinton, Lord, 132, 179

Tabouis, Genevieve, 44
Taylor, A.J.P., 1, 292-97, 299, 301, 303, 306
Temperley, Brigadier General A.C., 70-71
Templewood, Lord, 184
Thompson, Dorothy, 313
Thorez, Maurice, 282
Tilea, Viorel, 237
The Times, 94
Trotsky, Leon, 28
Tunisia, 196
Tyler, Wat, 37

325

Index